FootprintItalia

Naples & Amalfi Coast

Nick Bruno

Introducing the region

About the region

Naples

Campi Flegrei

Vesuvius, Herculaneum & Pompeii

Sorrentine Peninsula & Amalfi Coast

Capri, Ischia & Procida

Practicalities

Contents

About the author

Nick Bruno is Anglo-Italian, a journalist and travel writer, born and brought up in Islington, North London. He has lived in Naples, Venice, Manchester and Dundee, and travelled all over, kipping in barns, on mountainsides and in many a posh hotel. The childhood high of stumbling around in a fibreglass, orange alien suit on a Shepperton Studios moonscape, for a Milky Bar advert, has been hard to eclipse though. Dealing with Neapolitan bureaucracy for this book has been just as treacherous and memorable.

Acknowledgements

The biggest shout goes out to Shona, for all her help, but most of all for making me laugh.

Love and thanks to the Eames, Brunos and Mains, especially to Jack and Mary May, Gennaro and Anita Fontana, Ma Bruno, Babbo and Anita. Barbara e Pietro: Che matrimonio! In bocca al lupo per il futuro. I raise a cup of tea and cheeky chaser to chums in Dundee, London, Napoli, Verona, Venezia…A special thanks to: The Petrie - for lashings of hospitality, vino and great balls of hell-fire and horse; Vincenzo and Karin for great times in Anacapri and Chiaia; Michelle and Indra for their loveliness; Umberto Benvenuto, a real gentleman; Ennio Morricone, Nino Rota and Black Salt for the soundtrack.

Thanks to Stefania Gatta at ENIT, and the more charming and courteous cogs in the impenetrable beast that is Neapolitan bureaucracy, especially Giovanna Raffone for doing her best to promote Naples – and her family – in her own inimitable way. More appreciation goes to: Albert for an entertaining Spaccanapoli walk; Mariano e famiglia for their generosity; Mario for a tour of his stamperia; Massimo Di Porzio – un vero gentiluomo napoletano; i pizzaioli Mariano e Gaetano, e tutti Da Umberto; il grande Francesco di Coda (Soul Train); Roberto Addeo and the Presídio Vulcano Vesuvio for invaluable advice and a big day in the mouth of Vesuvius; Giovanni Visetti for all your help; Enzo and Peppino at La Tagliata for tasty plates and cakes; Giuseppe Lauro, Francesca Del Vecchio, Giovanni Benvenuto and Victoria Primhak for your suggestions and generosity; and Mimmo e la mamma for a delicious lunch. Not forgetting: Giuseppe Cafora, Monica Presti, la famiglia Gargano, Domenico di Meglio, Ernesto Cacialli, Gloria Morabello, Almamegretta, Anna Scrocca, Gabriella Russo, Giuseppe Cafora, Stefano of Pizzafest, la famiglia Scotti and Domenico Di Meglio.

Finally, a massive thank you goes to my brave editor, Tim Jollands, and to Alan, Kassia and Angus at Footprint for their fine work and saintly patience.

About the book

The guide is divided into four sections: Introducing the region; About the region; Around the city/region and Practicalities.

Introducing the region comprises: At a glance, which explains how the region fits together by giving the reader a snapshot of what to look out for and what makes this region distinct from other parts of the country; **Best of Naples & Amalfi Coast** (top 20 highlights); **A year in Naples & Amalfi Coast**, which is a month-by-month guide to pros and cons of visiting at certain times of year; and **Naples & Amalfi Coast on screen & page**, which is a list of suggested books and films. **About the region** comprises: History; Art & architecture; **Venice & Veneto today**, which presents different aspects of life in the region today; **Nature & environment** (an overview of the landscape and wildlife); **Festivals & events;**

Sleeping (an overview of accommodation options); **Eating & drinking** (an overview of the region's cuisine, as well as advice on eating out); **Entertainment** (an overview of the region's cultural credentials, explaining what entertainment is on offer); **Shopping** (what are the region's specialities and recommendations for the best buys); and **Activities & tours. Around the city/region** is then broken down into five areas, each with its own chapter. Here you'll find all the main sights and at the end of each chapter is a listings section with all the best sleeping, eating & drinking, entertainment, shopping and activities & tours options plus a brief overview of public transport.

Map symbols

[i]	Informazioni Information	**[▥]**	Monumento Monument
[○]	Luogo di interesse Place of Interest	**[▦]**	Stazione Ferroviaria Railway Station
[▥]	Museo/Galleria Museum/Gallery	**[▦]**	Escursioni a piedi Hiking
[▨]	Teatro Theatre	**[M]**	Metropolitana Metro Station
[○]	Negozi Shopping	**[▦]**	Mercato Market
[▨]	Ufficio postale Post Office	**[▦]**	Funicolare Funicular Railway
[✝]	Chiesa Storica Historic Church	**[▨]**	Aeroporto Airport
[▨]	Giardini Gardens	**[▨]**	Universita University
......	Percorsi raccomandati Recommended walk		

Picture credits

Superstock Pages 1, 3, 9, 20, 35, 37, 48, 92, 101, 151, 171, 207, 220, 222, 223, 224, 225, 226, 240, 257, 258, 259, 272: Age fotostock; pages 2, 9, 34, 72, 222, 261: Yoshio Tomii; pages 13, 227: De Agostini; page 18: Mauritus; page 116: Superstock Inc; page 126: Silvio Fiore; page 209: Witold Skrypczak; page 210: Colin Paterson; page 212: B. Zaro.

Julius Honnor pages 2, 6, 17, 121, 281, 282.

Shutterstock pages 2, 17, 26, 108, 128, 181: Alfio Ferlito; page 15: Nadejda Ivanova; pages 16, 85, 92, 219, 251: Danilo Ascione; page 19: Morozova Oksana; page 45: Khirman Vladimir; pages 49, 215: ollirg; pages 83, 185, 215: Einherjar; page 123: Quintanilla; page 127: Giovanni Colo; page 187: Mikhail Nekrasov; page 198: bravajulia; page 205: Irina Korshunova; page 244: Radek Smrcka; page 261: Dino.

Nick Bruno pages 2, 3, 9, 10, 11, 12, 14, 15, 29, 33, 36, 40, 41, 42, 46, 56, 57, 59, 60, 61, 65, 71, 74, 75, 77, 81, 82, 85, 88, 90, 91, 94, 95, 97, 98, 100, 102, 103, 104, 105, 106, 108, 109, 110, 111, 112, 113, 115, 119, 120, 122, 125, 130, 131, 132, 134, 135, 137, 138, 139, 141, 144, 145, 147, 148, 151, 152, 154, 155, 157, 158, 159, 160, 161, 162, 163, 165, 166, 167, 170, 176, 177, 179, 180, 182, 189, 190, 191, 195, 196, 199, 200, 201, 202, 204, 206, 208, 209, 211, 214, 216, 217, 221, 231, 233, 234, 236, 237, 238, 239, 242, 243, 247, 249, 250, 251, 252, 256, 265, 260, 265, 267, 270, 271.

Marina Spironetti pages 2, 9, 168, 173, 174, 175, 178, 186, 188, 191, 193.

tips page 21: Laurence Simon; pages 39, 80: Andrea Pistolesi; page 51: Guido alberto Rossi; page 68: Giuseppe Masci; page 129: Pedone; page 218: Stephano Scata.

Guido alberto Rossi page 51.

Ravello page 52.

Pizzafest page 54.

Alessandra Finelli, Rising Republic pages 64, 66.

Museo Cappella Sansevero page: 93.

EPT Napoli page: 115, 124, 127.

Giovanni Colo page: 127.

Miglio d'Oro Park Hotel page: 196.

Amalfi Hotel page: 229.

Genivs Loci page: 229.

Glow Images Front cover.
Shutterstock (Einherjar; Perov Stanislav) Back cover.

Contents

Reggia di Caserta gardens.

Introducing the region

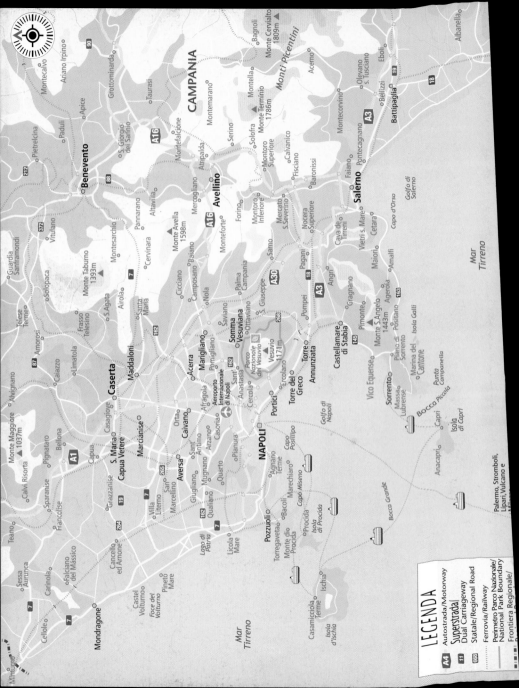

S et in the most spectacular and fertile bay imaginable, Naples oozes deadly gorgeous dollops of history, culture, food and vulcanism. Some 2500 years of life have created an intoxicating tragicomedy that is Napoli, La Città – Naples, the City. Living on their wits in this impossibly crazy and beautiful place, the irrepressible *Napoletani* have created Baroque customs and simple pleasures like *la pizza* and *il bel far niente*: the beauty of doing nothing.

Naples is not just one mad city with an addictive rhythm. Campi Flegrei – the Phlegrean Fields – fizz with fumaroles, springs and Graeco-Roman spas where emperors indulged, plotted and then often lost the plot. Feel the forces of nature around Vesuvius and the archaeological sites, walking on the crater rim of mainland Europe's only active volcano and exploring AD 79 time capsules at Pompeii, Herculaneum, Oplontis and Stabiae. Towering limestone cliffs shelter cute fishing villages, limpid emerald-blue inlets, fairytale castle gardens and majolica-domed churches on the Sorrentine Peninsula and Amalfi Coast. Serenity, glamour and shimmering beauty abound on the Islands of Capri, Ischia and Procida. Capri is all about drama, escapism and the *molto chic*; Ischia heals with its thermal springs, lush valleys and sandy beaches; while Procida has down-to-earth charm and pastel-painted villages straight out of a Neapolitan *presepe* (nativity scene).

At a glance

A whistle-stop tour of Naples & Amalfi Coast

Naples is one crazy *mamma* of a city that yields fascinating ancient baggage and stupefying surroundings: a natural bounty that an endless stream of foreign suitors has coveted. The sparkling gulfs of Napoli and Salerno have spectacular coastlines, islands and volcanoes that spawned Graeco-Roman myths, hedonistic shenanigans and seismic episodes. Despite its natural dangers and perennial troubles, the Campania region offers unparalleled drama, beauty and flavour – a life-affirming walk on the lip of snoozing Vesuvius.

Naples

Naples seeps into you: ignore the overstated negative reputation and experience it. Its relentless rhythm defies the rational as Naples makes its own rules. With 2500 years of foreign influence – including Greek, Roman, Norman, Arab, Swabian, Spanish and French – Naples is a city whose architecture, customs and language barely feel Italian let alone European. In his 1947 novel *La Pelle* (*The Skin*), Curzio Malaparte wrote: "Naples is the most mysterious city in Europe. It is the only city of the Ancient world that has not perished…It is not a city: it's a world – the ancient pre-Christian world, which has survived intact on the surface of the modern world." Naples is a tangle of intense flavours and vibrant culture. It's the home of pizza, coffee, ice cream, pasta and the fruits of

Above: Iconography and *caffettiera napoletana*.
Opposite page: *Gelati*.

The lowdown

Money matters

Naples has always been one of Italy's cheapest cities to visit. Not including entrance fees to the sights and transport costs, the cost of a typical day in Naples if you're flirting with frugality, is around €40-45. This might include: €2 for a cappuccino and *cornetto* in a back street café, *al banco* (standing at the bar); €0.45 for a large bottle of water from a supermarket; €1.50 for two scoops of a gelato; €15 for a simple two-course lunch with water and cover charge; €3 for a Peroni beer or aperitivo sitting down (nibbles are free); and €20 for dinner at a cheaper restaurant (two courses, wine, water and cover charge). If you are going to pad out your day with a bit of largesse by eating at some fancier restaurants then we are talking about €100 per person. Expect to pay for the privilege of consuming sitting down at a swanky cafés like Gambrinus and in tourist hotspots Positano and Capri.

Opening hours & holidays

Aperto or *chiuso*? It takes getting used to that shops, churches and some sights close for a long lunch. Shutters start coming down around 1230 and don't open until around 1600 onwards, although in busy city and touristy areas most of the sights and some shops stay open. Many places close on a Sunday and/or a Monday (or just the Monday morning). Family-run restaurants or bars may shut for a day during the week. Finally, the Italian holiday month is August. This means that shops, bars, restaurants and even some sights can be closed for a fortnight or longer, especially from 15 August (Ferragosto). They also close for Christmas, New Year and some of January too. August is definitely not the best month to visit Italy.

Combined tickets

Naples and the region of Campania's Artecard (see page 77) offers some free and otherwise discounted entry to many sights, plus savings on public transport.

Tourist information

The following official tourist information websites are useful places to visit before your trip: inaples.it, amalfitouristoffice.it, infocampiflegrei.it, capritourism.com, eptcaserta.it, infoischiaprocida.it, turismoinsalerno.it, sorrentotourism.com. If you're travelling by train, also check out trenitalia.it. Once you get to Italy, the regional tourist offices have plenty of leaflets and flyers on local sights and attractions and some offices will also help you to book accommodation.

Tip...

Download a PDF of the latest edition of *Qui Napoli* – the free handy bi-monthly listings booklet – from inaples.it before you arrive.

Introducing the region

Via dei Tribunali alfresco art.

the Campania Felix. Down in the old Graeco-Roman *decumani* streets, amid the layers of architecture and *arte d'arrangiarsi* ("arrange yourself": make ends meet), the languidly sensual *teatro napoletano* is played out with stop-start bursts of energy. Compelling atmospheres fill the city's *rioni* (quarters), from elegant Chiaia to palatial Capodimonte. The muggy air and glimpses of Vesuvius add to the dreamlike spectacle. Neapolitans infuse their Baroque everyday dealings with hedonism and macabre superstition laced with humour. Once Naples gets under your skin, that nonchalant Neapolitan shrug towards the city's perennial woes begins to make some sense. With Campania's beauty and fertility comes the Camorra's grip and volcanic menace. Neapolitans "dwell on the confines of heaven and hell-fire", as the Enlightenment scholar Edwin Gibbon said: so they are bound to behave a little differently. A T-shirt mimicking the warning on a cigarette packet sums up the city's deadly allure: *Napoli non è una città, ma uno stato d'animo* – Naples is not a city, it's a mood: an atmosphere.

Campi Flegrei

Dubbed the "Fiery Fields" by the ancients, this 13 km wide volcanic caldera west of Naples is picturesquely pocked with craters, steaming sights and Graeco-Roman ruins. Mythmakers Virgil and Homer saw this as a land of fatal contrasts: a heavenly Arcadian landscape scarred by a fiery Hades, the entrance to the underworld. Eerily beautiful Lake Averno and the sulphuric moonscape of Solfatara certainly have the whiff of myth about them. At Pozzuoli, Baia and Bacoli, remains of the most lavish spa resort and grandiose Roman buildings, including the Anfiteatro Flavio, mingle with a new wave of swanky beach clubs, restaurants and hotels. Amid the scenic architectural fragments at Cuma, where the Greeks founded Magna Graecia, is a trapezoidal tunnel with fantastical stories attached to a prophetess, the Cumean Sybil. Piscina Mirabilis, a cathedral-like underground cistern, held the water of one of Rome's finest feats of engineering, the Serino Aqueduct. At Bagnoli, an industrial wasteland is slowly being reclaimed as a destination of innovation and pleasure, while at Fuorigrotta, a piece of monumental Fascist architecture, the Mostra d'Oltremare, sits among theme parks, SSC Napoli's Stadio San Paolo and the zoo.

Vesuvius, Herculaneum & Pompeii

Below Vesuvius, compelling time capsules of Roman life continue to astonish archaeologists and visitors. This is *La Zona Rossa*, the Red Zone, the area that will feel the true force of mainland Europe's only active volcano one day. For a heart-pounding dose of humble pie, take a walk around the crater rim of Vesuvius and peer into its depths. There are incredible walks in the Parco Nazionale di Vesuvio and time-travel explorations at Pompeii, Ercolano, Oplontis, Boscoreale and Stabiae. Combine a walk around the ancient well-heeled beachside resort of Herculaneum, where skeletons, jewels and the Villa dei Papiri's priceless library of scrolls are still coming to light, with a journey around mind-blowing Pompeii. Along the *Miglio d'Oro* (the Golden Mile) there are dozens of 18th-century, Bourbon-era *Ville*

Vesuviane. Vesuvian soil yields the tastiest produce including San Marzano tomatoes, apricots, artichokes, persimmons, and grapes that produce the white Vesuvio DOC and Lacryma Christi wines.

Sorrentine Peninsula & Amalfi Coast

Tectonic forces lifted limestone rocks to create these spectacular coastlines. The *Penisola Sorrentina* extends from Roman spa-town Castellammare di Stabia to the wild headland of Punta Campanella, whose glittering splinter, the island of Capri, sits nearby. From Sant'Agata sui Due Golfi, which straddles the gulfs of Naples and Salerno, *la Costiera Amalfitana* and the meandering SS163 Amalfi Drive (beloved of coupé-car advertisers and slow coaches) begins. Soaring cliffs of the Monti Lattari plunge down to an azure sea studded with hidden coves and

grottoes – those natural hideouts of pirates and canoodling film stars. Rustic traditions and the tastiest produce thrive amid the terraced olive and citrus groves, campanile-chiming villages and fishing harbours. Pebbly beaches, dramatic ravines and stunning walks like the Trail of the Gods abound. Touristy Sorrento has its charms, especially towards Massa Lubrense. Positano defines the pastel-painted picturesque harbour turned chic resort. Amalfi basks in its glorious maritime past while lofty Ravello's Norman-Saracenic gardens and glorious vistas are a breath of ethereal air. The bedlam of the Second World War may have seized Salerno yet its *lungomare* and Moorish cathedral cloisters make it worth the detour. Towards the untamed Cilento Coast, Graeco-Roman Paestum and its ancient temples emerge like a vision of a lost civilization.

Capri, Ischia & Procida

These three islands offer their own unique dreams and adventures. Glamour, glitz and the jet-set are synonymous with Capri, the largest and bluest chip off the old Sorrentine Peninsula's limestone rock. So hilly and craggy is Capri that you can easily escape the daily invasion of mass tourism and bask in the island's wild wonders by ducking down a scented lane or by chartering a boat. Emperors Augustus and Tiberius, and writers like Graham Greene and Axel Munthe have all added to its allure as an idyllic retreat of rustic epicurean pleasures and hedonistic japes.

Both Ischia and Procida were plopped into the bay by the Campi Flegrei volcanic caldera. Vestiges of its heated volcanic past can be seen in Ischia's thermal springs, while Procida is made up of four curvy craters that form stunning bays backed by honey-hued tufa rock. Ischia's 46 sq km contain a dead volcano – Monte Epomeo – subtropical gardens and beaches of volcanic sand fizzing with fumaroles. Tiny Procida is all about intimacy, earthiness and relaxation – its leafy lanes lead to pastel-coloured fishing villages and beaches.

Left: Decorum in the forum.

Best of Naples & Amalfi Coast

Top 20 things to see and do

❶ Spaccanapoli & via dei Tribunali
The sticky flagstones of these long and atmospheric Graeco-Roman *decumani* streets are at the very heart of Naples. Weave between buzzing vespas and eavesdrop on Neapolitan street banter while unravelling the city's historic layers, discovering secret cloisters, pious sights, quirky shops, and many dark, esoteric tales and customs. Giving in to the delicious smells and tastes of pizza and pastries is part of the experience. Page 94.

❷ Santa Chiara cloisters
A few steps away from the nearby Spaccanapoli bustle is an enchanting cloistered world. Walking amid ornate arcades and faded frescoes, your eyes are drawn to the sparkling courtyard scene of wisteria creepers, citrus trees and vibrant majolica tiles with their whirls of blue, green and yellow. Page 91.

1 Piaggio & beast on via dei Tribunali.

2 Don't park your *culo* on the Santa Chiara majolica benches!

7 Steamy Solfatara, Pozzuoli.

❸ Cappella di Sansevero
Raimondo VII Prince of Sansevero, a learned Enlightenment figure, refurbished his family chapel filling it with some of the most exquisite statuary in Italy. A vibrant frescoed ceiling, *La Gloria del Paradiso*, full of mysterious Masonic symbols and two chilling anatomical figures allegedly created by princely alchemy, add to Raimondo's mystique. Page 93.

❹ Palazzo Reale & Museo di Capodimonte
A lavish Bourbon palace containing one of Italy's most impressive art collections and royal apartments crammed with gilt and Capodimonte porcelain. The lush landscaped gardens are a favourite for a kickabout and picnics. Page 81.

❺ Certosa di San Martino
This Carthusian monastery sits on the Vomero hill, with the most sublime views across the bay. Important artworks and various collections, including fascinating old maps and views of the city, chronicle Neapolitan history while its Baroque cloisters are studded with Cosimo Fanzago's skulls. Page 123.

❻ Reggia di Caserta
Carlo III of Bourbon's grandiose dream of a palace and adminstrative centre might not have gone quite to plan, but his Luigi Vanvitelli-designed, Versailles-aping vision is mightily impressive nonetheless. After dipping into a fraction of its five floors and 1200 rooms, there are expansive gardens to explore filled with fountains, statuary and Queen Maria Carolina's fantastical follies. Page 126.

❼ Pozzuoli
Pozzuoli, ancient Puteoli, was an important Roman harbour west of Naples. It retains a grimy charm, some fascinating Roman ruins – including the Anfiteatro Flavio – and a nearby crater, the Solfatara, full of bubbling, hissing, sulphurous menace. Page 158.

❽ Piscina Mirabilis
One of the Campi Flegrei's least visited sites is a subterranean Roman cistern with cathedral-like wonders, atmospheric light-effects and magical acoustics. Water was fed to it from the Apennines along another incredible feat of Roman engineering, the Aqua Augusta (Serino Aqueduct). Page 162.

11 Pompeii Scavi.

❾ Vesuvius

Mainland Europe's only active volcano may not have erupted since 1944 but don't underestimate 'Il Dominatore'. Vulcanologists reckon there's 400 sq km of molten rock 8 km below its fizzing fumaroles. A trip to its summit allows you to peer into its crater and down old lava fields to Pompeii and across the bay. Page 172.

❿ Herculaneum

The compact well-to-do Roman resort buried by over 15 m of pyroclastic debris by the AD 79 eruption reveals fine architectural details and artistic riches that allow you to imagine the cultured beachside lifestyle of its doomed inhabitants. Page 172.

⓫ Pompeii

Nothing prepares you for the scale of the most well-known archaeological dig of them all – a town buried in a searing volcanic time capsule for nearly 2000 years. Amid its villas and public spaces, filled with mosaics, frescoes and vulgar Latin graffiti, captivating insights into Roman life are still coming to light. Page 184.

⓬ Baia di Ieranto & Marina del Cantone

Towards wild Punta Campanella are the emerald and azure waters of the Bay of Ieranto and nearby Marina del Cantone, where yachts drop anchor, snorkellers and swimmers splash around and diners eat fresh seafood at beachside restaurants on stilts. Page 211.

⓭ Sentiero degli Dei

The Trail of the Gods consists of two trails (a lower trail and a higher ridge walk) and is best tackled going westwards, for backpack-dropping views of Capri and the Amalfi Coast – it reaches the most divine heights between Grotta Biscotto and Nocella. Page 212.

⑭ Ravello

Splendidly isolated and refined Ravello has inspired literary works and epic operas, including Wagner's *Parsifal*. Its lofty location and genteel atmosphere is the backdrop to the annual, highbrow cultural scrum, the Ravello Festival, but its real charm lies in its Norman-Saracenic villas with their magical garden terraces and shimmering coastal views, and an alluring Romanesque Duomo. Page 221.

⑮ Paestum

Mainland Italy's most important Greek ruins and its three impressive Doric temples emerge out of the wild meadows on the plains of the Sele River – a vision of a lost civilization. Arty adventurers like Shelley, Canova and Goethe made it the climax of the Grand Tour. Page 224.

⑯ Villa Jovis

Emperor Tiberius's infamous palace of pleasure and pain on the island of Capri, from where he ruled the Roman Empire from AD 27 to AD 37, is reached via twisting, scented paths with scampering lizards and abundant birdlife. There are dizzying views from the *specularium* terrace and atop the 300-m cliffs of Tiberius's Leap, where unfortunate victims were flung to the ocean below. Page 247.

⑰ Monte Solaro

As you rise serenely to the 600-m zenith of Capri on a single-seat chairlift, your feet dangle above terraced gardens and Anacapri's chiming bells fade into the distance. On top, you can only linger, enjoying an ice cream and surveying shimmering vistas of the Faraglioni Rocks and the bays of Naples and Salerno. Page 250.

⑱ Monte Epomeo

Ischia's dead volcano is reached on a wooded path that rises to otherworldly tufa rock formations pitted with volcanic bubbles. Clear days on the summit allow awe-inspiring views while cloudy ones evoke an eerie atmosphere that is just as memorable. Page 257.

⑲ Spiaggia dei Maronti

It's a water taxi ride away from Ischia's charming Sant'Angelo to this 2-km-long stretch of volcanic sand. The *spiaggia calda* (hot beach) is studded with steaming fumaroles and relaxing bar-restaurants. Just be careful not to get sizzled red like a lobster. Page 261.

⑳ Marina di Chiaiolella

Corricella may be lauded for its pastel-hued beauty beloved of film makers but crescent-shaped Chiaiolella, which sits in a volcanic crater, has oodles of harbour charm, some smart restaurants and nearby beaches. Page 261.

14 Villa Rufolo, Ravello.

15 Paestum's less ancient ruins.

Month by month

A year in Naples & Amalfi Coast

January & February

After the usual Neapolitan shenanigans at Capodanno (New Year's Eve) involving fireworks, firecrackers and *clacson* cacophony, and then the Epiphany celebrations with Befana treats for kids (6 January), the first month of the year is relatively quiet. Many hotels and restaurants in exclusively touristy spots remain closed but there is still plenty of life and culture in Naples itself. Expect relatively chilly weather (averaging 9°C) and some crisp, sunny days when views of a snow-covered Vesuvius and beyond are often unforgettable. The January sales are particularly good in Naples, with Chiaia the place to grab clothes bargains. The colder weather continues in February with Campania's mountains often sprinkled with snow. Temperatures seldom dip below 6°C in the city and there are spring-like days down here in Southern Italy as early as Shrove Tuesday, the climax of the Carnevale celebrations.

March & April

Although spring arrives during these months and days can be sunny and warm, there can be very

Above: Blooming wisteria vines, Campania.
Opposite page: Spiaggia Grande, Positano.

unsettled weather as well. From mid-April it's often warm enough to bathe and it's an ideal period for walking in the hills of the islands and on the Amalfi Coast and the Sorrentine Peninsula as wild flowers are in bloom and temperatures are not excessive. Big events include *NauticaSud* (early March), the Mezzogiorno's biggest boat show, held at the Mostra d'Oltremare, while at Paestum the town comes out and feasts for the *Festa Tradizionale dell'Annunziata* (24-25 March). For a week at the end of March, the *Settimana della Cultura* allows visitors to take advantage of free museum entrance, special guided tours and cultural events all over the country. Salerno stages its own film and cultural festival, *Linea d'Ombra* (mid-April).

Easter (*Pasqua*) celebrations and colourful processions dominate life across the region: Sorrento has a week of celebrations, Good Friday in Procida sees the macabre mix with the flamboyant, while the Procession of the Mysteries, on Easter Monday at Sant'Anastasia, at the foot of Vesuvius, commemorates a 16th-century miracle with barefooted men running through the streets asking for alms. It's the busiest time of year with backpack-toting *ragazzi* (youth) mimicking the disciples by jamming into the region's trains for a big day out. Amid the roaming herds of noisy teenagers and family day trippers are lots of traditional Neapolitan foods to sample including savoury *casatiello* and the now ubiquitous *pastiera* cake.

May & June

The bathing season officially starts on 1 May and from now until late October temperatures rarely dip below 20°C. Early May is arguably the best time to visit the region as the weather is pleasant, prices have yet to reach August heights and there are some fabulous cultural events. The *Maggio dei Monumenti* (May of Monuments), started in 1994 when Antonio Bassolino was mayor of Naples, sees free access to rarely seen sights and themed cultural events. Concerts and installations are held in historic spaces, sometimes with inspirational results, as when Brian Eno brought his multimedia

Above: Teatro San Carlo and the Galleria Umberto I. Opposite page: Totò on via San Gregorio Armeno.

work *77 Million Paintings* to the Grotta di Seiano. Music festivals appear all over the region, including the *Concerti al Tramonto*, sunset classical concerts held at Villa San Michele, Anacapri, from June to September; music recitals in La Mortella Gardens, Ischia; and *Festivalbar*, a series of televised concerts across Italy, comes to piazza Plebiscito with Italian acts like Ligabue and Jovanotti appearing alongside stadium-fillers Red Hot Chilli Peppers. June marks the beginning of *OPEN Estate a Napoli*, involving lots of cultural events throughout the city culminating in the recently reinstated Festa di Piedigrotta in September. Also of note is the *Regata Storica delle Quattro Repubbliche Marinare* (first Sunday in June), an ancient boat race that takes place at Amalfi every four years: after 2009, the fanfare and oarsmen will next return in 2013.

July & August

The holiday season gets into full swing and temperatures soar, averaging nearly 30°C, as do hotel rates. Oppressive heat, humidity and poor air quality, especially in Naples and Salerno, can make it a very uncomfortable time to visit. Boat services are at their peak so expect a sweaty scrum to get on your Capri-bound hydrofoil. Roads are often jammed throughout the region, especially along the Sorrentine Peninsula and Amalfi Coast at peak times; Sunday evenings can be gridlocked as people return after a weekend jaunt. Most Italians go on holiday in August and generally hit the beach – many businesses in the city close at this time. On 15 August the *Ferragosto* bank holiday, with origins in Roman Emperor Augustus's *Feriae Augusti*, heralds the biggest exodus of Italians on their holidays.

Of course, some big occasions provide reasons to be cheerful during this crazy time of year. The

Festa della Madonna del Carmine sees the Madonna del Carmine campanile in illusory flames. Fireworks and floats festoon the waters around the Castello Aragonese, Ischia, for the *Festa di Sant'Anna* (26 July), and Positano celebrates the *Festa dell'Assunta* (14-15 August) with re-enactments of Saracen raids. *Amalfi Estate* stages mainly classical and jazz concerts in dramatic settings including the Duomo and Grotta dello Smeraldo. For culture vultures there is no more spectacularly located classical music and arts programme than the Ravello Festival (until November). In mid-July the Neapolis Festival sees left-field acts like Massive Attack, Almamegretta and REM play at the Arena Flegrea.

September & October

Temperatures remain high in September, hovering around the mid-20s, while October is generally cooler, averaging around 20°C with more rainfall. Towards the end of October freakish cold snaps can arrive from the north. September is still busy in the tourist spots so prices for accommodation remain at high-season rates until early October.

Neapolitans come home in September, returning from their holidays to festivals and events that reflect the inhabitants' greatest passions: pizza, football, music and their favourite cult and saint, San Gennaro. *Pizzafest* fills ten days and thousands of stomachs with the best flat-bread meal known to man or yeast. The first encounters of SSC Napoli's footie season occupy the papers and discussions in late August onwards. Then there's the *Festa di San Gennaro* with its noisy celebrations, pyrotechnics and feasting on 19 September. In Anacapri, locals come together for the *Settembrata Anacaprese* to see which *quartiere* can produce the best food, sing the sweetest and laugh the longest. The *Festa di Piedigrotta* is back on the calendar in early September, on a smaller scale now, but still featuring a celebration of Neapolitan song and a colourful procession. Teatro San Carlo opens its classical music season.

November & December

Long sleeves, a waterproof jacket and an umbrella are definitely needed with temperatures dipping from an average 16°C to 11°C, while November sees the most rainfall – warm sunny days with temperatures up to 22°C are not uncommon though, especially in November. Food, nativities and Christmas become increasingly important. During the last week in November the region celebrates the pressing of the new olive harvest, and you can taste the new golden *olio di extra vergine* at Vico Equense. The *Festa di Santa Lucia*, the patron saint of the blind, is celebrated with fire, vino and sausages (12-14 December). In the run up to Christmas, the streets of Naples – via San Gregorio Armeno in particular – have extra magic, with twinkling *presepi* (nativity scenes) and stalls selling traditional Christmas treats. Most churches have a manger display and 'live' cribs with performers can be seen in the provinces, such as San Leucio outside Caserta.

Screen & page

Naples & Amalfi Coast in film & literature

Napule è mille culure, Napule è mille paure (Naples is a thousand colours, Naples is a thousand fears), sang Pino Daniele – many of its hues and cries fill books, screens and vinyl grooves, spanning three millennia.

Films

Paisà (Paisan)
Roberto Rossellini, 1946
A post-war neo-Realist classic consisting of six vignettes, one set in Naples.

Sciuscià (Shoeshine)
Vittorio de Sica, 1946
Neo-Realist flick, showing how the post-Second World War *scugnizzi* – Naples' street kids – ground out an existence.

Napoli Milionaria (Naples Millionaire)
Eduardo de Filippo, 1950
Playwright-actor de Filippo plays Gennaro Jovine, a well-meaning Neapolitan who gets caught up in people's troubles.

L'Oro di Napoli (The Gold of Naples)
Vittorio de Sica, 1954
Starring the comic genius Totò, Sophia Loren, Eduardo de Filippo and de Sica, this tribute to Naples explores the variety and moods of the city through its street characters, including a clown, a prostitute, a pizza seller and a gambler.

**Io Speriamo che me la Cavo
(Ciao Professore!)
Lina Wertmuller, 1992**
A teacher from the north struggles with a school of cheeky Neapolitan truants in this heart-warming comedy.

**Tutto Maradona
Rai/Logos TV, 1992**
Diego Maradona's goals for SSC Napoli plus interviews and insightful footage off the pitch.

**Libera
Pappi Corsicato, 1993**
Three tales about three 1990s Neapolitan women and their troublesome lives.

**L'Amore Molesto
Mario Martone, 1995**
An atmospheric film about a woman investigating the mysterious death of her mother.

**Gomorrah
Matteo Garrone, 2008**
Roberto Saviano's exposé of the Camorra's grip on Naples hits the big screen.

**It Started in Naples
Melville Shavelson, 1960**
Sophia Loren and Clark Gable fall in love on Capri to a swinging soundtrack that includes *Tu vuò fa l'Americano*.

**Le Mani sulla Città (Hands Over the City)
Francesco Rosi, 1963**
Leone d'Oro award winner about corrupt Neapolitan politicians and ruthless property speculators.

**Avanti!
Billy Wilder, 1972**
Jack Lemmon and Juliet Mills star in Wilder's dark romantic comedy in which Lemmon, an American business tycoon, travels to Ischia to collect the body of his father.

**Ricomincio da tre
Massimo Troisi, 1981**
Starring comic Massimo Troisi, who directs himself in this film about a Neapolitan in Florence.

Film locations of box-office hits

Ischia and Procida The fictional town of Mongibello in *The Talented Mr Ripley* is a mixture of Ischia Ponte and Procida's Piazza dei Martiri, Corricella and Pozzo Vecchio beach. Billy Wilder's comedy *Avanti!* was also shot on Ischia, while much of *Il Postino* was shot on Procida.

Naples and Capri *It Started in Naples*, a feel-good flick starring Sophia Loren and Clark Gable, was filmed in Naples and Capri. Jean-Luc Godard's arty-farty 1963 film *Le Mépris*, starring Brigitte Bardot, features Villa Malaparte, Capri.

Caserta The Star Wars prequels, *The Phantom Menace* and *Attack of the Clones*, feature the Reggia di Caserta's grand staircase.

Introducing the region

Books

Fiction
The Aeneid
Virgil, first century BC
Mantova-born Virgil lifted the Hellenistic hero Aeneas from Homer's *Iliad* and plonked him in a steamy, magical Campania in this epic poem that cunningly attaches illustrious Greek gods with Julius Caesar's heirs.

The Decameron
Giovanni Boccaccio, 1350
A collection of bawdy tales, many inspired by Boccaccio's time spent in Naples, told by a group of Tuscans who have fled from a plague-ravaged Florence.

Pentamerone (Tale of Tales)
Giambattista Basile, 1634
The 50 Neapolitan fairy tales collected and adapted by Basile were first published as *Lo Cunto de li Cunti* but later came to be known as the *Pentamerone* in deference to the structure of Boccaccio's *Decameron*. They include the first recorded versions of 'Cinderella', 'Sleeping Beauty', 'Rapunzel' and 'Hansel and Gretel'.

La Pelle
Curzio Malaparte, 1949
Describes the chaos and degradation after the Allied liberation of Naples.

Thus Spake Bellavista
Luciano De Crescenzo, 1989
Translated from the Italian, *Così Parlò Bellavista* (1984), De Crescenzo spins humorous yarns and entertaining theories through Professor Bellavista, who encounters a host of bizarre Neapolitan characters and their oddball survival techniques.

The Volcano Lover
Susan Sontag, 1992
This historical romance set in Naples in the late 1700s centres on the love triangle between Sir William Hamilton, his wife Emma and Lord Nelson.

Pompeii
Robert Harris, 2003
A well-researched and gripping novel that charts the life of a Roman engineer working on the Aqua Augusta from 22 to 25 August AD 79.

The Vesuvius Club
Mark Gatiss, 2004
Lucifer Box, an Edwardian secret agent, uncovers mysterious Masonic shenanigans amid the fleshy and sulphurous miasma of Napoli's hairy underbelly.

Non-fiction
New Science
Giambattista Vico, 1744
An influential humanist philosophical work, *Principi di Scienza Nuova d'intorno alla Comune Natura delle Nazioni*, that explores the development of language and society. It inspired James Joyce's *Finnegan's Wake* and continues to raise many brows.

The Essence of Aesthetic
Benedetto Croce, 1912
Rescued amid the rubble of the 1883 Ischia earthquake, Croce went on to become an influential philosopher. In *Breviario di Estetica* he opines that making art is an intuitive process.

The Story of San Michele
Axel Munthe, 1929
The story of a Swedish doctor's love affair with Capri.

Naples '44
Norman Lewis, 1978
Norman Lewis documents his incredible experiences as a British intelligence officer during the liberation of Naples, describing the atrocities of war and the city's starving yet forever resourceful population.

The Hand of God: the life of Diego Maradona
Jimmy Burns, 1996
An insightful trawl through El Pibe d'Oro's sublime and ridiculous moments.

Greene on Capri
Shirley Hazzard, 2000
A beautifully written and insightful memoir about the author's time spent with Graham Greene on his beloved Capri, from their first meeting in 1962 to Greene's last visit to the island in 1988.

See Naples and Die:
the Camorra & Organized Crime
Tom Behan, 2002
An academically researched account about the Camorra.

The Food and Wine Guide
to Naples and Campania
Carla Capalbo, 2005
Visits the region's food and wine producers, restaurants and pizzerias.

In The Shadow of Vesuvius
Jordan Lancaster, 2005
A readable account of Neapolitan history packed with facts and quirky stories.

Gomorrah: Italy's Other Mafia
Roberto Saviano, 2006
Roberto Saviano, from the notorious Camorra stronghold of Casal di Principe, investigates gangland life in Naples' suburbs. Weaving in disquieting stories and statistics from various sources, he paints a grimly fascinating picture of their far-reaching activities, in this journalistic 'non-fiction novel'.

Contents

About the region

Casa del Fauno mosaic.

History

Prehistoric tribes, the Etruscans & Greeks

While the history of Naples can be traced back to the seventh century BC, evidence of human existence in the Campania region goes back into prehistory. Fossilized footprints thought to belong to *Homo erectus* were found recently on the Roccamonfina volcano; in 2008 it was confirmed that these *ciampate del diavolo* (devil's trails) are the oldest known human footprints, dating back 385,000 to 325,000 years. In the caves of Capri and the Cilento coast Stone Age burials, bones and tools have been found spanning the Upper Paleolithic, Mesolithic and Neolithic periods (10,000-5000 BC).

Around 5000 BC southern Italy's hunter-gatherers were displaced by seafaring and agriculturally skilled settlers from Near Eastern territories Anatolia and Mesopotamia. Communities that could seed crops, rear animals and construct basic buildings produced Molfetta vases and worked metal. Around 3000 BC Italic tribes dominated Calabria, while Lucanians and Illyrians from the Balkans settled in nearby Basilicata and Puglia. Then, during the Bronze Age (after 1800 BC), Greek influence and trading links began: Mycenean and Minoan objects have been found as far north as the Etruscan territories in Lazio.

From the eighth century BC Greek settlers and Etruscans (a Mediterranean people with a rich culture and debatable origin) began to dominate the region. Colonizers from the Greek island Euboea established a trading settlement at Pithecusae (Ischia), then spread to the mainland, founding the colony Cumae (Cuma). The Cumaeans prospered, expanding along the coast to found Parthenope (near modern Pizzofalcone in Naples) before eventually building Neapolis – the 'new city' – alongside it, around 470 BC. Neapolis (Naples) became an important trading port and acquired its grid-like layout and walls, populated by over 30,000, swelled by more Greek colonists. Hellenistic culture – art, theatre, architecture, philosophy and literature – and its gods Dionysus (wine), Aphrodite (love) and Demeter (fertility and agriculture) flourished.

Magna Graecia – those parts of Italy and Sicily colonized by the Greeks – expanded through southern Italy with Spartans founding Tara (modern Taranto in Puglia) and Sybarites establishing Poseidonia (Paestum). Meanwhile the Etruscans, based at nearby Capua, established the towns of Herculaneum, Pompeii, Nola and Salerno. Something had to give and it did in 524 BC when a coalition of local tribes led by the Capuan Etruscans was defeated by the Cumaeans. The Greeks finally halted Etruscan expansion after a naval battle near Cumae in 474 BC. With Etruscan influence on the wane, hill tribes from the central Apennines, as well the Samnites, swallowed up large areas of Campania and threatened Magna Graecia's disunited Greek colonies.

Early Roman era

There seemed to be only one solution: alliance with the newly emerging power to the north, Rome, which greatly admired Hellenistic culture. Tara with the aid of Pyrrhus, King of Epirus, and then Carthaginian Hannibal (during the three Punic Wars) both aided by elephants, put up a fight, but by the third century BC southern Italy, including Campania, was under Roman control. Neapolis held out for a while, siding with Samnite tribes, but eventually agreed to become a federated city, with the Romans controlling commerce but not influencing the strong Greek identity. Indeed Hellenistic philosophy and art greatly influenced Rome, to the extent that, according to Strabo, writing in his first century AD work *Geographica*: "Greater vogue is given to the Greek way of life at Neapolis by the Roman people…taking delight in the way of living and observing the great number of men of the same culture as themselves sojourning there, happily fall in love with the place and make it their permanent home." The fertile soil of the so-called *Campania Felix* (Happy Land) yielded plentiful produce for the empire, and its coastal villas and spas at Baiae became the ultimate holiday resort. Romans revelled in the carefree Neapolitan lifestyle that contrasted with regimented Rome.

The Julio-Claudian emperors

Chroniclers Cicero and Plutarch talked of lavish villas, such as Vedio Pollione's '*Pausylipon*' (meaning 'freedom from pain'), located in modern Posillipo, and Lucullus's *Castellum Lucullanum* at Megaride (now the Castel dell'Ovo). The first Roman emperor, Caesar Augustus, built the Portus Julius naval port at Misenum and the nearby Piscina Mirabilis, the terminal reservoir of the 96-km-long Aqua Augusta (Serino Aqueduct), an immense engineering undertaking that supplied water to the cities in the Bay of Naples.

For those about to rock, Marcus Nonius Balbus salutes you.

At the wealthy resort of Herculaneum, the teachings of the Greek philosopher Epicurus and Philodemus of Gadara blossomed at the house of Piso, whose library of papyrus scrolls (see Villa dei Papiri, page 178) has yet to yield all of its ancient treasures. Epicureanism extolled the virtues of experiencing the pleasures of life in moderation and Virgil (70-19 BC), who spent much time in the Bay of Naples where he enjoyed his "studies in ignoble idleness", leaned on Greek culture to create the idea of Arcadia – an idealized simple life in a bucolic landscape. Perhaps more tellingly, his epic poem, the *Aeneid*, linked the imperial pretender Augustus with godly Greek ancestors from Troy.

About the region

The poem is ancient propaganda if you will; a classic example of Rome aping the Greeks to create a potent identity. Campania becomes the backdrop to this meeting of Greek and Roman mythology: through the soothsayer, the Cumaean Sybil, the hero Aeneas goes through Solfatara (see page 160) into Hades, the underworld, to meet the spirit of his father Anchises who tells him of the destiny of Rome.

From Suetonius's *De Vita Caesarum*, known as 'The Twelve Caesars', and Tacitus's *Annals* and *Histories* we have an idea, perhaps biased and exaggerated, of the decline of the Julio-Claudian dynasty's five emperors and successors between 27 BC and AD 68. Many of the most infamous dramas were played out in the Bay of Naples: Augustus (27 BC to AD 14) met Cassius and Octavian at Brutus's Nisida villa, where they plotted the assassination of Julius Caesar on the ides of March; Tiberius (AD 14-37) had a wild time holed up in his Capri villas and was suffocated at Misenum; Caligula (AD 37-41) famously rode horseback across a 3-mile bridge of boats and was later stabbed by conspirators; Claudius (AD 41-54) built a villa in Baiae for his first wife Messalina, who enjoyed herself too much for his liking – his second wife Agrippina may have killed him with a dodgy mushroom so that her son Nero (AD 54-68) would succeed him. Tubby megalomaniac Nero was a regular performer at a Neapolis theatre, and allegedly murdered his mother, then committed suicide, at his massive Baiae villa. Petronius also paints a picture of cruelty and debauchery during the reign of Nero in his notorious work *Satyricon*. Wild pagan celebrations borrowed from the Greek god Dionysius may have been outlawed by Rome, yet stories and evidence of wild orgiastic rites at Pompeii are rampant (see Villa dei Misteri, page 193). The next earth-shattering event helped seal the sauciness in the most captivating time capsule.

The eruption helped seal Pompeii's sauciness in a most captivating time capsule.

There may be intrigue and conjecture surrounding the Roman rulers, but the events of 26 August AD 79 are not disputed. The eruption of long-dormant Vesuvius engulfed Pompeii, Herculaneum and many nearby towns. Pliny the Elder and his nephew Pliny the Younger witnessed the cataclysmic events. The former perished trying to rescue friends at Stabiae while the younger Pliny stayed behind and wrote an invaluably descriptive account in a letter to Tacitus. Nearly 2000 years later Pompeii, Herculaneum and other buried towns below Vesuvius revealed their secrets.

Rise of Christianity

Roman power was on the wane in southern Italy and by the third century AD the city became a backwater as the Empire's power split into four administrative centres under Emperor Diocletian (AD 284-305). Christianity had been on the rise in Naples since the alleged visit of the apostle St Paul. Diocletian's persecution of the region's Christians created a very Neapolitan martyr when the Bishop of Benevento, Gennaro, was imprisoned, tortured, thrown to the bears in the Flavian amphitheatre at Pozzuoli (they weren't interested), then beheaded at nearby Solfatara in AD 305. Peculiarly Neapolitan paganism mixed with Christian idolatry created rituals involving blood and bones – in centuries to come the cult of San Gennaro (St Januarius) and the miracle of liquefying blood became its most popular example. The Edict of Milan signed by Emperor Constantine in AD 313 granted freedom of worship throughout the Roman Empire, so allowing Napoli's Palaeo-Christianity to develop.

Constantine took power east to Byzantium. In the fifth century the barbarians were making inroads in the north, with Huns and Vandals wreaking havoc and the Goths repeatedly sacking Rome. Romulus Augustus, the last emperor of the Western Empire, ousted from Rome by the Ostrogoths, was exiled at Lucullus's villa at Megaride and died there in AD 476. In 472 Vesuvius erupted and expelled so much ash that some fell in Constantinople, and not long after the Western Empire and ancient Rome fizzled out in Neapolis.

In search of the Greeks & Romans

For prehistoric and Graeco-Roman artefacts the Museo Archeologico Nazionale (see page 227) is peerless. Greek architectural remains can be seen at Cuma (see page 158), Paestum (see page 226), Ischia (see page 252) and piazza Bellini (see page 102) in Naples. Walking around Pompeii and Herculaneum's Roman streets and villas is mind-blowing (see pages 172 and 184).

Early Medieval Naples

Byzantine rule (AD 476-763)

Despite attempts by Emperor Justinian (527-565) to reunite the Western Empire by sending in the general Belisarius to expel the Ostrogoths in the sixth century, the hard-fought victories were fleeting. Instability followed. In 537 the Goths in Naples held out in a three-week siege but eventually cunning Byzantine troops entered the city via subterranean aqueducts and the Goths were massacred. The Gothic War (1535-1554) raged for many years until the last remnants of the Ostrogoth army were defeated in October 1553 at the Battle of Mons Lactarius, in the Monti Lattari mountains, near Vesuvius. Justinian's reconquest was shortlived as in 568 the Lombards arrived from the north, taking Benevento in Campania. When Ravenna, the centre of Byzantine power in Italy, was taken in 751 Byzantine rule ended.

Independent Duchy (AD 763-1139)

In 763 Naples became an independent duchy under enlightened Duke Stephen II who allied the city to the Papacy. Naples proudly kept its Greek traditions and prospered over the next four centuries. The city and its region flourished economically and culturally. A coin from this era in the British Museum depicts San Gennaro clutching the gospels with 'Neapolis' on the flip-side. Benedictine monk, historian and Carolingian renaissance man Paul the Deacon (720-800), who spent much time at Monte Cassino, wrote influential historical works and a hymn containing the first 'do-re-mi' scale. Enlightened Duke John IV ruled between 997 and 1002, and amassed an important library of books from Constantinople. In the late eighth century the south resisted the emerging Frankish influence and the advance of the Holy Roman Empire created by the coronation of Charlemagne in Rome. Maritime republics at Sorrento and Amalfi were founded and amassed great wealth. In 839 the landlocked Lombard Duchy of Benevento took Amalfi and by the year 1000 tiny Amalfi had a population of 70,000 – its influence extended as far as Constantinople and Jerusalem, and its maritime might rivalled Pisa, Genoa and Venice.

In the ninth century Saracen Arabs took Sicily from the Byzantines. Naples allied with the new maritime invaders and even helped take the ports of Puglia, including Bari, which had Muslim rulers for 30 years. When Rome fell in 846 Neapolitan general Cesarius joined a coalition of forces summoned by Pope Leo IV that defeated the Arabs. Neapolitan and Meridionale traditions, varieties of lemons and oranges as well as candied fruits and ice cream are of Arabic origin.

Normans & the Holy Roman Empire

The next threat arrived from Normandy and the Gallicized Vikings, who after stints as mercenaries on the Italian peninsula increased their influence and eventually usurped the Lombards and the various independent duchies. In 1139 Norman King Roger II de Hauteville united Naples and Sicily as the Kingdom of the Two Sicilies, with Palermo as its capital. Despite Naples' power waning it continued to be a cosmopolitan trading city. Many cultural institutions emerged, including Europe's first medical school at Salerno. Soon after the Hauteville line died out in 1189, Henry IV of Hohenstaufen, son of Holy Roman Emperor Frederick Barbarossa and married to a Norman princess Constance, took the crown. After the death of his mother in 1197, three-year-old Frederick II of Hohenstaufen became King of Sicily and then in 1220, after negotiations with two

Early medieval remains & artefacts

Byzantine interlaced arches and mosaics can be seen at the *duomi* of Ravello (see page 221), Amalfi (see page 214) and Salerno (see page 225). La Pietrasanta (see page 85) is the finest example of early medieval architecture in Naples.

popes (Innocent III and his successor Honorius III), he took the crown of Holy Roman Emperor.

Nicknamed '*Stupor Mundi*' ('Wonder of the World'), this orphaned only-child grew up in Palermo and developed an erudite mind that was way ahead of its time; he became fluent in six languages and was a scholar of the arts, sciences, mathematics and falconry. He produced the first medieval legal code and model of government, the Constitutions of Melfi, and in 1224 founded the first state university in Europe, the *Università Federico II*, which reinvigorated the city and made Naples an influential centre of independent thinking. (One of its most famous students was Thomas Aquinas, author of *Summa Theologiae*, which challenged Catholicism's disregard of scientific and philosophical enquiry.) Frederick's court attracted all the leading thinkers of the day and produced a 14-line poetry sonnet that influenced Dante, Petrach and Shakespeare. He built a chain of castles including the incredible octagonal hunting lodge-fortress Castel del Monte in Puglia, famed for its mysterious equilibrium that attracts many theories as to the recurrence of the number eight in its design. His excommunication by Gregory IX was lifted after a successful and bloodless crusade in 1228 that gave Christians access to holy places in Nazareth and Jerusalem. Frederick died in 1250 and his heirs, Conrad, Manfred and Conradin, were all ousted by the Pope who had a French Guelph (a supporter of the church opposed to the imperial Ghibellines) in mind for the vacant Neapolitan throne.

Angevins

Charles I & II to Robert the Wise

Charles of Anjou, youngest son of Louis VIII of France and King of Sicily since 1262, was crowned King of the Two Sicilies by Pope Urban IV in 1266 and made Naples his capital. Resentment grew in Sicily, culminating in the revolt known as the Sicilian Vespers (on Easter Monday 1282) and the eventual cession of the island to the Spanish Aragonese. While during the middle and late medieval period northern Italian city states began creating great wealth, it could be argued that Angevin rule in the south set the tone of economic backwardness here: the Guelph-controlled kingdom exempted the wealthy and the church from taxes, instead burdening its poorer subjects heavily to pay the 40,000 florin papal annuity. However, a period of cultural flowering and relative stability created an elegant capital with new city walls, French Gothic-style buildings and public works. Piazza del Mercato became the new civic space, Maschio Angioino was built and the population trebled (30,000 to 100,000) during nearly two centuries of Angevin rule.

Charles I's successors Charles II and Robert (the Wise) continued the royal patronage of the arts, especially Robert who through Guelph allegiances with Florence attracted artists such as Giotto. Boccaccio came to Naples to work in one of the Florentine banks that funded manufacture in cloth and silverware but soon realized his vocation was in writing. So enamoured was he with Naples and the Angevin courtly life that many tales in his playful masterpiece the *Decameron* are based on his time here. Roman poet laureate Petrarch was also a great admirer of the learned Robert and Naples. As well as constructing fabulous tombs and Gothic churches, the Angevins placed more emphasis on the cult of Gennaro by renovating the Duomo and creating a reliquary bust to preserve the saint's skull.

Neapolitan Monarchs

Norman kings
1130-1154	Roger II
1154-1166	William I
1166-1189	William II
1189-1194	Tancred
1194	William III

House of Hohenstaufen
1194-1197	Henry (VI, Holy Roman Emperor)
1197-1250	Frederick (II, Holy Roman Emperor)
1250-1254	Conrad (IV, Holy Roman Emperor)
1254-1258	Conradin (Holy Roman Emperor)
1258-1266	Manfred

Angevin Dynasty
1266-1285	Charles I of Anjou (Carlo I d'Angiò)
1285-1309	Charles II
1309-1343	Robert 'the Wise'
1343-1381	Joan I (deposed)
1381-1386	Charles III
1386-1414	Ladislaus
1414-1435	Joan II
1435-1442	René

Aragonese Dynasty
1442-1458	Alfonso I
1458-1494	Ferdinand I (Ferrante)
1494-1495	Alfonso II
1495-1496	Ferdinand II
1496-1501	Frederick IV

French rule 1501-1503, Spanish viceroyalty 1503-1713 and Austrian rule 1714-1734.

The Bourbons
1734-1759	Charles VII
1759-1825	Ferdinand IV and I (deposed *1806-1815* during *House of Bonaparte rule* under Joseph I and Joachim I)
1825-1830	Francis I
1830-1859	Ferdinand II
1859-1861	Francis II

Top: Carlo I d'Angiò (Charles I of Anjou). Above: *Carte Napoletane.*

Above: Santa Chiara Cloisters.
Opposite page: Alfonso d'Aragona's trumphal arch, Castel Nuovo.

It's a fact...

Angevin sovereigns were buried at Santa Chiara
(see page 91) and there are more examples of
exquisite funerary monuments from this era at San
Giovanni a Carbonara (see page 111).

Notorious Joans

When Robert the Wise died in 1343 he was
succeeded by the 16-year-old Princess Joan of Anjou
who as a child had been married to an Angevin
sovereign from Hungary, Andrew. Unlucky Andrew
was assassinated – perhaps at the Queen's request.
Cue a Hungarian invasion on Joan's coronation and
coups galore. Joan married a further three times and
was quite a handful according to the colourful
rumours. She lost three children as well, and to
add to her private ups and downs Joan also reigned
during the first of four outbreaks of bubonic plague
to strike the city over the next century. More twists
in the Angevin Neapolitan tale involving Hungarian
and French claimants to the throne ensued, and
Joan was imprisoned and died in tragic
circumstances in 1382.

According to many accounts, the sexual
appetites, lack of heirs and regal ineptitude of
Joan II, the last Angevin sovereign of Naples,
mirrored those of her namesake. Joan II was forced
to turn to Alfonso V of Aragon for help. After being
kidnapped by an alliance comprising powerful city
states and the pope, who preferred a French
claimant, Alfonso came to a strategic agreement
with the Duke of Milan, Philip Maria Visconti, and
took the throne of a reunited Kingdom of the Two
Sicilies in 1442.

Spanish Naples

The Aragonese dynasty (1442-1501)

Naples became the capital of the Kingdom of
the Two Sicilies and the Catalan dynasty lavished
money on the city, renovating and building new
piazzas filled with Baroque flourishes. Spain
encamped in Naples, with Spanish becoming

the official language of court, and under Alfonso (Alphonso/Alfons) the Magnanimous the city became a centre of the arts and humanism.

During Alfonso's reign, Francesco Laurana designed the triumphal arch at the Castel Nuovo and poet Jacopo Sannazaro wrote *Arcadia*, evoking the bucolic visions of an idealized Campania, reminiscent of that described by Virgil. Alfonso's successor Ferrante I (Ferdinand I of Aragon) was less of a charmer and more interested in government and law. He had difficulty learning Italian. Discontented nobles backed a brief return of the Angevins, under John of Anjou, that lasted seven months. On 13 August 1486 the aristocracy gathered for a wedding reception at Maschio Angioino, and Ferrante exacted his revenge by arresting and executing his enemies. After Ferrante I's death Alfonso II abdicated in favour of his son Ferrante II, but Ferrantino ('Little Ferrante') died at the tender age of 12. There followed more jostling for power between the French and Spanish royals, which flared into war.

Spanish viceroyalty (1503-1713)

A Spanish viceroyalty was established in 1503 which lasted until until the War of Spanish Succession in the early 1700s – over 40 viceroys held the post and six Spanish kings ruled during this time, starting with Holy Roman Emperor Charles V (Charles IV of Naples, Charles I of Spain), who famously declared: "I speak Spanish to God, Italian to women, French to men and German to my horse." The period saw a Neapolitan renaissance in music, arts and philosophy: Carlo Gesualdo (a noble who murdered his wife and lover in bed) invigorated the madrigal musical composition, Caravaggio's vivid brush strokes sparked the development of the Neapolitan naturalist school of painting, and the city became the centre of philosophy and science, producing Giordano Bruno, who challenged the church's view of nature.

The 16th century

The most notable viceroy was Don Pedro Alvarez de Toledo (1532-1553) who meted out severe punishments to criminals, repaired the Saracen tower defences against pirates and began construction of the Palazzo Reale and the Spanish quarters to house soldiers and their families. As Naples became the largest metropolis in Europe (300,000 in the early 17th century) a group of urban misfits, the *lazzaroni* (after St Lazarus, patron saint of lepers), emerged and when in 1646-1647 taxation soared, one of their number, Masaniello, led a revolt against the Spanish. He ruled for a week before being murdered by the viceroy's assassins.

Naples in the 17th century had more than its fair share of natural disasters. In 1631 the last Plinian eruption of Vesuvius rocked the region as did earthquakes in 1668 and 1694. Two-thirds of the population perished in the plagues of 1656 and 1691. Amid this destruction, San Gennaro was called upon time and time again, saints' day celebrations multiplied and charitable organizations – such as the Monte di Pietà, the Hospital of the Incurables and orphanages – were established.

Austrian Habsburgs (1713-1734)

The Enlightenment had an impact on a group of nobles who dreamed of an independent Naples. When Charles II of Spain (Charles V of Naples) died in 1700 without an heir they seized their chance. The nobles' leader Tiberio Carafa travelled to Venice and met with the Habsburg emperor, who agreed to place his second son Charles as king of an independent Naples. Meanwhile, French King

Historic remains & artefacts

The ornamental triumphal arch at the Castel Nuovo (see page 84), built in 1443 in honour of Alfonso V of Aragon (Alfonso I of Naples), is an imposing piece of early Renaissance artistry. Baroque fountains, church *campanali* and ceremonial spires built in this era include the Guglia di San Gennaro (see page 101), Santa Maria del Carmine (see page 113) and the Fontana di Monteoliveto (see page 106). La Capella di San Gennaro (see page 100) was erected after the 1527 plague.

Above: Liberty-style bandstand (1877), Villa Comunale gardens.
Opposite page: Piazza Plebiscito.

Louis XIV's grandson Philip of Anjou, to whom Charles II of Spain had bequeathed his possessions, claimed the throne and installed himself as Philip V of Spain (and therefore Philip IV of Naples). The aristocrats' coup failed, as it lacked popular support amongst the poor, but the nobles were later to get their wish when, after the War of Spanish Succession, the ensuing Treaty of Utrecht (1713) ceded more Italian territory to the Austrian Habsburgs, including Naples. However, the Austrians' policies in Naples made them very unpopular, so the invasion of a Spanish army in 1734 under the command of Philip V's teenage son Charles was celebrated, heralding a new era under Spanish Bourbon rule.

The Bourbon era

King Big Nose, the Lazzarone King & the Hamiltons (1734-1798)

In 1734 teenage Charles was crowned King of Naples. The following year he defeated the Austrians in Sicily, adding the crown of Sicily to that of Naples, with Naples his capital. Known as 'Re Nasone' (King Big Nose), Charles was a skilful ruler who employed the able administrator Bernardo Tanucci to oversee practical reforms, including taxing the church and cracking down on brigandage. Although the Bourbon reforms never quite fulfilled the vision of influential Neapolitan thinker Gaetano Filangieri (1752-1788), Charles's grandiose architectural projects gave the impression of a Neapolitan enlightenment taking place. The San Carlo opera house, royal palace of Caserta and *Albergo dei Poveri* (a huge hostel for the poor) were some of the era's notable buildings.

In 1759 Charles VII of Naples succeeded his brother to the Spanish throne to become Charles III of Spain. Unable under European law of the time to hold three crowns, he made his eight-year-old son Ferdinand King of Naples and Sicily, with Tanucci as regent in charge of state affairs. Ferdinand IV of Naples (Ferdinand III of Sicily), nicknamed 'Il Re Lazzarone', spoke and acted like Neapolitans on the street, enjoying hunting and fishing. In 1768 he married the powerfully connected Maria Carolina, an Austrian archduchess and sister of Marie Antoinette of France. Ferdinand's Habsburg queen was more focused on reform and still had the time to bear her husband 18 children. At this point the Bourbons became an Anglophile court, with Sir John Acton taking over from Tanucci as chief minister, and femme fatale Emma Hamilton, the young wife of British envoy Sir William Hamilton, becoming best friends with the Queen. Grand Tourists and characters like Goethe and Casanova were entertained at the Bourbon court. While Hamilton was absorbed in the frequent eruptions of Vesuvius and the discovery of its ancient buried treasures, his voluptuous wife danced in Greek costumes and had a fling with Admiral Nelson.

The Parthenopaean Republic (1799) & Napoleonic Naples (1806-1815)

After the French Revolution of 1789 European society split between royalists and liberals. In 1798 the Napoleonic French invaded Naples and a Parthenopaean Republic was declared. The Royal family, along with the Hamiltons and Nelson, escaped to Palermo during an almighty storm that took Prince Alberto's life. The royalists under Cardinal Ruffo's *Sanfedisti* (Army of the Faith) took the city back and in their savage treatment of the republicans the *ancien régime* created martyrs to the republican cause: there is an exquisite statuary memorial to them in piazza dei Martiri. In the midst of the mayhem was Admiral Nelson, who was largely welcomed as a hero for fighting the Napoleonic forces in Naples despite controversially executing his old colleague Admiral Caracciolo at the port. According to legend King Ferdinand's ship later passed Caracciolo's floating bloated corpse – an eerie omen you might say. Nelson's actions caused outcry in the House of Commons in London and the Royals had lost much support amongst the *lazzaroni*.

In 1806 the Bourbons again fled to Sicily as the French retook Naples and Napoleon placed first his brother Joseph and then his brother-in-law Joachim Murat on the Neapolitan throne. Reform of feudal laws and enlightened public works transformed the city during this period.

Bourbon Restoration & the Risorgimento (1815-1860)

After Napoleon's defeat and Murat's last stand ended in his execution, the Congress of Vienna in 1815 divided up the continent and restored the Bourbons and Ferdinand I King of the Two Sicilies to the throne.

Absolute monarchs found it increasingly tricky to hold onto power amid the growing liberalism and nationalism sweeping Europe – and the Bourbons in Naples would be toppled briefly by the largely middle class liberal secret society, the Carbonari in 1820 and 1848. Two figures – the idealist Giuseppe Mazzini and the swashbuckling general Giuseppe Garibaldi – were leading the Risorgimento, a popular movement that sought a

It's a fact...

Bourbon-era architecture includes the Palace of Capodimonte (see page 115), Albergo dei Poveri (see page 117) and the Reggia di Caserta. Murat commissioned the ceremonial square piazza del Plebiscito (see page 81), which was finished under the restored Bourbons.

united Italian nation, free of foreign rule. Meanwhile the astute Piedmontese statesman Cavour, with the help of Napoleon III of France, jettisoned the Austrians from Northern Italy in 1859. In 1860 Garibaldi took Sicily and Naples, but the wily Cavour wrested control of events by marching Vittorio Emanuele (Victor Emmanuel) of the House of Savoy to meet Garibaldi's redshirts and proclaim the northern sovereign the first king of a unified Italy. A plebiscite ratified the new Italy but there is much debate to this day about whether the largely illiterate population of the south understood what they were voting for.

Italian Naples

Unification & the early 20th century (1861-1922)

By 1871 the Veneto and the Papal States had joined the new state and in July 1871 Rome became Italy's capital. A unified Italy may have brought some political and social reforms to Naples but Garibaldi's promises to redistribute land never materialized and most new investment went into developing the northern economy. Poverty and illiteracy rates dwarfed those in Milan and Turin, and cholera and typhoid epidemics repeatedly ravaged the densely populated city. In 1884 a cholera epidemic claimed 15,000 Neapolitan lives. In response the authorities cleared lots of slum areas, widened streets, laid down a new water and sewerage system and paid for grand projects (such as corso Umberto I and Galleria Umberto I). However there was a gap in governance which organized crime filled – the Camorra thrived by collecting taxes in return for favours, including supplying work to the poor.

During this period hundreds of thousands of Campania's poor sought a better life in the Americas. Early emigrants were mainly single men, many under the age of 20; women and children usually joined them later. In the early years of the 20th century, Vesuvius erupted (in 1906) and a cholera epidemic in 1910-1911 claimed nearly 5000 lives, leading to over a million people from Campania emigrating to the Americas, mostly heading to New York. The pizzeria phenomenon, Enrico Caruso's crooning and *Saturday Night Fever* followed, not forgetting US-based Mafia's global activities.

The early 20th century saw some jobs created in Naples but at a huge environmental cost as the once idyllic bay of Bagnoli was choked by the Ilva (then Italsider) steelworks. Similarly, the First World War boosted jobs through munitions manufacture, but many Neapolitan families were affected by the loss of loved ones fighting on distant shores.

Fascist Naples & the Second World War (1922-1945)

The post-war humiliation of Italy at the Treaty of Versailles and an economic crisis sowed the seeds of Italian fascism. Despite healthy opposition, in 1922 60,000 blackshirts paraded in Naples and marched on Rome: King Vittorio Emanuele III and the Papacy allowed Benito Mussolini to assume autocratic rule. Aside from the atrocious violence and terror that followed and the disastrous alliance with Hitler, Il Duce's two decades of power had some surprisingly positive legacies, not all of which were taken advantage of by the post-war Italian republic.

Naples' port and transport system, as well as grandiose building projects, transformed the city. Significant scientifically based excavations at Herculaneum and Pompeii led by archaeologist Amedeo Maiuri were funded. Opponents of the regime included Neapolitan philosopher Benedetto Croce, who helped set up the journal *La Critica* and the *Comitato di Liberazione Nazionale* (CLN), which sought to influence Italy's post-fascist government.

Naples was ravaged by Second World War bombing, especially after the Allied invasion of 1943. Salerno was eventually secured by the Allies after an atrocious conflict. When the German commander placed Naples under martial law and decreed enforced labour of its citizens, the starving Neapolitans rose, up after a four-day battle and drove out the Germans. The retreating Germans sabotaged anything that would be of use to the approaching Allied forces and even callously destroyed the priceless Neapolitan state archives.

Threatened by communism, the Allies favoured a return to monarchy. Winston Churchill revealed the Allies' preference and dismissed Croce and the CLN in a bizarre but revealing analogy taken from a 1944 speech: "When you have to hold a coffee pot, it is better not to break the handle off until you are sure you will get another equally convenient and serviceable, or at any rate, until there is a dish cloth handy." Italian Resistance member and historian Claudio Pavone called it "immunity in return for obedience". Many Neapolitan fascists went unpunished and carried on as before within the new Italian republic, and organized crime (namely the Camorra), which was cracked down on during the fascist era, also went largely unchecked by the occupying Allies. In early 1944, Monte Cassino was the venue for one of the most notorious battles of the war. Then Vesuvius erupted in March 1944. British intelligence officer Norman Lewis's *Naples '44* is an illuminating account of this chaotic period and the consequences of the Allies' policy.

Post-war Naples (1946-present)

While the north voted unanimously for a republic in a 1946 referendum, some 79% of Neapolitans

Galleria Principe di Napoli.

It's a fact...

Urban renewal in Italian Naples included the building of the grand avenue corso Umberto I (see page 112) and the Galleria Umberto I (see page 83). The Mostra d'Oltremare (see page 156) and Palazzo delle Poste e Telegrafi (see page 107) are examples of fascist monumentalism. The Stadio San Paolo (see page 167) was built in the 1960s and had a roof added for the 1990 World Cup.

favoured a monarchy. Naples joined the republic but tension in the city teetered on the edge of civil war.

The increasing gulf between a prosperous north and backward south in modern Naples is still highlighted by the sight of unfinished flyovers, crime-ridden suburbs and abject poverty. *Clientelismo* politics and the all pervading state-within-a state, the Camorra, are the crippling mainstays of life in post Second World War Naples: corruption and the black market economy manifest themselves in the piles of refuse that have blighted the suburbs. A cholera outbreak struck in 1972 and then in 1980 an earthquake killed 3100 and left hundreds of thousands homeless. Money set aside for reconstruction and economic aid from the *Cassa di Mezzogiorno* (Fund for the South) was siphoned off by corrupt officials and the Camorra. Organized

crime profited from the boom in heroin and moved into the legitimate economy, setting up construction companies and taking control of public contracts such as refuse collection. In 1993 the Italian government, citing security reasons, dissolved the Naples city council. These *Tangentopoli* (bribesville) purges of corrupt politicians, taking place throughout Italy coincided with a Neapolitan revival under mayor Bassolino, which had many positive effects on the look and feel of the city. Indeed traffic-calming measures, new contemporary art museums and impressive developments – including a smart metro system and portside – make Naples a far more attractive city to visit these days. Bagnoli's industrial landscape is slowly being transformed and there is a real sense of civic pride in some areas. However, the continued influence of the Camorra and political corruption, exemplified by the ugly, stinking truth behind refuse collection and illegal dumping of waste in Campania revealed recently, means for Naples the old adage that "you can change the conductor but the music remains the same" rings tragically true.

Art & architecture

The complexity of Neapolitan history is reflected in the multi-layered nature of its buildings, none more so than in its darkly absorbing Centro Antico. Many foreign dynasties have left their mark on Campania's rich architectural and artistic heritage, an idiosyncratic legacy that makes this region of Italy so compellingly different.

Graeco-Roman

Naples itself has few sizeable Graeco-Roman ruins as most are either buried under the city or assimilated into later buildings. Indeed a tour with *Napoli Sotterranea* (see page 82) reveals the fascinating layers of the city deep underground at piazza San Gaetano, site of the *Neapolis agora* (main square) and even in a nearby garage, which contains the backstage part of the theatre where Emperor Nero performed. Other similarly incongruous sights include the remains of piazza Bellini's Greek city walls next to some trendy bars and the so-called *Ponti Rossi*, where Neapolitan traffic whizzes through the 2000 year-old arches of an aqueduct. Via dell'Anticaglia follows the *decumanus maximus* of Graeco-Roman Naples and is crossed by huge arched Roman walls.

Above: Ponti Rossi.
Opposite page: An audience with the Villa dei Papyri *peplophoroi*.

At Gaiola, off the Posillipo promontory, are remains of the Villa Pausilypon and its Roman theatre.

Outside Naples, the wealth of ancient remains is mind-blowing. In the Campi Flegrei you can see the Anfiteatro Flavio and Rione Terra at Pozzuoli; remains of lavish Roman villas at Baia; the cathedral-like wonders of the Piscina Mirabilis underground cistern – that held the waters of the Aqua Augusta (Serino Aqueduct) – at Bacoli; and the sprawling ruins at Cuma where the Greeks first settled. The most famous stones of them all are across the bay below Vesuvius. Nothing prepares you for the incredible time-capsule sights at Pompeii, Herculaneum and other archaeological marvels at Stabiae and Villa Oplontis along this coast. On the Sorrentine Peninsula are the crumbling remnants of a shoreline villa, the Bagno della Regina Giovanna. There are Greek remains at Lacco Ameno on Ischia and lots of Roman ones on Capri, including the infamous den of imperial iniquity, Villa Jovis, from where Emperor Tiberius ruled the empire. Heading south to Paestum are the magical remains of Greek Doric temples and a Roman forum.

Palaeo-Christian, Byzantine & Norman

As the power of the Western Roman Empire waned and that of Byzantium waxed, the influence of the East was expressed in art and architecture of this long period between the second and 12th centuries AD. The dawning of Christianity can be seen in the cool, atmospheric depths of the Palaeo-Christian catacombs of San Gennaro and San Gaudioso. In late antiquity, the church showed its increased influence on people and governance in the building of churches. While Naples was a natural home of Greek orthodoxy, the Latin West also grew here through the Catholic Church's bishopric in Rome. Churches were erected in honour of saints, such as Santa Restituta, whose remains were moved from the church at Lacco Ameno on Ischia to the Duomo, where there is a mosaic dedicated to the African female saint and San Gennaro.

The Normans, who ruled Naples between 1130 and 1194, made Castel dell'Ovo their administrative centre, and learned Holy Roman Emperor Frederick II enlarged the Castel Capuano. However little remains of the original architecture built by the Normans or Swebians, except the Romanesque La Pietrasanta tower on via dei Tribunali, which incorporates many Roman building fragments. Outside Naples there are lots of fine examples of the very Moorish Southern Italian Romanesque, especially in the increasingly

Graeco-Roman artworks

***Tomb of the Diver*, Paestum** A series of fresco panels including the alluring image of a youth diving gracefully into blue water (see page 227).

***Dionysian Cycle*, Villa dei Misteri, Pompeii** Nine scenes, painted on a rich red background, from a ritual dedicated to the Greek god of wine and revelry, Dionysus (see page 193).

***Alexander and Darius at the Battle of Issus*, Museo Archeologico Nazionale di Napoli, Naples** A massive Roman mosaic depicting an epic scene from the Battle of Issus (see page 108).

***The Farnese Bull*, Museo Archeologico Nazionale di Napoli, Naples** The most famous piece in the astounding Farnese Collection of statuary (see page 108).

***Villa dei Papyri statuary*, Museo Archeologico Nazionale di Napoli, Naples** A collection of busts, herms and statues including five female *peplophoroi* (mythical water-carriers), bronze runners, fawns, Greek philosophers and a drunken Satyr lounging on a lion skin (see page 178).

La Fontana di Monteoliveto.

Palaeo-Christian, Byzantine & Norman artworks

Capella di San Giovanni in Fonte, Duomo, Naples Remains of the Basilica di Santa Restituta, the oldest baptistery in Italy, with fifth-century mosaics depicting biblical scenes (see page 101).

Catacombe di San Gennaro, Naples Under a 20th-century church lie frescoes and mosaics from the second to 10th centuries and the tomb of the patron saint San Gennaro (see page 117).

Duomo di San Pantaleone, Ravello A stunning church with a 13th-century campanile, interlaced arches and Norman-period artworks, which influenced the twisting columns and mosaics of its Angevin-era pulpits (see page 221).

Duomo di San Matteo, Salerno Crosses and figures of niello work cover the bronze door cast in Constantinople and there are two elaborate 12th-century Byzantine-style ambones (see page 225).

prosperous maritime cities. In the 11th century keen art-lover and abbot Desiderius employed Lombard architects and craftsmen from Constantinople and masterminded a renovation of the Benedictine abbey of Monte Cassino that revolutionized arts in Campania. Through trading with the Orient, Amalfi, Ravello and Salerno were able to fund skilled artists trained at Norman schools in Sicily, who produced exquisite sculptures, thrones and mosaics that adorn their cathedrals. Arab-like arches and bronze doors cast in Constantinople can be seen amid the interiors and cloisters of both Amalfi's and Ravello's cathedrals. Norman-Saracenic architecture flourished during the 11th to 14th centuries in Ravello under the Normans and their successors the Angevins, most notably at the Duomo and Villa Rufolo. Much of Salerno's Duomo di San Matteo, rebuilt by Robert Guiscard (1015-1085) to celebrate Norman victory over the Lombards, was inspired by the abbey at Monte Cassino. Through the Romanesque doorway is an atrium containing 28 ancient columns pilfered from Paestum surmounted by Moorish arches and colourful inlaid decoration.

Angevin Gothic

Charles I of Anjou was the brother of the King of France and after assuming the Neapolitan throne in 1266 he strengthened the kingdom's links with the western world, importing many architects from France. Major Italian artists like Giotto from Florence, Tino da Camaino from Siena and Pietro Cavallini from Rome received Angevin commissions on the newly built Maschio Angioino and Duomo, and in various churches including the churches of Santa Maria di Donnaregina Vecchia, San Lorenzo Maggiore and San Domenico Maggiore.

Aragonese Renaissance

Under the Spanish Aragonese Naples underwent a cultural awakening, yet it was very different from the Renaissance in Tuscany, Rome and the Veneto as it was largely marked by a very Spanish imprint. Some Renaissance greats from the north – such as artist and sculptor Donatello (1386-1466), sculptor Benedetto di Maiano (1442-1497) and architect and sculptor Michelozzo (1396-1492) – were commissioned and their works can be seen in the Brancaccio tomb and Chiesa di Monteoliveto. However, few Renaissance palaces with their original bossed stonework façades have remained as many of them, including Sansevero and Filomarino, were eventually given the Baroque treatment.

Baroque

Renaissance preference for the classical orders was transformed into the hallmarks of the swirling naturalistic style of the Baroque with its riot of stucco work, marble and majolica. The Baroque's theatrical style lent itself to the demonstrative Neapolitan character and the extravagant religious rites of a period beset with natural disasters. In the 17th and 18th centuries Naples was brimming with churches and convents and there was no shortage of commissions for leading artists. The Counter-Reformation encouraged direct expression in popular themes such as the saints and Catholic virtues. Michele Merisi, better known as Caravaggio

About the region

(1571-1610), who fled Rome after killing a man, took refuge in Naples. His dramatic chiaroscuro style sparked the development of a Neapolitan naturalist school of painting. Meanwhile the Spanish Tenebrist (murky chiaroscuro style) painter Jusepe de Ribera (1591-1652) allied himself with Greek mannerist painter Belisario Corenzio (1558-1643) and Neapolitan Giovanni Battista Caracciolo (aka Battistello, 1578-1635) in the so-called Cabal of Naples that often used violent tactics to drive away competing artists so as to secure commissions.

The next wave of painters developed the Caravaggio-influenced yet more graceful style of Massimo Stanzione (1586-1656) and took the Baroque to a lighter, more colourful conclusion – the works of Luca Giordano (1632-1705) and Francesco Solimena (1657-1747) can be seen in the Museo di Capodimonte. During this period the Spanish viceroys and collectors such as the Flemish Gaspar Roomer helped disperse the Neapolitan Baroque style around Europe. A Neapolitan school of sculpture was founded in the 16th century and its famous students include Michelangelo Naccherino (1550-1622), Pietro Bernini (1562-1629) and Cosimo Fanzago (1591-1678) whose work can be seen in the city's many flamboyant statues, fountains and stone spires (guglie). Among the grand architectural projects carried out by the Spanish are Palazzo Reale, designed by Domenico Fontana (1543-1607); a broad new street, via Toledo, flanked by the Spanish Quarters to house troops and their families; and many noble palazzi along the Riviera di Chiaia.

Bourbon

During the Bourbon rule of Charles (Carlo) III grand building projects including the San Carlo Opera House, Royal Palace of Caserta and the Albergo dei Poveri transformed the city. The great architects of this period were still barmy about the Baroque style: Ferdinando Sanfelice (1675-1748) loved his sweeping staircases and exuberant façades (see San Lorenzo Maggiore); Domenico Antonio Vaccaro (1678-1745) enlivened his Santa

Chiara cloisters with vibrant majolica tiling; and Fernando Fuga followed his great public works like the Albergo dei Poveri with the very ornamental Girolamini. Prolific Luigi Vanvitelli (1700-1773), the son of a Dutch painter, tweaked the Baroque into Neoclassicism in the Reggia di Caserta, Villa Campolieto at Ercolano and Palazzo Calabritto in Chiaia. Meanwhile, Raimondo VII Prince of Sansevero (1710-1771) commissioned one of the most breathtaking collections of statuary and transformed his family funerary chapel, Cappella di Sansevero, into a compelling insight into his esoteric mind. When Ferdinand of Bourbon was restored to power in 1815 after Napoleon's defeat, he completed the building of the grandiose piazza del Plebiscito, started in 1809 by Joachim Murat.

Naples became synonymous with landscape painting, especially after the eruption of Vesuvius in 1631, which increased interest in the fashionable Grand Tour and images of Campania's Arcadian landscapes. Pietro Fabris (1740-1792) produced a famous series of topographically accurate gouaches to accompany Sir William Hamilton's vulcanological observations in *Campi Phlegraei: Observations on the Volcanos of the Two Sicilies* (1776). Inspired by the atmospheric landscapes of Turner, Dutchman Anton Sminck Pitloo (1791-1837) and Neapolitan Giacinto Gigante (1806-1876) formed the Posillipo School of painting.

Italian Naples: *stile Liberty* to contemporary

After Naples joined the new Italian state in 1861, and in response to the cholera epidemic of 1884, new technology, social policy and town planning came together in the construction of the neoclassical palazzi along the broad Corso Umberto I, Villa Comunale and two covered galleries in wrought iron and glass, the Galleria del Principe di Napoli (1870-1873) and the Galleria Umberto I (1887-1883). Belle époque and *stile-Liberty* buildings sprang up in the new middle-class suburbs of Vomero.

From Angevin Gothic to the Bourbon era artworks

Castel Nuovo, Naples A sturdy castle built by Angevin King Charles I in 1279 and remodelled by King Alfonso of Aragon in the 15th century, with a soaring Renaissance-style triumphal arch, two chapels (one Gothic and one Baroque) as well as some scratchy remains of frescoes by Giotto (see page 84).

Santa Maria di Donnaregina Vecchia and Museo Diocesano di Napoli, Naples This eighth-century monastery, rebuilt in 1293, is notable for a funeral

L'arco trionfale del Castel Nuovo.

monument by Tino da Camaino and frescoes by the Giotto school. Neapolitan religious iconography runs riot next door in paintings by Giordano, de Benedictis and Solimena (see page 102).

San Giovanni a Carbonara, Naples Sanfelice's sweeping double-flight staircase leads to Angevin funerary monuments, 15th-century frescoes and the elegantly rotund Cappella Caracciolo di Vico (see page 111).

Chiesa Sant'Anna dei Lombardi, Naples Otherwise known as the Chiesa di Monteoliveto, the Aragonese's favourite church has Naples' finest Renaissance artworks including frescoes by Vasari and *intarsia* stalls by Giovanni di Verona and Guido Mazzoni's *Lamentation of the Dead Christ*. Cosimo Fanzago's beguiling Baroque fountain is on the piazza nearby (see page 107).

Chiesa e Quadreria del Pio Monte della Misericordia, Naples Renaissance and Baroque artworks fill the galleries and church here: Caravaggio's chiaroscuro drama in *The Seven Acts of Mercy* altarpiece is the showstopper (see page 99).

Chiesa del Gesù Nuovo, Naples A Renaissance palazzo with Baroque reinterpretation whose original sparse Jesuit interior by Valeriano was embellished by many Mannerist and Baroque paintings. On piazza del Gesù stands the votive spire, La Guglia dell'Immacolata (see page 91).

Santa Chiara, Naples Bombed during the Second World War, this ravaged church has had its original austere Provençal-Gothic interiors resurrected, while its cloisters dazzle with colourful majolica tiles by Domenico Antonio Vaccaro (see page 91).

Certosa e Museo Nazionale di San Martino This 14th-century Gothic-style Carthusian monastery got a Baroque facelift and contains hundreds of important Neapolitan artworks including Jusepe de Ribera's *Moses*, the marble-inlaid Cappella di San Bruno by Cosimo Fanzago and 19th-century Posillipo School landscapes (see page123).

Museo di Capodimonte, Naples Charles (Carlo) III of Bourbon's massive hunting lodge (1738) brings together many important art collections, including that of Elisabetta Farnese, under one roof. Renaissance pieces include Titian's erotically-charged *Danae* and El Greco's atmospheric *El Soplón*. The presence of Baroque heavyweight Caravaggio broods in a dark alcove with *Flagellation* (see page 115).

Italian Naples: *stile Liberty* to contemporary artworks

Galleria Umberto I, Naples The cavernous *stile-Liberty* arcade was opened in 1887, just after the Galleria del Principe di Napoli, a smaller belle époque gallery (see page 83).

Villino Elena e Maria, Naples Look out for this handsome *stile-Liberty* building with nautical detailing at via Tito Angelini 41, not far from Castel Sant'Elmo (see page 124).

Piazza Matteotti, Naples Around the Fascist-built piazza is a cluster of imposing modernist buildings with state functions: Palazzo delle Poste e Telegrafi (1932-1936) (see page 107), Palazzo della Provincia (1934-1936), Casa del Mutilato (1938-1940) and Palazzo degli Uffici Finanziari e dell'Avvocatura di Stato (1937).

Casa Malaparte, Capri A striking red-hued piece of Italian rationalist architecture plonked in an idyllic Caprese landscape (see page 247).

Museo di Capodimonte, Naples Andy Warhol's colourful Pop Art depiction of an erupting Vesuvius is amongst the artworks in the contemporary art wing (see page 115).

Museo d'Arte Contemporanea Donnaregina (Madre), Naples Madre has all the big names in contemporary art from the 1950s to the Noughties including Gilbert & George, Andy Warhol, Jeff Koons, Lucio Fontana, Mimmo Paladino and Richard Long (see page 110).

Villino Elena e Maria, Vomero.

In the early 20th century the Santa Lucia district along the waterfront was lined with impressive neoclassical palazzi. Fascist urban renewal created the Mostra d'Oltremare (1940) and Stazione Marittima and swept away the old San Giuseppe-Carità quarter replacing it with bombastic state architecture centring on piazza Matteotti. The Novecento-style Banco di Napoli (1939) is on via Toledo.

Building after the Second World War saw modern apartment blocks fill the green spaces of Posillipo and Vomero, while the suburbs became a truly monotonous urban sprawl. Illegal building after the 1980 earthquake was equally dire. Notable post-war architecture includes the Fabbrica Olivetti e Case Popolari Olivetti (1951-1963) in Pozzuoli: this Rationalist-style factory and employees' housing estate lies in a breathtaking coastal area of the Campi Flegrei. Other examples include the Stadio San Paolo (1959) and Facoltà di Ingegneria in Fuorigrotta (1950-1960), and the skyscrapers of the Centro Direzionale (1982) business district. Since the 1990s the Italsider steel and chemical works at Bagnoli have been decommissioned and new developments have taken their place including the Città della Scienza.

Although the energy of futurism and its reaction to academic art and passéist culture is often seen as synonymous with the emergence of Fascism, its experimental nature is often overlooked. In Naples, there were various scenes during the 1920s and 1930s, first headed by Francesco Cangiullo (1884-1977), an artist and comedian who got involved in anarchic events (Piedigrotta was one of his explosive works) and collaborated with the likes of Giacomo Balla and Marinetti. Groups who embraced the new artistic developments of constructivism and surrealism emerged in the late 1920s, including the Pittori Circumvisionisti, who included artists Cocchia and Peirce.

Abstract expressionism and Arte Povera, notable post-war movements, can be seen in the Madre gallery. Lucio Fontana's abstract expressionist vision, known as *movimento spaziale*, involves lots of slashed canvases that evoke movement and depth, while Jannis Kounellis's found objects explore historical relationships. In 1985 the Museo di Capodimonte exhibited 16 paintings produced by Andy Warhol, in 2002 Sol LeWitt produced *White Bands in a Black Room* and in 2008 Louise Bourgeois scattered her life's work, including her spindly spiders, throughout the historic collection and palazzo courtyards. Coinciding with Mayor Bassolino's revival of the city, new initiatives including an annual Christmas installation in piazza del Plebiscito (memorable displays include Mimmo Paladino's *Salt Mountain*

and Anish Kapoor's towering red sculpture *Taratantara*) and artworks in the Metropolitana have enlivened the scene.

Small commercial galleries have sprung up in and around piazza dei Martiri in Chiaia, many representing a wave of emerging Neapolitan artistic talent. Michelle Lowe, who exhibits in her Chiaia boutique hotel Micalò, says: "Naples has an exciting arts scene and there's so much talent here with a very Neapolitan vision, including Ernesto Tatafiore, Daniela Politelli and Paola Margherita."

Architectural glossary

Columns The Greeks had three orders of columns: the **Doric** order, characterized by straight up-and-down plainness is meant to symbolize man (the grooves are called fluting); **Ionic**, characterized by scrolls, symbolizes women, and **Corinthian**, which has a bell-shaped top (or capital) and is adorned with acanthus leaves and volutes, symbolizes virgins. The Romans added the **Tuscan** order, which is without decoration, while the **Composite** order is a mish-mash of the three Grecian orders.

Aedicule A frame around a doorway or window made up of columns or pilasters and an entablature on top. It can also be a mini decorative structure housing a statue. It is used in both Classical and Gothic architecture.

Arcade A row of columns that support arches.

Architrave The lower part of an entablature, which meets the capitals of the columns.

Baldachin A canopy over a tomb, supported by columns.

Campanile Bell tower.

Capital The crown of a column adorned with scrolls (Ionic) or acanthus leaves (Corinthian).

Cloister Usually part of a church, this is a covered passage around a courtyard, lined with columns or arches.

Choir The chancel of a church, which is used by the clergy and the choir; it is occasionally separated from the nave by a screen.

Colonnade A series of columns.

Cornice A horizontal ledge or moulding. Practically, it's a gutter, draining water away from the building; aesthetically, it's a decorative feature.

Cupola A dome on a roof.

Entablature The upper part of an order that is held up by the column and includes the architrave, frieze and cornice.

Frieze The centre of an entablature; often decorated.

Loggia A recessed open gallery or corridor on the façade of a building.

Nave The central body of the church, between the aisles.

Narthex A long porch along the entrance wall of a church, before the nave.

Pediment The gable end or front of a Grecian-style structure, above the frieze and cornice, that supports the columns.

Pilaster A rectangular column that only slightly protrudes from a wall.

Pinnacle A small often ornate turret, popular in Gothic architecture.

Plinth The lower part or base of a column.

Portico A roofed space that serves as an entrance to a building.

Sacristy A room off the main or side altars in a church or, occasionally, a separate building that houses the sacred vessels, vestments and records.

Temple These are named according to the numbers of columns: a **distyle** temple has two columns, a **tetrastyle** temple has four, an **octastyle** temple has eight, etc.

Tracery Ornamental stonework that supports the glass in Gothic windows.

Naples & Amalfi Coast today

Just hanging around.

The Camorra and *La Munezza*

The sweet smell of optimism created by mayor Bassolino's so-called *Rinascimento Napoletano* of the early 1990s was overpowered by the acrid stink of uncollected rubbish – *La Munezza* – in 2007-2008. *Rifiutopoli* (Rubbishville) is a scandal that continues to threaten the health of Neapolitans – as insidious as the socio-political mess that is at the heart of the region's problems. The Camorra, the Neapolitan mafia, controls the transport of refuse and industrial toxic waste from all over Italy and Europe, which ends up in illegal dumps, including disused mines and agricultural land. In the neglected suburbs of the Caserta plain, dioxins and other cancer-causing toxins have leaked into the food chain. In 2008 high levels of dioxins were found in some mozzarella cheese, prompting alarm in delis and pizzerias worldwide. Meanwhile, lack of planning by local government – to establish new landfill sites – meant that there was nowhere to put the 50,000 tonnes of rubbish piling up on the streets. When newly elected Prime Minister Silvio Berlusconi staged his first cabinet meeting of his centre-right administration in Naples, in 2008, he promised to fix the rubbish crisis. Troops were sent in and arrests of Camorra members were made. More sinister were Berlusconi's measures to jail illegal immigrants and the much-maligned Roma, or Gypsy people, who he called "an army of evil". Largely Romanian, they live in squalid camps on the edges of Italian cities and are often blamed for increased violent crime.

Roberto Saviano's book *Gomorrah – Italy's Other Mafia* (2006) describes the all-pervading influence of the Camorra on life in Naples and beyond through drug dealing, the construction industry, prostitution, Chinese contraband, arms dealing and the dumping of toxic waste. Saviano's startling revelations about his home-town clan, and tales of savagery and greed, including the murder of the anti-Mafia priest Father Peppino Diana and the involvement of Italian fashion houses and corrupt politicians, painted a grim truth. Director Matteo Garrone's adaptation of the book captures the stark reality of life in the so-called 'Las Vegas' suburbs.

Naples experienced one of its dark phases recently, but it's a city that has to fight continually to survive. Certainly the gamble made at the start of the 90s (the so-called Neapolitan Renaissance) has been irreparably lost. At the moment we are very far away from evolving into a modern city of the Mediterranean.

Member of Neapolitan band, Almamegretta

View towards il Centro Direzionale.

Civic Pride and *La Creatività Napoletana*

While the city's complicated history and facets of Neapolitan character are inherent in the continued influence of the Camorra, there are many positive and creative aspects of *la Napoletanità* (Neapolitan-ness if you will) that makes Campania such a stimulating place to be. Recently opened contemporary art galleries the Madre and Pan have been followed by small independent galleries representing Neapolitan artistic talent. Stylish new hotels like Micalò and cultural centres cum bars like Culti in Chiaia, Rising in the Centro Antico and Kestè in the revitalized Campi Flegrei demonstrate this renewed *creatività Napoletana*. Recent refuse-collection problems have even reinvigorated a sense of civic pride and community initiatives, including an effort to improve the city's abysmal recycling provisions. In the absence of effective government it's perhaps this heroic collective spirit, when faced with disaster – a determination that drove out the Nazis – that is the city's only hope of fulfilling its

potential. Tourists who head straight to Campania's idyllic outposts like Capri, and the holidaymakers who are scare-mongered into staying in their colossal cruise liners at the docks, should be experiencing Napoli, the city. Perhaps by the time the adverse publicity of 2007-2008 fades a little from the memory, visitors will be able to enjoy the city's unparalleled cultural and culinary riches. By 2011 the €3.8 billion Metropolitana underground system with its art installations should be open and the once-polluted industrial wastelands of Bagnoli may have its long-overdue rebirth as a resort back on track. A new science centre, sports complex, spectacular pier and environmental study facility are complete but it remains to be seen when and if the planned grandiose spa resort and beaches will appear in a bay where Greeks and Romans made castles in the sand.

Nature & environment

The Bay of Naples sits on a geological fault line and is studded with a string of volcanoes that run towards Sicily. All this volatile vulcanism and resultant fertile soil, combined with the limestone rocks of the Appenine Mountains, that buckle to form the Amalfi Coast, produce a spectacular natural setting.

Campanian rocks

From Roccomonfina in the north to Vesuvius just south of Naples, Campania is dotted with volcanoes. Geological instability along the limestone rocks of the Apennines, where the Eurasian and African tectonic plates meet, caused the formation of the Campanian volcanic arc, including the Campi Flegrei caldera system, Vesuvius and four underwater volcanoes (Palinuro, Vavilev, Marsili, and Magnaghi) to the south. Debris spewed from these volcanoes make the plains of Caserta and around Naples incredibly fertile while enriching the marine waters of the *Mar Tirreno* (Tyrrhenian Sea). Inland are the earthquake-prone limestone mountains of Irpinia, around Avellino, which continue along the *Monti Lattari* (Milky Mountains) of the Sorrentine Peninsula and fall spectacularly to the sea.

Campi Flegrei, Procida & Ischia

West of Naples are the *Campi Flegrei*, or Phlegrean (Fiery) Fields, a vast area blistered by dozens of volcanic craters. Some display effusive volcanic properties (like the sulphurous cauldron of Solfatara that last erupted in 1198) while many others (including Agnano and Lucrino) have geothermal vents. Greeks and Romans exploited these hot fissures in their spa complexes, many of which are now under the sea at Baia. The whole area is subject to bradyseism (meaning 'slow shaking') which manifests itself in the ground slowly rising and falling over periods of time. After an earthquake in 1980 the ground at Pozzuoli rose to reveal more of the Serapis temple. Its ancient columns have a line of erosion made by molluscs from a previous period spent under the sea. Nearby is Europe's newest mountain, Monte Nuovo, formed after an eruption in 1538 that filled in Lake Lucrino. There are two notable protected park areas in the Campi Flegrei: the lush, wooded bowl of the Astroni crater, which teems with wildlife including woodpeckers and wolves, and the curved island of Vivara, a protected habitat whose birdlife is constantly under threat from local hunters. Off the tufa cliffs of Monte di Procida and Capo Miseno are the Phlegrean islands

Il Vesuvio.

of Ischia, Procida and Vivara, which display lots of curvy crater features. Ischia's Monte Epomeo is a dormant volcano whose flanks are particularly active with geothermal vents.

Vesuvius

Vesuvius's *Gran Cono* (Large Cone) is currently around 1281 m high. Apart from the odd rumble of an earthquake and the quietly fizzing fumaroles within its crater, there has been no activity since 1944. The Gran Cono sits within Monte Somma, the remains of a larger and higher crater that subsequently collapsed. Periods of eruption alternate with times of inactivity, with some five explosive Plinian eruptions taking place, the last of which happened in AD 79, witnessed and recorded by Pliny the Younger and his uncle.

The Vesuvius National Park authority has established nine colour-coded trails amid an otherworldly landscape of old lava flows. You can spot more than 600 species of flora including the all-important colonizing silver lichen *stereocaulon vesuvianum*, which allows plants to grow and animals to follow. Springtime is ablaze with yellow flowers of the Spanish broom and many orchids thrive on the older substrata. Lizards, snakes, martens, cuckoos, foxes and hares also thrive.

Sorrentine Peninsula, Amalfi Coast & Capri

The Monti Lattari mountains of the Sorrentine Peninsula rise to around 1000 m at Monte Faito, with its beech and cedar forests. Typical Mediterranean flora such as juniper, prickly pear and rosemary cling to the slopes while terraces and flat areas have abundant fruit trees – including lemon and orange trees (protected by straw *pagliarelle* matting), grape vines, apricots, pomegranates, peaches and walnuts. Limestone cliffs plunge down to a jagged coastline scarred by sheltered inlets, deep fjord-like ravines and marine caves. Just off the wild rocky tip of Punta Campanella is the island of Capri, which separated from the peninsula and took with it mammoths and wild boars (*kapri* in Greek). Capri is renowned for its plunging limestone cliffs and abundant wildlife, including rare orchids, the *lucertola azzurra* or blue lizard, and peregrine falcons that circle the skies above Villa Jovis and Monte Solaro.

Festivals & events

Catholic festivals, many with pagan origins and hundreds celebrating saints' days, dominate the Neapolitan calendar. Neapolitans certainly know how to party and display emotion so expect full-on fireworks, food, processions and histrionics. Traditional events celebrate the bounty of land and sea, while an eclectic array of cultural and music extravaganzas entertain locals and visitors across the region.

January

Capodanno (New Year)
Concert and fireworks in piazza Plebiscito and general mayhem all over. Positano sees in the New Year with the **Sagra della Zeppola**, which involves lots of fried pastries (*zeppole*) and festivities.

Festa Nazionale della Befana (6th)
Epiphany is celebrated in Italy with Italian children receiving more presents from *la Befana*, a good witch who leaves treats for the good kids and a lump of coal (now some honeycomb candy died black) for naughty ones.

Tinkling the ebonies and ivories, Ravello Festival.

Carnevale (14 days before Ash Wednesday)
The 'farewell to meat' festival is an excuse for excess that starts a fortnight before Ash Wednesday when Lent begins. All over Campania there are float parades, feasts and flamboyant shows throughout. Avellino, Capua and Paestum put on particularly full-on shows with masked revellers.

March

NauticaSud (early March)
The Mezzogiorno's biggest boat show is held at the Mostra d'Oltremare.

Festa Tradizionale dell'Annunziata (24-25th)
Paestum's feast day sees market stalls in the *centro storico* showcasing the area's bountiful produce and a procession led by an 18th-century statue of the Madonna.

Settimana della Cultura (late March)
The national week of culture allows visitors to take advantage of free museum entrance, special guided tours and cultural events.

April

Easter
Pasqua (Easter) in Naples is celebrated with processions and ceremonies, some dating from the Middle Ages and even pagan times. Celebrations at Sorrento/Massa Lubrense, Sant'Anastasia al Vesuvio and Procida are famously flamboyant, with the scoffing of lots of savoury and sweet pies – *il casatiello* and *la pastiera*.

Processione dei Misteri
Statues and contemporary depictions of scenes from the Passion of Christ are taken through the streets of Terra Murata, Procida on Good Friday.

Linea d'Ombra (mid-April)
Salerno's film and cultural festival (lineadombra.it).

Comicon (late April)
Comic and animation fans descend on Castel Sant'Elmo each spring (comicon.it).

May

Festa di San Costanzo (third week of May)
Càpri's patron saint and protector, who drove away Saracen attacks in the Middle Ages, is honoured with a flower-strewn procession and a host of cultural events.

Maggio dei Monumenti
Naples' historic sites can be visited free and some rarely seen sights are opened too. Themed cultural events including lots of concerts and installations in wonderful settings make May a stimulating month to visit.

June

Concerti al Tramonto
A season of concerts (June to September), classical and jazz, staged by the San Michele Foundation, custodians of Axel Munthe's enchanting Villa San Michele (sanmichele.org).

Regata Storica delle Quattro Repubbliche Marinare
Historic rowing regatta in which the four ancient maritime republics Venice, Amalfi, Genoa and Pisa celebrate their illustrious history with much pomp and ceremony during a week of events culminating in the rowing *palio*. The event, held on the first Sunday in June, rotates between the cities, with Amalfi next hosting the celebrations in 2012.

Pizzafest celebrations.

Festa di Sant'Andrea (27th)
The statue of Amalfi's patron saint, credited with saving the city by whipping up a storm, is paraded through the streets to commemorate the defeat of Barbarossa's fleet in 1544. On reaching the beach, fishermen return the statue to the Duomo as fast as they can as a mark of their strength and faith. The festival is accompanied by fish in all its forms – fresh and ornamental – music and fireworks.

Estate Amalfitana
A summer-long festival of cultural and foodie events including concerts at the Duomo and Grotta dello Smeraldo.

July

Ravello Festival
Classical music concerts and other artistic events are staged in spectacular Ravello from July to November (ravellofestival.com).

Festa della Madonna del Carmine (15-16th)
On the night before the saint's day, spectacular fireworks light up the Naples sky in a symbolic 'burning' of the campanile of the Chiesa di Madonna del Carmine in piazza Mercato. The following day, mass is celebrated every hour of the day.

Festa di Sant'Anna (26th)
Ischia's patron is honoured with a flamboyant procession of crazily adorned floats around the Castello Aragonese amid lots of fireworks (festadisantanna.it).

Festa di San Pantaleone Mass
Matinee performances and fireworks celebrate the liquefaction of the saint's blood in Ravello.

Neapolis Festival (late July)
The Arena Flegrea in Fuorigrotta stages concerts by established left-field acts such as Massive Attack, REM and Editors as well as Italian bands like Almamagretta.

August

Ferragosto (15th)
Summer bank holiday that heralds an exodus of Italians to the beach.

Sbarco dei Saraceni (14-15th)
Saracen raids of the ninth and 10th centuries are marked with spectacular re-enactments and fireworks on the water at Positano.

September

Settembrata Anacaprese
Anacapresi come together in late August to early September for themed events and good-natured competition to see which *quartiere* can deliver the finest food, sweetest song and heartiest laugh.

Festa di Piedigrotta
The old Piedigrotta festival, involving a Neapolitan song contest and religious procession, is back on the calendar in early September although on a smaller scale these days (festadipiedigrotta.it).

Pizzafest
In mid-September the Mostra d'Oltremare in Fuorigrotta hosts a celebration of the Neapolitan pizza with lots of competition between the best *pizzaioli* (pizzamakers) as well as much munching, music and general merriment (pizzafest.info).

Festa di San Gennaro (19th)
In and around the Duomo the faithful await the 'miracle of San Gennaro' which is considered a good omen for Naples. After much frenzied imploring and shaking, the reddish matter in the all-important ampoule (supposedly the saint's blood) usually liquefies and there's much relief, rejoicing and pyrotechnics into the evening.

October

Sagra della Castagna
All over Campania during the last weekend of October the harvest of sweet chestnuts is celebrated with street parties – at San Cipriano Picentino there's a donkey race (lasagradellacastagna.net).

November

Pane e Olio in Frantoio
On the last weekend of November, local producers of extra virgin olive oil and bread promote their goods at numerous tastings across Campania (cittadellolio.it).

Festa di Sant'Andrea (30th)
So good is St Andrew that the Amalfitani celebrate their patron saint twice, this time after his *manna* 'miraculously' liquefies, bringing much relief to the populace.

December

Festa di Santa Lucia (13th)
St Lucy's day is commemorated in Italy with fire and feasting. At Sorrento's Sagra della Salsiccia e Ceppone, a massive fire is prepared on the 12th, and the following night the feast is celebrated with copious amounts of barbecued sausages and local vino.

Presepi di Natale
Naples and Campania are famous for their nativity scenes (*presepi*). Via San Gregorio Armeno and its *presepi* shops make it a magic place to visit around Christmas and most churches have a tableau replete with Gesù, shepherds and livestock. San Leucio in the province of Caserta has a 'living nativity'.

Sleeping

Finding decent accommodation in Naples and its environs used to pose the usual dilemma of whether to fork out for a reliable old *albergo* (hotel) or risk it with a small and cheaper B&B-type *pensione*. Over the past 15 years lots of new small hotels, B&Bs and apartment-hotels have sprung up offering comfort, location and style at a reasonable price. New luxury hotels with a dash of contemporary chic are now going head-to-head with well-established hotels, which are having to up their game to attract increasingly demanding and savvy customers. Self-catering is often an economic option and offers flexibility – each chapter lists some recommended agencies.

Naples' grand old dames along the Santa Lucia waterfront and smart hotels like Grand Hotel Parkers in Vomero are now up against boutique hotels offering bags of character in the revitalized Centro Antico and swanky Chiaia. Leading the way is Costantinopoli 104 (see page 130), a *stile-Liberty* palazzo ensconced in a tranquil (for Naples!) courtyard near piazza Bellini, and the arty design-hotel Micalò (see page 132) on the riviera di Chiaia. For those on a budget there are lots of new small hotels in the atmospheric old city – such as Donnalbina7 (see page 131) and Piazza Bellini (see page 131) – offering modern style. B&Bs offer a slice of Neapolitan family life, such as the Raffone family's art-filled Donna Regina (see page 131 near the Madre art gallery and La Bouganville (see page 133) in lofty Posillipo.

Naples itself is split into various *rioni* (districts), each offering their own charms while some are just best avoided. The **Centro Antico** has lots of atmosphere and fascinating sights but can be a tad hairy after dark, while **La Sanità** and around piazza Garibaldi are best avoided because of petty crime. **Chiaia** is a good choice as it's handily located for many of the sights, has swanky shops and bars, and is relatively safe. **Posillipo** and **Vomero** are hilltop suburbs with wonderful views of the bay but can feel a little detached from the main action.

Above: Hotel Micalò, Naples.
Opposite page: JK Place terrace, Capri.

Perhaps due to their urban sprawl and history of volcanic events, **Campi Flegrei** and, on the opposite side of the bay, **Vesuvius**, **Ercolano** and **Pompeii** have less impressive accommodation. However, things are improving and prices are generally much cheaper, except perhaps at Pompeii which has a captive market. Pozzuoli is finally seeing some regeneration and will have a new luxury spa hotel soon, Baia's beach and bar scene has spawned the funky Batis (see page 164) and family-friendly Cala Moresca (see page 164), while right next to ancient Herculaneum is the excellent Hotel Miglio d'Oro (see page 196), housed in the grand Bourbon-era Villa Aprile.

The **Sorrentine Peninsula** and **Amalfi Coast** and **the islands** are well-established tourist destinations and have lots of choice for most budgets. Majolica tiles and shimmering views are standard at Amalfi's swanky Hotel Santa Caterina (see page 107) and homely Marina Riviera (see page 230), as well as at Ravello's posh Palazzo Sasso (see page 229) and Positano's elegant Le Sirenuse (see page 229). Down at Paestum, the Oleandri Resort (see page 230) resembles a Red Sea hotel. Budget options include Villaggio Nettuno (see page 229) at the Marina di Cantone and a Sant'Agnello hostel with boutique hotel fittings – Seven H (see page 228). On the islands, there are truly magical hotels for those with deep pockets. Capri has the new boutique darling J.K. Place (see page 262) while Anacapri's Caesar Augustus (see page 262) was King Farouk of Egypt's favourite retreat. Ischia has a glut of spa hotels (with varying standards of cleanliness) as well as the fabulous yet affordable Albergo Il Monastero (see page 263), housed in a castle convent. Procida's planning laws have resulted in a dearth of decent hotels, with La Vigna (see page 264) a standout choice.

Apartments and *agriturismi*

For those seeking freedom, whether it's in the city or on the coast, renting an apartment or villa is a great option. Small family-run outfits like Napoli Residence (napoliresidence.com) and Amalfi Vacation (amalfivacation.it) can be the easiest to

Tip...

When you check into your accommodation you have to hand over your passport by Italian law, so that they can photocopy your details for the police – don't leave it behind!

deal with while large brokers like **Ville in Italia** (villeinitalia.com) and **Cuendet** (cuendet.com) have hundreds of properties to choose from. Rustic *agriturismi* farm stays offer a taste of the rustic life and home-made food. Examples include Il Casolare (see page 164) in the Campi Flegrei, Bel Vesuvio Inn (see page 196) on the slopes of Vesuvius, and Il Castagno (see page 230) and La Ginestra (see page 228) on the Sorrentine Peninsula – all of which have basic and reasonably priced rooms.

Eating & drinking

Campania is a foodie's heaven. Its fecund volcanic soil and the waters of the Tyrrhenian Sea yield plentiful, tasty and healthy produce and seafood – the term 'Mediterranean diet' was first coined at the University of Salerno. The intense flavours of Campania's vegetables, fruits and seafood need little adornment. It's no coincidence that Graeco-Roman Naples was the natural home of Epicureanism – in its purest philosophical sense – and Bacchanalian revelry.

Neapolitan cuisine

Miseria e nobiltà – poverty and nobility – have shaped *la cucina Napoletana*. While the region's resourceful poor have created two simple world-conquering creations, dried pasta and pizza, 2500 years of foreign influence, especially French and Spanish, with a dash of Arabic, has spawned 'noble' dishes such as *timballi* and *sartù di riso* (see box opposite) as well as rich pastry and ice-cream making traditions.

Massimo di Porzio, vice president of the *Associazione Verace Pizza Napoletana*, is a purist when it comes to pizza making (see box opposite) but is always quick to enthuse about the incredible variety in Neapolitan cuisine. In the box opposite, he recommends 11 (this is Naples so everything, including cuisine, is turned up a notch) classic *piatti napoletani* to try as an introduction to *la gastronomia partenopea*.

Pasticcerie

Neapolitan pastries are world-renowned.
babà a rum-drenched bulbous sponge.
cornetto con crema/con marmellata sweet croissant usually filled with custard or marmalade. A breakfast favourite accompanied by coffee.
pastiera a large tart made with a filling of sweet ricotta and candied fruit.
sfogliatella meaning 'many leaves' or 'layers', *sfogliatelle* are made of thin layers of pastry and filled with ricotta often infused with orange. *sfogliatella riccia* has flaky pastry while *sfogliatella frolla* is the shortcrust version.
struffoli small deep-fried balls of dough covered in honey.
torta caprese chocolate-and-almond cake from Capri.
zeppole Neapolitan doughnuts or fritters, sometimes with cream but always crusted with sugar and served warm.

What the locals say

Eleven classic Neapolitan dishes

ragù di carne alla Genovese Not from Genova but invented by the Genovese family. Small pieces of beef cooked with onions and served with smooth and long tubular *pasta liscia* like *mezzanelli*.

spaghetti alle vongole The classic summer dish is often served with the freshest Vesuvian tomatoes combined with clams. Often called *vermicelli alle vongole*.

baccalà alla Napoletana Preserved cod fried and cooked with tomatoes and onions.

polipetti affogati/polipetti con pomodori Octopus cooked *in bianco* (stewed in its own juices) with wine and black olives, or cooked with tomatoes.

frittura di pesce Medley of lightly fried seafood served with a wedge of lemon.

mozzarella in carozza Mozzarella goes gooey in its fried bread 'carriage'.

parmigiana di melanzane Layers of fried aubergine slices, mozzarella, parmesan, basil and *passata di pomodoro*. Umberto's (see page 137) does a meaty *ragù* version.

zucchini alla scapece A *contorno* (side dish) of thin courgette slices marinated in garlic, vinegar and mint.

zuppa di soffritto di maiale A hearty soup of pig offal, tomatoes and chilli.

sartù di riso/timpano di maccheroni A tasty *ragù* sauce is poured over a mound of rice that contains pieces of *polpettine* (meat balls), aubergine, peas, sausage meat and sometimes provola cheese, then it's baked. There's an *in bianco* (literally white) version without the *ragù* sauce. It often takes the form of a *ciambellone* (large ring). On the same lines is the *timballo o timpano di maccheroni*, a 19th-century dish that consists of a mound of macaroni (a timbale mould resembling a kettle drum is used, hence the name) mixed with layers of filling typically including meaty *ragù*, *salsicciotto piccante* (spicy sausage), hard-boiled egg, tomato salsa and sometimes even brains. It's covered in *pasta frolla* (pastry).

bucatini alla Siciliana Long pasta tubes popular in Naples that are typically served with a rich sauce consisting of aubergine, meatballs, plus *ragù napoletano*, fried mushrooms, parmigiano and mozzarella. It's covered with more meaty *ragù* and baked in an oven.

"Naples was ruled by Ferdinando I di Borbone and the Regno delle due Sicilie," adds Massimo, "so everything was called 'Siciliano' for a while."

Massimo di Porzio, Ristorante-Pizzeria Umberto, Chiaia, Napoli (see page 137).

Paccheri pasta with seafood and tomatoes.

Tip...

A bar will charge a variety of prices for your coffee according to whether you're standing or sitting down, outside or inside. To avoid swallowing a big bill (*il conto*), just choose to consume your drinks and snacks at the bar (*al banco*).

Coffee

In Naples *caffè* is extra strong with a pre-sugared kick to complete the rush it gives. The barista may ask you '*già zuccherato?*' before he makes your caffeine hit, so ask for '*amaro*' (bitter) if you are sweet enough. A glass of water is served to clear your palate.

espresso/normale/un caffè a standard espresso – ask for a *doppio* espresso if you want a double.

ristretto an even stronger espresso made with less water.

caffè corretto espresso 'corrected' with a shot of alcohol, usually grappa.

macchiato espresso 'marked' or 'stained' with foamy milk on top.

caffè Americano or *lungo* espresso made or served with more hot water.

caffè shakerato iced espresso given the cocktail-shaker treatment.

cappuccino a frothy milky coffee seldom drunk after midday.

latte macchiato/caffè latte steamed milk 'marked' or 'stained' with a tiny shot of espresso.

caffè latte shakerato ice-cold *caffé latte* shaken.

When & where to eat

Breakfast (*colazione*) in Naples may include a caffè latte and/or an espresso accompanied by a pastry, usually a horn-shaped *cornetto* with fillings – *alla crema* (pastry cream), *al cioccolato* (chocolate) or *alla marmellata* (marmalade). On holiday and Sundays Neapolitans enjoy a long lunch (*pranzo*), perhaps followed by a cheeky siesta at the height of summer. An *aperitivo* is taken in the early evening, usually in a bar, and is served with *stuzzichini* (nibbles). Restaurants tend to serve lunch 1200-1530 and dinner (*cena*) 1900-2300. Traditionally *un ristorante* was posher than *una trattoria*, which in turn was generally more sophisticated than *un'osteria*, which was once just a rustic inn serving wine and simple dishes; however the distintion between each is blurred these days so the title is not a good indicator of quality, price or ambience.

Campania is one of the cheapest regions to eat out and standards are generally excellent. In Naples the Centro Antico has superb *pizzerie*, while the Borgo Marinari has waterside restaurants. Outside the city there are wonderful seafood restaurants in magical places. The cornucopia of *contorni* (side dishes) on Campanian menus is a great help for vegetarians.

Wines of Campania

Where once the Campania region was known for the quantity of richly coloured, alcohol-heavy wine produced, it is now creating quality wines with elegance and subtlety. Here are the best of Campania's DOC wines.

Aglianico del Taburno Rosso The Aglianico grape, cultivated in the Benevento province, is aged for two years; its bold taste goes well with cheese.

Campi Flegrei Falanghina Grown in the volcanic soil, the white Falanghina grape has a lightly aromatic bouquet with fruity notes. Goes well with seafood, especially mussels and crustaceans.

The €10 picnic

Head to a market, perhaps via Pignasecca in Naples' Quartieri Spagnoli district, or an *alimentari* (food store). Start with *pane casereccia* – rustic bread, sliced (*a fettine*) –and choose your toppings: salame and cheeses (such as *mozzarella di bufala*, Caciocavallo, pecorino, Provolone del Monaco, scamorza…) Slice your *pomodori* (tomatoes) and rub the flesh into the bread then build your feast. Invest in oil and condiments. Follow with seasonal fruits (apples, oranges, apricots, peaches, melon, grapes) and maybe a *babà*. Lubricate with a *vino Campano* (Falanghina, Falerno, Colli Irpini, Greco di Tufo).

Above: *Arance*. Opposite page: Bar Nilo, Spaccanapoli.

Capri Bianco A small, highly prized production of white wine mixing Falanghina, Greco and Biancolella grape varities. Best drunk young, its fresh, dry taste is a perfect match for seafood and cheeses like caciocavallo.

Costa d'Amalfi Bianco Falanghina and Biancolella vines grown on the terraces around Ravello, Furore and Tramonti produce a subtle wine that marries well with light seafood dishes and fresh cheeses. *Rosato* and *rosso* versions are also produced.

Fiano di Avellino A venerable white produced in the Avellino province with floral and hazelnut aromas. Goes well with fish and young cheeses.

Greco di Tufo Probably the best-known DOC along with Fiano. The Greco vine is grown in the Irpinia area, whose volcanic soil gives the wine a rich flavour and good acidity. It works well with Neapolitan seafood dishes, artichokes, rice dishes and soups.

Ischia Bianco Generally a mix of Forastera and Biancolella grapes, it has an intense yellow colour, subtle aromas and is a perfect accompaniment to delicate dishes and light antipasti. There is a sparkling *spumante* version.

Ischia Piedirosso The Piedirosso vine's reddish stalks resemble doves' feet, hence the name. With an aroma of violets, and a little tannic, it goes well with *coniglio all'ischiatana* (Ischian-style rabbit).

Taurasi Rosso Wine from the Aglianico vine grown in the Avellino province is aged for three years in barrels, giving it complex flavours and aromas; perfect for meat dishes and cheeses.

Vesuvio Lacryma Christi Bianco The white Coda di Volpe grape grown on the slopes of Vesuvius is blended with Falanghina and Greco varities. *Rosso*, *rosato* and *spumante* versions are also produced.

Tip…

The cover charge (*il coperto*) should be stated on the menu and can vary from €2 to €8. Some restaurants add a service charge (*servizio*) of 10%. If you're on a budget it's wise to work out the overall cost of your meal before you sit down.

Menu reader

General

affumicato smoked
al sangue rare
alla griglia grilled
antipasto starter/appetizer
aperto/chiuso open/closed
arrosto roasted
ben cotto well done
bollito boiled
caldo hot
cameriere/cameriera waiter/waitress
conto the bill
contorni side dishes
coperto cover charge
coppa/cono cone/cup
cotto cooked
cottura media medium
crudo raw
degustazione tasting menu of several dishes
dolce dessert
fatto in casa homemade
forno a legna wood-fired oven
freddo cold
fresco fresh, uncooked
fritto fried
menu turistico tourist menu
piccante spicy
prenotazione reservation
primo first course
ripieno a stuffing or something that is stuffed
secondo second course

Drinks (bevande)

acqua naturale/gassata/frizzante still/sparkling water
aperitivo drinks taken before dinner, often served
  with free snacks
bicchiere glass
birra beer
birra alla spina draught beer
bottiglia bottle
caffè coffee (ie espresso)
caffè macchiato/ristretto espresso with a dash of
foamed milk/strong
spremuta freshly squeezed fruit juice
succo juice
vino bianco/rosato/rosso white/rosé/red wine

Fruit (frutti) & vegetables (legumi)

agrumi citrus fruits
amarena sour cherry
arancia orange
carciofio globe artichoke
castagne chestnuts
cipolle onions
cocomero water melon
contorno side dish, usually grilled vegetables or
  oven baked potatoes
fichi figs
finocchio fennel
fragole strawberries
friarelli strong flavoured leaves of the broccoli
  family eaten with sausages
frutta fresca fresh fruit
funghi mushroom
lamponi raspberries
melagrana pomegranate
melanzana eggplant/aubergine
melone light coloured melon
mele apples
noci/nocciole walnuts/hazelnuts
patate potatoes, which can be *arroste* (roast),
  fritte (fried), *novelle* (new), *pure'di* (mashed)
patatine fritte chips
peperoncino chilli pepper
peperone peppers
pesche peaches
piselli peas
pomodoro tomato
rucola rocket
scarola leafy green vegetable used in torta di scarola pie.
sciurilli or *fiorilli* tempura courgette flowers
spinaci spinach
verdure vegetables
zucca pumpkin

Meat (carne)

affettati misti mixed cured meat
agnello lamb
bistecca beef steak
braciola chop, steak or slice of meat
carpaccio finely sliced raw meat (usually beef)
cinghiale boar
coda alla vaccinara oxtail
coniglio rabbit
coniglio all'ischiatana Ischia-style rabbit
involtini thinly sliced meat, rolled and stuffed

manzo beef
pollo chicken
polpette meatballs
polpettone meat loaf
porchetta roasted whole suckling pig
prosciutto ham – *cotto* cooked, *crudo* cured
salsicce pork sausage
salumi cured meats, usually served mixed (*salumi misto*)
  on a wooden platter
speck a type of cured, smoked ham
spiedini meat pieces grilled on a skewer
stufato meat stew
trippa tripe
vitello veal

Fish (*pesce*) & seafood (*frutti di mare*)
acciughe anchovies
aragosta lobster
baccalà salt cod
bottarga mullet-roe
branzino sea bass
calamari squid
cozze mussels
frittura di mare/frittura di paranza small fish, squid and
  shellfish lightly covered with flour and fried
frutti di mare seafood
gamberi shrimps/prawns
grigliata mista di pesce mixed grilled fish
orata gilt-head/sea bream
ostriche oysters
pesce spada swordfish
polpo octopus
sarde, sardine sardines
seppia cuttlefish
sogliola sole
spigola bass
stoccafisso stockfish
tonno tuna
triglia red mullet
trota trout
vongole clams

Dessert (*dolce*)
cornetto sweet croissant
crema custard
dolce dessert
gelato ice cream
granita flavoured crushed ice
macedonia (di frutta) fruit cocktail dessert with white wine

Useful phrases
can I have the bill please? *posso avere il conto per favore?*
is there a menu? *c'è un menù?*
what do you recommend? *che cosa mi consegna?*
what's this? *cos'è questo?*
where's the toilet? *dov'è il bagno?*

panettone type of fruit bread eaten at Christmas
semifreddo a partially frozen dessert
sorbetto sorbet
tiramisù rich 'pick-me-up' dessert
torta cake
zabaglione whipped egg yolks flavoured with
  Marsala wine
zuppa inglese English-style trifle

Other
aceto balsamico balsamic vinegar, usually from Modena
arborio type of rice used to make risotto
burro butter
calzone pizza dough rolled with the chef's choice of
  filling and then baked
casatiello lard bread
fagioli white beans
formaggi misti mixed cheese plate
formaggio cheese
frittata omelette
insalata salad
insalata Caprese salad of tomatoes, mozzarella and basil
latte milk
lenticchie lentils
mandorla almond
miele honey
olio oil
polenta cornmeal
pane bread
pane-integrale brown bread
pinoli pine nuts
provola cheese, sometimes with a smoky flavour
ragù a meaty sauce or ragout
riso rice
salsa sauce
sugo sauce or gravy
zuppa soup
zuppa di pasta e fagioli Neapolitan soup

Entertainment

Bars & clubs

In Italy the lines between restaurant, café, bar and club are often blurred. However there are various bar/club scenes around the city and in the Campi Flegrei. In Naples, the Centro Antico and university is the centre of the alternative, arty, student and gay scene, with piazza Bellini the starting point for a night out here. Bars like Intra Moenia and Perditempo are friendly places to find out what's going on by chatting to the locals, picking up flyers, and checking the *Napoli Zero* listings booklet. Chiaia and Santa Lucia (especially along via Parthenope) have the swankiest *locali* (nightspots), frequented by

cheesy piano bar tunes. Positano's Music on the Rocks plays house music and Anema e Core on Capri mixes Latin rhythms with Italian hits. Artis Domus is a basement bar in Sorrento featuring Italo house and live acts.

Children

In the centre of town via San Gregorio Armeno's *presepi* scenes and figurines capture the imaginations of kids and adults alike. There's often a child-friendly show or circus act appearing at piazza Dante on weekends and bank holidays.

The Acquario at the Villa Comunale is small but fascinating. Older kids and teens will be wowed by creepy underground adventures with Napoli Sotterranea and steamy volcanic visions at Solfatara and around the crater of Vesuvius. Pompeii and Herculaneum provide time-travel trips along Roman streets – the latter is a smaller archaeological site and best for small children. Fuorigrotta is lined with child-friendly attractions including the Edenlandia theme park, Naples Zoo and the Piscina Scandone swimming pool. Other rainy-day options include a trip to Bagnoli and its new leisure developments, including the Città della Scienza, an interactive 'Science City' filled with stimulating educational games. Nearby is the 900-m long Pontile Nord, an impressive pier perfect for bracing family walks. Footie-mad children are bound to be impressed by the atmosphere at a SSC Napoli match at the Stadio San Paolo.

Cinema

Foreign films in their original language are rarely shown in Italy and Naples is no exception – English-speaking flicks are dubbed into Italian. Warner Village shows the mainstream films whereas Amedeo, Astra and Modernissimo screen art-house films. The recently refurbished four-screen Modernissimo hosts left-field 'Videodrome' programmes including MaiGay.

Above: Clowning around in Piazza Dante.
Opposite page: Rising South club.

a dressed-up crowd. Smart bar/clubs include Be Bop Bar and S'Move. Enoteca Belledonne is a good spot to start a night out with a quality quaff of vino and some *stuzzichini* (snacks).

On summer weekends many people go out clubbing to the Campi Flegrei's chic beachside clubs including Arenile, Nabilah and Turistico Beach Club, where the likes of Jazzanova, Daft Punk, Atari and Gilles Peterson have done DJ sets. Things get going around 2230: you may be asked for a *tessera* (required of some establishments by Italian law), a membership card that rarely costs more than a couple of euros.

Each resort on the islands and coasts has at least one swanky bar playing dance music and

Rising Mutiny gig.

Tip...

The informative monthly *Napoli Zero* listings booklet is available at various bars including Enoteca Belledonne and Perditempo. Visit napoli.zero.eu.

Gay & lesbian

In Naples, Sputnik Club and Depot are late-night gay bars and there are quite a few club nights including Freelovers and Spirito Libero – good sources of information are napoligaypress.it and arcigaynapoli.org. Capri is well known for its gay scene, the Spiaggia Libera Via Krupp at Marina Piccola being the place where it all hangs out.

Music

Classical & opera

Grandiose operatic and classical productions are staged at the Teatro San Carlo while concerts of chamber music, organized by the likes of the Associazione Alessandro Scarlatti, are held in the famous Conservatorio di Musica San Pietro a Majella and various churches including the Chiesa di San Domenico Maggiore. On the Amalfi Coast,

Ravello hosts its famous festival of classical music (see page 54) while Suoni degli Dei features smaller concerts on the divine trail, the Sentiero degli Dei.

Contemporary

Live rock and alternative acts can be heard at Velvet, Doria 83 and Rising Mutiny – an 'arts club' that showcases indie, electronica and jazz acts. The Otto Jazz Club organizes concerts and Around Midnight is jazz central. Mu Mu Frequencies showcases live dance acts. Outdoor summer festivals include Neapolis at the Arena Flegrea, which attracts top left-field acts such as Massive Attack, as well as the more mainstream pop-rock TV event Festivalbar and Festa di Piedigrotta, the traditional showcase for *Canzone Napoletana* (Neapolitan song).

Outside Naples, most places have a nightclub playing piano bar tunes and occasional jazz/pop acts. In Sorrento Artis Domus stages rock and latino music gigs, L'Ecstasy at Ischia Porto is a venue for the Ischia jazz festival in September while Arenile at Bagnoli hosts indie/dance-electro acts like Atari.

Theatre & dance

Naples has grand theatres and fiercely independent ensembles. Every night there is something different to see, from mainstream TV spin-offs to edgy and experimental works. The productions are mainly in Italian and often in dialect. Neapolitan theatre can be traced from Nero's Graeco-Roman performances, through the 16th-century *commedia dell'arte* and the masked Neapolitan archetypal character Pulcinella, to the 20th-century Teatro Umoristico of the de Filippo family and Totò, ending with the comic genius Massimo Troisi and his modern-day descendants. Neapolitan offbeat humour and quick wit can be seen in productions at the Sancarluccio and Sannazaro theatres.

Contemporary dance productions appear occasionally on many of the city's theatre programmes while the most lavish ballet productions are staged at the Teatro San Carlo.

Music ancient & modern

Napoli's ancient musical traditions blossomed in the 1500s when the first conservatories were established, nurturing abandoned children and training them as musicians. Great composers such as Rossini, Donizetti and Bellini as well as *castrati* singers like Farinelli followed. When the Teatro San Carlo was opened in 1737, Naples became the fashionable home of opera. In the 20th century Caruso and Pavarotti would revel in the Neapolitan folk tradition, taking *O Sole Mio*, *Torna a Surriento* and *Santa Lucia* to a worldwide audience.

Neapolitan Baroque Naples was the centre of the flamboyant Baroque opera during the 17th and 18th centuries. Influential composers include Alessandro Scarlatti (1660-1725) and Giovanni Battista Pergolesi (1710-1736) who transformed the *opera buffa*. Maestro George Friederic Handel (1685-1759) drew heavily from this period of Neapolitan music.

La Canzone Napoletana Popular song in Naples lives on in contemporary musical styles such as the garbled crooning of Neomelodica. From the late 1870s up until the 1970s the city stopped during September's Festa di Piedigrotta to listen to the newest songs by the likes of Sergio Bruni and Peppino di Capri, presented at the Festival della Canzone Napoletana.

Alternative music An alternative music scene emerged in the 1970s when artists like James Senese, Napoli Centrale, Pino Daniele, Musicanova and Nuova Compagnia di Canto Popolare (NCCP) mixed jazz, Latin rhythms, rock and Neapolitan folk styles. Multi-instrumentalist Daniele Sepe mixed classical arrangements and 12th-century Latin texts with jazz and rap (bands Bisca and 99 Posse feature) on *Vite Perdite* (1994, Polo Sud-Piranha label). The band Almamegretta mix dub and rock interlaced with Arabic and Neapolitan influences, most successfully on the Adrian Sherwood produced *Sanacore* album (1995) and on *Karmacoma (Napoli Trip)* with Massive Attack. Today, rap artists Co'Sang and Lucariello reflect the realities of life in the Camorra-ridden suburbs while Epo forge a more mainstream rock and electronic path.

What the locals say

Almamegretta's favourites
Modern Neapolitan classics:
Napoli Centrale's first album, *Napoli Centrale* (1975) and Pino Daniele's early 1980s albums, *Nero a Metà*, *Vai Mò* and *Bella Mbriana*.
New bands: Filocalia, Co'Sang, Lucariello and EPO.

Shopping

Bancarella in the Centro Antico.

Being a port city with 2500 years of history, crafts and trading behind it, you can get just about anything in Naples. In the Centro Antico, particularly on Spaccanapoli and via dei Tribunali, there are lots of interesting independent outlets, *bancarelle* (stalls) and *rigattieri* (bric-a-brac sellers) peddling everything from pasta to fading gouaches, *corni collaudati* (charmed horns for the superstitious) and marble busts. Via San Gregorio Armeno is the world-famous home of skilled artisans who make presepi (nativity scenes) and figurines.

Port'Alba, off piazza Dante, is renowned for its second-hand and specialist bookshops and stalls. Via Santa Maria di Costantinopoli and via Domenico Morelli are famed for their *antiquariati* (antique dealers), who stock anything from Capodimonte porcelain and Posillipo School paintings to period furniture and historic prints. The main shopping drag is via Toledo, part of which is pedestrianized these days – it's good for window shopping while you do the evening *passeggiata*.

A good introduction to Neapolitan market life can be found in the nearby Quartieri Spagnoli, around via Pignasecca and Montesanto, where you'll find food, clothing and household goods – perfect for the budding barista or for anyone after Italian spoons and kitchenware. For a more full-on experience head to Mercato di Porta Nolana and piazza Mercato which have just about everything, legal and otherwise. For food, the market at Porta Capuana (aka Mercato dei Vergini) is entertaining, edgy and teeming with tasty produce. The Mercato dei Fiori (flower market) is at Maschio Angioino while the Fiera Antiquaria is an antiques market held once or twice a month in and around the Villa Comunale.

Chiaia (via Chiaia, piazza dei Martiri, via della Cavalarizza and via dei Mille) is the best place to go if you are after swanky fashion, designer labels and interiors shops. The best clothing sales are held here in January. On a larger scale, out of town towards Nola is a recently opened (2008) shopping centre full of designer labels and world famous brands – the rotund Renzo Piano-designed Vulcano Buono resembles Vesuvius, has ample parking and is also reached via a free shuttle bus run by City Sightseeing Napoli from piazza Vittoria and piazza Fanzago.

Further afield, Sorrento is well known for its inlaid-wood products, Positano for its loose-fitting fashions, Amalfi for its paper and classy stationery and Vietri for its colourful ceramics. Little boutiques on Capri still feature that sandals-and-cotton Caprese look. The big designer labels may have moved into Capri Town but there are still lots of tempting gastronomic shops and quirky outlets. Anacapri has even more family-run outlets. Ischia's Il Corso and Procida's via Vittorio Emanuele have an earthier selection.

Food for home

Although many of the touristy resorts like Sorrento, Ischia Ponte and Amalfi have a few reasonably priced shops for the locals, Naples is easily the best place to pick up regional food bargains for taking home – there are lots of small outlets selling wine

Tip...

Shops are open Monday to Saturday from around 0900 until 1300 and then again from 1600 to 2000. Most of them close between 1330 and 1600; on Monday mornings in the winter; and Saturday afternoon in the summer. Sales are held in January and in mid-July to August.

(enoteche) and food shops (alimentari) where you can pick up Lacryma Christi wine, taralli biscuits, mozzarella cheese and fresh pasta at a fraction of the price charged at the airport. Supermarkets are often even cheaper, with lots of exotic labels and quirky products to catch the eye. Pasticcerie (pastry shops/bakers), many with bars attached, are full of delicious Neapolitan pastries. Specialist gourmet food shops are crammed full of smelly goodies including hand-made chocolates, cheeses, salami and fennel-infused digestivo (an alternative to limoncello perhaps).

Bringing home the grapes

Airport restrictions on fluids in hand luggage make it trickier than in the past to take a few bottles of olive oil or wine home with you. You can still buy alcohol and other bottled liquids after security at the airport itself but it is likely to be much pricier than in the shops. Any bottles in your hold luggage should be covered in bubble wrap, sealed in a zip-lock bag and padded out with towels or clothing to prevent breakages. Shipping is an option if you're planning to take home a case of wine or more, although you will need to prove to Customs that the wine is strictly for personal consumption and you should bear in mind that the shipping price per bottle may be more than the value of the wine itself. For the best advice, ask the enoteca or dealer when you buy the wine.

Activities & tours

Boat trips

A fabulous way to see Campania's coastline and marine caves, with some swimming and sunbathing thrown in, is to hire a boat or join a tour. All around the Sorrentine Peninsula, Amalfi Coast and the islands, small operators explore natural wonders like the Emerald, Blue and Green grottoes and the rocky islets of the Li Galli islands and the Faraglioni rocks. Vessels including flash yachts and traditional *gozzo* Sorrentine sailing boats can be hired with or without a captain if you have suitably salty sea-dog skills. If you want to go fishing with the locals, Pasquale Saurino runs various trips from Ischia's harbours including squid fishing at night and a fishing trip combined with a tour around the island's coves.

Cultural tours

Getting around all the sights of Naples, with its insane traffic and incomplete public transport system, would take weeks but there are tour companies and friendly local guides who make things easier. For those on a budget, City Sightseeing Napoli's four open-top bus routes are excellent, with commentary available in eight languages. Another option, especially if you are in a group so that you can share the cost, is to hire a driver with local knowledge. Multilingual speakers Francesca Del Vecchio's Itinera and Francesco Coda's Soultrain Tours are reliable options – they will also drive you around the Campi Flegrei and along towards the Sorrentine Peninsula. Besuited and gentlemanly drivers Giovanni and Umberto Benvenuto, of Benvenuto Limos are perfect for doing the Amalfi Drive in cool air-conditioned style. Ischia can be explored with Giuseppe Lauro and his Ischia Taxi Service.

For an unusual, atmospheric experience amid Roman ruins, *L'Ultima Notte di Ercolano* combines an evening tour of Herculaneum with a theatrical performance. On a similar goose-pimple-raising trip is the *Sogno Pompei*, an under-the-stars jaunt filled with the sights and sounds of ancient Pompeii. As well as organizing group excursions around Campania's archaeological sights, Arethusa runs night-time walks around the magical Reggia di Caserta palace gardens – the combination of 18th-century music, atmospheric lighting and theatrical performance amid the Bourbon statues and fountains makes this a special Baroque evening.

The *Parco Sommerso di Gaiola* is a protected stretch of Posillipo coastline rich in Roman structures including the Villa Pausilypon and the Grotta di Seiano. CSI Gaiola runs various themed tours around the archaeological site above and below water – some by boat, others involving snorkelling, diving and birdwatching.

Food & wine

Every Neapolitan cook worth his/her salt thinks their own culinary *fantasia* can improve at least one of the region's fabulous dishes. The ever-artful Giovanna Raffone of Posillipo Dream, who has appeared with celebrity chefs (some of whom she doesn't rate), loves to share her culinary secrets during her entertaining cookery courses in her Posillipo kitchen. For her lesson on how to make *frittura di pesce* (fried seafood medley) Giovanna takes you to her local *pescivendolo* to see the art of bartering before learning how to make the crispiest *calamari fritti* known to man or marine beast. Elsewhere CucinAmica and Ciao Laura run a host of structured courses in Vomero and on the Amalfi Coast respectively.

Walking

Campania has some of the most spectacular walking trails anywhere, including the Amalfi Coast's *Sentiero degli Dei* (Trail of the Gods), a truly divine walk. Experienced guide Giovanni Visetti suggests that the best periods for walking are mid-April to mid-June, when the weather is usually good with mild temperatures, longer days and lots of flowering plants to enjoy, and mid-September to mid-October, when temperatures and the weather in general are usually fair – although on the downside days are shorter, less flowers are in bloom and there's the risk of coming across areas damaged by wild fire. Giovanni lives in Massa Lubrense and leads walks all over the Sorrentine Peninsula and Amalfi Coast; he also ventures to

Marina Grande boat trips, Capri.

Capri. Luigi Esposito of Capri Trails guides groups along the island's trails, including the coastal walk *Il Sentiero dei Fortini* that takes in old French forts. Roberto Addeo, who is in touch with this friendly network of outdoor specialists (whenever.it), is a vulcanologist guide responsible for treks amid the rare species, old lava flows and fizzing fumaroles of the *Parco Nazionale del Vesuvio*.

Wellbeing

The volcanic springs of the Campi Flegrei, beloved of the ancient Greek and Roman glitterati, still provide curative waters and treatments. The famous spa waters at Baia may bubble elsewhere after centuries of earthquakes, but there's still lots of natural steam, hot pools and mud treatments at the *Terme Stufe di Nerone* at nearby Bacoli. For a choice of spa resorts for all budgets head to Ischia which has the 85°C iodine-rich springs of Casamicciola Terme (Terme Manzi and Parco Termale Castiglione are the swankiest establishments here) and the most naturally radioactive waters in Italy at Lacco Ameno. Pick of the resorts is the Spa & Resort Negombo, which overlooks the stunning Bay of San Montano near Lacco Ameno.

Contents

Piazza Plebiscito.

Introduction

Over 2500 years of human life and much volcanology have created the intoxicating tragicomedy that is Napoli. It's dirty, loud, chaotic and infuriating at one turn, then compelling, exhilarating and gorgeous. Labyrinthine layers of history have created architecture, customs and language that barely feel Italian let alone European.

Greek-founded Neapolis lies in the most naturally blessed yet deadly bay imaginable, which perhaps explains its inhabitants' lust for life's joys and dark obsessions. Simple pleasures like *la pizza, la sfogliatella* and *il bel far niente* (the beauty of doing nothing) are deeply ingrained. In the Centro Antico, beside shiny bronze skulls of a religious cult, the grimy flagstones of the old Graeco-Roman *decumani* buzz and spit with vespas and the clipped vowels of gesticulating *scugnizzi* – Neapolitan 'street kids'. On the Santa Lucia waterfront you gaze out across the shimmering bay towards Vesuvius, the Sorrentine Peninsula, Capri, the islands… Colours and tastes are vivid, the natural fruits of the fertile volcanic soil and ocean. Bright red tomatoes and azure blue seas contrast with shadowy layers accumulated by centuries of history.

Napoletanità (being Neapolitan) is truly a way of life. "Ccà nisciuno è fesso" they say: "Nobody is stupid here." Living on their wits the irrepressible Napoletani create Baroque customs and cults. Macabre miracles like San Gennaro's liquefying blood gave Naples the title *L'Urbs Sanguinum*: the City of Blood. It could be applied to today's Camorra clan wars. Fortunately, for the visitor at least, Napoli's life-affirming culture and cuisine, as well as the bay's natural wonders, overshadow the criminal state-within-a state that infects its troubled suburbs.

Cinquecento on the basalti approaching San Domenico Maggiore.

What to see in…

…one day

Kick off your day at **Bar Gambrinus** and then explore the **Monumental City**, the **Centro Antico**, the **Madre gallery** and **Museo Archeologico**, eating pizza at **Il Pizzaiolo del Presidente** on via dei Tribunali, drinking an aperitvo in **Chiaia**, **Borgo Marinari** or on via Orazio, and then dining below **Castel dell'Ovo** or at **Rosiello** in Posillipo.

…a weekend or more

Spend further days exploring the area's natural and archaeological wonders on day trips or overnighters: **Vesuvius**, **Pompeii** and **Capri** are must-dos. There's plenty more sightseeing and shopping, including incredible art and gardens at **Capodimonte**, the **Certosa di San Martino** and gastronomic goodies aplenty.

Essentials

❶ Getting around

By foot The easiest way to get around the Centro Antico is on foot. Traffic in Naples is notoriously anarchic and takes some getting used to. Drivers obey a very Neapolitan game plan which is much like playing bumper-cars at the fair: whizzing scooters and vehicles largely ignore traffic lights, and *clacsons* are used constantly to communicate a laconic "oi watch it!" All this makes crossing the road in Naples an art form in itself.

By public transport Naples has a comprehensive transport system of buses, trams, funiculars and metro trains. For up-to-date timetables consult the latest *Qui Napoli* booklet, given away free at tourist offices and elsewhere. Tickets are available from *tabacchi* (tobacconists – look out for the big 'T') as well as from ticket offices, some bars and news-stands. The **UnicoNapoli** travel cards provide unlimited travel in the city and beyond over various timescales: 90 mins for €1; 24 hrs on weekdays for €3; 24 hrs at the weekend for €2.50; 72 hrs throughout Campania including the islands for €20 and 72 hrs in conjunction with the Artecard for €25.

Napoli's metro system, **Metronapoli** (metro. na.it), is currently undergoing redevelopment and when finished (2011 or thereabouts) will consist of 10 lines. Two lines are particularly useful: **Linea 1** or *Metro d'Arte*, with contemporary art installations, runs from piazza Dante and Museo to Vomero; **Linea 2** crosses the city from east to west, linking Pozzuoli to Gianturco. When completed Linea 1 will run in a circle between Napoli Centrale train station and Capodichino airport.

Buses and trams run from 0500-2400. There are three colour-coded types: red buses (marked 'R') are supposedly fast and frequent; orange buses are the most common; blue buses serve the outlying areas. Night buses (*linee notturne*) are best avoided. Useful buses include **R2** linking piazza Garibaldi and piazza Trieste e Trento; **R3** running from piazza Carità to Mergellina via the Galleria Umberto I and Chiaia; and **R4** linking the port area with Museo Archeologico.

Four **Funicolari**, cable railways, connect Napoli's hills (Vomero and Posillipo) with downtown areas: **Centrale** (via Toledo to piazza Fuga), **Montesanto** (piazza Montesanto to via Morghen), **Chiaia** (Parco Margherita to Cimarosa) and **Mergellina** (via Mergellina to via Manzoni). They are a fun and handy way to get around.

Taxis Taking *un tassi* is often convenient, and can be an entertaining if hair-raising insight into *Napoletanità*. If the meter isn't switched on, agree to a fixed price before you set off and ask for the regulated price list that should be on view in the back of the cab. Taxis can be hailed at the 90 taxi ranks or by phoning these companies for a €1 booking fee: **Consortaxi** (T081-552 5252); **Consorzio Taxi Vagando** (CoTaNa, T081-570 7070, taxivagando.it); **Radio Free Taxi** (T081-551 5151). **Francesco Coda** (T338-945 3222) also provides a reliable taxi service as well as tours of the city (see page 150).

❷ Bus station
Regional and local buses go through **Napoli Centrale**, piazza Garibaldi, T081-554 3188. **CTP** (T081-700 1111) and **STP** (T081-552 2176) are the big bus operators.

❸ Train station
The main train station, connecting with major cities, is **Napoli Centrale**, piazza Garibaldi, T081-554 3188.

❹ ATMs
Cash machines are available throughout the city. Be careful of pickpockets and card-reading scams, especially at train stations. **Banco di Napoli** has a *bancomat* (ATM) at via Toledo 177.

❺ Hospital
Both of these have 24-hr *pronto soccorso* (casualty departments): **Ospedale Cardarelli**, via Cardarelli 9, T081-546318; **Ospedale Fatebenefratelli**, via Manzoni 220, T081-769 7220.

❻ Pharmacy
For information on the rota of night-time opening pharmacies (*farmacie di turno*) ask your hotel or telephone T1100 for nearest ones. The newspaper *Il Mattino* and the doors of pharmacies also have lists.

Post office The Central Post Office (Ufficio Postale) is housed in the Fascist-era building at piazza Matteotti, T081-551 1456, Mon-Fri 0800-1830, Sat 0800-1230.

Tourist information offices The handiest offices are: the **EPT Napoli Centrale** (T081-268 799, Mon-Sat 0900-1900); **EPT Stazione Mergellina** (piazza Piedigrotta 1, T081-761 2102, Mon-Sat 0900-1900) and **UIT Piazza Plebiscito** (piazza del Gesù, T081-551 2701, Mon-Sat 0900-2000, Sun 0900-1500).

Campania Artecard The Campania Artecard (T800-600601, from mobiles T06-3996 7650, artecard.it) enables visitors to see the region's attractions at a discounted price, with public transport thrown in. There are four different cards:

The **Ordinaria** card allows 'three days all sites' of discounted sightseeing at €25 for adults or €18 for 18-25 year olds with the first two attractions free (pick the pricey ones first) and then 50% off entry to other sights, plus free use of all public transport – including regional trains and certain buses. A **seven-day** card costs €28 (€21 for 18-25s), while an **annual** card is €40 (€30 for 18-25s). Then there's the **three-day Naples and Campi Flegrei** card (€13 adults, €8 18-25s), which gives you the same deal but only within Naples and the Campi Flegrei. The following sights are included in the scheme: Castel Sant' Elmo, Certosa e Museo di San Martino, Città della Scienza, Complesso Museale di Santa Chiara , Museo Archeologico Nazionale, Museo Civico di Castel Nuovo, Museo Nazionale di Capodimonte, Palazzo Reale and all five major attractions in the Campi Flegrei (counted as one admission). Additionally, lots of other sights offer small discounts on presentation of the card. It's available at major transport hubs, tourist offices, at participating attractions and at some *edicole* (news-stands).

Neapolitan driving tips

Rimane calmo! The most important thing is to stay calm so that you can get used to the way Neapolitans drive.

Try and look into the eyes of the drivers to see their intention. If they are wearing sunglasses, then that's unlucky!

Neapolitan drivers hoot their horn a lot, like a reflex action. It's a friendly warning.

The old adage that at traffic lights in Naples, "Green means take care and red means go!" is not as prevalent as it used to be as the Vigilanza Stradale (traffic police) actually dole out fines these days.

Don't leave valuables or luggage unattended, in your car – ever!

Tassista Francesco Coda

Right: Targa napoletana.

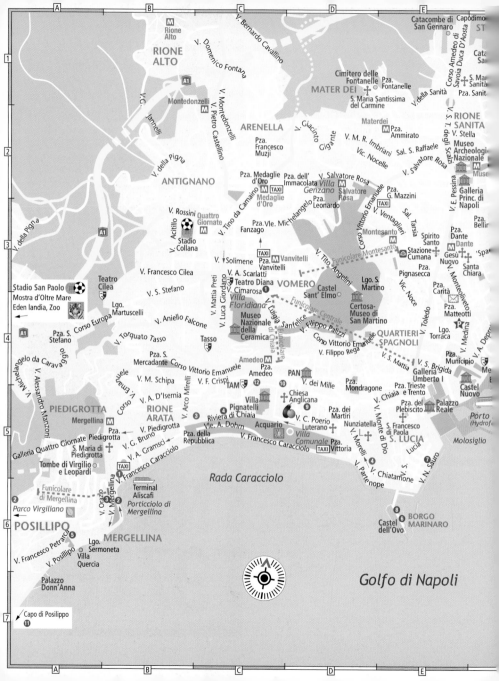

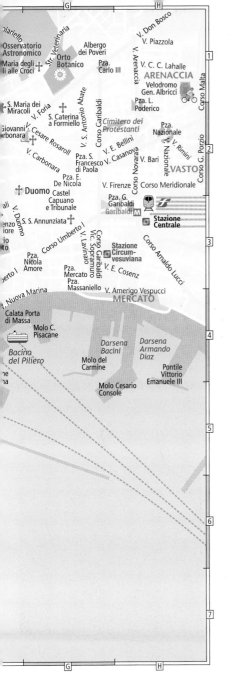

Naples listings

Sleeping

1 Ausonia *via Caracciolo 7* B5
2 La Bouganville *via Manzoni 155* A6
3 Micalò *Riviera di Chiaia 88* C5
4 Napoli Residence *via Chiatamone 6* D5

Eating & drinking

1 Acunzo *via D Cimarosa 64* C3
2 Chalet Ciro *via Mergellina 11* B6
3 Ciro a Mergellina *via Mergellina* B6
4 Gran Bar Riviera *Riviera di Chiaia 183* C5
5 Gran Caffè Cimmino *via Petrarca 147* A6
6 La Bersagliera *borgo Marinari 10/11* E6
7 La Cantinella *via Cuma 42* E5
8 La Scialuppa *borgo Marinaro 4* E6
9 Moccia *via San Pasquale di Chiaia 21/22* D5
10 Osteria La Cucinotta *via G. Bausan 32* C4
11 Rosiello a Posillipo *via Santo Strato 10* A7
12 Trip *via Giuseppe Martucci 64* C4

Santa Lucia & around

Piazza Plebiscito is the grand focal point of the city. A semicircular colonnade sweeps on either side of the San Francesco di Paola church and a huge pedestrianized space, beloved of football-playing kids, lies in front of the statue and shrapnel-studded Palazzo Reale façade. Grandiose buildings including the Galleria Umberto I and Teatro San Carlo and smart cafés surround intimate piazza Trieste e Trento and its elegant, artichoke-adorned fountain. Nearby, the muscular hulk of Castel Nuovo (Maschio Angioino) overlooks muddled piazza Municipio and the port. Buildings cling to the tufa rock of Monte Echia, also known as Pizzofalcone, where Greek settlers founded Parthenope. Santa Lucia is no longer the old fishermen's quarter immortalized in song, although it does have the Borgo Marinari's swanky yachts and restaurants beside the honeycomb-like blocks of the Castel dell'Ovo.

Calcio kids on piazza Plebiscito.

Piazza del Plebiscito & Chiesa San Francesco di Paola

Chiesa T081-764 5133.
Mon-Fri 0800-1200, 1530-1800, Sat-Sun
0800-1300. Bus R3, C18, 140, 152.
Funicolare Centrale: Piazza Augusteo.
Map: Central Naples, C7, p86.

Now the traffic has gone and it's no longer used as
a car park, the city's largest square and its dramatic
architecture is once again the focal point of grand
Neapolitan occasions. The Pantheon-aping San
Francesco di Paola church (1817) designed by Pietro
Bianchi (1787-1849), with its three wide drum-like
domes and sweeping portico, is the backdrop of
celebrations, demonstrations, concerts, state visits
and quirky contemporary art installations. Begun
by the Bonapartist ruler Joachim Murat and finished
by Ferdinand of Bourbon, the royal basilica has a
circular plan and a rather formal feel, like a severe
Palladian mausoleum. Back on the piazza there
are equestrian statues of Carlo III and Ferdinando IV
by Antonio Canova and Antonio Calì. The Doric
colonnades are flanked by lounging lions who draw
your eyes to the long façade of the Palazzo Reale,
where you can admire eight statues of some of the
city's most renowned rulers replete with bulbous
breeches, armoury and bullet holes. From left to
right, and in chronological order, they are: Roger II,
Frederick II, Charles of Anjou, Alfonso of Aragon,
Charles V of Hapsburg, Charles III of Bourbon,
Joachim Murat and Victor Emmanuel II of Savoy.

Palazzo Reale

Piazza del Plebiscito 1, T081-400547.
Thu-Tue 0900-1900, €4, free under-18s, discounts
with Artecard, guided tour by reservation.
Bus R3, C18, 140, 152. Funicolare Centrale:
Piazza Augusteo. Map: Central Naples, C7, p86.

Chances are your introduction to the enormous
Royal Palace will come on piazza Plebiscito where
a walk along the 167 m-long façade and its eight
regal statues makes for an amusing introduction
to Neapolitan history and the city's rulers.
Designed by Domenico Fontana (1543-1607), it was
built for a planned visit by King Charles III of Spain,
who never got around to a sojourn in Naples let
alone sliding down (not advised) the banisters of
its **Scalone Monumentale** (Grand Staircase). The
Royal Apartments are crammed with tapestries,
frescoes, paintings, sculpture, period furniture,
chandeliers, porcelain and clocks, with pots of
gilt and drapes thrown in. Don't miss the Throne
Room's chair with lions to rest divinely chosen
elbows on and an eagle designed to soar above

Tip...

Students and professors often swing open a door
in the Biblioteca Nazionale to have a smoke on the
chessboard-tiled roof terraces outside. Superb views
of the port and beyond can be enjoyed from here but
be warned, your enjoyment may be cut short by one
of the officious janitors.

Chiesa di San Francesco di Paola.

Biblioteca Nazionale terrace.

Around the city

the sovereign's crown. More fabulously overblown decor can be seen in the **Teatrino di Corte** (Court Theatre), where there are no prizes for guessing where the king sat, the relatively understated **Studio del Rè** (King's Study) and the **Cappella Palatina** with its preposterously grand *presepe* (nativity scene).

You won't find a fustier old library anywhere than the **Biblioteca Nazionale** (piazza del Plebiscito 1, Mon-Fri 0830-1930, Sat 0830-1330), frequented by university students and lucky scholars who get to see the priceless papyrus manuscripts rescued from Herculaneum.

Piazza Trieste e Trento & Caffè Gambrinus

Piazza Trieste e Trento.
Bus R3, C18, 140, 152.
Funicolare Centrale: Piazza Augusteo.
Map: Central Naples, C7, p86.

Amidst the roundabout traffic and lollypop-wielding *poliziotti* of this piazza near the Galleria Umberto is an alluring fountain with water sprouting from an artichoke, the Fontana del Carciofo. Historic Caffè Gambrinus (see page 135) on the corner makes a charming espresso stop with its dapper baristas, Neapolitan pastries and grand *fin di secolo* interiors.

Napoli Sotterranea & the Acquedotto Carmignano

Tours start outside Caffè Gambrinus, piazza Trieste e Trento, T081-400256, lanapolisotterranea.it.
Tours cost €10, last about 1 hr and run Thu 2100; Sat 1000, 1200, 1800; Sun 1000, 1100, 1200, 1800. Bus R3, C18, 140, 152. Funicolare Centrale: Piazza Augusteo. Map: Central Naples, C7, p86.

Trace Napoli's fascinating history by taking a guided tour of the city's ancient Carmignano aqueduct, visiting atmospheric spaces once occupied by Greeks, Romans and sheltering families during the Second World War, and filled with 2500-year-old bricks and intriguing graffiti.

Top: Caffè Gambrinus.
Above: Fontana del Carciofo, Piazza Trieste e Trento.

Galleria Umberto I

Piazza Trento e Trieste.
Entrances on via San Carlo, via Toledo, via Santa Brigida and via Giuseppe Verdi. Bus R3, C18, 140, 152. Funicolare Centrale: Piazza Augusteo. Map: Central Naples, C6, p86.

Despite the present-day scaffolding and grime, the glass and wrought-iron elegance of this 1887-built, *stile-Liberty* arcade will leave you with a sore neck and wide eyes. The cruciform structure is accessed via one of four grand entrances and is worth lingering in to admire its colossal space, ever-changing lighting effects from its curvy skylights, architectural detailing and coloured marble floors. Its rather drab electronics outlets and overpriced cafés do not quite match the swanky smugness of its Milanese twin, the Galleria Emanuele II.

Teatro San Carlo

Via San Carlo 93, T081-400300.
Bus R3, C18, 140, 152. Funicolare Centrale: Piazza Augusteo. Map: Central Naples, C6, p86.

Europe's oldest working opera house was built for King Carlo I in 1737 and its interiors and acoustics still impress. At its height its sumptuous interiors, including Bourbon blue-upholstered seats (now the customary red), and world-famous performances sealed the city's reputation for glamour and worldly pleasures. The present façade was added in 1812 before a fire in 1816 destroyed much of the interior. Among the greats to have graced the stage are Puccini, Rossini, Donizetti, Mascagni, Verdi and Pavarotti, foreign composers Mozart and Haydn, and the smooth castrato falsettos of Farinelli and Velluti.

Raccolta de Mura

Piazza Trieste e Trento, T081-795 7736.
Mon-Sat 0930-1330, free. Bus R3, C18, 140, 152. Funicolare Centrale: Piazza Augusteo. Map: Central Naples, C6, p86.

Neapolitan music is celebrated at this small basement museum where old *canzoni* classics from the halcyon days of the popular Piedigrotta Festival (see page 55) are piped through speakers. Ettore de Mura's collection of vinyl, posters, lyric sheets and assorted documents introduces you to the heady days from 1834 when the people of the Campania region stopped to hear the new festival tunes. Emotive lyrics and catchy arrangements made songs like *Te voglio bene assaje* (1839) by Sacco and Donizetti, *Funiculì, Funiculà* (1880) by Turco and Denza, and the much-covered classic *'O Sole Mio* (1898) by Di Capua and Capurro massive hits across Neapolitan society and beyond.

Galleria Umberto I.

Tip...

Don't miss the often overlooked **Galleria del Principe di Napoli**, a smaller *belle époque* gallery (1870-1873), opposite the Museo Archeologico.

'O Sole Mio

By Di Capua and Capurro (1898)

Translation

Che bella cosa è na jurnata 'e sole,
n'aria serena doppo na tempesta!
Pe' ll'aria fresca pare già na festa...
Che bella cosa na jurnata 'e sole.

What a wonderful thing a sunny day
The serene air after a thunderstorm
The fresh air, and a party is already going on...
What a wonderful thing a sunny day.

Ma n'atu sole
Cchiù bello, oje ne'.
O sole mio
Sta 'nfronte a te!
O sole
O sole mio
Sta 'nfronte a te!
Sta 'nfronte a te!

But another sun,
that's brighter still
It's my own sun
that's in your face!
The sun, my own sun
It's in your face!
It's in your face!

Quanno fa notte e 'o sole se ne scenne,
Me vene quase 'na malincunia;
Sotto 'a fenesta toia restarria
Quanno fa notte e 'o sole se ne scenne.

When night comes and the sun has gone down,
I start feeling blue;
I'd stay below your window
When night comes and the sun has gone down.

Ma n'atu sole
Cchiù bello, oje ne'.
O sole mio
Sta 'nfronte a te!
O sole, Ohhh sole mio
Sta 'nfronte a te!
Sta 'nfronte a te!

But another sun,
that's brighter still
It's my own sun
that's in your face!
The sun, my own sun
It's in your face!
It's in your face!

Castel Nuovo (Maschio Angioino)

Piazza Municipio, T081-420 1241.
Mon-Sat 0900-1900, €5. Bus R2, R3, C25.
Funicolare Centrale: Piazza Augusteo.
Map: Central Naples, D6, p86.

The muscular bulk of the New Castle (or the Maschio Angioino, the Angevin Fortress, as it's known to the locals), with its five cylindrical towers, now stands sentinel over the road and harbour traffic in piazza Municipio and nearby Molo Beverello. Angevin monarch Charles I built it in 1279 and it was remodelled by King Alfonso of Aragon in the 15th century. After hopping over the moat where crocodiles once snapped, you can join tour groups photographing the **Triumphal Arch**

Tip...

If time is pressing forego a look inside the castle but do take a close-up view of the triumphal arch at the entrance, which you don't need to buy a ticket for. If you feel like tackling Napoli's traffic in a horse-drawn carriage, bring your best bartering skills to the man outside the castle entrance nonchalantly holding the reins in one hand and a cigarette in the other.

(1454-1467), built to commemorate Alfonso's conquest of Naples in 1443. Zoom in on the highest arch to see the four Cardinal Virtues (Prudence, Justice, Temperance and Fortitude) and at its zenith a statue of St Michael. Many of the historical events that took place here are hardly

virtuous or saintly; an infamous event involved King Ferrante I, Alfonso's son, who invited some troublemaking barons to a mock wedding, then arrested and condemned them to death. You can stand in the grandiose, octagonal **Sala dei Baroni** (Barons' Hall) where this happened but sadly nothing is left of the Giotto frescoes that once decorated its walls and 28 m-high vaulted dome. More recently, until 2006, it was a council chamber and witnessed modern-day cloak-and-dagger episodes, often involving the Camorra, the local government and mountains of *munezza* (rubbish).

The **Museo Civico** (Civic Museum) on the first and second floors of the castle contains Angevin and Aragonese interiors, including 14th- and 15th-century sculptures, some rather dreary 15th- to 19th-century paintings and a mighty bronze door complete with cannonball damage. Don't miss the two chapels: the overblown Baroque **Cappella delle Anime del Purgatorio** and **Capella Palatina** with its tall, stark and handsome Gothic windows and some remnants of Giotto's genius.

Monte Echia & Pizzofalcone

Map: Central Naples, B7, p86, and Naples, D5, p78.

The extinct volcano of Monte Echia was where the Greeks put down their curious odds and gods, and named a colony after the winged siren Parthenope. This lofty perch (renamed Palaeopolis

Above: Castel Nuovo and its Renaissance arch.

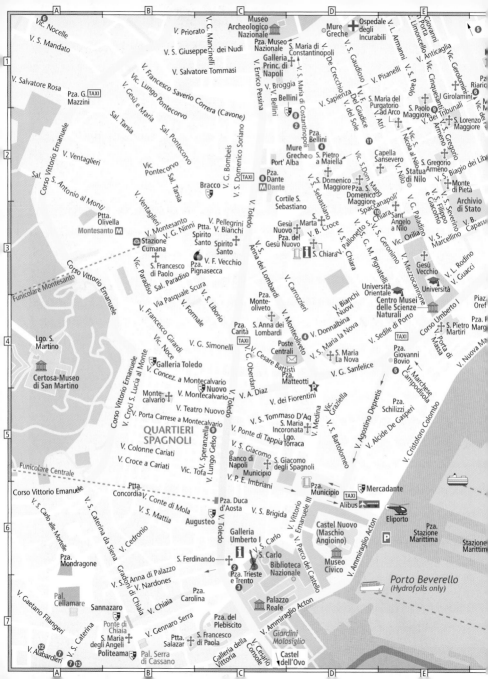

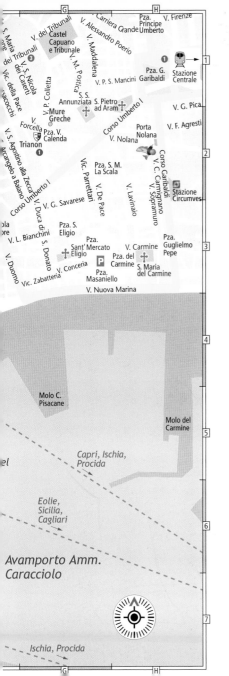

Central Naples listings

● Sleeping

1 Clarean *piazza Garibaldi 49*, **H1**
2 Costantinopoli 104 *via Santa Maria di Costantinopoli 104*, **D2**
3 Decumani Roof *via Tribunali 197*, **G1**
4 Donnalbina7 *via Donnalbina 7*, **D4**
5 Donna Regina *via Luigi Settembrini 80*, **F1**
6 La Controra *piazza Trinita' Alla Cesarea 231*, **A1**
7 Palazzo Alabardieri *via Alabardieri 38*, **A7**
8 Piazza Bellini *via Costantinopoli 101*, **D2**
9 Toledo *via Montecalvario 15*, **C5**

● Eating & drinking

1 Antica Pizzeria da Michele *via Cesare Sersale 1/3*, **G2**
2 Caffè del Professore *piazza Trieste e Trento 46*, **C6**
3 Caffè Gambrinus *piazza Trieste e Trento*, **C7**
4 Caffè Letterario Intra Moenia *Intra Moenia, Piazza Bellini 70*, **D2**
5 Europeo di Mattozzi *via Marchese Campodisola 4*, **E4**
6 Il Pizzaiolo del Presidente *via Tribunali 120/121*, **F1**
7 La Caffettiera *piazza dei Martiri 25*, **A7**
8 Mexico *piazza Dante 86*, **C2**
9 Pizzeria di Matteo *via dei Tribunali 94*, **E1**
10 Scaturchio *piazza San Domenico Maggiore 19*, **D3**
11 Sorbillo *via dei Tribunali 32*, **D2**
12 Umberto *via Alabardieri 30/31*, **A7**
13 Vinarium *vico Santa Maria Cappella Vecchia*, **A7**

Around the city

or Old City, when Neapolis – the New City –
was founded nearby) is a great place to get your
bearings on the city and its history. To reach the
summit, also known as Pizzofalcone, head up the
hill behind piazza Plebiscito. Some crumbling
ancient Greek remains can be seen and nearby
is the Baroque **Church of Santa Maria Egiziaca**,
designed by Fanzago, and the mighty pink-
plastered **Nunziatella** – a former convent turned
military academy built by Ferdinando Sanfelice
(1675-1748). Don't miss Sanfelice's imposing
Palazzo Serra di Cassano and its double staircase
at via Monte di Dio 14: today it houses the Italian
Institute for Philosophical Studies, Naples being
one of the chin-stroking capitals of the world.

Castel dell'Ovo & Borgo Marinari

Borgo Marinari, T081-240 0055.
Castle Mon-Sat 0830-1800, Sun 0830-1400, free.
Bus R3, 140. Map: Naples, E7, p78.

The malleable tufa rock of the ancient island of
Megaride, with its two islets connected by a natural
arch, attracted Greek settlers who established their
colony Parthenope here. Today the Castle of the Egg
is attached to the once atmospheric Santa Lucia
district via a causeway and looks over the Borgo
Marinari, the old fishermen's district turned swanky
restaurant quarter – a relaxing and scenic spot for
drinks and dining, and a backdrop to many a
Neapolitan wedding photograph. The citadel's
strategic position has been put to many uses down
the centuries: Roman patrician Lucullus built a villa
here, monks of the order of St Basil had a monastery
and subsequent incumbents – Frederick II's
Hohenstaufen dynasty, Normans, Angevins,
Aragonese and Bourbons – put it to various uses
including royal palace and prison. Impressive castle
spaces can be admired in the Hall of the Columns
and Loggiato, while the outside ramparts offer
views across the bay and down to the jetties where
the Camorra's speedboats ferried contraband in
the 1980s. The uninspiring **Museo di Etnopreistoria**
(T081-764343, Mon-Fri 1000-1300 by appointment,
free) contains prehistoric tools and ceramics.

Vesuvio and Castel del'Ovo at dawn.

Tip...

To get back down
to sea level take the
steps of the **Rampa
di Pizzofalcone** that
zig-zags between
houses hewn out
of the rock and
plunges you onto
via Chiatomone and
Santa Lucia, near
Castel dell'Ovo.

Magic eggs & other legends

Legends are two-a-*denarius* in Naples and the Castel dell'Ovo has picked up a few. The most popular myth, begun in the medieval period, is that the Roman poet Virgil, author of the *Aeneid*, hung a magic egg within an iron cage under the castle – if the egg should break, the city's fortunes and those of its citizens would shatter also. Another theory smashes this by positing that the 'ovo' is a corruption of the German word for lion (*lowe*), and derives from Frederick II's insignia which hung here up to the late 13th century.

Centro Antico – the Ancient City

The ancient heart of the city combines medieval atmosphere, dazzling churches, serene cloisters, eclectic shopping and quirky sights aplenty. Street vendors, boisterous students and scooters rattling along the sticky, pitted flagstones of the dark, narrow Graeco-Roman *decumani* and *cardi* add to the dreamlike spectacle. Most of the main sights and dark delights lie on or just off two of the three original east-west streets of the grid layout of Neapolis: long and straight Spaccanapoli ('Split Naples') follows the *decumanus inferior* and consists of via Benedetto Croce, via San Biagio dei Librai and via Vicaria Vecchia, while parallel via dei Tribunali is the *decumanus major*. Three Baroque *guglie* (spires) mark calamitous plagues and earthquakes with swirls and cherubs.

Chiesa del Gesù Nuovo

Piazza del Gesù, T081-551 8613.
Mon-Sat 0900-1300, 1600-1900, Sun 0900-1300,
free. Bus C57. Metro: Dante.
Map: Naples, D3, p86.

The austere diamond-pointed stones of the
church of Gesù Nuovo's façade hardly hints at
the ornamental richness and piety awaiting inside.
The Jesuits transformed the battle-hardy
15th-century Palazzo Sanseverino into a
sumptuous church with the help of architect
Giuseppe Valeriano (1542-1596) and a collection
of celebrated Neapolitan artists including Cosimo
Fanzago (1591-1678), Andrea Vaccaro (1605-1670)
and Francesco Solimena (1657-1747). Its flamboyant
frescoes, coloured marble, gilt and stucco work
continue to be a very popular backdrop to
Neapolitan worship every day. A side chapel
contains votive offerings to San Giuseppe
Moscati (1880-1927), the renowned doctor
who was canonized in 1987: queues of pious
Neapolitans flock here to pray to the saint who
dedicated his life to the city's poor and infirm.
Two rooms are filled with metallic ex-voto hearts
and body parts with imploring messages for
miracle cures. Twisted shards of a Second World
War bomb that pierced the barrel-vaulted ceiling
dangle above these poignant offerings near
Moscati's old office, which you can peer into.

Tip...

Remember not
to park your *culo*
(backside) on the
majolica-tiled
benches, or you'll be
reprimanded by one
of the attendants.

Above: Gesù nuovo.
Opposite page: Arte e creature,
via dei Tribunali.

Santa Chiara

*Via Santa Chiara 49, church T081-552 6280, cloisters
and museum T081-792156, santachiara.info.*
Church Mon-Fri 0930-1300, 1430-1800,
Sat-Sun 0900-1300, free. Cloisters and museum
Mon-Sat 0930-1830, Sun 0930-1430, €4, discount
with Artecard. Bus C57. Metro: Dante.
Map: Central Naples, D3, p86.

Beyond the robust-looking campanile that towers
over bustling Spaccanapoli is one of the most
evocative spaces in Naples: cloisters filled with
wisteria, citrus trees and vibrant majolica tiles.
Before entering this magic world, you can visit

the 14th-century Santa Chiara church built for
Robert of Anjou's wife Sancia di Maiorca. A Second
World War bomb and a devastating fire destroyed
the church's 18th-century Baroque flamboyance.
The reconstruction recalls the original Provençal-
Gothic Franciscan character. Highlights include a
Tuscan-style tomb of Robert the Wise behind the
high altar and the Coro delle Clarisse (Choir of the
Poor Clares) where the nuns stood apart from the
public congregation.

The layout of the complex is typically
Neapolitan, and a vestige of the Graeco-Roman
world, where a cosseted environment lay behind

a street façade. A walk amid the cloisters' arcades designed by Domenico Antonio Vaccaro (1678-1745) and the striking tiles with their vivid whirls of blue, green and yellow majolica is uplifting. Hundreds of pastoral scenes created by father and son team Donato and Giuseppe Massa during the 18th century adorn the cloisters' 72 octagonal pillars and benches, while faded frescoes cover the walls under the arcades. The museum housed within the nuns' old quarters is worth a look for its Roman baths and some interesting artefacts tracing the complex's history.

Chiesa di San Domenico Maggiore

Piazza San Domenico Maggiore, T081-449097. Daily 0900-1200, 1700-1900, free. Bus C57, R2. Metro: Dante. Map: Central Naples, D2, p86.

The bulky back-end of the church of San Domenico Maggiore dominates one of the city's most attractive squares and its Baroque monument, the Guglia di San Domenico (1737). The church and monastery were begun by the Angevins (1283-1324) and have been much altered after earthquakes and fires. Enter via a staircase on the piazza or at the true main entrance on the *vicolo* (side street). The interior is 76 m long and contains 14th-century frescoes by Pietro Cavallini, who influenced Giotto, in the Cappella Brancaccio. A copy of Caravaggio's *Flagellation* (1607) by Andrea Vaccaro in the north transept can be compared to the original in the Museo di Capodimonte. Remains of the ancient Chiesa di Sant'Angelo a Morfisa can be seen in the atmospheric crypt. Don't miss the Cappellone del Crocifisso and a reproduction of the 13th-century panel painting through which – legend has it – Christ spoke to the influential theologian Thomas Aquinas. Aquinas, along with many a radical philosopher, studied at the adjoining monastery and original seat of the University of Naples Federico II. Another influential alumnus, Giordano Bruno who promoted the idea of a solar system and an infinite universe, was burnt as a heretic by the Roman Inquisition in 1600.

Top: Santa Chiara cloisters.
Above: Majolica magic.

Capella di Sansevero

*Via Francesco de Sanctis 19, T081-551 8470,
museosansevero.it.*
Mon, Wed-Sat 1000-1740, Sun 1000-1310, €6,
€4 with Artecard, €2-4 concessions. Bus R2, C57.
Metro: Dante. Map: Central Naples, E2, p86.

Containing some of Italy's most extraordinary
sculptures as well as fascinating clues to the life of
an infamously mysterious Neapolitan prince, the
Sansevero chapel is a must-see. Also known as the
Pietatella, it was built as a votive chapel dedicated
to Santa Maria della Pietà in what was once the
gardens of the Palazzo Sangro di Sansevero in
piazza San Domenico Maggiore. Then Raimondo
VII Prince of Sansevero remodelled it into a family
funerary chapel, commissioning gifted artists
including Giuseppe Sanmartino, who created the
spine-chillingly lifelike *Cristo Velato* (*Veiled Christ*) as
the centrepiece. The darkly furtive imagination of
the locals reckoned that after the figure was carved
from a single block of marble the alchemist prince
mixed up a home-brew to petrify a sheet laid over
it – another entertainingly fantastical Neapolitan
theory. Beside the main altar is Antonio Corradini's
sensuous and immodest masterpiece *La Pudicizia*
(*Modesty*), dedicated to the patron's mother, who
died at just 23 years. Francesco Queirolo's
Disinganno (*Disillusion*, otherwise known as
Freedom from Sin) depicts a man disentangling
himself from a rope net, and honours di Sangro's
father who chose to go all monastic after an
action-packed life had ensnared him in sin.
Mysterious Masonic symbols abound in both
the original labyrinthine-patterned floor (still in
situ in the mausoleum) and the vibrant frescoed
ceiling (by Francesco Maria Russo). Its vibrant hues,
including a ghoulish green illuminating the family
worthies (saints), were allegedly created by the
Prince himself. In the vault stand two anatomical
figures displaying original skeletons and
cardiovascular systems, with a ceramic organ
or two thrown in.

Raimondo VII Prince of Sansevero

Orphaned at an early age, Raimondo di Sangro
(1710-1771) was raised by his grandfather. His esoteric
studies, scientific exploits and Masonic activities
brought him infamy and led to excommunication
by Pope Benedict XIV in 1751. Among his many
pioneering projects were a rudimentary submarine,
an eternal lamp, sophisticated weaponry and an
intricate timepiece. He even managed to extract
phosphorus from urine. Superstitious Neapolitans
have attached many stories to him: that he was
a sorcerer who could miraculously liquefy San
Gennaro's blood, and that he administered mercury
to petrify the circulatory systems of two trusty
servants and in so doing killed them.

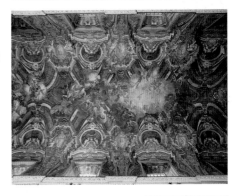

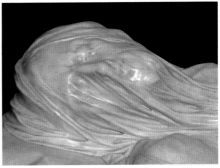

Top: Ghoulish green fresco hues.
Above: Veiled Christ.

Spaccanapoli

Through the heart of Naples

The walk along Spaccanapoli and the parallel via dei Tribunali is captivating and a little hair-raising. These are two of the three main east-west streets (*decumani*) that cut through the heart of the ancient Graeco-Roman city of Neapolis. Leave your preconceptions and valuables behind and go with the crazy Neapolitan flow.

Start at piazza di Gesù with its Guglia dell'Immacolata spire and colourful palazzi, then visit the **Gesù Nuovo** church and **Santa Chiara** cloisters before heading into narrow via Benedetto Croce and Spaccanapoli. The streetlife buzz of weaving vespas and animated *napoletani* along these sticky flagstones provide a dizzying spectacle. Behind grimy Renaissance palazzi are hidden courtyards, including Palazzo Filomarino at No 12, the home of historian and philosopher Benedetto Croce. Passing intriguing outlets and *bancarelle* you come to the *pasticceria* Scaturchio (see page 136) and its sweet offerings, and then piazza San Domenico Maggiore with its palazzi, Baroque obelisk and **Chiesa di San Domenico Maggiore**. A side street to the east of the piazza leads to the mysterious family chapel, the **Cappella di Sansevero**.

Above: Spaccanapoli from Vomero.
Opposite page: Benvenuti a Spaccanapoli!

Imaginations spiked by strange tales and astonishing sculptures, rejoin Spaccanapoli which is now called via San Biagio dei Librai. There are more intriguing outlets and antique stalls to see. Beside the endearing **Sant'Angelo a Nilo** church, which contains Cardinal Brancaccio's tomb by Donatello, is piazzetta Nilo and Bar Nilo, a fine place to take a caffeine fix. Next to the lounging **Statua del Nilo** is a humorous mini-chapel dedicated to Diego Maradona. Further east there is the San Nicola a Nilo church, which sits opposite the Palazzo Carafa Santangelo with its equine bust gifted by Lorenzo de' Medici. Drop into the grandest old pawnshop and its adjoining chapel at the **Pio Monte di Pietà** before entering the magical world of **Via San Gregorio Armeno** and its *presepe* nativity-scenes, figurines and fake mossy trees. Serenity and pious relics await at the churches and cloisters of **San Gregorio Armeno**, **San Lorenzo Maggiore** and **San Paolo Maggiore**. If you have 90 minutes free and a head for confined spaces go deep into the city's past at **Napoli Sotterranea** on piazza San Gaetano, the heart of the ancient city of Neapolis.

Reaching via dei Tribunali there is a choice: head east to plunge into oodles of art and pious relics at the **Girolamini**, **Monte della Misericordia** and magnificent **Duomo** or else go west in the open air. If you pick a visit to San Gennaro's congealed blood you can backtrack afterwards, along edgy via Tribunali and end up at the Intra Moenia bar beside the old Greek city walls, on leafy and lefty piazza Bellini. Along this stretch of the old *decumanus major* be prepared for the creepy sight of shiny bronze skulls and bones outside the **Purgatorio ad Arco** church, some fabulous *palazzi* (including Sanfelice's Palazzo Spinelli at No 362) and Roman architectural fragments below the city's oldest campanile, the 10th- to 11th-century **La Pietrasanta**. Along via dei Tribunali are the upper crust of *scugnizz'* – street kids' – pizzerias: Di Matteo, Il Pizzaiolo del Presidente and Sorbillo.

Slowly but surely, some of the cracks in the *chiese* and *palazzi* of this UNESCO World Heritage Site, caused by centuries of skirmishes, neglect and

Tip…

You can easily spend a whole day here but an early morning start should give ample time to see the main sights before lunch, at the hottest part of the day. Evenings on the old streets are lively, with students joining the boisterous Neapolitan throngs in the many bars and pizzerias.

earthquakes (including one in 1980 that left thousands homeless), are being patched and properly propped up. Improvements are welcome but thankfully the Centro Antico is unlikely to lose in the near future its edginess and become a sanitized, twee and overly touristy zone. Students, working-class *rigattieri* (rag-and-bone men cum antiquarian dealers), artists and well-to-do diners rub along together here; many congregate in the cafés on piazza Bellini, a leafy haven of Neapolitan esoteric and anti-establishment expression.

Around the city

Sant'Angelo a Nilo

Piazzetta Nilo, T081-551-6227.
Mon-Sat 0830-1300, 1645-1900, Sun 0830-1300,
free. Bus R2, C57.
Metrò: Dante. Map: Central Naples, E3, p86.

Just east of piazza Domenico on piazzetta Nilo,
Cardinal Brancaccio instigated the construction of
this peachy-hued church in 1384 although much of
its exterior was transformed in the early 1500s. Inside
is the cardinal's early Renaissance tomb, sculpted in
Pisa by Donatello and Michelozzo in the 1420s and
brought to Naples by Cosimo de' Medici. The
adjoining courtyard, part of the Palazzo Brancaccio,
contains the city's first public library (1690).

Statua del Nilo

Piazzetta Nilo.
Map: Central Naples, E2, p86.

In piazzetta Nilo an enigmatic ancient Egyptian
statue of the Nile river god, with overflowing
cornucopia tucked under his arm, lounges atop a
Latin-inscribed plinth. The reclining figure was
brought to Naples by Alexandrian merchant
settlers in Graeco-Roman times, then went missing
and reappeared minus its head in the 15th century.
A local sculptor produced the present head
although the original may have had the head of
a beast. Neapolitans still call it *O Cuórpè Napule*
(*Il Corpo di Napoli* in Italian or Body of Naples).
A vendor used to display his jazz magazines on
the statue, which faces a humorous mini-chapel
dedicated to that other Neapolitan deity, Diego
Maradona, outside Bar Nilo.

Cappella del Monte di Pietà

Via Biagio dei Librai 114, T081-580 7111.
Sat 0900-1900, Sun 0900-1400, free. Bus R2, C57.
Metro: Dante. Map: Central Naples, E2, p86.

Duck into this rather refined courtyard along lively
Spaccanapoli to view a 16th- century palazzo,
chapel and old pawnshop. Jewellers and
moneylenders once rubbed together along

this stretch of the via Biagio dei Librai, while the
state-run **Pio Monte di Pietà** offered the best deals
to impoverished debtors in the form of interest-
free loans. It's now owned by the Banco di Napoli.
Two sculptures by Bernini entitled *Charity* and
Security flank the entrance and a triangular
tympanum frames Naccherino's Pietà and a
couple of angels. Inside, the ceilings are filled with
colourful frescoes, including the *Misteri del Passione*,
painted in 1601-1603 by Belisario Corenzio. The
courtyard hosts regular live jazz and classical
concerts for a diverse chin-stroking crowd.

Via San Gregorio Armeno

Map: Central Naples, E2, p86.

At right-angles to Spaccanapoli, via San Gregorio
Armeno's famous *presepi* (nativity scene) shops spill
onto the street with bizarre stage sets animated by

Tip…

Bar Nilo, on piazzetta Nilo, is a great little place to
grab refreshments and mingle with local characters.

Ladri di Presepi

18 December 2006. A very Neapolitan story of theft,
piety and tragicomedy unfolds. On the small vicolo
just off bustling via Toledo the thieves set themselves
up in a blue workman's tent, sheltering themselves
from the heavy rain and passers-by on via Toledo.
Away from the public gaze they blowtorch open the
old iron door of the Chiesa di San Nicola alla Carità
and fill their sacks with around 300 antique *presepe*
figures from the 18th century, estimated to be worth
over a €1 million. The priceless Gesù Bambino may
have been left untouched, but public outcry follows
the next day. The story is all over the press. *"La gioia
dei bimbi rubata!"* – "Children's joy robbed!" – says the
tearful parish priest, Mario Rega.
  22 December 2006. Mass is being held in the church
when a policeman thunders in and cries: "Padre Mario,
we have found the *presepe*!" Elated, the priest thanks
God and the police, and even has some good words
for the thieves for having not vandalized the precious
presepi – leaving baby Jesus and the shepherds intact.

Move on up!

mains-powered water features, hypnotic mechanized movements of tiny figurines and twinkling lights behind fake plastic shrubberies. You may be charmed and amused by these imaginative visions, but be prepared to part with huge sums for the traditional hand-made figurines made by the area's *figurari* craftsmen. More affordable is the good old-fashioned tat sold alongside caricatures of political figures and celebrities – Northern League firebrand Umberto Bossi gets a witty Neapolitan work-over while Pavarotti is given a more dignified treatment. Napoli's nativity tableau tradition flourished in the 18th century, filling churches, palaces and homes, and the **via dei Pastori** (Road of the Shepherds) is still the place for enthusiasts seeking a lovely hand-painted bunch of miniature bananas to pimp their Christmas crib.

Chiesa e Chiostro di San Gregorio Armeno

Church via San Gregorio Armeno 44, cloisters piazzetta San Gregorio Armeno 1, T081-552 0186. Daily 0900-1200, free. Bus C57, R2, 24. Metro: Cavour/Museo. Map: Central Naples, E2, p86.

First sight of this Benedictine convent is of its Baroque red-hued bell tower (1716) that straddles via San Gregorio Armeno, looming over its pastoral scenes and figurines. It is named after the Armenian St Gregory whose remains were brought here in the eighth century by nuns fleeing persecution in Constantinople. Santa Patrizia also came from Byzantium and her congealed blood is said to liquefy here every Tuesday. Amongst the artworks of the sadly neglected yet sumptuous Baroque church interiors are gilt stucco work, vibrant frescoes by Luca Giordano and a carved wooden ceiling. The reclusive nuns that traditionally lived here were daughters of nobles and were not averse to knocking up delicious confections in the refectory

Around the city

including ice-cream desserts and the *sfogliatella* pastry. A walk around the atmospheric cloisters, with their citrus trees and a curvy marble fountain flanked by statues of Christ and the Samaritan (1733), is often punctuated by the chatter of schoolchildren playing next door.

Chiesa e Scavi de San Lorenzo Maggiore

Piazzetta San Gaetano/via dei Tribunali 316, T081-290580/T081-211 0860 (museum), sanlorenzomaggiorenapoli.it.
Church daily 0900-1330, free. Excavations and museum Mon-Sat 0930-1730, Sun 0930-1330, €5, €3 concessions, discounts with Artecard. Bus C57, R2, 24. Metro: Cavour/Museo. Map: Central Naples, E2, p86.

Below this Franciscan religious complex located at the intersection of via dei Tribunali and via San Gregorio Armeno are the remains of the Graeco-Roman agora or forum, and a Roman basilica. You can even see part of the old *macellum* (market) in the dimly lit and rather spooky excavations. In the 13th century Charles of Anjou hired a team of French craftsmen to rebuild the complex in Gothic style and after suffering damage in a spate of earthquakes it got the Baroque treatment in the 17th and 18th centuries. More recent restoration (1882-1944) returned much of the church to its Gothic form, although the exuberant 1743 façade built by Ferdinando Sanfelice (1675-1748) and the multicoloured marble-inlaid side chapels by Cosimo Fanzago (1591-1678) remain.

Chiesa di San Paolo Maggiore

Piazza San Gaetano, T081-454048.
Daily 0800-1200, 1700-1900, free. Bus C57, R2, 24. Metro: Museo/Cavour.
Map: Central Naples, E1, p86.

The 16th-century church was built over a Roman temple dedicated to Castor and Pollux, Zeus's twin sons. The 1688 earthquake may have destroyed much of the original façade and most of its Corinthian columns, but the replacement

Fiammetta

In 1336 the writer Giovanni Boccaccio (1313-1375) met his Fiammetta (Little Flame) at San Lorenzo Maggiore. So smitten was Boccaccio with Maria d'Aquino, illegitimate daughter of King Robert the Wise in Naples, that her vision inspired the character Fiammetta in *Filocolo*, *L'Elegia di Madonna* and, most famously, the *Decameron*. In Boccaccio's medieval masterpiece of a hundred tales Fiammetta is one of the wittiest of the 10 storytellers who have fled to the countryside to avoid a bubonic plague-ridden Florence.

Chiesa di San Paolo Maggiore.

Baroque double staircase provides grandstand views of via Tribunali street-life. Highlights of the rather anodyne post-Second World War restoration are Francesco Solimena's (1689-1690) frescoes in the sacristy and a couple of flamboyant chapels with mother-of-pearl, coloured inlaid marble and paintings by Massimo Stanzione (1585-1656).

Napoli Sotterranea

Piazza San Gaetano 68, T081-296944, napolisotterranea.it.
Tours depart Mon-Fri 1200, 1400, 1600 (also Thu 2100), Sat-Sun 1000, 1200, 1400, 1600, 1800. €10, discounts with Artecard. Bus R2, R3, C25. Metro: Cavour/Museo. Map: Central Naples, E2, p86.

For a sense of the city's multi-layered history take a 90-minute tour with Underground Naples and descend 40 m into the tufa rock labyrinth of

Graeco-Roman cisterns. A visit to the dank, cool depths makes a refreshing break on a sweltering day plodding the sticky Centro Antico flagstones – bring a warm top though as it can get chilly. Enthusiastic guides, including the charming English-speaking Ilaria, let groups trace the Greek foundations of ancient Neapolis, its aqueducts and the myth of the *monastini* – the little monks – who cleaned the tunnels and entertained the wives. An extra excursion (30 minutes) to a theatre where Nero performed Greek plays is accessed via someone's garage and is now overlooked by a kitchen window. The truly bizarre hotchpotch history of Naples begins to make sense amid the ancient compacted mud and flaking bricks. In the caverns transformed into a Second World War air-raid shelter city you are told that 5 m of 20th-century rubbish is buried under your feet. It's not for claustrophobics but don't miss out on the optional walk by candlelight through a cramped tunnel to a spookily lit cistern. Napoli Sotterranea also run tours of the atmospheric Acquedotto Carmignano, the Graeco-Roman aqueduct that runs under via Chiaia (see page 82).

Chiesa e Quadreria dei Girolamini

Church piazza Girolamini 107, Cloisters, library and gallery via Duomo 142, T081-449139, girolamini.it. Mon-Sat 0930-1230, free. Bus C57, R2, 24. Metro: Cavour. Map: Central Naples, E1, p86.

The monastery complex was founded by the San Filippo Neri order, of the San Girolamo alla Carità convent in Rome, hence the name 'Church of the Girolamini'. The real highlights here are the two cloisters (a grand space with fragrant orange trees and an intimate one with majolica tiles), the 18th-century, wood-panelled library and the Quadreria (gallery). You can easily spend a relaxing half-hour spotting familiar faces in the chiaroscuro images of saints and sinners on canvas. The church (1619) has paintings by Francesco Solimena and Luca Giordano, sculpture by Pietro Bernini and the tomb of Giambattista Vico, the influential Neapolitan philosopher.

Chiesa e Quadreria del Pio Monte della Misericordia

Via dei Tribunali 253, T081-446944, piomontedellamisericordia.it. Mon-Sat 0930-1230, €5, discounts with Artecard. Bus R2, 24, C57. Metro: Cavour. Map: Central Naples, E1, p86.

Renaissance artworks fill the galleries of this charitable organization and adjoining octagonal church. Beyond the five-arch loggia, the Our Lady of Mercy church contains the brooding *The Seven Acts of Mercy* (1607) altarpiece by Caravaggio (1571-1610). Step next door to view 150 canvasses by 17th- and 18th-century Baroque masters while learning about the charity set up by seven noble gentlemen in 1601 to help the city's needy and oppressed Christians in the Ottoman empire. Just as uplifting as the displayed works by Vaccaro, Giordano and Ribera is the building itself, and particularly the way that light streams into the cavernous space beneath its dome.

Tip...

Upstairs you can peek outside at the nearby obelisk, La Guglia di San Gennaro (1660), erected as thanks to the patron saint for protecting Naples from the eruption of Vesuvius in 1631.

Giambattista Vico (1668-1744)

Born to a bookseller and the daughter of a carriage-maker on Spaccanapoli, Giambattista Vico was an autodidact, Professor of Rhetoric at the University of Naples, royal historiographer for Charles III, who wrote the influential philosophical discourse *Scienza nuova* (1725). His humanism and belief in the importance of history, memory and imagination to human thought and action went against the grain of the Enlightenment rationalists like Descartes who believed wholeheartedly in scientific analysis. Vico's deadpan one-liners include: *"Verum esse ipsum factum,"* – "Truth itself is made"; *"Verum et factum convertuntur,"* – "The true and the made are convertible"; and "Man makes himself the measure of all things."

Around the city

Duomo

Via Duomo 147, T081-449097, duomodinapoli.it.
Duomo Mon-Sat 0800-1230, 1630-1900, Sun
0800-1330, 1700-1930, free. Excavations Mon-Sat
0900-1200, 1630-1900, Sun 0900-1230, €3
(including entry to baptistery). Bus R2, E1. Metro:
Cavour. Map: Central Naples, E1, p86.

Napoli's cathedral is the focus of veneration of
the city's patron saint and the thrice-annual public
outpouring of Neapolitan piety that is the Miracle
of San Gennaro. It was begun by Angevin King
Carlo I in the 13th century on the site of the Basilica
di Santa Restituta, a Palaeo-Christian structure and
the city's oldest surviving basilica. Mosaic floors,
Greek flagstones and Roman remnants including
ancient pipes inscribed with the name Aurielie

Utician can be viewed in the **Scavi del Duomo**
(Duomo Excavations). Earthquakes, changes of
rule and artistic fashion have erased much of
the original French Gothic interior and façade.
A richly painted ceiling and Latin-cross structure
are supported by 110 granite columns.

Beyond the tombs of Angevin kings at the
entrance is the lavishly adorned **Cripta di San
Gennaro** (also known as Succorpo or the Cappella
Carafa), the most apt expression of the Neapolitan
Baroque. Above you'll see a fresco cycle by
Domenichino depicting the life and miracles of the
city's top saint. The highlight of the visit, for pious
Neapolitans especially, is the altar tabernacle with
its silver bust encasing the skull of San Gennaro
and two phials containing his congealed blood.
The atmosphere around the venerated relics is

Above: Lavish Duomo interiors.
Opposite page: Il Duomo.

San Gennaro

Little documentary evidence survives about Napoli's patron saint but that doesn't diminish the profound hold that the ancient cult of San Gennaro has on Neapolitans. What we do know is that Gennaro (Januarius) was born in the late third century and became Bishop of Benevento. His martyrdom and subsequent fame came about during Emperor Diocletian's persecution of Christianity (AD 303-311): Gennaro was discovered taking communion to an imprisoned deacon and was decapitated on 19 September 305 near Solfatara, where the Santuario di San Gennaro stands today. According to the legend, a pious lady – Eusebia – collected his blood in two ampoules. A version of the story says that after Constantine allowed freedom of worship, Eusebia presented the ampoules to Gennaro's family, upon which Vesuvius erupted and the blood liquefied. According to another tale, the blood first liquefied in the hands of Bishop Severus when Gennaro's body was brought to Naples. And so the popular belief grew that the liquefaction was a sign that the saint would protect the city from disaster, be it earthquake, famine, plague or even relegation of the SSC Napoli football team to Serie B.

In 1338, around the time the Duomo was being built, the first documented liquefaction happened. The saint's relics were housed in the atmospheric catacombs near Capodimonte, before being moved to Benevento and then finally to the Duomo in 1497 by Archibishop Carafa, who helped popularize the cult by entombing them in the sumptuous Succorpo. Three times a year – on the Saturday preceding the first Sunday in May in a procession to Santa Chiara, on 16 December and on the Saint's Day 19 September – there is a solemn ceremony followed by a frenzy of emotional outpouring by the faithful imploring the miracle. The vigil can last many hours and the fate of the city is believed to depend on the speed of the liquefaction. If the 'miracle' takes a while it's a bad omen for Naples. Many pious Neapolitans may not agree but recent scientific studies posit the idea that the ampoules do not contain solely blood and that liquefaction is due to a bit of kinetic energy. These scientists reckon that the miracle is not unlike the phenomenon of ketchup becoming runny after a good old shake…

always charged with extraordinary emotion. Head to the north transept to see the tomb of Innocent IV, who was pope during the esoteric rule of Fredrick II of Hohenstaufen, founder of the University of Naples. The remains of Prince Andrew of Hungary who was brutally strangled in 1345 in front of his wife, Joan I, are also housed here.

The oldest baptistery in Italy, the fifth-century **Capella di San Giovanni in Fonte**, has colourful mosaics depicting biblical scenes including *Christ Saving Peter from the Waters* and the *Miracle of the Fish*. Further chapels include the **Tocco**, with Gothic frescoes (1312), and **Minutolo**, which is paved with majolica and contains the tomb of a cardinal.

Museo del Tesoro di San Gennaro

Via Duomo 149, T081-421609, museosangennaro.com.
Tue-Sat 0900-1500, Sun 0900-1400, €6, €3.50 concessions, discounts with Artecard. Bus R2, E1. Metro: Cavour. Map: Central Naples, E1, p86.

For those seeking more religious relics and ancient bling, head to the Museum of the Treasure of San Gennaro next door to the Duomo, containing seven centuries of shiny treasure donated to the patron saint including lots of golden cherubs and silvery saints.

Around the city

Santa Maria di Donnaregina Vecchia

Vico Donnaregina 25, T091-441 806.
Sun-Fri 0900-1200, Sat by appointment. Bus R2,
E1. Metro: Cavour.

This monastery, founded by an Italo-Graeco order in
the eighth century, was totally rebuilt in 1293 under
the reign of Carlo III of Anjou. It is built on two levels,
to keep the nuns and public separate, with the lower
part containing a funeral monument to Maria
d'Ungheria by Tino di Camaino (1325-1326) with the
upper section containing the largest 14th-century
cycle of frescoes in Naples, painted by the Giotto
school (1332-1335).

Bony souls in purgatory.

Museo Diocesano di Napoli alla Chiesa Santa Maria di Donnaregina Nuova

Largo Donnaregina 7, T091-441 806,
museodiocesanonapoli.it.
Museum Mon, Wed-Fri 0930-1630, €5.
Bus R2, E1. Metro: Cavour.

At the start of the 17th century Clarissan nuns
from the neighbouring Donnaregina monastery
commissioned this church with its imposing
façade (1640-1650) and rich interiors of colourful
marble and artworks by Giordano, de Benedictis
and Solimena. The museum here explores Naples'
relationship with religious iconography – Maria
and San Gennaro especially – as well as Baroque
artworks by the likes of Andrea Vaccaro, Mario
Stanzione and Aniello Falcone.

Santa Maria delle Anime del Purgatorio ad Arco

Via dei Tribunali 39.
Church Mon-Sat 0900-1300; Ipogeo Museum Sat
1000-1230, €2. Bus R2, C57. Metro: Museo/Dante.

Heading west along the atmospheric via Tribunali,
which traces the ancient *decumanus major*, you
come across the spine-tingling street-side sight
of skulls and crossbones, given a shine by millions
of superstitious strokes by devoted Neapolitans,
below a brooding 17th-century church façade.
A typically dark Neapolitan cult of the dead –
where *capuzzelle* (skulls) and souls in purgatory
are worshipped – is apparently still practised
here in the catacombs below the church.
Amid the Baroque interiors is a suitably macabre
sculpture of a winged skull (*Teschio alato*) by
Cosimo Fanzago (1591-1678).

Piazza Bellini

Bus E1, R1, C57. Metro: Dante.
Map: Central Naples, D2, p86.

At the western end of the dark, throbbing via
dei Tribunali is this lively and leafy square with a
sunken section containing the old Greek city walls,

surrounded by handsome university buildings including the peach-coloured former **Sant'Antoniello a Port'Alba** monastery and the Baroque **Palazzo Firrao** by Fanzago. Local artists and students often place an action-painting between the ancient tufa blocks and decorate the grubby statue of composer Vincenzo Bellini (1801-1835) with a traffic cone. There's often a whiff of exotic tobacco amid the flaky grand buildings, palms and orange trees. Despite the slightly edgy vibe added by local *guaglioni* (kids) on scooters, it's a laid-back haven. An array of drinks and snacks are served at the cafés here, their tranquil cobblestoned terraces filled with parasols, potted plants and a friendly mix of arty and alternative types, students and tourists.

Santa Maria la Nova

Largo Santa Maria la Nova 1, T081-552 3298.
Bus R1, R4, C57. Map: Central Naples, D4, p86.

The church and its adjoining convent were built by Giovan Cola di Franco in 1596 on a site given to the Franciscan order by Carlo I d'Anjou in recompense for having demolished one of their churches to make way for the Castel Nuovo. Beyond the handsome Florentine-style façade the sumptuous interiors include an exquisite marble relief, *The Adoration of the Shepherds* (1524), by Santacroce and a coffered ceiling (1598-1603) with lots of gilt framing some 46 paintings by the likes of Imparato, Corenzio and Curia. The former monastery is now a local governmental building and contains two cloisters with Renaissance frescoes and tombs.

Galleria dell'Accademia di Belle Arti

Via Costantinopoli 107, T081-551 0547, accademianapoli.it.
Mon-Thu 1000-1400, Fri 1400-1800, €5, €3 concessions. Bus C57, R1, 24.
Metro: Dante/Museo.

The former convent building of San Giovanni delle Monache (1673-1732) was turned into the Academy of Arts by Enrico Alvino in 1864. It still attracts

Piazza Bellini.

students looking to enter the world of art as well as art conservation and restoration. Indeed the recently opened (2007) Gipsoteca section has many important plaster casts that have inspired its sculpture students. A sweeping staircase with busts set in balustrades sets the classical tone. The gallery exhibits span the 17th to 20th centuries and include works from the influential Posillipo School including idyllic landscapes by Carelli, Gigante and Duclere. Two rooms contain a collection of 20th-century works including Manlio Giarrizzo's Matisse-inspired paintings and some experimental works of the 1960s by Neapolitan artists.

Perfect Pizza

Ask a Neapolitan what their favourite food is and you'll get myriad replies. Some go for the textures and candied sweet filling of a *sfogliatella*, others prefer the seafood tang of *spaghetti alle vongole*. However, no orange-infused ricotta or heap of juicy clams can compete with the major Parthenopean preoccupations and deities: *caffè*, San Gennaro, Diego Armando Maradona and the city's most successful export: *la pizza*.

Pizza, in its modern form was invented by impoverished Neapolitans and there is still no better place to sample its original and flavoursome simplicity than in Napoli itself. Most Neapolitan pizzerias have an open pizza-making area, complete with wood-burning oven, where skilful *pizzaioli* (pizza makers) are often happy to share their knowledge of and enthusiasm for *la vera pizza napoletana*: the true Neapolitan pizza.

Deep in the Centro Antico, on via dei Tribunali, a dark, narrow, buzzing street with layers of history and superstition, displayed on and hidden up Neapolitan sleeves is the kneading, slapping and stretching ground of Ernesto Cacialli, who has been a *pizzaiolo* since the age of 12. Cacialli barks orders at his team working around the wood-fired oven – while displaying as many facial folds as the malleable pizza dough he is expertly manipulating on the marble counter.

He shows a more youthful and perky face to Bill Clinton, recorded in a copy of *Time* magazine which he proudly flashes in front of his two sons on dough-ball duty. Cacialli hit the headlines when he dragged the president off via dei Tribunali into the Pizzeria di Matteo during a G7 walkabout in 1994. He has cleverly profited from this notoriety by opening **Il Pizzaiolo del Presidente** (the President's Pizza Maker) just up the road.

Cacialli's story encapsulates the fly, charming yet steely *scugnizz'* (street kid) character and inventiveness that is central to the whole pizza story. By the time Vittorio De Sica's 1954 film *L'Oro di Napoli (The Gold of Naples)*, in which Sophia Loren stars as a seller of *pizze a credito*, southern Italians who had emigrated to America had started a whole new chapter in the pizza story. Back in the 18th century canny street vendors devised a way of making starving Neapolitans regular customers: *pizze*

Below: Pizza al forno di legna. Opposite page: Preparation at Il Pizzaiolo del Presidente.

fritte (fried *calzone*-style pizzas) were eaten and paid for eight days later, on picking up their next pie. *Pizzaioli* turned this into theatre for visiting Grand Tourists, who brought home exotic images of delicious pies, ovens balancing on heads and frenzied tarantella dancing.

And the Neapolitan pizza beat goes on. Cacialli's quick hands and nimble wrists stretch the dough into a flat base. You won't find a rolling pin or any machine to mix the dough in a proper Neapolitan pizza kitchen. He adds the *trecolori combo* of tomato passata, chunks of mozzarella and a couple of basil leaves. Olive oil completes this simple topping. Using a wooden paddle he plunges the pizza into the bulbous oven. After no more than 90 seconds he pulls out a bubbling *Margherita* (named in honour of the first Queen of Italy), with a slightly charred, blistered *cornicione* (raised rim).

Cacialli's *cornicione* is thin while at **Umberto's**, an elegant restaurant with pressed yellow tablecloths in upmarket Chiaia, a thicker base reigns. The besuited Massimo di Porzio is not your regular Neapolitan. His tall, wiry frame and an earnest, amiable nature contrasts with Cacialli's stocky street-fighter demeanour. The gangly *guaglione* is just as passionate about his city and its pizza though.

Signor di Porzio is vice president of the Associazione Verace Pizza Napoletana set up in 1984 with the aim of safeguarding the essential characteristics needed to make a real Neapolitan pizza. "Follow these principles," he says, "and you're on the way to making a perfect pizza: leaven the dough twice over eight to nine hours;

use your hands to allow air into the dough, to give those yummy, smoky cornicione bubbles; cook the pizza for about a minute in a *forno a legna* (wood-fired oven) – at 450-480°C; and use only natural ingredients – including '00' flour mixed with 5-10% Manitoba American flour, which gives the dough stretch and flavour."

Of course Cacialli insists that his newer organization, **La Regina Margherita**, is the real flag bearer of authentic Neapolitan pizza. He helped design the cavernous oven that produced the biggest ever wood-fired pizza in 2004 – the *Margherita* measured over 5 m in diameter and weighed 124 kg.

Away from the flying pizza-related quips and stunts, amid the kitsch marina lights and canoodling couples, is **Ciro a Mergellina**. Behind lurid yellow chalet lettering is a sprawling dining-room stage set, where little Neapolitan dramas take place at dozens of tables. Dapper, bow-tied waiters with the cheeky grins of 1970s comedians glide around. The Eric Morecambe lookalike with heavy specs reckons that you'd be really unlucky to find a bad pizza in Naples. "Our Agerola mozzarella is the best buffalo mozzarella in the world," he adds. Ciro's pizza *Margherita* has a pleasing puddle of passata, mozzarella and olive oil. They also serve a fist-sized octopus swimming in its meaty juices, which is plonked on the plate. That's the great thing about eating in Naples: if you're not a sucker for the yummiest pizza on the planet, there are plenty of tasty alternatives.

Five of the best

Pizzerias

❶ **Pizzeria di Matteo** Smoky crust that President Clinton enjoyed *piegata in quattro (folded in four)*. See page 136.

❷ **Antica Pizzeria da Michele** Purists' pizzeria serving only *Margherite* and *marinare*. See page 136.

❸ **Il Pizzaiolo del Presidente** Thin bases and popular for its *pizze fritta*. See page 136.

❹ **Sorbillo** A youthful place serving large rectangular pizzas. See page 136.

❺ **Umberto** Sophisticated atmosphere, smaller pizza but with a thicker than usual *cornicione* and superb Neapolitan dishes served as well. See page 137.

Via Toledo to piazza Cavour

Partly pedestrianized via Toledo (still called via Roma by most locals) is popular for shopping and an evening *passeggiata*. The maze of narrow lanes of the Quartieri Spagnoli rise up the hill to the west while to the east there are wider blocks lined with Fascist era and modern buildings. Towards the Centro Antico in piazza Monteoliveto, the Tuscan-style Renaissance church of Sant'Anna dei Lombardi sits next to a fountain replete with water-spouting lions and a statue of a jaunty-looking King Carlos II of Spain as a child.

Further up via Toledo, where the traffic returns, recently spruced-up piazza Dante's Foro Carolino is a handsome backdrop to family-friendly events and concerts. Nearby is the Museo Archeologico Nazionale, a colossal building containing mind-blowing finds from antiquity. Going west along via Foria is the chaotic piazza Cavour, a transport hub. Respite from the mayhem can be found at the Madre contemporary art gallery and the green haven of the Orto Botanico (see page 116).

Palazzo delle Poste e Telegrafi.

Quartieri Spagnoli

Buses R1, 24, C57. Metro: Dante.
Map: Central Naples, B5, p86.

The network of streets running up the hill on the western side of via Toledo is known as the Spanish Quarters as the tall tenements were built to house Spanish troops in the 16th century. Despite stories of Camorra shoot-outs and warnings to avoid the area, it's no worse than other districts. The sight of a Rolls Royce with blacked-out windows crawling along a crowded, narrow street can be unnerving though. Just off piazza Carità is via Pignasecca which is well worth exploring for its small shops and market stalls selling fish, fruit, veg as well as bargain homeware and clothing.

Chiesa Sant'Anna dei Lombardi

Piazza Monteoliveto 44, T081-551 3333.
Mon-Fri 0900-1200, Sat 0900-1200, free.
Bus R1, R4, C57. Metro: Dante.
Map: Central Naples, C4, p86.

Just east of via Toledo, not far from piazza Gesù and near a playful Baroque fountain, is this unassuming-looking church containing some of the city's most important Florentine-style Renaissance treasures. It was begun in 1411 and became thereafter the favourite church of the Aragonese rulers, who employed leading artists of the time to decorate its chapels and tombs. In the **Sacrestia Vecchia** (Old Sacristy), Giorgio Vasari's (1511-1574) sumptuous ceiling frescoes and the intricate *intarsia* stalls (1506-1510) by Giovanni di Verona are astonishing. The chapels are no less dazzling with the bas-relief *Nativity* (1475) by Antonio Rossellino in the **Capella Piccolomini** (dedicated to the Duke of Amalfi's wife) and the eight life-size terracotta figures of Guido Mazzoni's *Lamentation of the Dead Christ* (1492) in the **Cappella Orilia** worth seeking out. Bombing in 1943 caused severe damage, and restoration work aimed at bringing the church back to its former glory continues. On the intimate piazza nearby you can relax beside white marble lions and eagles spouting water on the curvy Baroque lip of Cosimo Fanzago's beguiling fountain (1699), with a statue of a young tousle-locked King Carlo II of Aragon looking westwards.

Palazzo delle Poste e Telegrafi

Piazza Matteotti 3.
Mon-Fri 0800-1830, Sat 0800-1230. Bus R1, R4, C57. Metro: Dante. Map: Central Naples, D4, p86.

Fascist urban renewal swept away the old San Giuseppe-Carità quarter and replaced it with bombastic architecture like the brooding Banco di Napoli building on via Toledo and a cluster of civic buildings on piazza Matteotti, including the Central Post Office (1932-1936) by Giuseppe Vaccaro (1896-1979). Its curvilinear façade, clad in a combination of light and dark marble and smooth lines, makes it one of the most alluring (or alienating, depending on your point of view) examples of modernism in Naples. It's also a suitably edifying venue to get yourself acquainted with Neapolitan-style bureaucracy, the Italian *Poste* and the accompanying shrugs of the shoulders.

Piazza Dante

Via Toledo.
Metro: Dante. Map: Central Naples, C2, p86.

The grand piazza on via Toledo is backed by the large semicircular palace **Foro Carolino** topped with 26 statues, designed by Luigi Vanvitelli (1700-1773) in 1757 for Carlo III of Bourbon. After years of neglect, the cars have been given the boot and it has been scrubbed up, erasing much of the graffiti and mess around the statue of poet Dante Alighieri. It's now once again a meeting place and venue for public gatherings where juggling clowns on stilts and political sideshows vie for the attention of local footy-playing kids and day-tripping families.

Tip...

Don't miss the nearby gateway to the Centro Antico (Ancient City) at via Port'Alba, which is an area filled with interesting antiquarian bookshops.

Around the city

Museo Archeologico Nazionale di Napoli

Piazza Museo 19, T081-440166,
napolibeniculturali.it.
Wed-Mon 0900-1930, €6.50, €3.50 under-25s,
free under 18/over 65, €4 audioguide in English.
Bus C57, 24, R4. Metro: Museo.
Map: Central Naples, C1, p86.

Prepare to be blown away by the scale and quality
of the National Archaeological Museum of Naples's
collection of ancient Greek, Roman and Egyptian
artefacts. Formerly a riding school and then a
university seat, this enormous building was
modified in the 18th century by Bourbon
monarchs Carlo III and then Ferdinand IV to house
the ever-increasing number of objects discovered
at Pompeii, Herculaneum and in the Campi Flegrei.
Many of the statuary antiquities of the **Farnese
Collection**, begun by a 16th-century pope and
ending up in Bourbon Naples through Elisabetta
Farnese, can be seen on the ground floor. The
imposing presence and beauty of the statues
never fails to impress. One of the masterpieces is
the *Toro Farnese* (*Farnese Bull*), a 4 m-high Roman
copy of a Greek sculpture from second century
Rhodes depicting five figures, a dog and a bull.
Pliny the Elder wrote about the original sculpture
in his *Naturalis Historia*, while this colossal version
by Apollonius was unearthed at the Baths of
Caracalla in Rome. Walking amid the marbled
giants and contemplating the lives, myths and
journeys surrounding them is electrifying –
in a chin-stroking way.

You can spend many hours taking in the
priceless treasures upstairs so here are a few pieces
to look out for. Among the many Roman mosaics is
the massive *Alexander and Darius at the Battle of
Issus*. As so little Greek painting survived, this
Pompeian mosaic is important as it's a copy from
the Hellenistic period. There are lots of mosaic
animals (the Romans loved their birds, fish, dogs,
cats and ducks it seems) as well as skeletons –
La Ruota della Fortuna (*The Wheel of Fortune*) has
a grinning skull – and paved floors, many with
black-and-white geometric patterns. Seek out

Top: Museo Nazionale courtyard.
Above: Villa dei Papyri statuary.

Nile river scene mosaic from the House of the Faun.

Tip...

It makes sense to visit the museum at the hottest part of the day to escape the sun. Allow at least three hours to see the main exhibits. An inner courtyard café with towering palm trees is a good place for a breather before tackling the other floors.

the *opus vermiculatum* (vermiculated mosaic) *Fauna Marina*, and imagine its colourful crustaceans and marine creatures rippling lifelike below the water of a recessed pool between Pompeian dining couches in the House of the Faun. Similarly alluring are the bronze statues from the Villa dei Papiri, of tousle-haired dancing girls striking a pose and perfectly poised athletes.

Many of the paintings from Pompeii and Herculaneum were based on older Greek works, including the *Sacrificio di Ifigenia* (*Sacrifice of Iphigenia*) which has a stark quality reminiscent of 20th-century surrealism and characters displaying lots of grief, flailing arms and vacant looks. It was found at the fun-sounding House of the Tragic Poet and is a copy of a lost fourth-century painting by Timanthes that Pliny the Elder raved about. Elsewhere, connoisseurs of ancient hooliganism will get a frisson from the fresco

documenting the AD 59 punch-up between the home crowd and Nucerians at the amphitheatre.

You could spend weeks exploring the vast collections of ancient inscriptions, metalwork, furnishings, glassware, coins and gems on the first floor. Seek out the intricate cameo-work on the *Tazza Farnese*, an exquisite bowl from Hellenistic Egypt and on *Il Vaso Blu*, a wine amphora with delicate cupids crushing grapes on cobalt-blue glass, found at Pompeii. A large collection of Egyptian relics, largely amassed by Cardinal Borgia, includes lots of mummies and funerary statuettes.

For those flagging, the sight of the **Gabinetto Segreto** (Secret Cabinet) and its erotic contents should raise eyebrows. At various times during its history the collection of saucy relics was reserved

Five of the best

Ancient treasures

❶ The *Toro Farnese* (*Farnese Bull*) is a 4 m-high Roman copy of a second-century Greek sculpture representing the myth of Dirce, who was shackled to a wild bull by Antiope's sons Amphion and Zethus as retribution for the maltreatment of their mother.

❷ The enormous *Alexander and Darius at the Battle of Issus* mosaic from Pompeii depicts Alexander the Great (in profile on the left with bulbous eyes and a sideburn) defeating Darius (right, fleeing on his chariot). The mosaic measures 582 x 313 cm and contains over a million individual *tesserae*.

❸ The *Tazza Farnese* (*Farnese Cup*) is an exquisite bowl from Hellenistic Egypt (spot the Nile god with cornucopia) that ended up in Italy after Octavian's conquest of Egypt in 31 BC.

❹ Among the elegant statues from Herculaneum's Villa dei Papyri is a tipsy **Satyr** lounging on a lionskin-covered boulder, who seems to be saying "You're me best mate, you are!"

❺ The **Gabinetto Segreto** (**Secret Cabinet**) contains an eye-popping statue of Pan copulating with an attractive goat.

Top: Il Gabinetto Segreto.
Below left: Totò and Pulcinellas.

for the eyes of male visitors of 'mature age and proven morality'. Eye-bulging pieces include painted scenes from Pompeii, advertising *lupanare* (brothel) services; some erotic statues; and an enormous array of average-sized penises belonging to ubiquitous Graeco-Roman fertility god Priapus.

As for the building itself, the central stairway, below a dome and giant compass, is breathtaking but is eclipsed by the cavernous **Salone della Meridiana**, replete with sundial, celestial ceiling frescoes and a chunky Atlas carrying a globe: the *Farnese Atlante* statue. Back down to earth are the up-to-date Neapolitan displays of abandoned masonry dumped in corners that no doubt vex visiting health and safety officers from out of town. Like Naples, it's all very captivating, amusing and hazardous.

Museo d'Arte Contemporanea Donnaregina (Madre)

Via Settembrini 79, T081-292833, museomadre.it. Mon, Wed, Thu and Sun 1000-2100, Fri-Sat 0900-2400, closed Tue, €7, €3.50 concessions, free Mon. Bus CS, E1. Metro: Cavour.

Napoli's newest contemporary art gallery, Madre, is housed in the handsome Donna Regina palace amidst the traffic mayhem near piazza Cavour. Portuguese architect Alvaro Siza has transformed

the old palazzo interiors into a series of white cubes: its two main floors of thought-provoking exhibits make a refreshing antidote to the ancient treasures in the nearby Archaeological Museum and the lavish religious relics of the Duomo. Standouts from the permanent collection on the first floor are Jeff Koons' bold and brassy *Pop Art*, Richard Long's mud installation, Sol LeWitt's simple yet pulsating wall drawings and the primitive, childlike scratches of Mimmo Paladino. On the second floor there are 100 works from the 1950s to the 1990s including Andy Warhol's *Early Coloured Liz* (*Chartreuse*), Gilbert & George's in-your-face *Shitty World* and Lucio Fontana's *Attese* series of monochrome canvases and precise slashes. Recent temporary exhibitions have included Brian Eno's experiments in music and video, and a group show exploring Napoli's relationship with the cross. Take a breather from the mind-blowing art in the two large courtyards and on the roof terrace with views over the city and Paladino's *Cavallo* (horse) sculpture. It's just a shame the staff are so lax.

San Giovanni a Carbonara

Via San G a Carbonara 5, T081-295873.
Daily 0900-1300. Bus CS, E1. Metro: Cavour.

A double-flighted staircase (1700s) by Sanfelice leads to impressive church interiors that include a towering funerary monument (1428) to Angevin King Ladislao di Durazzo, who had enlarged the original Augustinian structure. Also of note are 15th-century frescoes by Leonardo da Besozzo and bas-reliefs, statuary and inlaid-marble work in the Renaissance-style Cappella Caracciolo di Vico (1517).

Its two main floors of thought-provoking exhibits make a refreshing antidote to the ancient treasures in the nearby Archaeological Museum and the lavish religious relics of the Duomo.

Top: Fishy business, Casa del Fauno.
Above: Mimmi Paladino's rooftop *Cavallo*.

Corso Umberto & around

Corso Umberto I, known as the *rettifilo* (straight line), is the broad, clogged artery running southwest from the monstrous confusion that is piazza Garibaldi to piazza Bovio, centre of the old financial district and stock exchange. To the north is the Università degli Studi di Napoli Federico II and its fascinating museums with their whiff of formaldehyde, dust and scientific finds. The Mercato di Porta Nolana provides pure Neapolitan theatre with its sea of contraband, fish, produce and humanity, while to the south are the nowhere lands of the Mercato district that stretches down to the industrial port area. Between the odd historic attraction, including the Sant'Eligio Maggiore and Santa Maria del Carmine churches, there are grimy outlets selling doorknobs and fork handles, while behind closed doors old tenement apartments have been turned into a warren of warehouses for contraband Chinese goods, run by the Camorra.

Mercato di Porta Nolana

Corso Garibaldi, between piazza Garibaldi and Circumvesuviana terminal
Bus 1, 152, 172. Metro: Garibaldi.
Map: Central Naples, H2, p86.

Leave your valuables and preconceptions behind when visiting this general market southwest of Napoli Centrale station. Nicknamed *'sopra le mura'* as it's right under the city walls, it's an exhilarating open-air *teatro napoletano*. Taking in the sights, sounds and smells: wriggling octopuses get the chop, shellfish are stacked high under plastic fountain displays, toothless *fruttivendoli* juggle pineapples while bartering, and everywhere you look there are contraband goods that have fallen off the back of Chinese cargo ships. In June 2008 the authorities closed the market down temporarily and enforced a clean-up of the contraband and *munezza*. A sign neatly summed up the situation: "Church entrance: Don't leave rubbish."

Above: Guaglione! Where's your moto helmet?
Opposite page: Market banter.

Piazza Mercato

Bus 1, 152, 172. Map: Central Naples, G3, p86.

Looking more like a shabby car park and flanked by run-down apartment blocks, at first glance it's hard to believe that piazza Mercato is such an important Neapolitan square. In the 13th century commercial activity thrived around the two Angevin-built churches here, **Sant'Eligio Maggiore** and **Santa Maria del Carmine**. Both have been rebuilt, the latter having a 75-m campanile topped with majolica tiles. Inside there are frescoes by Solimena and a venerated effigy of Madonna Bruna, whose feast day is celebrated with an eardrum-bursting firework display on 16 July. Also worth a gander are the striped towers of the **Porta del Carmine** and remnants of the **Castello del Carmine**, scene of Masaniello's revolt and short-lived republic of 1647.

Centro Musei delle Scienze Naturali

Anthropology, Mineralogy and Zoology at via Mezzocannone 8, Paleontology at largo San Marcellino 10, T081-253 5164, musei.unina.it.
Mon-Fri 0900-1330, Mon and Thu 1500-1700, Sat-Sun 0900-1300, €4.50 for all 4 museums, €3 concessions. Bus E1, R2.
Map: Central Naples, E4, p86.

Slightly off the Spaccanapoli trail are the University's Natural Sciences Museums dedicated to animals, minerals, humans and dinosaurs. The bulk of the collection is housed in the Gesù Vecchio, a Jesuit college turned university complex. Fascinating finds include Bolivian mummies, Bourbon King Charles III's Indian elephant skeleton, half-ton Madagascan quartz crystals and *Metaxytherium medium* – that's an extinct relative of the herbivorous sea cow or manatee. Top of the bill goes to the carnosaur, *Allosaurus fragilis*, suspended over a beautiful majolica floor in the nearby Palaeontology museum.

Capodimonte & La Sanità

North of the city, up on the hill, are the grand open spaces of the Parco di Capodimonte, containing one very fancy Bourbon hunting lodge, Palazzo Reale, with its world-class art collection and regal interiors. This is a must-see sight. Nearby on the Miradois Hill stand the three classical pavilions of the Osservatorio Astronomico, while below in the down-at-heel Rione Sanità (birthpace of Antonio de Curtis, the legendary comedian known as Totò) poverty, piety and the macabre mix. Amid the scruffy piazzas are ancient catacombs and cemeteries brimming with mosaics, frescoes and skulls: top billing goes to the catacombs of San Gennaro and San Gaudioso and the Cimitero delle Fontanelle and their spine-chilling chambers that reveal the origins of the Neapolitans' superstitious psyche. Above ground in the light, you can escape the traffic haze of piazza Carlo III at the wonderful Orto Botanico, which provides an earthy, botanic oasis for the soul, while nearby the immense 18th-century poorhouse, the Albergo dei Poveri, is being resurrected after years in purgatory and near ruin.

Palazzo Reale & Museo di Capodimonte

Palazzo Capodimonte, via Miano 2, or accessed via the park from via Capodimonte, T081-749 9111, museo-capodimonte.it.
Thu-Tue 0830-1930, last entry 1830, €7.50, €6.50 after 1400, €3.75 concessions, free under 18/ over 65. Bus R4, C57, C63.
Map: Naples Greater, C7, p86.

Art, nature, architecture, history, astronomy, garden design, and fancy porcelain all come together at the world famous Royal Palace and Museum of Capodimonte. The imposing scarlet and grey *palazzo* was commissioned by Carlo III of Bourbon in 1738 and designed by Giovanni Antonio Medrano as a lavish hunting lodge and a gallery for the exceptional Renaissance art collection inherited by Elisabetta Farnese, the king's mother. More fabulous works and furnishings from across Europe have since been added by Bourbon successors, Italy's post-unification royals – the House of Savoy – Joachim Murat's Napoleonic regime and the Italian government, who opened it to the public in 1957. You can easily spend half of a brain-bursting day here just skimming the surface of this world-class collection – which can be a tad taxing, so the wonderfully lush 124-ha park grounds provide much needed fresh air and views.

After climbing the epic staircase to the *piano nobile*, a series of sumptuous rooms and Royal Apartments contain the **Collezione Farnesiana** (Farnese Collection) as well as Armoury and

Above: Louise Bourgeoise's *Maman*. Right: Caravaggio's *Flagellation*.

Porcelain collections. Among the many artistic highlights are: Titian's (1477-1576) erotically charged *Danae*, depicting Jupiter seducing the daughter of the king of Argos; Masaccio's (1401-1428) *Crucifixion*, part of a polyptych from a Pisan church; Bellini's (1432-1516) wintry *Transfiguration*; Bruegel the Elder's (1528-1569) haunting *Misanthrope* with the cheery Flemish proverb, "As the world is deceitful, I am going into mourning;" and El Greco's (1541-1614) *El Soplón*, an atmospheric chiaroscuro piece showing a young man diligently blowing on an ember to light a candle. For a real eyeful of rococo-style Capodimonte porcelain pop into the Salottino della Porcellana, Queen Amalia's parlour (1757) brought here from the Royal Palace at Portici.

The **second floor** galleries provide the most dramatic works and arguably the most rewarding viewing for the visitor by sketching the development of Neapolitan painting, including the city's astounding 17th-century creativity when the city's

Around the city

Baroque painting was famed throughout the world. The rather flat emotion and pious detachment of many earlier works suddenly gives way to brutality and raw human expression in both Caravaggio's influential *Flagellation* and Artemesia Gentileschi's (1593-1652/3) *Judith Slaying Holofernes*. Billowing clouds, tumbling angels and celestial shafts of light fill Titian's *Annunziazione (Annunciation)*. Giuseppe Recco's (1634-1695) series of brooding fish-market scenes capture the slimy textures of life wriggling with death. On a tenderer note is Niccolò Colantonio's 15th-century Flemish-influenced oil painting *San Gerolamo nello Studio* in which St Jerome removes a thorn from the wounded paw of a lion amid the scattered trappings of study.

On the **third floor**, there is a complete change in atmosphere as more modern, converted spaces under the roof are filled with 19th-century Realists and Impressionists, temporary shows,

Tip...

One visit is not nearly enough to take in all the fabulous works here, so use your time wisely. In three hours you can cover the major works and skim over the rest, by which time you'll probably be whacked. Escape the hottest part of the day in Capodimonte's cool galleries, combined with a mid-morning or late afternoon spent in the relaxing grounds – a perfect spot for a picnic, kickabout and sprawling out.

Colantonio's *San Gerolamo nello Studio*.

photography by Mimmo Jodice and contemporary art, including Warhol's colourful pop-art *Vesuvius*.

On the **ground floor** the **Gabinetto dei Disegni e delle Stampe** (Collection of Drawings and Prints) includes absorbing works by Michelangelo (1475-1654), Solimena (1657-1747), Tintoretto (1518-1594), Rembrandt (1606-1669) and Raffaello (1483-1520).

Museo dell'Osservatorio di Capodimonte

Via Moiariello 16, T081-557 5111, oacn.inaf.it.
By appointment only, free. Bus C63.
Map: Naples, F1, p78.

On the Miradois Hill to the south of the Palazzo Reale stand three classical pavilions belonging to the Museum of the Capodimonte Observatory. Arcane Neapolitan bureaucracy can make a visit to see the fascinating collection of historic astronomical instruments (lots of shiny old telescopes, intricate time pieces and globes) problematic – don't expect much help unless you phone and make an appointment. However there is ample charm in the tranquil grounds that teem with fruits and flowers, and contain a curious collection of buildings including a contemporary glass pavilion, the handsome neo-classical Specola building and bulbous metallic sheds containing telescopes.

Orto Botanico

Via Foria 223, T081-449759/T081-445654, ortobotanico.unina.it.
Mon-Fri 0900-1400, Sun/holidays by appointment only, guided visits Mar-May 0900-1100 by appointment. Bus C57, R4. Metro: Cavour. Map: Naples, G1, p78.

Escape the traffic fumes on via Foria by taking a walk amid some 9000 species and 25,000 plants at the city's Botanical Gardens, established in 1807 by Joseph Bonaparte. There are some 12 ha to explore and many themed areas, including an arboretum, with rare prickly paperbark trees, a citrus orchard, a section filled with native Mediterranean plants, a palm grove, and ponds bursting with colourful

Bourbon Court

The 18th-century Bourbon court was so starry-eyed about astronomy that Carlo III set up the first European university department dedicated to its study in 1735. Later in 1791 Ferdinand I commissioned the building of an observatory at the ex-Palazzo degli Studi (which later became the Museo Archeologico), before realizing that the surrounding buildings deep in the Centro Antico blocked sections of the heavens – so the building work was shifted to lofty Capodimonte, which was a more suitable vantage point for a celestial vault.

water lilies. Impressive greenhouses imitate temperate, hot-humid and hot-dry climates. The neoclassical Serra Merola, built in 1820, drips with tropical fronds while the Serra Califano contains succulents, cacti and *Cycadales*, the primitive tree fern. A red-hued castle-like building houses a museum that includes plant fossils and human creations made of plant material – the giant lutes, Amazonian weapons and canoes from Borneo's mangrove swamps are particularly fascinating.

Albergo dei Poveri

Piazza Carlo III.
Bus C57, R4. Metro: Cavour.
Map: Naples, G1, p78.

Designed in 1751 by Ferdinando Fuga and Luigi Vanvitelli as a poorhouse for the down-at-heel subjects of Carlo III of Bourbon, this colossal structure covering over 100,000 sq m is undergoing restoration. Originally, five courtyards and a church were planned as part of a massive self-contained village, but the project was never fully realized. Nevertheless, at one time it was the largest building in Europe. Having been put to many uses – including state archive and venue for kick-abouts and acts of vandalism – it fell into almost complete ruin after the 1980 earthquake. So far the 300-m façade has scrubbed up handsomely and it has started to host theatre productions and exhibitions. The city's long-term plans for the building are yet to be set in stone.

Catacombe di San Gennaro

Via Capodimonte 13, T081-741 1071.
Guided tours Tue-Sun 0900-1000, 1100-1200, €5.
Bus R4. Map: Naples, E1, p78.

Plonked in the middle of nowhere on the busy road to Capodimonte, the 20th-century Chiesa dell'Incoronata Madre del Buon Consiglio (inspired by St Peter's in the Vatican) is the starting point of a descent into the atmospheric Catacombs of San Gennaro. Guided tours go into the dank, spooky depths to peer at second- to 10th-century frescoes, fifth-century mosaics and the tomb of the haloed San Gennaro. Pilgrims used to flock here to venerate Napoli's patron saint and his relics, until they were moved to the city's Duomo.

Catacombe di San Gaudioso

Piazza della Sanità, T081-483328,
santamariadellasanita.it.
Daily tours 0930, 1015, 1100, 1145 and 1230, €5.
Bus R4. Map: Naples, E1, p78.

Under the church of Santa Maria della Sanità (1603-1613) lie fifth- and sixth-century catacombs with Paleo-Christian frescoes, mosaics and sculpture, including some spine-chilling paintings of skeletons.

Cimitero delle Fontanelle

Chiesa della Maria Santissima del Carmine,
via Fontanelle 77, T081-549 0368.
By appointment only – phone in advance.
Metro Mater Dei. Map: Naples, D1, p78.

Nothing prepares you for the bizarre and chilling sight of the thousands of bones and skulls lining the walls of these tufaceous caves dug into the Materdei Hill. Small coffin-like shrines called *teche* attest to the cult of the dead that flourished here: anonymous skeletal remains were adopted by devotees who prayed for the deceased in exchange for favours. Restoration teams found votive slips with imploring messages from devotees in the orbits of skulls.

Chiaia, Mergellina & Posillipo

Heading west from piazza Trieste e Trento, the sticky paving stones of pedestrianized via Chiaia rise and loop around to piazza dei Martiri, with its handsome lion statues representing republican ideals – namely martyrdom at the uprisings of 1799, 1820, 1848 and 1860. The swanky streets to the west are lined with boutiques, bars and restaurants while up on via dei Mille is the PAN arts centre. The Riviera di Chiaia has pockmarked grandeur in its handsome *palazzi* that once peered onto a beach – hence the name Chiaia which derives from the Spanish *playa*. The gentrified air and horses and carts may have been replaced by roaring traffic and a hotch-potch of businesses, yet the Riviera retains some majesty in the Bourbon-built Villa Comunale gardens (with its aquarium, fountains and antiques market) and the well-hidden Villa Pignatelli museum and gardens.

Along the scenic rat-run that is via Caracciolo you arrive at the marina at Mergellina, a favourite for island escapes and Neapolitan *passeggiate* with ice cream. Posillipo is a well-heeled district, where villas flirt with the coast and sweeping roads named after poets Petrarca (Petrarch), Orazio and Mazzoni give giddy views.

Villa Comunale

Riviera di Chiaia.
Bus 140, C9, R3. Metro: Amedeo.
Map: Naples, D5, p78.

Trapped between the cacophonous traffic claxons of Riviera di Chiaia and via Caracciolo is this royal park popular with joggers and families. The Spanish viceroys first laid out a park here in the 1690s but it was Bourbon monarch Ferdinand IV who gave it its present layout when in 1780 he commissioned architect Luigi Vanvitelli and landscape designer Felice Abate to create the **Passeggio Reale** (Royal Promenade). Its long gravel paths are punctuated with fountains and Baroque statues amid exotic and Mediterranean trees including palms and monkey puzzles. At the end of a broad avenue near piazza Vittoria is the **Fontana della Tasca di Porfido** with its shoreline shells and lounging lions. Its alternative name Fontana delle Paparelle (Fountain of the Ducks) alludes to the fact that ducks once splashed here. Kids' playgrounds, a bandstand and handsome neoclassical buildings are its main attractions these days.

The Villa Comunale houses the Stazione Zoologica Anton Dohrn, established by the German scientist in 1872, which has research labs studying marine environments. On the ground floor is the **Acquario** (T081-583111, szn.it, Tue-Sun 0900-1700, €2.50), Europe's oldest aquarium, containing the slightly unsettling spectacle of 23 huge leaking tanks filled with Mediterranean marine life. Illustrated posters give serving suggestions for each fruit of the sea. Nearby is another elegant edifice (1870), the **Casina Pompeiana** (T081-245 1050, Mon-Sat 0900-1900, free), which once contained views of Pompeii and now hosts art exhibitions and cultural events. Every third and fourth weekend of the month sees the gardens and surrounding streets given over to a fabulous antiques market, the **Mercato Antiquariato** (see Shopping, page 144).

Villa Pignatelli

Riviera di Chiaia, T081-761 2356.
Tue-Sun 0830-1400, €2. Bus 140, C9, R3.
Metro: Amedeo. Map: Naples, C5, p78.

Peering through the iron gates on the traffic-ridden Riviera di Chiaia, the sight of the Doric columns of Villa Pignatelli (1826) offers a glimpse into how fabulous this road must have once looked. Designed by Pietro Valente, pupil of Antonio Niccolini who created the Teatro San Carlo, and built at the behest of Ferdinand Acton of the influential Anglo-Italian family, the villa is set in lush gardens and displays a passing nod to a grandiose Pompeian residence. Subsequent owners, the Rothschilds and Pignatellis, made changes to the villa's interiors and it was eventually bequeathed to Italian state in 1952.

Francesco – il fioraio – and son.

Tip...

Between PAN and piazza Amedeo, on via dei Mille, the dizzying sight of the overblown Baroque church **Santa Teresa a Chiaia** (1620) and the chance to meet one of Chiaia's great street characters await. Opposite the towering façade by Cosimo Fanzago (rebuilt after the 1688 earthquake and containing sculpture and paintings by Fanzago and Luca Giordano) is a florist stall run by grinning 90-year old Francesco and his equally amiable son. Dextrous Francesco has been dodging the traffic and cutting flowers for over half a century. Their vibrant bouquets and posies cost peanuts, and their spirit is priceless.

Around the city

The two museums housed in the villa – the second-floor **Museo Diego Aragona Pignatelli Cortes** and **Museo delle Carozze**, housed in a garden pavillion, contain 16th- to 20th-century paintings and collections of porcelain (with some fine Japanese Edo vases), antiquarian books in the leather-clad library, as well as horse-drawn carriages from Italy, France and Britain. The real draw, however, are the lush gardens with their towering palms.

Palazzo Delle Arti di Napoli (PAN)

Via dei Mille 60, T081-795 8605, palazzoartinapoli.net.
Mon, Wed-Sat 0930-1930, Sun/public holidays 0930-1400, closed Tue, €5, concessions €3.50. Bus C22, C25. Metro: Amedeo.
Map: Naples, D4, p78.

Worlds away from the traffic mayhem on via Mille, yet often just as disquieting, are PAN's three floors of contemporary works by up-and-coming artists. Beyond the perkily pink-and-grey façade of the tastefully renovated 18th-century Palazzo Roccella is a relaxing yet vibrant world of temporary themed exhibitions, cultural events and Napoli's leading art documentation centre. PAN's archives and workshops cover such diverse subjects as theatre, photography, architecture, design and comics. Recent group shows have included *Bellezza Pericolosa* (Dangerous Beauty), which explored extreme themes to do with body image, while *Impresa d'Arte* (the Business of Art) tackled the relationship between art and economics. Recharge your batteries in the courtyard where you can view towering apartments rising up the Vomero hill and imagine what it must have looked like 200 years ago when it was just *prati* (fields) around the palazzo.

Porticciolo di Mergellina

Bus C16, C24, R3. Metro: Mergellina.
Map: Naples, B6, p78.

At the western end of busy via Caracciolo, along the waterfront, the Mergellina marina is an atmospheric slice of Neapolitan life: you can sit down at the breakwater amid canoodling couples watching the ebb and flow of the sea and the comings and goings of hydrofoils, yachts and fishermens' boats, with stunning views of Vesuvius and the bay, and then wander around the neon-lit

Above: Parco Virgiliano, Posillipo. Opposite page: Diego Armando Maradona.

chalet restaurants, ice-cream parlours and bars near the funicular station. A favourite Neapolitan pastime is to watch the sunset here and then visit one of the local restaurants, such as Ciro a Mergellina (see page 137). The marina is served by lots of buses and the Mergellina Funicular, and is a 10-minute walk from the Mergellina metro station.

Tombe di Virgilio e Leopardi & Parco Virgiliano

Via Piedigrotta 20, T081-669390.
Daily 0900 till dusk, free. Bus R3, 140.
Metro: Mergellina. Map: Naples, A5, p78.

Next to the church of Santa Maria di Piedigrotta, tucked away from the roaring traffic passing through the Mergellina–Fuorigrotta tunnel, is the Parco Virgiliano – not to be confused with the park of the same name in Posillipo (see below). Tombs of the poet **Giacomo Leopardi** (1798-1837) and of Mantova-born poet **Virgil** (19-70 BC) can be seen here, though it's doubtful that the author of the *Aeneid* was actually buried here. Legend has it that Naples-mad Virgil used his magic gaze to create the impressive tunnel, the **Cripta Neapolitana**, nearby. However, Roman bricks and inscriptions suggest that architect Lucius Cocceius Auctus designed this incredible feat of engineering that burrows through tufa rock for 700 m, opening out in the Campi Flegrei. It is undergoing restoration so you can only peer into it.

Parco Virgiliano, Posillipo

Viale Virgilio, Posillipo.
Bus C27. Map: Naples, A6, p78.

A series of terraces offer jaw-dropping vistas of the entire Bay of Naples including the Campi Flegrei, Capo Miseno, Capri, Ischia and Procida. It's a popular spot for families and joggers, who huff and puff between the parkland trees and around the running track within the extensive grounds. On the way, roads via Orazio and via Petrarca have swanky cafés and similarly spectacular views.

Napoli-Maradona mania

Maradona and Napoli: take a flawed footballing genius, a perennially troubled yet intoxicating city with the most passionate *calcio* fans, and you have perhaps the most intense people-player relationship in world sport. On 29 October 2008, nearly 25 years after Maradona did some centre-circle kicky-ups at his introduction to 70,000 *tifosi impazziti*, SSC Napoli went back to the top of Serie A and within a week 'El Pibe de Oro' ('The Golden Boy') was announced as manager of Argentina. In 1991, Maradona left the club in a cloud of cocaine- and Camorra-fuelled controversy having secured two Scudetti (1986-87 and 1989-90) and a Uefa Cup (1989). Napoli's decline mirrored Maradona's personal struggles – yet after years of financial mismanagement that ended in bankruptcy, the club's film-producer president Aurelio de Laurentiis steered the club back into top flight competition. Befitting the quasi-religious devotion of Neapolitans to him, the club retired Maradona's number 10 shirt and plans to rename Stadio San Paolo in his honour.

Vomero

Up on the hill above the city is the Vomero with its pastel-hued mix of *fin di secolo* palaces and modern apartment blocks, punctuated by some uplifting sights: the parkland and museum of Villa Floridiana and the twin delights of Castel Sant'Elmo and the Certosa di San Martino. Access to the battle-worn castle and fabulous monastery complex give spectacular vistas of the bay. A walk around San Martino's sumptuous interiors, panoramic terraces and spellbinding art collections provides the most fascinating insight into Neapolitan history and the minds that dreamt up this city.

Below: Piazzale San Martino. Opposite page: Chiostro Grande.

Certosa e Museo Nazionale di San Martino

Piazzale San Martino 5, T081-558 6408.
Thu-Tues 0830-1930, €6, free under 18/over 65,
discounts with Artecard.
Metro/Funicular: Piazza Vanvitelli, then either a
15-min walk to the Certosa or take Bus V1.
Map: Naples, D4, p78.

This former Carthusian monastery, begun in
the 14th century, now houses fabulous artworks and
various interesting collections as part of the National
Museum of St Martin. It's especially worth a visit for
the handsome Baroque cloisters and sublime views
across the bay from the terraced gardens.

Charles of Anjou, Duke of Calabria, built the main
part of the sprawling Gothic complex, including the
lavishly decorated church, between 1325 and 1368.
From the 16th to the 18th centuries Mannerist-style
revetments and Baroque flourishes were added.
The original triple-naved interior of the church was
modified by Florentine Giovanni Antonio Dosio and
then by local architect Giovanni Giacomo di Conforto,
who created lots of side chapels adorned with inlaid
marble and artworks, including statues by Giuseppe
Sanmartino and Cosimo Fanzago and many frescoes
by Vaccaro, Giordano, Torelli, Caracciolo and d'Arpino.
Seek out Ribera's painting of *Moses*, who is depicted
with curious horns of light, and the exquisite inlaid
wood panels in the *Sacrestia*. The **Quarto del Priore**
was the lavish residence of the prior who governed
monastery life and was the sole person allowed
contact with lay persons. Its recently restored interiors
recreate as it may have looked and contain stunning
artworks including the *Madonna con Bambino e San
Giovannino* by Gian Lorenzo Bernini (1598-1680), the
Virgin and Child triptych (1494) by Jean Bourdichon
and ceiling frescoes by Micco Spadaro.

Tip...

Approaching the monastery, look out for some
handsome *stile-Liberty* (Italian art nouveau) buildings
including an impressive example of *eclettismo,*
the Villino Elena e Maria at via Angelini 14, with its
flamboyant nautical motifs.

Tip...

Avoid the traffic with a serene funicular ride
up to these Vomero sights on one of three lines:
Centrale, Chiaia and Montesanto all stop on or near
piazza Vanvitelli. It's then a short 10-minute walk
westwards to Villa Floridiana or a 15-minute stroll
to the castle and monastery. For the adventurous
there are two alternative return routes that involve
a meandering walk down old steps to the city
below. The oldest, dating back to the 1500s, is the
Pedamentina di San Martino, which starts at the
piazza outside the monastery and ends up at the
Corso Vittorio Emanuele, towards the western end
of the Spaccanapoli. Another staircase is the Salita
del Petraio, which starts further westwards at via
Caccavello, near Castel Sant'Elmo, and follows
roughly the route of the Funicolare Centrale,
ending up on Corso Vittorio Emanuele at the
Suor Orsola Benincasa University complex.

Around the city

Take a breather walking around the **Chiostro Grande** (Great Cloister), with its Florentine-style gardens, saintly statues and macabre marble skulls by Fanzago. The monks had their cells here. Among the museum collections are historic *presepi* (nativity scenes) and carriages, as well as exhibitions detailing the history of the complex, Naples and Neapolitan theatre. The fascinating section *Immagini e Memorie della Città* is filled with maps and images of Naples made during various periods, including the remarkable *Tavola Strozzi*, a 15th-century view of the city, and *Veduta della Darsena*, a dockside scene by Gaspar Van Wittel painted in 1702. Neapolitan artworks from the 19th century include lots of Arcadian landscapes by artists of the Posillipo School including *Panorama of Naples Viewed from the Conocchia* by Giacinto Gigante.

Castel Sant'Elmo

Via Tito Angelini 20, T081-578 4030.
Thu-Tue 0900-1830, €3, free under 18/over 65.
Metro/Funicular: Piazza Vanvitelli, then either a
15-min walk to the castle or take Bus V1.
Map: Naples, D4, p78.

Next to the Certosa di San Martino is the Sant'Elmo Castle, worth a visit for the views from its ramparts. Apart from opening a floor or two for temporary art exhibitions, cultural events and for special *Maggio dei Monumenti* open-doors visits, you can't see much else of the interiors. 'Sant'Elmo' derives from the 10th-century St Erasmus church that stood here and which in typically Neapolitan linguistic fashion has lost some letters. In the 16th century, Spanish Viceroy Pedro Toledo transformed the Angevin construction (1329-1343) into its present star-shaped form. For many centuries it was used as a prison, incarcerating insurgents and outspoken figures including the Renaissance philosopher Tommaso Campanella – author of an outlandish-at-the-time Utopian treatise, *City of the Sun*.

Villa Floridiana & Museo Nazionale della Ceramica Duca di Martina

Via Domenico 77, T081-478 8418.
floridiana.napolibeniculturali.it.
Wed-Mon 0830-1330, guided tours of museum
0930, 1100 and 1230, €2.50, free under 18,
discounts with Artecard.
Map: Naples, C4, p78.

Landscaped royal gardens with some of the best views in town plus the National Ceramics Museum are the refined attractions to be found at Villa Floridiana, a 15-minute walk from Vomero's piazza Vanvitelli. In 1817 Bourbon monarch Ferdinand I gifted the estate and the neoclassical villa to his second wife, Lucia Migliaccio, Duchess of Floridia, and named it in her honour. Connoisseurs of camellias can spot rare varieties in the lush gardens although the fabulous views of the city are likely to divert everyone's attention. Placido de Sangro, the Duke of Martina, was potty about porcelain and ceramics, amassing some 6000 valuable pieces which were donated to the city on the death of his grandson in 1891. As well as the fine examples of Wedgwood, Capodimonte and Ming there are precious objects including tortoiseshell pieces and some 17th- to 19th-century paintings by the likes of Francesco Solimena and Domenico Antonio Vaccaro.

Below: Castle and monastery.
Opposite page: Villino Elena e Maria.

COL VENTO   IN POPPA   PER OGNI   ROTTA

Easy side trips in Campania

Caserta & Santa Maria Capua Vetere

Although the region's seaside attractions largely overshadow Campania's stunning mountainous areas of Irpina, Benevento, Avellino and the Cilento, for example, a tour of the interior is recommended, if time allows. Campania's spectacular and earthquake-ravaged inland territory warrants a book in itself, and a car is essential for exploring it. However, two places are within half an hour's striking distance from Napoli Centrale by train or via the A1 Autostrada: Caserta has an old medieval centre and a Bourbon royal palace to rival Versailles in scale and ambition, while Santa Maria Capua Vetere contains the second-largest Roman amphitheatre, an ancient temple and an archaeological museum.

Reggia di Caserta

Viale Douhet, T0823-277430, reggiadicaserta.org. Royal Apartments Wed-Mon 0830-1930, last admission 1900. Park Wed-Mon 0830 till sunset, last admission 2 hrs before sunset. English Gardens Hourly guided tours 0930 to 3 hrs before sunset. Palace €5, gardens €3, both €7, free under 18. Audio guides €6/€4. Bus shuttle to Diana Fountain €1 round trip. Guided tours with Arethusa (T0823-448084, arethusa.net), €4. The entrance to the palace is opposite the train station.

Out of the scruffy, traffic-ridden modern suburbs of Caserta appears the incongruous sight of a colossal royal palace with a few typically Neapolitan rough edges. The scale of the frontage impresses but nothing prepares you for the expansive gardens and fountains that rise spectacularly up a verdant hill. Carlo III of Bourbon commissioned Baroque behemoth Luigi Vanvitelli to build the palace that was part of his plan for a new administrative centre. He abdicated and returned to Spain in 1759, leaving the project in the hands of his less high-minded son Ferdinand and faithful regent Tanucci. As the ancien regime declined and Italy was unified in 1860 the military occupied the palace; later it was to play an important role as Allied HQ and venue of official Fascist and Nazi German capitulation in 1943-1945.

The five-storey palace occupies over 45,000 sq m, has two principal façades 247 m long and 36 m high with 243 windows, and took 22 years to build (1752-1774) and another 73 years to garnish with much gilt. Its 1200 rooms and 43 staircases are arranged around four monumental courtyards. The 20-km monumental avenue to Naples was never completed. Amid the sumptuous yet rather garish **Royal Apartments** is the striking throne room containing a frieze with medallions depicting the kings of Naples and a smaller version of Naples' Teatro San Carlo. More uplifting are the expansive **gardens**, with gravel paths, a long fish pond and lots of fountains including La Fontana di Eolo (Fountain of Eolus) with fantastical grottoes, zephyrs and gods. La Cascata Grande impressively apes a natural waterfall cutting through a wooded hill and the **Giardino Inglese** (English Gardens), designed by English botanist Andrea Graefer, mixes 2500 sq m of naturalistic parkland scattered with Roman stautues from Pompeii and some curious follies with Masonic references that were all the rage when Queen Maria Carolina of Austria commissioned the project in 1786.

The Reggia and its grand staircase appeared as the Naboo Royal Palace in the Star Wars prequels, *The Phantom Menace* and *Attack of the Clones*.

Below: La Fontana di Diana e Atteone. Bottom: Scalone d'onore.
Opposite page: La Reggia.

Tip...

Each September Casertavecchia hosts an arts festival, **Settembre al Borgo** (settembrealborgo2008.org), which sees Italian writers, musicians and film-makers join international artists of the calibre of legendary Brazilian singer Caetano Veloso, who played a sell-out concert at the Reggia di Caserta in 2008.

Great days out

Casertavecchia

Built around its sombre 12th-century cathedral is the old hilltop town of Casertavecchia, some 10 km north of Caserta. It retains lots of medieval atmosphere and is a popular place for dining. The **Duomo di San Michele Arcangelo** (piazza Vescovado, T082-337 1318, daily 0900-1300, 1530-1800, free) is built of volcanic tufa stone in a Norman-Arabic style. It has a Moorish *tiburio ottagonale* (octagonal roofed tower) as well as a 13th-century campanile, a façade with strange carved animal sculptures with Lombardic origins, and gracefully stark interiors. There are 18 Roman columns and colourful marble mosaic details on the apse paving and on the elegant pulpit. Also worth seeking out is the Gothic church, **Chiesetta dell'Annunziata**, and the crumbling yet commanding six-pack of tower ruins of the 11th-century **castle**, begun by the Normans in 879.

San Leucio

Piazza della Seta, Strada Statale SS87, T082-330 1817, comune.caserta.it/belvedere. Mon-Sat 0930-1730, €6.

A few kilometres northwest of Caserta on the SS87 is the model silk workers' community of San Leucio set up by Ferdinando I in 1789, which had liberal laws based on the theories of Neapolitan philosopher and jurist Gaetano Filangieri. It takes its name from the small church on the hill here. As well as superb views from the belvedere, orderly rows of workers' houses and the handsome **Casino Reale** palace with its sumptuously frescoed royal apartments, there's a **Museo della Seta** (Silk Museum) that displays historic fabrics and weaving machines. The privately owned **Stabilimento Serico de Negri** still produces plush fabrics here today.

Above: Duomo di San Michele Arcangelo. Opposite page: Anfiteatro Campano.

Santa Maria Capua Vetere

Museo Archeologico: Via Roberto D'Angio 48,
T0823-844206.
All sites opening times Tue-Sun 0900-1730.
€3 to see all sites. Frequent trains from Napoli
and Caserta. A1 Autostrada Exit Caserta Nord.
From Caserta head westwards along the Via
Appia (SS7)

Seven km west of Caserta through nondescript
suburbs is Santa Maria Capua Vetere, where the
Thracian gladiator Spartacus is said to have
launched his rebellion against Rome in 73 BC.
There are evocative archaeological sites to
investigate including the **Arco di Adriano**, a
triumphal arch of the ancient via Appia, and –
most famously – the **Anfiteatro Campano** (piazza
Ottobre, T0823-798864), started by Hadrian in the
first century AD. Despite being looted for its stone
and metal, the ruins of this arena, which held
around 60,000 spectators, are mightily impressive.
Highlights include traces of frescoes and
Palaeo-Christian remnants in the passages under
the arena, a **Museo dei Gladiatori** displaying suits
of armour, and architectural fragments scattered
around the picturesque grounds. The **Museo
Archaeologico dell'Antica Capua-Mitreo** (via
Roberto d'Angio 48, T0823-844206), housed in the
Torre di Sant'Erasmo, displays artefacts from the
Bronze Age as well as lots of ceramics, artworks,
weaponry and trinkets made by Etruscans,
Samnites, Greeks and Romans. Ask a member of
the museum staff for access to the nearby **Mitreo
temple**, dedicated to a Persian god, which has a
fresco depicting the ritual sacrifice of a bull.

Acquedotto Carolino

The most impressive stretch of architect Luigi
Vanvitelli's 38-km aqueduct designed to feed the
thirsty fountains and communities of the Reggia
and San Leucio can be seen 8 km west of Caserta.
Near the SP3354 road loom three-tiers of galleries
of the 50-m-high Ponti della Valle (Bridges of the
Valley) designed to convey water from sources up in
the hills across the Maddaloni Valley. Remnants of
the Roman aqueduct Acqua Giulia were discovered
during the epic construction between 1753 and 1770.
A triangular obelisk memorial at the Ponti della Valle
marks the deaths of Bourbon troops and Garibaldi's
Red Shirts, who fought at the 1860 Battle of Volturno,
a key battle of the Risorgimento, the movement
behind the unification of Italy.

Sleeping

In the past 10 years lots of B&Bs and mid-range hotels have appeared in the suburbs and deep in the old city. Many of the big swanky hotels are not happy about the competition, but it's good news for visitors. Generally prices remain lower than the rest of Italy. There are now some very stylish conversions of old apartments, in Chiaia and the Centro Antico especially, while around Santa Lucia lots of well-established hotels live off past glories and business customers, and tend to disappoint. It's best to avoid places on Corso Garibaldi and near piazza Garibaldi because of the traffic noise, pollution and crime.

Santa Lucia & around

Palazzo Turchini €€€€
Via Medina 21/22, T081-551 0606, palazzoturchini.it.
Bus R1, R2. Metro: Dante.
Located off piazza Municipio in a 1590s building that once formed part of the Royal Conservatory, this well-appointed hotel offers a comfortable, air-conditioned stay within easy reach of the Monumental City, the port and the Centro Antico. The modern interiors include lots of marble and hardwood, giving the place a sleek but warm feel, and creams, whites and warm wooden tones fill the 27 guest rooms, which have decent facilities including air conditioning, internet and TV.

Centro Antico

Costantinopoli 104 €€€
Via Santa Maria di Costantinopoli 104, T081-557 1035, costantinopoli104.com.
Metro: Museo/Dante.
Map: Central Naples, D2, p86.
Take one *Stile Liberty* palazzo with a gorgeous palm-fronded garden in the throbbing heart of the Centro Antico then add a pool and attractive interiors to make one very special hotel package. Beyond the art nouveau ironwork and stained-glass windows is an elegant yet homely reception area/lounge and equally alluring breakfast room. The 19 bedrooms all have individual flair, mixing carefully chosen artworks, luxurious bathrooms and smart

furnishings. Napoli's ancient sites, arty shops and cool hang-outs are all within walking distance.

Piazza Bellini €€
Via Santa Maria di Costantinopoli 101, T081-451732, hotelpiazzabellini.com.
Metro: Museo/Dante.
Map: Central Naples, D2, p86.
Ensconced in the Bohemian heart of Naples, Hotel Piazza Bellini delivers a suitably stylish package of minimalist contemporary interiors with lots of colourful flourishes. The young, knowledgeable staff know the word-on-the-piazza when it comes to Napoli's cultural events and recommend the nearby Pizzeria di Matteo (see page 136) for the best pizza.

Donnalbina 7 €
Via Donnalbina 7, T081-1956 7817, donnalbina7.it.
Bus R1, R4, C57.
Metro: Dante.
Map: Central Naples, D4, p86.
Donnalbina is a great-value find, smack-bang in the Old City, near all the best pizzerias, historic sights and via Toledo shops. The six unfussy, whitewashed rooms have vibrant artworks by local artists and decent bathrooms. You can even have breakfast in bed, which is a real treat in this price bracket. Excellent facilities include free Wi-Fi connection and use of internet on the hotel's PC.

Decumani Roof
Via dei Tribunali 197, T333-600 9627, decumaniroof.net.
Metro: Cavour.
Map: Central Naples, G1, p86.
These smart new flats at the Castel Capuano end of the Decumanus Maggiore have original artworks and stunning rooftop views. However the climb to the tiled terrace is not really suitable for families with young children or the less mobile. A small one-roomed apartment for three people costs €90-120; a two-roomed apartment for four to six people is €100-€180.

Via Toledo to piazza Cavour

Donna Regina €
Via Luigi Settembrini 80, T081-442 1511.
Metro: Cavour.
Map: Central Naples, F1, p86.
Don't be put off by the traffic mayhem around via Foria and the dodgy old lift as this B&B housed in a crumbling 14th-century convent building offers lots for anyone wanting to learn about Neapolitan art, history and culture. Donna Regina is owned by the ever-clever Raffone family, who number quite a few sculptors, painters, printers and cooks in their ranks. Think large rooms crammed with oddities, antiquarian books, prints and paintings. It's very handy for the

Below: La cucina di Donna Regina.
Opposite page: Piazza Plebiscito lion.

Madre gallery (next door) and the Museo Archaeologico Nazionale which is nearby.

Toledo €
Via Montecalvario 15, T081-406800, hoteltoledo.com.
Bus R1, R4, C57. Metro: Dante.
Map: Central Naples, C5, p86.
Just off the bustling shopping street, via Toledo, and near the famous Teatro Nuovo, this well-run place offers reasonably priced and comfortable accommodation. Its 33 rooms are functional and fairly well soundproofed – when you close the shutters – from the Quartieri Spagnoli streetlife outside. The amiable manager explains that before the 1980 earthquake this old palazzo once housed a brothel. Breakfast can be taken on the leafy roof terrace and there's a café cum lounge where you can check your email and relax.

Listings

Corso Umberto & around

Clarean €
*Piazza Garibaldi 49,
T081-553 5683, clarean.
hotelsinnapoli.com.*
Metro: Garibaldi.
Map: Central Naples, H1, p86.
If you need a place near the station this place is a good bet: it's close to the Alibus stop, so it's great for an overnight stop or early start, when being close to the transport links is the priority. Be aware that it's in the seedy piazza Garibaldi area so it's not recommended for more than one night. Guest rooms have modern furniture and smart parquet floors, and feel surprisingly light and fresh. The bar-breakfast area is a pleasant place to start the day and overall the service is very good.

Capodimonte & La Sanità

Villa Capodimonte €€
*Via Moiarello 66, T081-459000,
villacapodimonte.it.*
Bus 24, C66.
Opened in the mid-1990s, this modern hotel is conveniently located near the Museo di Capodimonte and Osservatorio Astronomico though it's a bit out of the way for those without a car and relying on public transport to see the downtown sights. There may be sleek, art deco inspired marble and parquet flooring, but the business-orientated feel may

Galleria Umberto I.

disappoint those seeking real character and charm. However, on the plus side it's a quiet hotel away from the Naples hubbub, with relaxing public areas include a piano bar, rooftop terrace and lush gardens.

Chiaia, Mergellina & Posillipo

Ausonia €€
*Via Caracciolo 11,
Mergellina, T081-682278,
hotelausonianapoli.com.*
Bus B. Metro: Mergellina.
Map: Naples, B5, p78.
The Ausonia is in the perfect spot for those using the Mergellina hydrofoils to and from Ischia. Traffic may roar along the via Caracciolo waterfront rat run outside but once inside the large palazzo there are restful rooms with a nautical theme. Porthole windows, framed knots and prints of ships give it a slightly kitsch yet charming feel. There's a cosy little bar with internet access, and you get to go away with a maritime-themed key ring at the end of your stay.

Micalò €€
*Riviera di Chiaia 88, Chiaia,
T081-761 7131, micalo.it.*
Bus R3, 140, 152.
Map: Naples, C5, p78.
Micalò's Anglo-Italian owners commissioned a talented young architect to create the city's most inspiring boutique hotel in a 17th-century palazzo opposite the Villa Comunale Gardens. Its cool marble floors and curvy walls are sprinkled with interesting objects and artworks by Neapolitan artists. The cavernous guest rooms have huge beds below minimalist-style mezzanine bathrooms. Scrambled eggs and fresh *cornetti* are on the healthy yet hearty breakfast menu which is served in the Art Bar – another relaxing space to take in the art, read up on the city and chat while drinking a cocktail or a coffee.

Hotel Micalò.

Palazzo Alabardieri €€
Via Alabardieri 38, Chiaia, T081-415278, palazzoalabardieri.it.
Bus C25. Metro: Amedeo.
Map: Central Naples, A7, p86.
Chiaia's chic shops, smart restaurants and swanky bars are on the doorstep of this smart hotel. Guest rooms are spacious and soundproofed, with traditional furnishings and botanical prints. A reading room filled with lots of armchairs and historic Neapolitan scenes leads to a cream-hued dining room with coved ceiling. Attentive staff, a great location and lots of handy services make this a good choice for both couples and families.

Riviera 281 €€
Riviera di Chiaia 281, Chiaia, T081-764 1427, riviera281.it.
Bus R3, 140, 152.
Metro: Amedeo.
Opposite the Villa Comunale Gardens is the handsome 19th-century Palazzo San Teodoro, which now contains a stylish B&B. Cool hues on the walls contrast with vibrant contemporary artworks and funky furnishings. Guest rooms have flat screen TVs and elegant marble bathrooms. A relaxing lounge leads to a smart roof terrace where you can sip an aperitivo and drink in the seaside views.

La Bouganville €
Via Manzoni 155, Posillipo, T081-769 2205, labouganville.com.
Funicolare di Mergellina: Manzoni.
Map: Naples, A6, p78.
Take a breather from Napoli's traffic mayhem up in this small and tranquil Posillipo B&B run by the helpful host Giuliano. Staying in a Neapolitan home gives you a real taste for the city and Giuliano does not disappoint, having lots of quips, stories, tips and recipes at the ready. The two guest rooms are cosy and open onto a leafy garden – there's no en suite though. The B&B's near the via Manzoni funicular stop, so it's handy for Mergellina and not too far from the Parco Virgiliano.

Platamon B&B €
Via Chiatamone 55, Chiaia, T081-764 3203, bebnaples.com.
Metro: Amedeo.
Just up the road from Napoli Residence (see below), Marco Platamon has a small B&B containing three largish guest rooms with tiled floors, fresh white walls and some exuberant artworks. Doubles cost €80-100.

Self-catering
Napoli Sweet Home
T081-282510/245 2431, napolisweethome.com.
Napoli Sweet Home is a lettings agency with dozens of apartments and B&B options starting from €35 per person for an apartment in Mergellina.

Napoli Residence
Via Chiatamone 6, Chiaia, T081-406404, napoliresidence.com.
Metro: Amedeo.
Map: Naples, D5, p78.
Friendly owner Marco Platamon has two well-maintained one- and two-roomed flats in Chiaia (and one in the Centro Storico), with simply furnished rooms and ethnic artworks. Prices start at €100 for up to three people sharing.

Vomero

Grand Hotel Parkers €€€€
Corso Vittorio Emanuele 135, T081-761 2474, grandhotelparkers.it.
Bus C16. Metro: Amedeo.
The stunning view of the bay from the swanky terrace restaurant George's is the biggest draw of this grand old five-star hotel. English aristocrat George Parker Bidder acquired the hotel in 1889 and it still maintains some *belle époque* elegance despite some uninspiring recent refurbishments. Guest rooms have art nouveau decorative flourishes but lack character somehow and are a tad disappointing. Overall the level of service, style and atmosphere is not quite what you would expect from an historic hotel that once hosted illustrious guests such as Oscar Wilde and Virginia Wolfe.

Eating & drinking

Vomero lift.

Weekend a Napoli €€
Via Enrico Alvino 157, T081-578 1010, weekendanapoli.com.
Metro: Vanvitelli.
Switched-on owners Paolo and Patrizia have created a truly comfortable hotel with superb-value accommodation in a quiet residential corner of Vomero. Its big boon is that you just don't get this kind of personal service and Neapolitan family warmth in the big hotels. Guest rooms have soundproofing, calming hues and top-notch facilities including plasma TVs, air conditioning and free Wi-Fi. There are various room options available and even a small apartment. Some of the small doubles lack natural light but the suites are spacious and bright, and some ave large jacuzzi baths.

La Controra €
Piazza Trinità alla Cesarea 231, T081-549 4014, lacontrora.com.
Metro: Salvator Rosa.
Map: Central Naples, A1, p86.
Hostel buildings don't often come as grand as this 17th-century convent building near a crumbling old Baroque church. Recent refurbishments have added a smart modern café and landscaped gardens which are venues for DJ sets and art exhibitions. As well as well-maintained mixed dorms there's a selection of en suite doubles and family rooms at very reasonable rates. The rooms have recently been refurbished, and you'll find pieces of contemporary sculpture alongside retro furniture. Prices start at €16 for a bed in a dorm.

Santa Lucia & around

La Bersagliera €€€
Borgo Marinari 10/11, T081-764 6016.
Wed-Mon 1200-1500, 1900-2400. Bus B, 152, C25.
Map: Naples, E6, p78.
Opened in 1919 and frequented by Neapolitan geniuses Totò and Eduardo de Filippo, as well as Sophia Loren and the late Luciano Pavarotti, this historic eatery at Borgo Marinari is still pulling in the punters. Book a table outside overlooking the harbour or in the elegant dining room and sample seafood specialities including *insalata di polipo* (octopus salad), *frittura di paranza* (fried marine medley) and their homemade *pastiera*. Main courses €9-20. Reservations recommended.

La Cantinella €€€
Via Cuma 42, T081-764868, lacantinella.it.
Mon-Sat 1230-1530, 1930-2400. Bus B, 152, C25.
Map: Naples, E5, p78.
Located on the Santa Lucia *lungomare* (promenade) on the corner of via N Sauro, La Cantinella has the hint of an exotic 1970s Bond set with its bamboo-bedecked dining room. The cuisine is a little out of the ordinary as well: creative, experimental Neapolitan dishes like champagne-infused courgette risotto and pilaf of curried prawns go a little further

than simply prepared Neapolitan food. Grilled seafood connoisseurs are also in for a treat here.

La Scialuppa €€€
Borgo Marinari 4,
T081-764 5333, lascialuppa.it.
Tue-Sun 1200-2400.
Bus B, 152, C25.
Map: Naples, E6, p78.
Down on the Borgo Marinari, La Scialuppa has bags of character, wonderful views and arguably the best dining experience on the marina. With its nautical decor and harbourside location it's like being on a boat, without the motion of the ocean to disturb your enjoyment of their specialities, which include *rigatoni al pesce spada* (chunky pasta tubes with swordfish) and *linguine al scialuppa* (linguine, scampi, prawns, tomatoes and parsley).

Da Patrizia €
Borgo Marinari 24,
T081-764 6407.
Tue-Sun 1230-1530, 1930-2300.
Bus B, 152, C25.
Among the swanky eateries is the ever-reliable Patrizia's, which has just half-a-dozen tables on the quayside. It's tiny, popular and only open in the warmer months so book in advance. Neapolitans in the know rate its quality seafood dishes at reasonable prices. Expect classics like *spaghetti alle cozze* (with mussels and tomatoes), *frittura di gamberi e calamari* (lightly fried

prawn and squid) and *polipo alla Luciana* (octopus cooked in garlic, wine and its own juices).

Cafés & bars
Caffè del Professore
Piazza Trieste e Trento 46,
T081-403 0410.
Daily 0700-0200.
Map: Central Naples, C6, p86.
This refined bar near piazza del Plebiscito is famed for its *caffè ai gusti di nocciola e cioccolata* (coffee flavoured with hazelnut and chocolate) and delicious *sfogliatelle*.

Caffè Gambrinus
Via Chiaia 1, T081-417582,
caffegambrinus.com.
Daily 0800-0130.
Map: Central Naples, C7, p86.
Take in the handsome *stile-Liberty* (Italian art nouveau) interiors of this historic café, with its dazzling display of mirrors, gilt and chandeliers, while watching the entertaining interaction of the dapper baristas and Neapolitan clientele. Prop up the long marble bar or pay for the privilege of

sitting in an elegant corner or on the terrace, sipping espresso and munching on a few of their excellent pastries: it's famed for *babà al rhum, coda d'aragosta* (*sfogliatella* in the shape of a lobster's tail) and the creamy topped cake *Il Vesuvio*. Fancy cocktails are accompanied by *stuzzicherie* (savoury nibbles). Among the illustrious guests who have chatted and chomped here are Oscar Wilde, Benedetto Croce and Lucifer Box (Mark Gatiss's dashing fictional secret agent in *The Vesuvius Club*).

Busy barista at Caffè Gambrinus.

Centro Antico

Antica Pizzeria da Michele €
*Via Cesare Sersale 1/3,
T081-553 9204.*
Mon-Sat 1000-2400.
Metro: Dante.
Map: Central Naples, G2, p86.
Pizza purists flock to this
no-nonsense pizzeria for just two
classic varieties, the *Margherita*
and *marinara*. Thin crusts with
wonderful charred bubbles are
the order of the day. Pick up a
ticket and join the queue that
disappears almost as quickly as
you can say *"pizza pizza ca'
pummorala 'ncoppa".*

Il Pizzaiolo del Presidente €
*Via dei Tribunali 120/121,
T081-210903,
ilpizzaiolodelpresidente.it.*
Mon-Sat 1230-1530, 1930-2400.
Metro: Dante.
Map: Central Naples, F1, p86.
The 'President's Pizza Maker',
Ernesto Cacciali, handed Bill
Clinton a *pizza-piegata* during
the G7 summit in 1994 and, on
the back of his fame, the fly
pizzaiolo opened this no-frills
pizzeria, just up from his old
place Di Matteo. Take a seat at
the paper-clothed tables in the
cosy basement and order from a
couple of dozen pizza varieties
including their famed *pizza fritta*
(fried pizza).

Pizzeria di Matteo €
Via dei Tribunali 94, T081-455262.
Mon-Sat 0900-2300.
Metro: Dante.
Map: Central Naples, E1, p86.
It's one of the city's top pizzerias
– President Clinton dropped in
during the G7 summit of 1994. As
well as making a tasty *Margherita*
that spills over your plate, they
do an excellent *ripieno al forno* –
a folded *pizza calzone* with a
choice of fillings.

Sorbillo €
*Via dei Tribunali 32,
T081-446643.*
Mon-Sat 1200-0100.
Metro: Dante.
Map: Central Naples, D2, p86.
Step into the flagstone ground
floor of this historic pizzeria
opened in 1935 and you sense
a friendly, youthful vibe.
Red-shirted Neapolitan
waitresses glide around while
boss Gino Sorbillo conducts
the *pizzaioli* music behind the
counter. The huge rectangular
and very thin-based pizzas spill
over the plates: *passata di
pomodoro* makes the *Margherita*
swimmingly delicious while two
pizzas named after the founding
grandparents Luigi and Carolina
retain an elastic, charred base
reminiscent of naan bread.

Cafés & bars
Caffè Letterario Intra Moenia
*Piazza Bellini 70, T081-290988,
intramoenia.it.*
Daily 1000-0200.
Map: Central Naples, D2, p86.
Art, music and books combine
in this boho bar popular with
students, academics and creative
types who sit at the tables on
leafy piazza Bellini or browse
through the fascinating
collection of books and
prints inside.

Scaturchio
*Piazza San Domenico Maggiore
19, T081-551 6944, scaturchio.it.*
Daily 0730-2030, closed Tue.
Map: Central Naples, D3, p86.
Opened in 1921, this Neapolitan
institution is famed for its
pastries and cakes including
sfogliatelle, the papal-approved
pastiera cake (Pope John Paul II
was a big fan apparently) and *lo
zefiro* (orange-flavoured
semifreddo cake).

Via Toledo to piazza Cavour

Antica Pizzeria Port'Alba €
Via Porta Alba 18, T081-459713.
200-1600, 1800-0100.
Metro: Dante.
One of the oldest pizzerias
(allegedly opened in 1738 as
an open-air pizzeria stand,
with interiors and tables added
in 1830), Port'Alba serves all the
classics as well as various pasta
and seafood dishes, at very
reasonable prices. The crust

Above: Blop, blop, blop.
Below: Squadra Umberto.

here is a little thicker than your average *pizza napoletana.*

Cafés & bars
Mexico
Piazza Dante 86, T081-549 9330.
Mon-Sat 0730-2030.
Map: Central Naples, C2, p86.
Café connoisseurs from near and far flock to the Passalacqua family's bars on piazza Dante and piazza Garibaldi to sample coffee made with roasted arabica beans, which you can buy here.

Europeo di Mattozzi €€
Via Marchese Campodisola 4, T081-552 1323.
Mon-Sat 1200-1530, Thu-Sat 1930-2300. Bus R1, R2, R4.
Map: Central Naples, E4, p86.
Opened in the 1930s, this elegant establishment on piazza Bovio serves fine food amid colourful ceramics and old prints. Perennial favourites include *polpo in casseruola* (octopus casserole), *pasta e patate con provala* (pasta and potatoes with smoky melted cheese) and baba for dessert.

Rosiello a Posillipo €€€
Via Santo Strato 10, Posillipo, T081-769 1288.
Thu-Tue 1230-1600, 1900-2400.
Bus B, C23, 140.
Map: Naples, A7, p78
It may be pricey and a bit out of the way in Posillipo (catch the 140 bus from Mergellina or, better still, take a cab), but the wonderful terrace views of Capri and Vesuvius and their gorgeous food and wine make Rosiello a very special place to dine. Vegetarians can enjoy their flavoursome *parmigiana di melanzane* and carnivores can savour the *braciole* (rolls of beef) served with a tomato ragout. Their bianco, rosso and rosato wines are produced at their Varriale vineyard.

Ciro a Mergellina €€
Via Mergellina 18/21, Mergellina, T081-681780.
Tue-Sun 1330-2330.
Metro: Mergellina.
Map: Naples, B6, p78.
Close to the Mergellina *lungomare* this Neapolitan favourite does classic Neapolitan dishes including seafood and pizzas. The entertaining dining experience in this open-plan 1960s chalet is enhanced by the dapper waiters who whizz around with a quip, smile and suggestion at the ready. You can order your *Margherita* topped with either *pomodorini di Vesuvio* (the tasty

tomatoes grown below Vesuvius) or *passata.* Their *ripieno al forno* – baked *calzone* style – is very filling and their *insalate di mare* (seafood salad) is a popular antipasto choice with the locals. For something a bit different try the delicious *polipo affogato* – a huge octopus cooked simply in its own brick-red juices.

Umberto €€
Via Alabardieri 30/31, piazza dei Martiri, Chiaia, T081-418555.
Tue-Sun 1230-1530, 1930-2400.
Metro/Funiculare di Chiaia: Amedeo.
Map: Central Naples, A7, p86.
The di Porzio family have run this elegant restaurant-pizzeria for three generations. Current boss Massimo is president of the Associazione Verace Pizza Napoletana, which safeguards the methods needed to make a proper pizza (see page 104). The spacious rooms have interesting artworks for sale and often host cultural events, as befitting a place close to piazza dei Martiri in upmarket Chiaia. Expect slightly smaller pizzas here but excellent quality, pressed

What the locals say

Moccia (*Via San Pasquale di Chiaia 21/22, Chiaia, T081-411348, Wed-Mon 0730-2030, Map: Naples, D5, p178*) is a wonderful place to get a box full of Neapolitan pastries (*babà, sfogliatelle, pastiera* and *torta caprese*) and local school kids queue for their *pizzette* (small pizzas). A 97-year-old *nonna* still runs the place and always keeps an eye on me when I come in.

Vincenzo, Chiaia and Anacapri resident

tablecloths and friendly service from dapper waiters. Their Pizza DOC is topped with San Marzano tomatoes and the best buffalo mozzarella. As well as classic fishy *frittura* and meaty *ragù alla Genovese* with pennolini pasta, they do delicious *contorni* (side dishes) like *mozzarella in carozza* (in a breaded carriage), *zucchini alla scapece* (marinated courgettes) and tasty *friarelli* (bitter broccoli-like shoots).

Osteria la Cucinotta €
Via G Bausan 32, Chiaia, T081-405400.
Mon-Sat 1200-1500, 1900-2400.
Metro/Funiculare di Chiaia: Amedeo.
Map: Naples, C4, p78.
Empty picture frames hang from an antique workshop opposite this cosy osteria in a narrow Chiaia backstreet. Great value *primo piatto* dishes at €4, such as linguine with squid and *rigatoni al ragù*, are always available on the *menu del giorno*. A main course of fish and meat does not cost much more.

Vinarium €
Vico Santa Maria Cappella Vecchia 7, Chiaia, T081-764 4114.
Mon-Sat 1100-1600, 1900-0200.
Bus C25.
Map: Central Naples, A7, p86.
There's a bar and *enoteca* serving fabulous wine at the front of this busy place in Chiaia. It's great for lunch and late-night diners and drinkers. A sheet with the day's choices includes hearty pasta dishes, abundant salads and seafood. A combination of that classic Neapolitan wedge of carbohydrate, *pasta frittata*, followed by a baked fish and a tempting *semifreddo* cake served with hot chocolate sauce is great fuel for a trawl around Naples.

Cafés & bars
Chalet Ciro
Via Mergellina 11, Mergellina, T081-669928.
Open 24 hrs.
Map: Naples, B6, p78.
Ciro has been pulling in the punters to sample their yummy dollops of gelato on the Mergellina waterfront since the

1950s. Choose from hundreds of *coni, coppe, semifreddi* and *sorbetti* combinations and flavours, including the fantabulous *pizza al gelato* (ice-cream pizza) and the exotic fruit-filled *coppa Tarzan*.

Gran Bar Riviera
Riviera di Chiaia 183, Chiai, T081-665026.
Open 24 hrs.
Map: Naples, C5, p78.
Day and night this Neapolitan café is filled with Neapolitans enjoying its refreshments, pastries, ice cream and cakes. Their famous *buondì notte* combo of nutella and *semifreddo* zabaglione is a treat well worth trying.

Gran Caffè Cimmino
Via Petrarca 147, Posillipo, T081-575 7697.
Daily 0700-0100.
Map: Naples, A6, p78.
There are wonderful views from the scenic via Petrarca, a favourite of tour buses and luvved-up couples – this fabulous place has the *sfogliatelle* and famed *babà alla frutta* to match.

La Caffettiera
Piazza dei Martiri 25, Chiaia,
T081-764 4243.
Daily 0700-2230.
Map: Central Naples, A7, p86.
This popular café with refined
interiors and outside tables looks
onto the lions in piazza dei Martiri.
Great little pizzas, savoury cakes
and lots of sweet pastry treats.

Trip
Via Giuseppe Martucci 64, Chiaia,
T081-1956 8994, new.cra.na.it.
Map: Naples, C4, p78.
"Trip is not an ordinary café,"
explains Chiaia resident Michelle
Lowe, "it's a kind of cultural
meeting place…great for having
a drink and snacks, to meet
people, see interesting artworks
and arty films." Their Saturday
brunch (1300-1600) is particularly
popular with families as it
combines an excellent menu with
arty events for parents and film
fun, and games for the *bambini*.

Vomero

Acunzo €€
Via D Cimarosa 64, T081-578 5362.
Mon-Sat 1300-1500, 1930-2330.
Metro Vanvitelli.
Map: Naples, C3, p78.
Open since 1964 and often full –
for good reason, as this place
serves great pizzas (try their
pizza pulcinella piled with mince,
prosciutto, mozzarella, ricotta and
mushrooms) as well as tasty fried
foods from their traditional
Neapolitan *friggitoria* cookbook.

Pick of the picnic spots

Pick up savoury picnic goodies
and refreshments from a local
alimentari (a deli or food shop
like Gastronomia L.U.I.S.E.,
see page 147), fruit from a
bountiful market (via Pignasecca,
see page 148) and *dolce* treats
from a *pasticceria* (Moccia, see
page 138) and seek out some
shade between larking about
and sightseeing in one of these
leafy retreats.

Parco Virgiliano, Posillipo
Race the joggers and snap the
shimmering views around the
bay from this sprawling tree-
filled park on the Posillipo hill.

Reggia di Caserta Gardens
Fountains, follies and a
fantastical English Garden make
the palace gardens an epic stage-
set for a nosh-up *napoletano*.

Capodimonte Gardens
Oodles of art in the museo and
lush gardens made for lazy
afternoons.

Villa La Floridiana
A green oasis blooming with
exotic plants – including rare
camellias – in the heart of
residential Vomero.

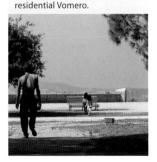

Left: Parco Virgiliano.

Entertainment

Be Bop Bar
Via Ferrigni 34, Chiaia,
T081-245 1321.
Daily 1800-0200, usually later
at weekends, free.
Metro: Amedeo.
Less posy and packed than many
of Chiaia's swanky *locali*, Be Bop
Bar attracts a wider age range of
punters who come for the
relaxed atmosphere and eclectic
tunes.

Enoteca Belledonne
Vico Belledonne a Chiaia 18,
Chiaia, T081-403162.
Daily1200-0200.
Metro: Amedeo.
Locals cram into and gather
outside this popular wine bar
to quaff the quality *vino* and to
nibble on tasty *stuzzichini* snacks
before moving on. It's a buzzing
spot for an *aperitivo*.

Kinky Klub
Vicolo delle Quercia 26,
T335-547 7299, kinkyjam.com.
Daily 2200-0300, €3 for
mèmbers. Metro: Dante.
After 15 years of the Kinky Bar,
the reggae, dub and wacky
baccy have moved to bigger
premises. The Caribbean feel
is enhanced by top live acts
including Mad Professor and
Mr Dennis Alcapone.

Living *La Vita Notturna*

Neapolitans often eat their evening meal (*cena*) late and quite a few relaxed eating places including **Vinarium** (see page 138) provide a place for late-night eating and social drinking. Indeed the lines between restaurant, café, bar and club are often blurred. Chiaia and Santa Lucia (especially along via Parthenope) have the swankiest *locali* frequented by a dressed-up crowd. In the Centro Antico, especially around the university, there are lots of small places that attract mainly alternative, arty and student types: piazza Bellini is often the starting point of a night out here. You'll hear more poppy dance music where *la bella gente* go while, in the old city, alternative, rap, reggae and indie sounds can be heard, often accompanied by the smell of exotic tobacco. Things get going around 2230 and you may be asked for a *tessera* (required of some establishments by Italian law) – a membership card that rarely costs more than a couple of euros. On summer weekends, many people go out clubbing in the Campi Flegrei or down to the Cilento Coast, which both have bar-clubs, some right on the beach.

Tip...

Neapolitan band Almamegretta's top hangouts are: **Perditempo, Kinky Klub, O Core e Napoli** and **Bar del Madre**, all in the Centro Antico.

Le Bar
Via Eldorado 7, piazzetta Marinari 18, Borgo Marinari, T081-764 5722.
Open 24 hrs during the summer but only weekends in the winter. Bus B, 152, C25.
Down by the yachts amid some fine restaurants, Le Bar is a glamorous place to mix some excellent cocktails with a bit of socializing.

Madrenalina
Museo Madre, via Settembrini 79, T081-1931 3016, museomadre.it.
Phone for upcoming events.
Metro: Cavour.
A white cube in the Madre contemporary art gallery often turns into a stylish bar, with experimental visuals and eclectic DJ sets (jazz, electronica, deep house, pop).

Perditempo
Via San Pietro a Maiella 8, T081-444958.
Daily 1000 till late, free.
Metro: Dante.
A favourite "waste of time" of the Neapolitan band Almamegretta, the Perditempo is a kind of cultural centre cum bar that combines a bookshop, record store and venue for left-field events including live music acts.

Rising South
Via San Sebastiano 19, T335- 879 0428, risingrepublic.com.
Tue-Sun 2000-0300.
Set up as a cross between a *centro sociale* and an ethnic-styled club by a professor of music anthropology, aided by a member of the Neapolitan rap band 99 Posse, this atmospheric place entertains a diverse crowd with its cocktails and experimental electronica acts, including Daddy G from Massive Attack and ex-Fugazi front man Joe Lalli.

S'Move
Vico dei Sospiri 10A, Chiaia, T081-764 5813.
Daily 1000-0300.
Metro: Amedeo.
Opened in 1992, S'Move's stylish three floors serve food and drink throughout the day while by night it hosts mainly house music DJs who get the dressed-up crowd waving their hands in the air, like they just don't care.

Superfly
Via Cisterna dell'Olio 12, T347-127 2178.
Tue-Sun 1700-0300.
Metro: Dante.
Chilled-out lounge and jazz tunes combine with the sleek contemporary decor, making this tiny place a Parthenopean poseurs' paradise. It's worth

popping in for a daiquiri or mojito in the evening when the crowd spills out onto the Centro Antico street.

Velvet
Via Cisterna dell'Olio 11, T328-957 7115, velvetzone.it.
Tue-Sun 2400 till dawn.
Metro: Dante.
Opened way back in the mid-1980s, this historic club has hosted many top indie acts over the years including Massive Attack, and still features an eclectic programme of club nights and gigs.

Cinema
Foreign films in their original language are rarely shown in Italy and Naples is no exception. Warner Village shows the mainstream flicks whereas **Amedeo** (via Martucci, T081-680266), **Academy Astra** (via Mezzocannone, T081-552 0713) and **Modernissimo** screen art-house films. Between June and August the **Cinema d'Estate** festival has outdoor screenings in piazzas and parks such as Parco del Poggio.

Modernissimo
Via Cisterno dell'Olio 23, T081-580 0254, modernissimo.it.
Metro: Dante.
The recently refurbished four-screen Modernissimo in the Centro Antico is the most stylish venue, screening art-house films and hosting left-field

'Videodrome' programmes including MaiGay, which explores sexuality and gender.

Warner Village Metropolitan
Via Chiaia 149, T081-4290 8225, warnervillage.it.
Mainstream Italian films and the latest Hollywood blockbusters dubbed into Italian are screened here.

Gay & lesbian
Although conservative and strongly family orientated, Naples has always been a city with many influences and a free-thinking, open and tolerant core lies at the heart of *Napoletanità*. There may not be exclusively gay venues but there are many club nights. Outlying areas of Naples may have more traditional values but the university quarter and piazza Bellini is the centre of many of the left-field scenes and is a meeting place for the gay community, with **Caffè Letterario Intra Moenia** (see page 136) being particularly popular. However, violent homophobic episodes in 2007 and 2008 highlighted the increasing presence of extreme right-wing elements in the city and all over Italy.

Leone di piazza dei Martiri.

Tip...
A good source of information is **napoligaypress.it** which has up-to-date listings, a gay guide to the city and articles about the gay scene in Naples.

ArciGay Circolo Atinoo & ArciLesbica Circolo le Maree
Vico San Gerolamino 19, T081-552 8815, arcigaynapoli. org, arcilesbica.it/napoli.
Open Mon, Wed, Fri for ArciGay and Tue, Thu, Sat for ArciLesbica, 1730-2030.
Metro: Dante.
The city's main gay and lesbian organizations organize cultural events, parties and political demonstrations. They welcome visitors to their offices in the Centro Antico.

Depot
Via della Veterinaria 72,
T081-780 9578.
Metro: Cavour.
Leather vests and bare chests are
all the rage at this the self-styled
leather cruising bar.

Evaluna
Piazza Bellini 72,
T081-292372, evaluna.it .
Mon-Sat 0930-1400, 1800-2200,
Sun 1800-2200. Metro: Dante.
A relaxing meeting place and
cultural centre that specializes in
womens' books, arty gifts, courses
and esoteric tours of the city.

Freelovers
Freelovers.it, myspace.com/
freelovers.
A full-on partying crowd comes to
these nights organized at various
venues including **Underbridge**
(via San Domenico, T333-334 6216)
and **Arenile** (see page 166).

Spirito Libero at Sud
Terranea Club
Via Quercia 3, T349-674 8557.
Sun 2200 till late. Metro: Dante.
A Sunday *Gay-Lesbo* night
playing Eurodance, Dance
and party tunes.

Sputnik Club
Via Santa Teresa degli Scalzi 154
bis, T081-1981 3222, sputnikclub.it.
Daily 1600 till late.
Metro: Museo.
An intimate internet and gay bar
that opens till the wee early
hours every day.

Music
Classical & opera
As well as grandiose operatic
and classical productions at the
Teatro San Carlo, various
organizations stage chamber
music concerts across the city,
including the Associazione
Alessandro Scarlatti, named after
Naples' most famous composer.

Associazione Alessandro
Scarlatti
Piazza dei Martiri 58,
Chiaia, T081-406011,
associazionescarlatti.it.
Metro: Amedeo.
Check out this well-established
(1918) organization's website for
details of their programme of
chamber concerts held at various
venues including Villa Pignatelli,
Castel Sant'Elmo and the Chiesa
di San Domenico Maggiore.

Centro di Musica
Antica Pietà de' Turchini
Via Santa Caterina da Siena 38,
T081-402395, turchini.it.
Bus C16, E3.
Funicolare: Centrale.
Corso Vittorio Emanuele II.
Baroque music concerts are
staged in the former
Conservatorio della Solitaria,
in the Convent and Church of
Santa Caterina da Siena.

Chiesa Anglicana
15 Via San Pasquale a Chiaia,
Chiaia, T081-411842.
Metro: Amedeo.
The neo-Gothic Christ Church
hosts choral concerts, organ
recitals and renditions of
Handel's *Messiah* at Christmas.

Chiesa Evangelica Luterana
Via Carlo Poerio 5, Chiaia,
T081-663207, lutero.org.
Metro: Amedeo.
Established by the Franco-
German evangelical community
in the 1820s, this Lutheran
church off Piazza dei Martiri
hosts ecclesiastical concerts.

Conservatorio di Musica San
Pietro a Majella
Via San Pietro a Majella 35,
T081-564 4411,
sanpietroamajella.it.
Metro: Dante.
Students and teachers often play
amid the grand surroundings of
this famous conservatory in the
heart of ancient Naples.

Teatro di San Carlo
Via San Carlo 98f, T081-797 2331,
teatrosancarlo.it.
Metro: Dante.
Founded in 1737, this prestigious
opera house attracts discerning
audiences to its lavish ballet and
opera productions and
large-scale classical concerts
staged in the grandest of
settings. Tickets start at around
€25. See also page 83.

Contemporary

There are a few decent small venues around the city like **Velvet** (see page 141), **Doria 83** and **Rising Mutiny** (an offshoot of Rising South, see page 140). The **Otto Jazz Club** organizes concerts including intimate weekend sessions in the Monte di Pietà courtyard (infoline T081-344 3655). Tens of thousands turn out for the likes of Massive Attack, Laura Pausini and R.E.M at outdoor summer festivals **Neapolis** (at the Arena **Flegrea**, see page 166), **Festivalbar** and **Festa di Piedigrotta** – the last two are both staged in piazza Plebiscito.

Around Midnight

Via Bonito 32A, T081-742 3278, aroundmidnight.it.
Tue-Sun 2200 till late.
Metro: Vanvitelli.
Vomero's historic jazz club serves food and hosts mainstream jazz and blues gigs six nights a week.

Doria 83

Via G Doria 83, T081-556 6960, myspace.com/doria_83.
Metro: Vanvitelli.
Alternative live acts, from the mellow indie of Lara Martelli to electro 'parteno-pop' outfit Plastic Penguin, play at this popular venue in Vomero.

Mu Mu Frequencies

Piazzetta Monteoliveto 10, T081-552 4103.
Tue-Sun 1030-2000, 2230 till late. Metro: Dante.
A café cum record shop and second-hand store by day, at night it comes alive with all sorts of live music and DJ shenanigans from Psychobilly to Deep House.

Officina 99

Via Gianturco 101, T081-734 9091, officina99.org.
Metro: Gianturco.
Ska, rock , dub, hip hop, folk and industrial sounds can be heard at this social centre that produced the 1990s rap group 99 Posse.

Rising Mutiny

Via V Bellini 45, T335-879 0428, risingrepublic.com.
Events season runs from late Oct to May. Metro: Dante.
The very intimate 'Arts Club' venue invites the most interesting music acts to its atmospheric cushion-strewn room. Acts to have played number the emerging electro band Fluydo, jazz duo Dave Burrell and Leena Conquest, Brazilian songstress Rosalia De Souza as well as acoustic sets by Neapolitan artists NCCP, Raiz and Teresa De Sio. See Rising South, page 140, for more top acts.

Naples has grand theatres and fiercely independent ensembles, and every night there is something different to see from mainstream TV spin-offs to edgy and experimental works. The productions are mainly in Italian and often in dialect.

Contemporary dance productions appear occasionally on many of the city's theatre programmes while the most lavish ballet productions are staged at the **Teatro San Carlo** (see Music, page 142). Venues include **Teatro Acacia** (via Tarantino 10, T081-556 3999), **Teatro delle Palme** (via Vetriera 12, T081-658 1925), **Teatro San Carlo** (via San Carlo 93, T081-416305) as well as **Teatro Elicantropo** and **Nuovo Teatro Nuovo** (see Theatres, page 144). **Napoli Danza** (napolidanza.com) promotes contemporary dance and runs an annual festival featuring dance videos.

Bellini

Via Conte di Ruvo 14, T081-549 1266, teatrobellini.it.
Metro: Dante.
Epic musicals, classic dramas and occasional concerts are staged at this grand theatre in the Centro Antico.

Shopping

Elicantropo
Vico Gerolimini 3, T081-296640, teatroelicantropo.com.
Metro: Cavour.
Experimental theatre and contemporary dance get a run-out at this tiny space near piazza Cavour.

Mercandante
Piazza Municipio 1, T081-551 3396, teatrostabilenapoli.it.
Metro: Dante.
Innovative writers including the acclaimed musicologist Roberto de Simone and Roberto Saviano, creator of the internationally acclaimed book-turned-play-turned film *Gommora*, are amongst the talent to have recently staged productions at this famous theatre opened in 1779.

Nuovo Teatro Nuovo
Via Montecalvario 16, T081-406062, nuovoteatronuovo.it.
Metro: Dante.
Plays by celebrated playwrights such as Shakespeare, Goldoni, Ionesco and Pinter fill the programme of this innovative theatre.

Sancarluccio
Via san Pasquale 49, Chiaia, T081-405000, teatrosancarluccio.com.
Metro: Amedeo.
Opened in 1972, Teatro Sancarluccio mounts avant-garde productions from Italy and elsewhere – it provided the debut performance of comic actor Massimo Troisi in *La Smorfia*.

Sannazaro
Via Chiaia 157, T081-411723, teatrosannazaro.it.
Metro: Dante.
Although comic productions have always been the mainstay at Sannazaro, one-off events including Burlesque cabaret and unplugged concerts are staged at this elegant theatre.

Napoli has lots of small independent shops and *bancarelle* (stalls) selling all sorts. The main shopping drag is via Toledo, part of which is pedestrianized these days. Bargain hunters should check out the nearby Quartieri Spagnoli, particularly around via Pignasecca and Montesanto, where there's a market. Via della Cavallerizza and via dei Mille have most of the swanky fashion, designer labels and interiors shops. Spaccanapoli, via dei Tribunali and the Centro Antico area are full of family-run businesses selling everything from pasta to historic prints, *presepi* (nativity scenes) and antique marble busts. Port'Alba, off piazza Dante, is famed for its second-hand and specialist bookshops.

Art & antiques
Not surprisingly, given its rich history and artistic heritage, there are lots of *antiquariati* (antique dealers) in Naples, with clusters of antique shops along via Domenico Morelli in Chiaia and all over the Centro Antico, especially on via Santa Maria di Costantinopoli.

Antiquariato Florida
Via Domenico Morelli 13, Chiaia, T081-764 3440.
Mon-Sat 1000-1400, 1630-1930.
Metro: Amedeo.
It's pricey but well worth a look around to see the neoclassical paintings and interesting

portraits, as well as handsome period furniture and the occasional Parisian chandelier.

Il Rigattiere
Via dei Tribunali 281 and 87, T081-299155.
Mon-Sat 1000-1330, 1630-1930. Metro: Dante.
Brigida d'Amato, the spiky and spirited owner of these bric-a-brac shops, is passionate about her city and is happy to tell you about her cornucopia of dusty treasures, which often appear as props in films and on stage.

Quagliozza Salvatore
Via S Biagio dei Librai 11, T081-551 7100.
Mon-Sat 1000-1330, 1630-1930. Metro: Dante.
Antiques and ephemera addicts love the eclectic items often displayed on church steps along Spaccanapoli and this *rigattiere* (second-hand dealer cum rag-and-bone man) is crammed with intriguing oddities from the recent and distant past.

Books
Being the home to an illustrious and influential university, Naples has lots of interesting bookshops. Just off piazza Dante, via Port'Alba is famed for its second-hand and specialist outlets and stalls.

Feltrinelli
Via Santa Caterina a Chiaia 23 (Piazza dei Martiri), T081-240 5411, lafeltrinelli.it.
Mon-Thu 1000-2100, Fri 1000-2200, Sat 1000-2300, Sun/public holidays 1000-1400, 1600-2200. Metro: Amedeo.
The nationwide chain's flagship Naples shop has it all covered including an English-language section and stacks of CDs, DVDs magazines and stationery. There's even a café, which hosts regular cultural events including appearances by musicians such as Almamegretta and Daniele Sepe.

Tip...
Shops are open Monday to Saturday from around 0900 to 1300 and then from 1600 to 2000. Most of them close 1330-1600; Monday mornings in the winter; and Saturday afternoon in the summer. Sales are held in January and in mid-July to August.

Above: Centro Antico *rigattieri*. Opposite page: *Musica napoletana*.

Five of the best

Fashion outlets in Chiaia

Jossa (via Carlo Poerio 43, T081-240 5207) Nook, Diptyque, Costume National and Yohji Yamamoto are amongst the trendy labels sold here.

Marinella (Riviera di Chiaia 287, T081-764 4214, marinellanapoli. it, Mon-Sat 1000-1330, 1630-1930) Kennedy, Gorbachev, Gabriele d'Annunzio and Caruso have all touched the cloth at this famous old shop approaching its centenary. It's still the place to purchase a quality *cravatta* (tie), and they also do cashmere sweaters, jackets and accessories for gents.

Maxi Ho (via Nisco 23/27, T081-427530) Men's and women's designer *vestiti* (clothes including the odd string vest) at reasonable prices.

Mercatino di San Pasquale di Chiaia (via San Pasquale di Chiaia) Italian market stalls are often only full of cheap imports but this one has some quality garments at bargain prices. Remember to barter though. Near the Scuola Umberto there are fruit and veg stalls.

Nennapop (via Nardones 22, T081-1956 9000) Colourful accessories and lots of quirky clothes and shoes by emerging designers, including Maria Grazia.

*As selected by **Michelle**, resident of Chiaia and Capri*

Intra Moenia
Piazza Bellini and via Benedetto Croce 38, T081-290 988.
Daily 1000-0200. Metro: Dante.
The arty café-shop (see page 136) and its right-on sister shop Edizioni Intra Moenia stock lots of Napoli-themed black-and-white postcards, excellent books of photojournalism as well as unusual prints and books, many with an historical, political or cultural slant.

Libreria Neapolis
Via San Gregorio Armeno 4, T081-551 4337.
Mon-Fri 1000-1630, Sat 1000-1400. Metro: Dante.
All things to do with Naples and its culture, and the south of Italy, fill the pages of the publications in this interesting little bookshop in the midst of via San Gregorio Armeno's nativity scene frenzy.

Treves
Via Toledo 249-250, T081-415211.
Mon-Sat 0930-1330, 1630-2000.
Metro: Dante.
Along the pedestrianized section of via Toledo, this long-established shop (opened in 1861) has a great selection of books including lots of cookery and guide books, some in English.

Chocolates
Gay Odin
Via Toledo 124, T081-400063, gayodin.it.
Mon-Sat 0930-1330, 1630-2000.
Metro: Dante.

Gay Odin's chocolates are as flamboyant as its famous name, which first hit the street in the 1920s: *Vesuvio* is laced with rum and *la foresta* is the poshest, crumbliest and flakiest chocolate log ever tasted. There are eight other outlets in Naples, including one at via Benedetto Croce 61.

Clothing
If you're after the designer labels like Armani, Prada and Bulgari then head to the Chiaia area and these streets: via Chiaia, via della Cavalerrizza, via Poerio, via Filangeri and via dei Mille. Before entering some designer-label shops in and around piazza dei Martiri you may be vetted before they buzz you in. It's nice clobber if they like the cut of your jib.

London Outlet
Via del Nilo 33 and 71, T081-295494, londonsas.it.
Mon-Sat 1000-1400, 1630-2000.
Metro: Museo.
Urban clothing, art and music come together at this shop in the Centro Antico.

Department stores
Coin
Via Scarlatti 86/100, T081-578 0111, coin.it.
Metro: Vanvitelli.
Mon-Fri 1000-2030, Sat 1000-2030, Sun/holidays 1030-1400, 1630-2030.
Italy's ubiquitous department store is always good for a

browse. There are usually bargain accessories to be found, while the excellent kitchen department stocks plenty of stylish gadgets and cutlery.

Doll repairs
Ospedale delle Bambole
Via San Biagio dei Librai 81, T081-563 4744, ospedaledellebambole. Sun-Fri 1030-1400, 1700-2000. Metro: Dante.
You might not be in possession of a doll requiring emergency treatment, but don't let that put you off a visit to the Dolls Hospital, a magical shop crammed with old dolls and doll parts.

Food & drink
Augustus
Via Toledo 147, T081-551 3540. Mon-Sat 0930-1400, 1630-2000. Metro: Dante.
As well as wonderful pastries, Augustus has lots of ready prepared snacks and meals including *pizze, arancini, parmigiane di melanzane* and *pasta al forno.*

Above: Babà. Top: *Frutta e verdura.*

Charcuterie Esposito
Via Benedetto Croce 43, T081-551 6981. Mon-Sat 0930-1400, 1630-2000. Metro: Dante.
Should you need some Neapolitan delicacies like mozzarella or even unusual pasta shapes to take home, this place on Spaccanapoli is full of gastronomic goodies.

Enoteca 2000
Via Tribunali 33, T081-211 0079, professionevino.it. Metro: Dante.
This is a good spot in the Centro Antico to pick up wines and spirits at very reasonable prices.

Gastronomia L.U.I.S.E.
Piazza dei Martiri 68, Chiaia, T081-551 6944. Mon-Sat 0830-1400, 1630-2000. Metro: Amedeo.
This posh deli is packed with local specialities and has a tiny bar manned by one barista.

Mercadante
Corso Vittorio Emanuele, 643/644, T081-680964. Mon-Sat 0930-1330, 1630-2000. Metro/Cumana: Corso Vittorio Emanuele.
With over 2000 wine labels from all over the world and especially strong on Southern Italian and Tuscan wines, Mercadante have now added a wine bar to their wine shop, so you can sit down, quaff and snack on quality cheeses, *salume* and chocolate

while you're selecting your *etichette* (wine labels).

Homeware
Bonetti
Piazzetta Carolina 16/17, T081-764 5433. Mon-Sat 0930-1330, 1630-2000. Metro: Amedeo.
Rows of shiny *caffetiere* in the shop window beckon you into this place near piazza Plebiscito. Pick up and feel the quality of their Italian kitchen products including weighty pans, elegant glassware and stylish espresso cups.

Culti Spacafé
Via Carlo Poerio 47, T081-764 4619. Daily 1000-1400, 1600-2000. Metro: Amedeo.
Japanese-style goods for the home and stylish accessories are on display at the front and there's also a smart café, a spa and a hammam.

Spina
Via Pignasecca 62, T081-552 4818. Daily 1000-1400, 1600-2000. Metro: Montesanto/Dante.
If you fancy recreating your very own Italian bar at home or need

Listings

new kit for the kitchen, this shop in the Quartieri Spagnoli, established in 1870, is a must-visit.

Markets
Naples has some fantastic markets including the ever-entertaining **Mercato di Porta Nolana** (see page 113) which has just about everything legal and otherwise. For food, the markets at **Porta Capuana** (sometimes called **Mercato dei Vergini**) and **Via Pignasecca** (off via Toledo) are superb. Under the towers of the Castel Nuovo there is the daily **Mercato dei Fiori** (flower market) – get there at the crack of dawn for the freshest petals. The **Fiera Antiquaria** (fieraantiquariana poletana.it,

T081-761 2541), the antiques market, is held in and around the Villa Comunale from 0800 to 1400, usually on the third Sunday of each month and the preceding Saturday – check for the latest details.

Multimedia & music
Fnac
Via Luca Giordano 59, T081-220 1000.
Mon-Sat 0930-2000, Sun 1000-2000.
Metro: Vanvitelli.
Time wasters will enjoy browsing through the multimedia gadgets, cameras, music and DVDs here. You may even find a Morricone soundtrack, Pasolini flick or Zucchero collaboration to enhance your life.

Outdoor equipment
Arbiter
Via Toledo 268, T081-416463.
Mon-Sat 0930-2000.
Metro: Dante.
According to vulcanologist guide Roberto Addeo and walking expert Giovanni Visetti, Arbiter is the best shop for outdoor equipment in Campania.

Wellbeing
Farmaceutica di Santa Maria Novella
Via Santa Caterina a Chiaia 20, Chiaia, T081-407176.
Mon 1630-2000, Tue-Sat 1000-1315, 1630-2000.
Metro: Amedeo.
This branch of the 800-year-old Florentine pharmacy is famed for its herby perfumes and almond hand cream.

Il Rigattiere, via dei Tribunali.

Souvenirs

Via San Gregorio Armeno is the world-famous home of skilled artisans who make *presepi* (nativity scenes) and figurines. For those wanting to pimp their crib there are dizzying lines of miniature shepherds, animals and fake moss-and-bark trees. These shops also do a roaring trade in caricature figures of the famous. On Spaccanapoli the curious trappings of Neapolitan superstition are sold everywhere: horns of many sizes and charts to help you live by *la smorfia* – an amusing yet, to many, deadly serious system of using images seen in dreams to win the *lotto*.

Tip...

Perennially unlucky? You never know, a visit to one of the curious *bancarelle* (stalls) and outlets along Spaccanapoli may change your fortunes. It will certainly give an insight into Neapolitan superstitions and their accompanying trinkets to ward off *il malocchio* (the evil eye). Among the *corni* (horns of many sizes), incense, *munacielli* (little monks) and amulets you'll also spot illustrated charts to help you live by *la smorfia*: an amusing yet deadly-serious-to-many numbering system, where images seen in dreams were first used in the 19th century to win the Tombolata, nowadays the Lotto. Key numbers include: 3 *Gatta* (cat); 13 *Sant'Antonio* (St Anthony); 21 *Femmena annura* (naked woman); and 83 *Maletiempo* (bad weather).

Via Costantinopoli has interesting antique shops and a very special *stamperia* (printing press).

Giuseppe Ferrigno
Via San Gregorio Armeno 8, T081-552 3148.
Mon-Sat 0930-1900.
Metro: Dante/Museo.
Only traditional materials – including terracotta, wood and silk – go into the making of these hand-crafted *presepi* figurines. After the death of world-renowned *maestro del pastore* Giuseppe Ferrigno in 2008 at the age of 73, his son Marco continues the family tradition begun in 1836.

Mario Raffone
Via Costantinopoli, T081-459667.
Mon-Fri 0930-1330, 1600-1930
Metro: Dante.
This *stamperia* (printer) once supplied the Bourbon royal family and is a wonderful place to see old Heidelberg presses in action and to meet charming Mario Raffone. They produce exquisite prints and cards, including limited edition *incisioni* (etchings) of Vesuvius and prints of nativity figures.

Activities & tours

Cultural

Arethusa
T0823-448084, arethusa.net.
This company provides group tours all over Italy including guided visits to Reggia di Caserta, and a night-time walk around the palace gardens, Il Percorsi di Luce, accompanied by 18th-century music, atmospheric lighting and theatrical performance.

City Sightseeing Napoli
T081-551 7279, napoli.city-sightseeing.it.
€22 adults, €11 children 6-15, family ticket for 2 adults and 3 children €66 valid for all city routes.
Four open-top city bus tours departing from piazza Municipio allow you to hop on and off at various sights. Headphone commentary is available in eight languages. Line A visits the principal artistic attractions (11 stops including piazza del Gesù and the Museo di Capodimonte) and lasts 75 minutes. Line B tours 12 panoramic spots in 75 minutes including Posillipo and the Castel dell'Ovo. Line C (weekends only) includes San Martino and the Vomero sights, the streets of the Centro Antico, and Chiaia's piazza dei Martiri. The new Line R is a 45-minute tour of the Centro Monumentale and Centro Antico. They also run tours to the new shopping centre near Nola, Vulcano Buono, from piazza Vittoria and piazza Fanzago, and three tours of the Vesuvian sights (see page 201).

Francesco Coda's Soultrain Tours and Taxi Service
T338-945 3222, soul_train@alice.it.
Charming autodidact and English, German and Turkish speaker Francesco is a font of knowledge about Naples, the Campi Flegrei and the *costiera*. He's also a reliable choice for airport transfers. Tours from €35 per hour.

Gaiola
Discesa Gaiola 27-27, T081-570 9499, gaiola.org.
Tours from €5, snorkelling from €15 , diving from €35. Bus 140.
The Parco Sommerso di Gaiola is a protected stretch of Posillipo coastline studied by marine biologists. The friendly Gaiola study group runs fascinating tours of the area and its ruined Roman structures – including the Villa Pausilypon – by land and sea. Other excursions are snorkelling, diving and bird-watching in and around the Pausilypon archaeological site, Marechiaro, the island of Nisida, the Grotta di Seiano and the Baia di Trentaremi.

Tip...
To play sports in Naples you invariably need to head to the hills and suburbs of Naples. The Parco Virgiliano in Posillipo has plenty of space for exercise and there's even a running track, while the lofty Capodimonte park is a wonderful spot for a kickabout and other activities.

Itinera
Corso Vittorio Emanuele 663, T081-664545, itineranapoli.com.
Metro: Corso V Emanuele.
Friendly, English-speaking Francesca Del Vecchio organizes tours around the city and beyond, including trips around the Campi Flegrei sights (see page 166).

Museo Aperto Napoli
Via Pietro Coletta 85, T081-563 6062, museopartonapoli.it.
Thu-Tues 1000-1500.
Metro: Garibaldi/Cavour.
MAN hires out audio guides to 81 Neapolitan monuments and has created four signposted routes around the city's sights. Drop in for information and to use their luggage-deposit service.

Cookery courses
La Cucina di Posillipo Dream
Via Manzoni, 214/O, T081-575 6000, posillipodream.it.
Funicolare di Mergellina: Manzoni.
Enterprising cook Giovanna Raffone runs personalized cookery courses from her B&B kitchen in Posillipo, where you can learn how to make frittura di mare (fried seafood medley) and survey stunning views over the Campi Flegrei.

CucinAmica
Via Solimena 80, T081-589 3973, cucinamica.it.
€300 for a 3-lesson weekend course, €400 5-lesson course.
Metro: Vanvitelli.

Carmela Capote, biologist by profession and gluten-free specialist, runs courses teaching both the basics of Neapolitan cuisine and Italian haute cuisine from her Vomero villa.

Cycling
Napoli Bike
Riviera di Chiaia 201, Chiaia, T081-411934, napolibike.com.
Metro: Amedeo.
This friendly shop on the Riviera rents out mountain bikes for €5 for the first hour, €2.50 thereafter, on weekdays 0930-1830. Cycling in Naples is a pretty scary proposition unless you can get your bike out of town by car, so avoiding the dangers of freewheeling on anarchic roads. A good place to cycle is the Parco Virgiliano in Posillipo. Otherwise, a couple of hours in the Villa Comunale gardens opposite the shop and then along the *lungomare*, via Posillipo, to Marechiaro is an option. Good luck!

Diving & snorkelling
See Gaiola above.

Football
Having won two *scudetti* in the late-1980s with Diego Maradona, **SSC Napoli** have been mired in financial woes and mismanagement while rebounding between Serie A and Serie B. The 60,000-capacity San Paolo stadium had a roof added for the 1990 World Cup

Transport

Finals, for which it staged the infamous semi-final between Italy and Argentina, in which Maradona called on Napoli fans to support his nation. Tickets to see SSC Napoli play are available from the stadium in Fuorigrotta (see page 167) and in agencies around town.

Virgilio Club
Via Tito Lucrezio Caro 6, T081-575 5261, virgilioclub.it.
There's a full-size astroturf football pitch, two *calcetto* (5-a-side pitches) and a *discoteca* at this smart club in Posillipo.

Swimming
The sea on the *lungomare* adjacent to the Villa Comunale gardens has been cleaned up of late although it hardly looks enticing. There are fabulous swimming spots outside the city though – mainly on the Amalfi Coast and the Islands. Two public baths with irregular opening hours provide the safest city swimming: **Piscina Collana** (via Rossini 8, Vomero, T081-560 0907) and **Piscina Scandone** (via Giochi del Mediterraneo, Fuorigrotta, T081-570 2636.)

Tennis
Tennis Club Napoli
Viale Dohrn, Villa Comunale, Chiaia, T081-761 4656, tennisclubnapoli.it.
The poshest club in town hosts prestigious tournaments and hires out its clay courts.

Naples

Frequent train services to Ercolano Scavi (20 mins), Pompei (40 mins), Caserta (40 mins), Sorrento (55 mins), Salerno (1 hr) and Rome (2 hrs). Frequent hydrofoils to Capri (35 mins), Procida (40 mins), Ischia (45 mins) and Positano (75 mins). Buses to Pompeii (35 mins), Sorrento (45 mins), Caserta (45 mins), Salerno (70 mins), Benevento (90 mins), Foggia (2 hrs) and Bari (3 hrs).

Right: Ponti Rossi bus.
Below: A pong behind the green car.

Contents

Campi Flegrei

Pozzuoli Baths.

Introduction

A few miles west of Naples, just over the Posillipo hill, are the Campi Flegrei – the Phlegrean (Fiery) Fields. Its Arcadian landscapes may be a tad scruffy these days and don't offer quite the same epic drama as described by Virgil in the *Aeneid*. However, exploring this bubbling volcanic landscape and its colourful Graeco-Roman past, you get the feeling that the Roman poets and chroniclers like Petronius, author of the *Satyricon*, had the juiciest material to inspire their mythical tales and saucy prose. Campi Flegrei's palaces of pleasure witnessed dastardly deeds including the pact that sealed Julius Caesar's fate on the Ides of March.

Dozens of craters lie within the Campi Flegrei caldera system, including steamy Solfatara and eerily beautiful Averno, which the ancients believed to be the entrance to Hades: the Hell that inspired Dante's *Divine Comedy*. Roman Puteoli (modern-day Pozzuoli) was the empire's most important port and has an amphitheatre, Baia has Roman spas above and below the waves, and amid the atmospheric ruins at Cuma there are fantastical stories of an immortal prophetess, the Cumean Sybil.

Through ancient tunnels you emerge at SSC Napoli Stadio San Paolo and traffic-ridden Fuorigrotta, with its curiously Neapolitan theme parks and the monumental, Fascist-era Mostra d'Oltremare, venue of Pizzafest and the Carpisa Neapolis Festival. Ancient and modern mix again at Bagnoli, where the incredible Serino aqueduct passes rusty chimneys and new leisure developments.

Eggy whiff – che puzza!

What to see in...

...one day
Head straight to **Pozzuoli** to see the **Anfiteatro Flavio** and **Solfatara**, followed by **Baia**'s archaeological sites and **Cuma**'s ruins.

...a weekend or more

Linger for longer at **Pozzuoli** and **Baia**, taking in the **Rione Terra** and **Parco Archeologico di Baia** by boat, then visit **Piscina Mirabilis** at Miseno followed by lunch at one of Bacoli's beachside restaurants. **Cuma** and add excursions to the **Astroni** reserve and Bagnoli's changing post-industrial landscape. **Fuorigrotta**'s theme parks, Fascist-era **Mostra d'Oltremare** and an **SSC Napoli** fixture at **Stadio San Paolo** will excite some. Move on to **Procida** and **Ischia** from the port at **Pozzuoli**.

Around the region

First impressions are not great. Traffic, pollution and heavy industry have taken their toll on an area once famed for its lavish roman spa resorts and villas. Fuorigrotta ('beyond the grotto') is accessed via a tunnel that burrows through the hill of Posìllipo. Despite its shabby appearance, there are some stimulating attractions: the Fascist-era Mostra d'Oltremare exhibition centre, Stadio San Paolo (home of SSC Napoli) and the Neapolitan take on the theme park, Edenlandia, next to the zoo. The coastline at Bagnoli is poised to be resurrected from recent industrial ruin. Once a beauty and bathing spot, it was blighted by Second World War bombing and the enormous Eternit/Italsider steel and chemical works, the largest in southern Italy. After years of political wrangling, parts of the rusty *cantieri* are finally being transformed into an aquarium, sports complex, media park and environmental study centre. Already opened is a Science City and the Pontile Nord, a spectacular pier that juts 900 m into the sea. The islet crater of Nisida, where Lucullus and Brutus had villas, is now the home of a juvenile prison and NATO. Within two nearby dead volcanoes, Agnano and Astroni, are a racecourse and a WWF nature reserve.

Mostra d'Oltremare

Viale Kennedy 54, T081-725 8000, mostradoltremare.it.
Metro: Campi Flegrei.

Built by the Fascist government in 1940 and redeveloped in the 1990s, the Oltremare Exhibition Centre stages trade shows and festivals including Pizzafest. There are lots of modern structures in typically bombastic and fantastical Fascist style, including a couple of theatres, pavilions – including the Padiglione America Latina, home to occasional art exhibitions – as well as the monumental Fontana dell'Esedra, whose colossal fountain columns are often lit up in lots of juicy colours. The 6000-seater

Essentials

❶ **Getting around** The Campi Flegrei are 20 mins away by rail or 30 mins by road from Naples.

❷ **By road** Two tunnels emerge at Fuorigrotta. The more scenic Discesa Coroglio descends from Capo Posillipo to Bagnoli, while the inland A56 Tangenziale di Napoli (Naples circular) heads towards Cuma.

❸ **By bus** SEPSA bus route 152 from piazza Garibaldi in Naples is cheap but tortuous. The open-topped Archeobus, also run by SEPSA, is a circular 90-min route that starts and ends at piazza della Repubblica, Pozzuoli, visiting the main archaeological sites (with Artecard). Buses depart on the hour Fri-Sun and public holidays 0900-1900, but check in advance as they are notoriously unreliable. City Sightseeing run a similar service, Retour Campi Flegrei, starting at piazza Municipio, Naples (see page 149).

❹ **Metro and trains** The Metropolitana Linea 2 is handy for Solfatara, Bagnoli and Agnano. The Ferrovia Cumana and Circumflegrea railway lines run from Montesanto station in Naples and are excellent for travelling to and from Pozzuoli and Baia but it's quite a hike (a bus is available) to the ruins from the station at Cuma.

❺ **Train/bus station** Piazza Vincenzo Oriani, Pozzuoli, SEPSA T800-001616, sepsa.it.

❻ **ATM** Banco di Napoli, piazza della Repubblica, Pozzuoli, T081-526 1386.

❼ **Hospital** Ospedale Santa Maria delle Grazie, Pozzuoli, via Domiziana, T081-855 2111.

❽ **Pharmacy** Farmacia Carella, via Terracciano 69, Pozzuoli, T081-526 1162.

❾ **Post office** Corso Umberto 1 63, Pozzuoli, T081-526 1560, Mon-Fri 0830-1830, Sat 0830-1300.

❿ **Tourist information** Main Campi Flegrei tourist office at via Matteotti 1, Pozzuoli, T081-526 6639, icampiflegrei.it, daily 0900-1530. Also at via Risorgimento 28, Baia, T081-868 7541.

Tip…

Save yourself a lot of hassle by buying a **Napoli Artecard** (artecard.it). The *archeologia del golfo* version costs €30 for three days' sightseeing and travel on public transport around the Campi Flegrei and the Vesuvian sights.

Arena Flegrea hosts concerts including gigs by the likes of Massive Attack and REM during the annual Neapolis Festival.

Edenlandia

Via JF Kennedy 76, T081-239 1348, edenlandia.it.
Mon-Fri 1500-2000, Sat-Sun and holidays 1030-1200, €2.50, free children under 110 cm, €2 per ride or €10 for a bracelet that allows unlimited rides.
Ferrovia Cumana: Edenlandia-Zoo.

An entertaining insight into Neapolitan family life with a few fairground rides along the way. Dodgems, carousels, a flight simulator, video arcades, tenpin bowling, water flumes and family-friendly restaurants keep the hordes happy.

Zoo di Napoli

Via JF Kennedy 76, T081-610 7123, lozoodinapoli.it.
Apr-Oct 0930-1800, Nov-Mar 0930-1600, €5, free children under 80 cm. Ferrovia Cumana: Edenlandia-Zoo.

Naples Zoo nearly joined the extinct list a few years back but was saved after a high-profile campaign. A walk around provides a real eye-opener into the Neapolitan relationship with animals and the natural world. You can see exotic animals including Indian elephants, lions, tigers, leopards, deer, llamas, buffalo and bears as well as many bird species including pelicans and pink flamingos. There's also a *fattoria* (farm) where you can pet ponies, cuddle rabbits and feed goats.

Città della Scienza

Via Coroglio 104, Bagnoli, T081-735 2111, cittadellascienza.it.
Tue-Fri 0900-1700, Sat-Sun 1000-2100 (Mar-May also open Mon), €7, €5 3-18 years. Ferrovia Cumana to Bagnoli, then bus C9, or Metro to Campi Flegrei, then bus C10.

Bagnoli's rebirth as a resort was kick-started with this multimedia science centre. A former Italsider factory building now contains an impressive series of exhibition spaces that are especially suitable for families. There are themed sections – including Signs, Symbols & Signals and Science & Nutrition – and lots of interactive displays. In the Planetarium, the heavens are projected onto a huge cupola. Elsewhere, contemporary artists including Sol Lewitt explore the relationship between art and science.

Ippodromo di Agnano

Via Raffaele Ruggiero, T081-735 7111, ippocity.info.
Bus C2 or Ferrovia Cumana to Agnano; if driving, take the Agnano exit off the A56 Tangenziale, then follow signs for Ippodromo.

Gallopo and *trotto* (horseracing and chariot racing) are staged within a dead volcano crater that has been turned into a hippodrome. Most weeks there are four meetings: check the calendar on the website or call them for the latest. Between races you can visit their contemporary art gallery, which continues the equine theme.

Grotta di Seiano.

Around the region

Riserva Cratere degli Astroni

Via Agnano agli Astroni, Pianura,
T081-588 3720, wwfnapolinord.it.
Daily 1000-1600.
Ferrovia Circumflegrea to Pianura, then bus C14;
if driving, take the Agnano exit off the A56
Tangenziale, then it's 1 km to Pianura.

Lush woods interspersed with lakes, streams and a
network of paths make up the 300-ha WWF Astroni
Nature Reserve. You wouldn't know it but the former
Bourbon royal hunting grounds and its three hills –
Imperatrice, Pagliaroni and Rotondella – sit within a
long-dead volcano that last erupted 4000 years ago.
You can hire bikes and explore the landscape which
is teeming with rare plants, handsome trees such as
red oak, lots of birdlife ranging from blackcaps to
geese and heron, as well as mammals including
wolves, dormice and rodents. One of the Astroni's
loudest residents is the greater spotted woodpecker,
which is the symbol of the park.

Busy port town Pozzuoli (Roman Puteoli) is
beset by volcanic ups and downs, and awash with
ancient ruins – including the Anfiteatro Flavio. The
curving bay has ancient, grimy charm. After years
of neglect following an earthquake in 1980, the
childhood home of Sophia Loren has attracted
investment recently and is now on the up,
economically. Further west are Baia and Bacoli,
where there's the Museo Archeologico dei Campi
Flegrei and the remnants of once-lavish Roman
villas, gardens and thermal baths that can be
seen under the sea. There are dead volcanic craters
turned into eerie lakes (Averno, Lucrino, Fusaro and
Miseno), incredible feats of Roman engineering
(Piscina Mirabilis, Cento Camerelle and Arco Felice)
and – perhaps topping them all for atmosphere –
the picturesque Graeco-Roman ruins at Scavi di
Cuma. Some bonkers mythology and the juiciest
history imaginable, which spawned Satyricon and
satire, add to the bubbling pot of wonders here.

Above: Capo Miseno and beyond. Opposite page: Il Serapeo.

Serapeo (Tempio di Serapide)

Via Serapide, Pozzuoli, T081-526 6007.
Wed-Mon 0900 to 1 hr before sunset, closed Tue,
€4, €2 18-25, free under 18/over 65.
Metro/Ferrovia Cumana: Pozzuoli.

Not far from the Cumana station lie the sunken
remains of a Roman *macellum* (market), complete
with the imprints of 36 shops, dating back to the
first and second centuries AD. The site is usually
referred to as the Temple of Serapis, named after
the discovery of a statue of the Egyptian deity
much venerated under Emperor Vespasian.
The architectural fragments, including marble
columns, are sometimes submerged after a deluge.
Look closely and you'll discover tiny holes created
by marine molluscs, which tells us that the site
once lay under the sea. This is prime evidence of
the bradyseism – the gradual subsiding and lifting
of the earth's surface – that has affected the Campi
Flegrei over the centuries.

Rione Terra

Largo Sedile di Porto, Pozzuoli, T848-800288.
Sat-Sun 0900-1800, €3, €2 6-18 years, free under
6/over 65; €4 guided tour 45 mins.
Metro/Ferrovia Cumana to Pozzuoli, then a
10-min walk towards the old town.

Archaeological excavations in the 1990s uncovered
underground Roman streets filled with shops and
fountains on this tufa outcrop, currently 33 m
above the sea. Visitors can now go on a fascinating
tour following the old *decumanus* (the main
east-west high street), dipping into grain stores,
side-street taverns and gladiators' quarters.
Incredible artefacts found here can be seen at
the Museo Archeologico dei Campi Flegrei at Baia.

Anfiteatro Flavio

Via Terracciano 75, Pozzuoli, T081-526 6007.
Wed-Mon 0900 to 1 hr before sunset, €4, €2
18-24, free under 18/over 65.
Metro/Ferrovia Cumana to Pozzuoli, then a
10-min walk up hill or bus 152 or P9.

Built between AD 67 and 79 during Vespasian's
reign, the Flavian Amphitheatre's impressive
40,000-capacity structure looms out of busy
roads and a scruffy modern backdrop. It measures
147 x 117 m, making it the third largest Roman
amphitheatre. A strange scene unfolds while
exploring the overgrown grounds, which are
strewn with toppled columns and ancient
fragments – including the odd oversized marble

Tip...

Get the most out of a visit to the Campi Flegrei by
hiring a driver and tour guide (see page 166). With
a driver you can linger at the lakes, pass through
the arches of the Arco Felice aqueduct and visit the
colossal Roman cisterns Piscina Mirabilis and Cento
Camerelle at Bacoli.

Tip...

A *biglietto cumulativo* (combined ticket) includes entry to the Anfiteatro Flavio and Serapeo in Pozzuoli, the Museo Archeologico di Baia and Scavi di Cuma. It costs €4 and is valid for two days.

foot. An open corridor offers glimpses of the gladiatorial arena, and a rectangular ditch at its heart once housed wild beasts who were hoisted into the melee. In late antiquity the nearby Solfatara volcano spewed ash and other volcanic debris into the amphitheatre, preserving the underground chambers' architectural features. It has staged many a drama: San Gennaro, patron saint of Naples, was imprisoned here in AD 305 alongside other Christian martyrs; notorious exhibitionist Nero lanced a bull here; and some scholars believe that the arena used to be flooded for mock sea battles.

Solfatara

Via Solfatara 161, Pozzuoli, T081-526 2341, solfatara.it.
Daily 0830-1900, €5.50, €4.40 Artecarde €4 4-10, free under 4.
Metro/Ferrovia Cumana to Pozzuoli, then bus P9 or an 800-m walk up hill.

Northwest of Pozzuoli, this 4000-year-old sulphurous volcanic crater splutters, hisses and froths sulphurous geysers and mud. Recent seismic studies have found increased activity in the Campi Flegrei area but the good news is that Solfatara, the most currently active of the volcanoes of the Phlegrean Fields, hasn't erupted since the 12th century and its energy is on the wane. Bocca Grande (Big Mouth) jettisons water vapour at 70°C and the hollow-sounding ground is stained with luridly red arsenic and yellow sulphur deposits. Hydrogen sulphide vapours with the whiff of rotten eggs did not deter ancient spa-goers and Grand Tourists from bathing in and drinking from the mineral-rich springs and fumaroles. The otherworldly, scalding landscape (don't wear rubber soles or flip-flops!) combined with hissing and gurgling noises, and foul smells make it all very disorientating but thrilling. A well purportedly produces medicinal water, and you can peer into ancient *sudutoria* (steam grottoes) aptly named Purgatory and Hell.

Parco Archeologico di Baia

Via Fusaro 75, Baia, T081-523 3797.
Tue-Sun 0900 to 1 hr before sunset,
€4 valid for 2 days including entrance to Museo Archeologico di Baia, Anfiteatro Flavio, the Serapeo and Scavi di Cuma.
Ferrovia Cumana to Baia then stairs on piazza de Gasperi to entrance.

The most fashionable and decadent of all Roman resorts – *Baiae* – can be explored on the slopes behind Baia station. Bulbous domed baths of Diana, Venus, Sosandra and Mercury, and the ruins of a first century BC imperial Roman palace built by Ottaviano make up part of this sprawling site, part of which is under the sea (see Baia Sommersa page 166). Learned Holy Roman Emperor Frederick II reopened many of the establishments in the 1400s as did the Spanish viceroys in the 18th century. Alas, the land has since subsided and most of the hot water emerges elsewhere. For eerie and muddy echoes of the ancient past dust off your best Latin dialect and pour water over yourself below the world's oldest large-scale dome within the Tempio di Mercurio, part of the old spa complex. More strange acoustics can be experienced underneath the arches of the Cryptoporticus, a large cistern that fed the baths.

Right: Bocca Grande strikes again.
Opposite page: Baia Sommersa boat – *Cymba*.

Craters full of secrets

Campi Flegrei's *crateri vulcanici* yielded lots of secrets. Many of them are filled with water now, and Roman sources describe them being put to use as oyster farms and military harbours. Virgil described one such lake, Lago d'Averno (Lake Avernus), in his epic poem the *Aeneid*. Avernus derives from the Greek name Aornus ('without birds'), alluding to the noxious fumes that asphyxiated birds flying over the lake. Lago del Fusaro (Lake Fusaro), famed for its wildfowl and mussel farming, is graced by the elegant Bourbon hunting lodge **Casina Vanvitelliana** (T081-868 7635, guided tours only Sun 1030-1330 and 1530-1830, €2) whose guests have included Mozart. Lago Miseno (Lake Miseno), also known as Mare Morto (Dead Sea), was the home of the Roman fleet dockyards, Portus Julius. Tiberius was suffocated at Misenum. Lago Lucrino (Lake Lucrino) – also known as Piriflegetonte, the River of Flames – where Cicero had a Roman villa is a mere tenth of its size since the 1538 eruption of Europe's newest mountain, Monte Nuovo, nearby. Astroni is now a nature reserve and Agnano, the area's oldest volcano, was once a lake and a Roman thermal bath complex – it now stages chariot horseracing.

Fiery Fields legends

❶ The soothsayer Sibyl cast spells at her Cumaean bolthole.

❷ Caligula built a 3-mile bridge of boats from Baiae to Puteoli, and rode across it on horseback.

❸ Cleopatra, who according to some was no oil painting, bathed at Baiae.

❹ Hellish Lake Avernus was the entrance to Hades, the mythical underworld.

❺ Claudius was poisoned with a dodgy mushroom.

Museo Archeologico dei Campi Flegrei

Via Castello 45, Baia, T081-523 3797.
Tue-Sun 0900 to 1 hr before sunset, €4, €2 18-25, free under 18/over 65. Ferrovia Cumana to Baia, then 15-min walk or local bus up the hill.

The 15th-century Aragonese castle housing the Campi Flegrei Archaeological Museum commands fabulous views over the Baia promontory and archaeological area. Highlights of the collection include the Ninfeo di Punta Epitaffio, a recreated Nympheum with statues found in the sea; the Sacello degli Augustali (a shrine dedicated to the emperor's cult, found at Misenum); and the Sala dei Gessi with its plaster-casts of celebrated Greek statues used as models by a sculptor's studio during the first to second centuries AD. In between there are lots of salvaged mosaic floors, ceramics, jewellery and coins.

Piscina Mirabilis

Via A Greco 10, Bacoli, T081-523 3199.
Generally open Mon-Fri 0900 to dusk.
Ferrovia Cumana to Baia, then bus.

You wouldn't believe it from the messy Bacoli neighbourhood and its exterior but within this hump of tufa and weeds is a subterranean structure with cathedral-like wonders. The largest known Roman freshwater reservoir impresses with its scale, acoustics, atmosphere and bare facts: it's 15 m high, 72 m long and 25 m wide. Only mossy dribbles penetrate its vaulted ceilings and a few puddles gather amid its 48 cruciform pillars, yet it once contained around 12,000 cu m of water to feed the area's villas, spas and the Imperial fleet at Portus Julius. The water came from the Apennines near Avellino, some 160 km away, travelling along the Aqua Augusta (Serino Aqueduct) and serving Pompeii, Pozzuoli and Naples on the way.

Cento Camerelle

Via Cento Camerelle 165, Bacoli, T081-523 3199.
Call in advance for opening hours.
Ferrovia Cumana to Baia, then bus.

The remains of a once lavish two-storey Roman villa belonging to Ortensio Ortalo, dating from the Republican era and the first century AD, contains atmospheric vaulted passageways and cisterns hewn out of the tufa rock.

Bacoli & Capo Miseno

Bacoli has a curving bay and beach that attracts families and weekend hedonists who enjoy the smart bars and clubs along here. At the head of the promontory is Capo Miseno (Roman Misenum), with its 78-m-high cliffs and a 19th-century lighthouse

Tip...

A word of warning at Piscina Mirabilis: you may have to track down the key holder who lives nearby and is sometimes held up making her pasta sauce.

overlooking Lake Miseno. Misenum became the home of the Roman fleet and its admirals, including Pliny the Elder, when the original Portus Julius at Lake Lucrino, Baia silted up. The Miliscola beach here is popular with Neapolitans.

Scavi di Cuma

Via Monte di Cuma 3, Cuma, T081-854 3060. Daily 0900 to 1 hr before sunset, €4, €2 18-25, free under 18/over 65. Ferrovia Cumana to Baia then bus, or Circumflegrea to Fusaro then bus.

The ancient Greeks settled here in 730 BC, making Cumae the first colony of Magna Graecia. Its picturesque ruins spark the imagination with its ancient myths. A couple of hours are enough to explore the parkland, with its crumbling remains and a creepy cavern. Fabulous views of the coastline and architectural fragments belonging to an acropolis (two large temples dedicated to Apollo and Jupiter that were transformed into churches in the fifth and sixth centuries) can be seen atop a hill – it's a breathtaking spot for a picnic. These basilicas were toppled by 10th-century Saracen raiders. Most of what you see dates from Roman and early Christian times.

The biggest draw is the 130-m-long trapezoidal tunnel, the Antro della Sibilla (Cave of the Sibyl). Hewn out of tufa rock, the gallery has an otherworldly ambience that Virgil described in the *Aeneid*, although in truth the structure probably had a funerary or military use. It contains a three-room chamber from where, according to legend, the Cumaean Sibyl helped Aeneas descend into the underworld.

Above: Cave of the Sibyl.
Opposite page: Porto di Baia.

Myth-making & soothsaying

Virgil's *Aeneid* tells of the Trojan hero Aeneas visiting the Sibyl at Cumae. The prophetess falls into a trance and tells Aeneas that he will be the founder of Roman civilization. He then descends into the underworld and talks to his father. Of course the *Aeneid* is a piece of ancient propaganda that, by claiming descent from Aeneas's son Ascanius, created a myth attaching the Greek legends of Troy to the Roman Julio-Claudian dynasty. So Virgil's epic bolstered the imperial claim of Julius Caesar's heirs by making them out to be from gloriously Greek stock. Sibyl's Cave may not contain a supernatural portal to hell but there is evidence that soothsayers were influential in this period, and a Cumean Sibyl probably did exist. Some scientists believe that volcanic gases with psychoactive properties circulated in the chamber, perhaps explaining the stories of wild visions and freaky dancing.

"…you reach the town of Cumae
the sacred lakes, the loud wood of Avernus,
there you will see the frenzied prophetess
deep in her cave of rocks she charts the fates
…She will unfold for you…
the wars that are to come and in what way
you are to face or flee each crisis…"

From Virgil's *Aeneid*, first century BC.

Sleeping

The Campi Flegrei is not renowned for its excellent hotels but things are changing, slowly. Remember, you can get here from nearby Naples quite easily so the area can be visited on day trips and may include a foray to the nearby islands of Procida and Ischia.

Pozzuoli, Baia, Bacoli & Cuma

Cala Moresca €€
Via Faro 44, Bacoli, T081-523 5557, calamoresca.it.
Located on a hill above Miseno, this hotel is set amid gardens with a large pool, tennis court and a kids' playground. There's also a gym and access to a private beach. Many of the 36 functional rooms and nine mini-apartments have balconies with views towards Procida and Ischia.

Villa Giulia €€
Via Cuma Licola 178, Pozzuoli, T081-854 0163, villagiulia.info.
If you have the use of a vehicle this is a great base. The neighbourhood may not be beautiful but within the high walls of this historic townhouse garden there are citrus trees, a pool and a Neapolitan summer kitchen, where you can make a proper pizza. There are doubles and five apartments of various sizes. The English-speaking owner can provide meals and arrange activities including golf, tennis and horse riding.

Batis €
Via Lucullo 101, Baia, T081-868 8763, batis.it.
There's a youthful vibe at Batis and well-priced, attractive rooms – some have mezzanine bedroom areas. It makes a good, sociable base from which to explore Baia's archaeological sites as the spa ruins are nearby and there's a self-styled 'art lounge' bar that hosts latino dance nights and live music.

Hotel Miseno €
Via della Shoah 21, Porticciolo Casevecchie, Bacoli, T081-523 5000, hotelmiseno.it.
The harbourside hotel is nothing special inside but it's the serene location and unfussy vibe that charms. You may not get immaculate rooms and state-of-the art facilities but the family-run bar-ristorante **Miseno a'mmare** is tops for quality seafood and samba music. Excursions, boat trips and airport transfers can be easily arranged as well.

Hotel Relais Villa Oteri €
Via Lungolago, 174, Bacoli, T081-523 4985, villaoteri.it.
Villa Oteri provides elegance and a great location at a very affordable price. Close to Bacoli's beach and bars, it has nine well-turned-out rooms and a restaurant, and offers discounted entry to the Stufe di Nerone spa up the road. Discounts are also available for use of nearby pool and beach facilities.

Self-catering

Averno Damiani Camping, Hotel & Apartments
Via Montenuovo Licola Patria 85, Pozzuoli, T081-804 2666, averno.it.
It's not a luxury Imperial complex but you get good value accommodation and lots of activities and facilities here, including spa, gym, *campo di calcetto* (five-a-side football pitch), swimming pools, go-karting, restaurant and a disco. There are pitches for tents and caravans, as well as hotel rooms (€85-105) and apartments with kitchenettes (€100-140).

Il Casolare
Via Pietro Fabris 12/14, Bacoli, T081-523 5193, sibilla.net/ilcasolare.
Agriturismo goes boho in this rustic 19th-century *masseria* (grand farmhouse). Colourful artworks and knick-knacks give the place an earthy and eccentric feel. Four functional rooms (€55-65) provide good value, especially for families. Tobia Costagliola and his friendly troupe create tasty dishes using their homegrown produce.

Eating & drinking

Il Tempio €€€
Via Serapide 13, Pozzuoli,
T081-526 6519.
Tue-Sun 1230-1500, 1900-2300.
Next to the Temple of Serapis,
this pricey place is famed for its
freshly caught *pescato del giorno*
(catch of the day) creations.

Capitello €€
Via Serapide 33, Pozzuoli,
T081-526 879.
Thu-Tue 1230-1500, 1900-2300.
Reliable ristorante serving
classics like *insalate di mare*
(seafood salad), *frittura* (seafood
medley) and *polpettoni*
(Neapolitan-style meat balls).

Garibaldi €€
Via Spiaggia 36, Bacoli,
T081-523 4368.
Tue-Sun 1200-1500, 1900-2300.
Opened in the early 1900s, this
fisherman's favourite beside the
curving bay of Bacoli serves
classic Neapolitan dishes such
as *spaghetti alle vongole veraci*

(spaghetti with mussels) with a
peperoncino (chilli) kick to boot.
The *dolci* include chocolate
mousse and panna cotta with
frutti del bosco (forest fruits).

Lucullo €€
Via Montegrillo 8, Baia di Bacoli,
T081-868 7606.
Oct-May Tue-Sun 1200-1500,
1900-2300.
Francesca di Vecchio, Naples
resident and local tour guide,
reckons Lucullo is "in one of the
most beautiful spots – on a pier
by the sea at Bacoli". Indeed the
varnished wood-filled interior is
reminiscent of a yacht. After
eating their sublime seafood,
there are often some poptastico
piano bar acts to enjoy.

La Villetta €
Via Lungolago 58, Bacoli,
T081-523 2662.
Daily 1200-1500, 1900-2300.
A ristorante-pizzeria that
regularly features in Italian
restaurant guides for its
well-prepared Neapolitan fare:
featuring pizza, seafood, grilled
vegetables and meat dishes.
It overlooks Lake Miseno, has a
leafy courtyard and is close to
Bacoli's bars and nightspots.

Cafés & bars
Buono
Corso Umberto I 43, Pozzuoli,
T081-526 0472.
Thu-Tue 0630-0300.
Good for a savoury or sweet
morning *merenda* (snack) at

the bar or on the terrace
overlooking Pozzuoli's
lungomare. As well as *pizzette*
(mini pizzas) and pastries like
sfogliatelle, they do delicious
ice cream.

Monkey Café
Via Lucollo 2, Bacoli,
T081-868 7082.
Daily 0700-0200.
Popular with the Bacoli *ragazzi*,
they serve all sorts of *spuntini*
snacks including panini, brioche
and roast meats.

Enoteca Partenopea
Viale Augusto 2, Fuorigrotta,
T081-593 7982.
Daily 0900-1330, 1630-2000,
closed Sun afternoon.
Southern Italian specialities,
including wines from Irpinia,
swordfish purée, mozzarella
and Campanian salame fill this
wine bar-deli near the Stadio
San Paolo.

Entertainment

Clubs

Arenile
*Via Coroglio 14/B,
Bagnoli, T081-570 6035,
arenilereload.com.*
A chic beach club overlooking the *pontile nord*, popular with sunbathers by day and clubbers by night, featuring emerging bands and top DJs. Also hosts Napoli jazz festival gigs in August.

Kestè d'Inner
*Corso Umberto I 51/A, Pozzuoli,
T081 551 3984, keste.it.*
Opened in 2008, this stylish arts club hosts contemporary art exhibitions, gastronomic evenings and eclectic musical events.

Nabilah
*Via Spiaggia Roma 15, Bacoli,
T081-868 9433, nabilah.it.*
During the summer, the swankiest beachside bar-club in Italy attracts top DJs like Gilles Peterson.

Turistico Beach Club
Via Miliscola 21, Bacoli, T081-523 5228, lidoturistico.com.
Raucous, hands-in-the air house music on at weekends followed by laid-back tunes after mass, on the *domenica*.

Music

Arena Flegrea
*Viale Kennedy 54, Fuorigrotta,
T081-725 8000.*
The 6000-seater venue stages concerts throughout the year including the Neapolis Festival (neapolis.it) each July.

Shopping

Food & drink

Daber
*Via Anfiteatro 1, Pozzuoli,
T081-526 7443.*
A handy *supermercato* for picnic supplies near the train station and amphitheatre.

Dolci Qualità
*Via Carlo Rosini 45, Pozzuoli,
T081-526528, dolciqualita.com.*
Campanian wine including Per' 'e Palummo (red) and Falanghina DOC (white), as well as Miele d'Acacia – honey produced in the Campi Flegrei/ Castelvolturno area.

Il Mercato Ittico
Pozzuoli.
Pozzuoli's wholesale fish market, one of the biggest in Italy, is next to the Temple of Serapis. The area generally has excellent fishmongers.

Activities & tours

Boat trips

Baia Sommersa
*Porto di Baia, T081-524 8169,
baiasommersa.it.*
Mid-Mar to mid-Nov Tue-Sun 0930-1330, 1530-1930. Artecard discounts on excursions.
Glass-bottomed boat *Cymba* does tours of the underwater archaeological area, including Roman villas and Portus Julius, at 1000, 1200 and 1500 (€10, €9 4-12 years, free 0-3). Their Arkeotour daily tour includes a trip on *Cymba* as well as visits to Baia's and Cuma's archaeological sights (€35 plus €15 for optional lunch). Booking in advance is recommended.

Bus tours

Retour Campi Flegrei
*Largo Castello, piazza Municipio,
Napoli, T081-1930 5780,
retourcampiflegrei.com.*
Fri-Sun (check latest seasonal timetables), €10 1-day ticket, €15 2-day ticket.
Billed as a "Slow journey through myth, history and nature" these bus tours run by City Sightseeing are divided into four itineraries (Puteoli, Cuma, Discesa agli Inferi and Baiae) covering Campi Flegrei's fabulous sights. You even get to drive under the Arco Felice, a Roman arch that forms part of the via Domitiana, an ancient road that linked the Phlegrean Fields to Rome.

Left: *Napoli in Bocca*, Neapolitan cook book.
Opposite page: *Le stufe* – ancient saunas.

Transport

Cultural
Francesco Coda's Soultrain Tours and Taxi Service
T338-945 3222,
soul_train@alice.it.
Engaging autodidact and English, German and Turkish speaker Francesco is a font of knowledge about the Campi Flegrei, Naples and the *costiera*. He's also a reliable choice for airport transfers. Tours from €35 per hour.

Itinera
Corso Vittorio Emanuele 663, Napoli, T081-664545, itineranapoli.com
Friendly English-speaking Francesca Del Vecchio organizes a host of tours around the Campi Flegrei and beyond. From €30 per hour.

Diving
Baia Sommersa
Porto di Baia, T081-524 8169, baiasommersa.it.
Mid-Mar to mid-Nov Tue-Sun 0930-1330, 1530-1930. Artecard discounts on equipment hire. Scuba-diving and snorkelling amid the molluscs and mosaics

of the underwater archaeological area of Portus Julius, including submerged Roman villas, one of which belonged to Lucius Piso, Julius Caesar's father-in-law.

Football
SSC Napoli
Stadio San Paolo, piazzale V Tecchio, Fuorigrotta, T081-239 5623, sscnapoli.it.
Metro: Campi Flegrei/Mostra. Tickets to see SSC Napoli play cost around €25 and are available from the stadium and in agencies around town. The *tribuna laterale*, along the touchline, offers good views of the action.

Swimming
Piscina Scandone
Via Giochi del Mediterraneo, Fuorigrotta, T081-570 2636.
Metro: Campi Flegrei/Mostra. Olympic-size pool, diving areas and regular *pallanuoto* (water polo) matches can be enjoyed at this pool in Fuorigrotta.

Wellbeing
Terme Stufe di Nerone
Via Stufe di Nerone 45, Bacoli, T081-868 8006, termestufedinerone.it.
Subscription €150 for 10 visits. Ferrovia Cumana: Lucrino. This spa complex, near Emperor Nero's sprawling villa, is not the most luxurious but it is very popular and offers 52°C natural steam, outdoor pools and mud treatments. Its steamy reputation would make Nero blush.

Fuorigrotta
Frequent Ferrovia Cumana train services to Napoli Montesanto (6 mins), Bagnoli (7 mins), Pozzuoli (17 mins), Fusaro (27 mins). Bus Linea 1 to Napoli piazza Garibaldi (24 mins) and Solfatara (34 mins).

Bagnoli
Frequent Ferrovia Cumana train services to Napoli Montesanto (13 mins), Fuorigrotta (7 mins), Pozzuoli (9 mins), Fusaro (20 mins).

Pozzuoli
Frequent Ferrovia Cumana train services to Napoli Montesanto (22 mins), Fuorigrotta (16 mins), Bagnoli (9 mins), Fusaro (11 mins). **Caremar** (T081-017 1998, caremar.it), **Medmar** (T081-333 4411, medmargroup.it) and **Procidalines** (T081-896 0328) run hydrofoil and ferry services to and from the Porto di Pozzuoli, Ischia (50 mins) and Procida (15 mins).

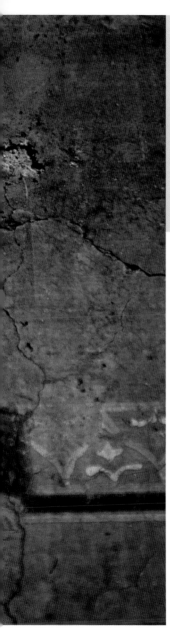
Salve, curly!

Contents

Vesuvius, Herculaneam & Pompeii

Introduction

Nature's awesome power blisters the Neapolitan landscape and psyche. Wherever you are in the Bay of Naples, Vesuvio (Vesuvius) appears in the corner of your eye. A walk around Vesuvius's crater to gaze into its serenely steamy, sulphurous depths is both a humbling and heart-pounding experience. Mainland Europe's only active volcano is 9 km east of Naples. It hasn't erupted since 1944 but it could blow at any time. You can combine an ascent of the mountain with time-travel explorations of its ancient Roman victims – Pompeii, Herculaneum, Oplontis, Stabiae and Boscoreale – buried in the infamous eruption of AD 79 witnessed and recorded by Pliny the Younger. The treasures and revelations, preserved and revealed in the 1700-year-old volcanic time capsules at Pompeii and Herculaneum are particularly brain-blowing. Set aside one day at least to visit Vesuvius and explore the ancient Epicurean resort of Herculaneum. Sprawling Pompeii was a grubbier commercial town and deserves a whole day at least to explore. There are trekking opportunities amid rare species (including 20-odd varieties of wild orchids) and otherworldly-coloured rocks in Vesuvius National Park. The Ville Vesuviane – 18th-century aristocratic residences – dot the Miglio d'Oro (Golden Mile) near its coastal slopes. Juicy fruits of the fecund Vesuvian soil can be sampled everywhere, including the tastiest tomatoes – *pomodorini del piennolo* and *san marzano* – apricots, artichokes, persimmons and grapes that produce the white Vesuvio and Lacryma Christi wines.

Column, Casa del Rilievo di Telefo, Herculaneum.

What to see in…

…one day

Pack a visit to Roman beachside resort **Herculaneum** and the steaming lip of dozing volcano **Vesuvius** into a day. Knee-tremblers are guaranteed scrambling into the crater with a vulcanologist guide.

…a weekend or more

Set aside at least a day to explore the vast remains at **Pompeii** and visit the **Santuario della Madonna del Rosario** nearby. Enjoy a themed tour with **Sogno Pompei**. Use extra days to explore hidden corners of Pompeii, to visit the Vesuvius Observatory and archaeological sites **Oplontis**, **Stabiae** and **Boscoreale**. Experience cultural events at the **Miglio d'Oro** Bourbon-era villas and treks in the **Vesuvius National Park**.

Ercolano & Vesuvius

You can squeeze two stupefying sights and a whole lot of history and geology into a day here. In AD 79 the good, the bad and the scholarly (most Romans were squat and ugly according to the Ercolano guides) of Herculaneum were seared by the instant karma of a 482°C pyroclastic surge that roared down Vesuvius at 400 kph. The depth and heat of the blistering debris that swept into the elegant resort helped preserve organic matter including wooden beams supporting roofs, papyrus scrolls of Greek wisdom, and boats filled with the skeletons of those fleeing for their lives. Herculaneum's intimate scale means you need only a few hours to see the wonders of this Roman time capsule.

Grand Tourists were carried to Vesuvius's summit on sedan chairs or aboard the famous funicular railway, whereas today you are now more likely to use less stylish transport to reach the lip of the volcano. Scientists estimate there to be 400 sq km of molten rock 8 km under the well-monitored volcano, and the authorities reassure Neapolitans that there should be ample warning to evacuate the 600,000 people living in the Zona Rossa (Red Zone) nearest the volcano. Imagine living on the slopes with the threat of a Plinian eruption: in 2007 some scientists controversially posited that an event like the cataclysmic Avellino eruption 3780 years ago is not out of the question.

Herculaneum

*Ercolano scavi (Herculaneum excavations),
corso Resina, Ercolano, information T081-857 5347,
ticket office T081-777 7008, pompeiisites.org.*
Apr-Oct daily 0830-1930, Nov-Mar daily
1000-1700, last entry 90 mins before closing
time, closed 1 Jan, 1 May, 25 Dec.
€11, €5.50 18-25, free under 18/over 65.
Audioguide €7, €4 for children. See below for
details of combined ticket for all 5 Vesuvian sites.
The entrance to the site is a 5-min walk downhill
from Ercolano station.

Herculaneum was a well-to-do Roman town of
around 5000 residents, with elegant seaside villas,
many of which were buried to a depth of over 15 m
by the huge pyroclastic flows of the AD 79 eruption.
In 1709 Emmanuel de Lorraine, Prince d'Elbeuf,
came across the back of the Roman theatre while
digging a well and shortly afterwards the first
haphazard excavations began. The nature of the
volcanic deluge resulted in fewer roofs collapsing
here than in Pompeii, and the searing heat
carbonized organic materials, meaning that
extraordinary architectural details, bodies and

Late morning, early October.

Tip...

You can visit all five archaeological sites – Herculaneum,
Pompeii, Oplontis, Stabiae and Boscoreale – within
three days by buying a *biglietto cumulativo* (combined
ticket) for €20, €10 18-25, free under 18.

Essentials

❶ **Getting around** Reaching Ercolano by train is
easy but ascending Vesuvius is less straightforward:
the Vesuviana Mobilità bus service is the most reliable.

By road Take the A3 Napoli–Salerno Autostrada
and exit at Ercolano.

By tour guide Itinera (T081-664545, itineranapoli.
com) run tours around Vesuvius.

By bus A bus service run by **La Vesuviana Mobilità**
(T081-963 4420, vesuvianamobilita.it) operates between
Naples (piazza Piedigrotta at Mergellina, via Marina at
Molo Beverello and Hotel Terminus on piazza Garibaldi)
and the Vesuvius National Park entrance (€13.30).
It also connects Vesuvius with Ercolano (€7.70) and
Pompeii (piazza Anfiteatro, €8.70). Alternatively take
an infrequent public bus or a small minibus outside
Ercolano station. Combined tickets including entry to
the national park cost €15. Note however that these
minibuses are cramped and do not allow much time
at the summit.

By train From Naples or Sorrento, take the
Ferrovia Circumvesuviana Railway to Ercolano
from the Stazione Vesuviana (Corso Garibaldi;
Metro: Garibaldi); there are stations as far as Sorrento.

❷ **Bus station** piazzale stazione 1, Ercolano.
ANM Autobus T081-7631111.

❸ **Train station** Circumvesuviana Ercolano, piazzale
Stazione 1, T800-053939, T081-772 2444, vesuviana.it.

❹ **ATM** Banco di Napoli, via IV Novembre Ercolano 3,
T081-777 3466.

❺ **Hospital** Ospedale Maresca, via Montedoro 2,
Torre del Greco, T081-849 0191.

❻ **Pharmacy** Corso Italia 9, Ercolano, T081-739 0021,
daily 0900-1300, 1600-2000.

❼ **Post office** Via Panoramica 298, Ercolano, T081-739
5385. Mon-Fri 0800-1330, Sat 0900-1230.

❽ **Tourist information** Via IV Novembre 82, Ercolano,
T081-788 1243. For information about Herculaneum,
check out pompeiisites.org. **Parco Nazionale del
Vesuvio** (piazza Municipio 8, San Sebastiano al Vesuvio,
T081-771 0939, parconazionaledelvesuvio.it) has
information about the park and guided walks in
the area, including night time visits to the crater.
Vesuvius Information Point, Contrada Osservatorio,
T081-777 8069.

objects are still being discovered. Around 300 skeletons were found huddled together in boathouses along with fine jewellery in the 1980s, and it's reckoned that archaeologists have only brushed the surface of the so-called Villa dei Papiri (see page 178) and its fascinating library of Graeco-Roman scrolls. Indeed some hope that papyri will be revealed containing the lost works of Greek writers such as Epicurus, Aristotle and Euripides.

The broad sloping path that curves around and descends into the archaeological site allows you to appreciate the enormity of the AD 79 eruption and the vast amount of debris that buried the town. It also provides an overview of the Roman grid layout of the streets and blocks. The roads orientated north-south are the *cardi* while the east-west routes are called *decumani*. These define the six rectangular *caseggiati* (blocks or sections) of the city, known as *insulae*.

Above: Dramarama.
Opposite page: Fountain head.

Tip...

In the summer months it's best to visit Herculaneum first and then Vesuvius. Off-season, the scarcity of buses may necessitate a trip to the summit in the morning.

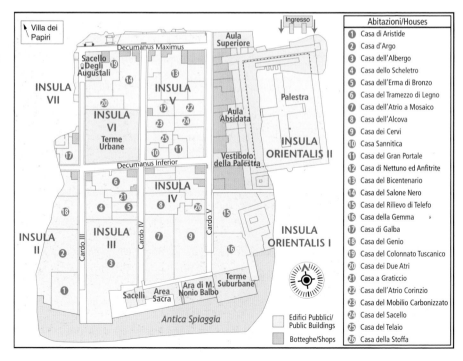

Abitazioni/Houses
① Casa di Aristide
② Casa d'Argo
③ Casa dell'Albergo
④ Casa dello Scheletro
⑤ Casa dell'Erma di Bronzo
⑥ Casa del Tramezzo di Legno
⑦ Casa dell'Atrio a Mosaico
⑧ Casa dell'Alcova
⑨ Casa dei Cervi
⑩ Casa Sannitica
⑪ Casa del Gran Portale
⑫ Casa di Nettuno ed Anfitrite
⑬ Casa del Bicentenario
⑭ Casa del Salone Nero
⑮ Casa del Rilievo di Telefo
⑯ Casa della Gemma
⑰ Casa di Galba
⑱ Casa del Genio
⑲ Casa del Colonnato Tuscanico
⑳ Casa dei Due Atri
㉑ Casa a Graticcio
㉒ Casa dell'Atrio Corinzio
㉓ Casa del Mobilio Carbonizzato
㉔ Casa del Sacello
㉕ Casa del Telaio
㉖ Casa della Stoffa

Insulae II & III The first building on Cardo III Inferiore is the **Casa di Aristide** (House of Aristides) where fleeing victims' skeletons were found. One of Herculaneum's finest villas (discovered in 1828) is next door, the **Casa d'Argo** (House of Argus), named after a painting depicting the myth of Argus, which sadly was stolen. Opposite is the back entrance to the **Casa dell'Albergo** (House of the Inn), not an inn at all but a sprawling villa that was undergoing refurbishment at the time of the eruption. The only private *thermae* (thermal baths) were found here, while a carbonized pear tree trunk was found in the garden.

No prizes for guessing what was found in the **Casa dello Scheletro** (House of the Skeleton). The less palatial **Casa dell'Erma di Bronzo** (House of the Bronze Herm) has a bronze sculpture of the owner and a Tuscan-style atrium. On Cardo IV the

Casa del Tramezzo di Legno (House of the Wooden Partition) is a grand Roman dwelling named after the wooden partition that closes the *tablinium* (main room). Seek out the mosaic paving, corniced façade and dog's-head spouts on the compluviate roof that channels rainwater to a sunken pool. There were shops, including one used by a *lanarius* (fabric maker), known as the Bottega del Lanarius (Store with a Clothes Press) – you can see the instrument inside.

Insulae IV & V You get a feel for the might of tectonic forces at work when you see the geometric mosaic flooring rippled by the eruption in the **Casa dell'Atrio a Mosaico** (House of the Mosaic Atrium). Next door, the **Casa dell'Alcova** (House of the Alcove) has a lavish room with paintings and wooden couches.

Tip...

Allow at least three hours to take in the excavations at Herculaneum. It's an exposed site, so protect yourself from the sun and stock up with cool water from the shop opposite the entrance.

The **Casa dei Cervi** (House of the Deer) was an opulent waterfront residence named after two marble groups of deer being savaged by dogs in the garden (the originals are in the Archaeological Museum in Naples, see page 108). A drunken Hercules relieves himself nearby.

The **Casa Sannitica** (Samnite House) has the layout of a pre-Roman dwelling, with an imposing portal of Corinthian capitals and a graceful open gallery with Ionic columns and fabulous frescoes. Just as grand is the elegant façade of neighbouring **Casa del Gran Portale** (House of the Great Portal) with its two pilasters, demi-columns and carved capitals with winged Greek-style Victories.

Under the **Casa di Nettuno ed Anfitrite** (House of Neptune and Amphitrite) is a well-preserved wine store with intact wooden fittings, counter and shelves for amphorae. Along the east wall is the remarkably vivid Neptune and Amphitrite glass wall mosaic. The much-photographed *nymphaeum* has elaborate decoration depicting hunting scenes and attractive motifs, all topped with a head of Silenus (best mate of wine god Dionysus). On the *decumanus maximus* is the **Casa del Bicentenario** (House of the Bicentenary), found in 1938 by top archaeologist Amedeo Maiuri, 200 years after Charles III began the official digs.

Insula VI The **Terme Urbane** (Thermal Baths) date back to the first century AD, during the reign of Augustus. Separate baths and entrances for men and women are on Cardi III and IV respectively. Unusual red and black interiors mark out the **Casa del Salone Nero** (House of the Black Hall). Worth checking out are the two large panels depicting Jupiter, Hercules, Juno, Minerva and the Etruscan god Acheloo in the **Sacello degli Augusti** (College of the Augustali), the seat of the cult of Emperor Augustus.

Insulae Orientalis I & II Head eastwards to the **Palaestra**, the public sports centre, with its monumental vestibule, a lower terrace with porticoes, a long pool for breeding fish and part of a cruciform swimming pool. Seek out the mythical

Garden of thermal delights

Roman plumbing meets idle pleasures at the Terme Urbane. A large *praefurnium* (furnace/boiler room) heated the baths and water was drawn from an 8-m-deep well. The men's baths have an *apodyterium* (dressing room) with basins for washing and niches for storing clothes. To the left is a round *frigidarium* (cool plunge pool) with a blue vaulted ceiling painted with fish and pierced by a skylight. The temperature rises in the *tepidarium* and *caldarium*. Roman plumbing prowess and engineering ingenuity are displayed in the exposed pipes and smoke vents.

On Cardo IV Superiore is the entrance to the women's baths. It has a magnificently decorated *apodyterium* with mosaic floors depicting Triton swimming with dolphins, a cuttlefish, an octopus and a cherub with a whip. On to the *tepidarium* with its labyrinthine mosaic floor, and then the *caldarium* with white and red marble benches. Check out the grooves in the vaulted ceiling, designed for channelling condensation.

After a stint in the baths the patrons would relax in the porticoed garden, perhaps exercising in the outdoor *palaestra* (gym) or shooting *pila* (a ball game) in the *sphaeristerium*, a covered hall.

five-headed serpent, Hydra, entwined around a tree trunk. The 18th-century Bourbon excavation tunnels run beneath the avenue here, offering an insight into the scale of the excavations.

Moving to the SE corner of the excavations is three-storey **Casa del Rilievo di Telefo** (House of the Relief of the Telephus), Herculaneum's largest villa, named after a bas-relief depicting the myth of Telephus – the son of the god Hercules – founder of the city. Don't overlook the circular plaster cast copies of the original marble *oscilla* (discs depicting satyrs to ward off evil) hung between the red-hued columns. Also on Cardo V is the **Casa della Gemma** (House of the Gem), named after an engraved stone found here, where there are large frescoed panels and refined graffiti in the toilets recording the visit of a renowned physician.

Suburban district On the western fringes of the south terrace are the **Sacelli** (Sacred areas) which have two temples – one dedicated to Venus and the other to four gods: Neptune, Minerva, Mercury and

> 66
>
> You must remember that the Romans were not tall and good looking as they are depicted in the films: the tallest man was 165 cm and the tallest woman was 155 cm – because they all bred with their cousins. And Cleopatra was no beauty either.
>
> 99
>
> *Ercolano tour guide*

– most fittingly – Vulcan. The **Terme Suburbane** (Suburban Baths) has a *frigidarium* with white marble flooring and a *tepidarium* with a stuccoed wall depicting warriors. There's an extraordinary impression made by a *labrum* (washing tub) on the volcanic material that immersed the *caldarium*. Nearby is a half disrobed and handless statue of the senator M Nonius Balbus, an ally of Octavian (who reigned as Augustus from 27 BC to AD 14).

A theatre is buried nearby accessed via 18th-century tunnels dug by Prince d'Elbeuf's speculative excavators – its *scaenae frons* (monumental stage backdrop) was unceremoniously stripped of its lavish

Thermopolium.

decoration and statuary. This area was right on the beach: boat storehouses and warehouses line the old shoreline. In the early 1980s, 300 human skeletons and then a 9-m-long Roman boat containing an oarsman, soldier, swords and a pouch of coins were found here. In 2008 work began on recreating the beach.

Dead city scrolls

Around 1800 papyrus rolls were unearthed in the Villa dei Papiri library, believed to have been collected by the Epicurean scholar and philosopher Philodemus of Gadara. Many of the carbonized scrolls were clumped together and badly damaged by well-meaning conservators attempting to separate the leaves. In the 1990s multispectral imaging techniques developed by NASA were used to decipher the text on the opened scrolls. Most of the scrolls are kept at the Palazzo Reale library in Naples. Astounding discoveries are still being unearthed – in 2007 a throne was found with exquisite ivory bas-reliefs depicting Greek mythological figures.

Villa dei Papiri

Northwest of main excavation.
The villa is currently not open to the public.

Historians believe that this most opulent villa, where a priceless library of papyrus scrolls was discovered, belonged to Lucius Calpurnius Piso Caesoninus, father-in-law of Julius Caesar. In the 1750s engineers dug into the multi-storey villa when excavating a well. The scale and beauty of the residence is mind-blowing: covering almost 3000 sq m, the villa had a 250-m-long shoreline frontage, rooms filled with exquisite art and statuary, a porticoed garden and terraced grounds brimming with vineyards, orchards and fountains. The Archaeological Museum in Naples (see page 108) houses a collection of marble and bronze busts from the villa.

Five of the best

Mosaics in Herculaneum

❶ Terme Urbane

Disrobing females and flies on the steamy walls of the *apodyterium* (changing room) would have got an eyeful looking down at the floor in the Public Baths: floating centre stage is the mermaid-like Greek god Triton wielding a trident in one hand and clasping a fish in the other, while a naughty cherub is ready with a whip. A maelstrom of maritime beasts, including dolphins, a cuttlefish and an octopus, whirl around.

❷ Casa di Nettuno ed Anfitrite

Head to the *triclinium* (a kind of summer dining room/lounge) for a look at vibrant glass paste mosaic designs studded with seashells. On the east wall stands a languid-looking Neptune, the god of water and the sea, grasping his triton alongside his scantily clad queen Amphitrite, who leans on a plinth. On the north wall a *nymphaneum* (fountain and shrine) has similarly vivid tiles depicting dogs chasing deer amid garlands of fruit, flowers and birds. The niche would have held statues and fountains fed by a tank set into the wall.

❸ Palaestra

Mosaic swimmers and an anchor motif once shimmered beneath the water of the gymnasium pool. Although now accessed by cool tunnels excavated from the massive pyroclastic debris (look at the layers and depth!) from the AD 79 eruption, the large alfresco cross-shaped pool here was surrounded by a grandiose colonnade.

❹ Casa dell'Atrio a Mosaico

The rippled geometric designs in the House of the Mosaic Atrium reveal the full force of the AD 79 eruption – the combination of meandering lines and mysterious motifs in the entrance followed by an expanse of chequerboard design buckled by seismic forces strikes an alluring yet unsettling note. Over wavy floors you are led into a grand space with pillars resembling a basilica – this is the Egyptian *oecus* (reception room) that the Roman architectural writer Vetruvius described as being all the rage with nobles wanting to wow their tight curly big-wig guests.

❺ Villa dei Papiri

Archaeologists await further funding and the go-ahead to discover yet more geometric-patterned mosaics and crazy paving in this most exquisite "casa delle Muse": House of the Muses.

Top: Mosaic of Neptune and Amphitrite.
Above: Triton in the Terme Urbane.

Around the region

Museo Archeologico Virtuale (MAV)

Via IV Novembre, Ercolano,
T081-1980 6511, museomav.com.
Tue-Sun 0900-1700, €7.

Opened in July 2008, this €10 million museum near the ruins takes visitors on a virtual journey around the villas and public spaces of ancient Herculaneum. There are lots of interactive multimedia displays to explore as well as some intriguing sights, smells and temperature fluctuations thrown in to get you into the Roman mood.

Ville Vesuviane including Villa Campolieto

Corso Resina 283, Ercolano, T081-732 2134,
villevesuviane.net.
Tue-Sun 1000-1300, free, a 5-min walk heading east from the entrance to Herculaneum.

In the 1700s, sumptuous aristocratic residences were built along the coast from San Giovanni a Teduccio to Torre Annunziata. The celebrated stretch of road from Resina to Torre del Greco known as the *Miglio d'Oro* (Golden Mile) has many a classical pile but alas most are privately owned or in disrepair. Collectively they are known as as the Ville Vesuviane. In Ercolano you can visit the Villa Campolieto, home of the Ente per le Ville Vesuviane that overlooks the restoration and preservation of these mansions – 122 of them – and organizes guided tours, by appointment, of many villas including Villa Favorita. Opportunities to hobnob with the Bourbon descendants are best during the annual events: *Emozioni Vesuviane* (late April to June), the *Festival delle Ville Vesuviane* (when classical concerts are held at mansions built by the likes of Vaccaro and Vanvitelli) and *Natale nelle Ville* at Christmas. The Royal palace **Reggia di Portici** (via Università 100, Portici, T081-775 5109) and its Villa d'Elbeuf by Sanfelice are also open by appointment:

Parco Nazionale del Vesuvio

Park headquarters Ente Parco Nazionale del
Vesuvio, piazza Municipio 880040, San Sebastiano
al Vesuvio, T081-771 0911, vesuviopark.it; visitor
centre at summit T081-777 5720/T081-739 1123.
Public buses run from Ercolano Scavi station at 1010, 1130 and 1240, returning from Vesuvius at 1240, 1350 and 1500 (tickets at Bar Vesuvio). Compagnia Trasporti Vesuviani has a small office outside Ercolano Scavi station and runs regular minibuses (often cramped, so don't bring luggage) to the National Park car park for €10 return or €15 including entrance to the park. The minibus departs for the volcano when full and waits for about an hour at the car park, so there's not that long to enjoy the visit. The park path is open daily from 0900 and closing times vary throughout the year – last admission is about 90 mins before sunset. €7, €5 under 18/student, free under 8 accompanied by an adult.

Summit walk The route to the summit of Vesuvius involves motor transport to the entrance car park followed by a walk over volcanic rocks. All vehicles, bar the jeeps driven by official guides, stop at the car park at 1017 m. The climb to the summit is around 250 m over rough ground, which combined with the heat of a summer's day or high winds can make for an uncomfortable walk for even the fittest person. The Vesuvius National Park

Below: Villa Campolieto. Opposite page: In the crater.

authority looks after the protected area around the volcano and their nature trail (No 5 of nine routes, see page 183) incorporates part of the ascent to the summit and halfway around the crater. Upon reaching the visitors' centre you pay an admission charge to enter the park and go to the crater's rim.

The views along the steep, wide gravelly path and around the mountain are incredible. Inside the crater (out of bounds unless accompanied by a guide, see Great days out, page 182) fumaroles steam amid luridly coloured rock crystals and silver-grey pumice. The 200-m chasm to the floor of the crater adds to the dizzying spectacle. A rusty, makeshift handwritten sign points the way to Pompeii down below. A souvenir stall-cum-bar sells assorted tat, snacks, postcards, refreshments and Lacryma Christi wine.

Osservatorio Vesuviano

Via Diocleziano 328, T081-610 8483, ov.ingv.it. Sat-Sun 0900-1400, free.

Built by Bourbon monarch Ferdinand II in the 1840s, the neoclassical Vesuvian Observatory has an exhibition exploring volcanology, with lots of video, observatory instruments and interesting collections of volcanic rock. Eyes are fixed nervously on the instruments that record the seismic and geochemical activity across 300 sq km – they are monitored closely from the surveillance centre in Fuorigrotta.

A tectonic timebomb

When the Eurasian and African tectonic plates met it was murder: the superheated earth's crust spilled magma into the Bay of Naples, forming the Campanian Volcanic Arc and the volcanoes of Sicily. Vesuvius's Gran Cono (Large Cone) is 1281 m high, 200 m deep and has a diameter of 600 m. It sits within the caldera of Monte Somma, the remains of a larger and higher (1149 m) crater that formed some 18,000 years ago and subsequently collapsed. Between Monte Somma and the Gran Cono is the Valle del Gigante (Valley of the Giant), which is in turn divided between the Valle del Inferno (Valley of Hell) to the east and the Atrio del Cavallo (Hall of the Horse) in the west.

Vesuvius's violent eruptions are called 'explosive' or 'Plinian' eruptions – they propel ash and smoke high into the atmosphere in the shape of an umbrella pine tree, and include the event of AD 79, witnessed and described by the Plinys. The last such explosion in 1631 killed some 4000 people. Recent findings of Bronze Age footsteps and buried skeletons as far away as Afragola and Avellino paint a disquieting picture of the 1780 BC eruption*, dubbed "a first Pompeii". On that occasion a sonic boom accompanied the propulsion of molten rock, cinders and ash at 100,000 tons per second some 30 km into the stratosphere. Northeasterly winds carried pumice and weighty lapilli rocks as far as Nola and Avellino, where over several hours it reached up to 3 m in height. After 12 hours the column collapsed and caused a blistering pyroclastic surge that laid waste to everything in its path – it deposited 20 m of debris some 5 km away.

Alarmingly, the volcano has been dormant for more than 60 years now, the longest period of inactivity in nearly 500 years: the longer the wait, the more the pressure builds below. There have been many 'effusive' eruptions (these spew lava) over the past 25,000 years, including the last eruption in 1944 which killed 26 people. The question is: will the next eruption be effusive or Plinian?

A fascinating piece by Stephen S Hall in the National Geographic (Sept 2007) describes this eruption and the controversial theories of vulcanologists Mastrolorenzo, Petrone, Pappalardo and Sheridan.

Scrambling on cooled magma

Adventurous types will relish a trek in the otherworldly volcanic landscape of Vesuvius National Park or a scramble into the crater itself, accompanied by an expert guide. You can combine a trip to Herculaneum with a trip to the summit, perhaps followed by a trek along one of the designated trails around the park. Sturdy walking boots with ankle support, outdoor kit (from mid-October to May especially) and food supplies are essential.

Into the crater with vulcanologist Roberto Addeo

Special guided tours can be taken from the visitor centre with the likes of amiable Guida Vulcanologica, Roberto Addeo. Roberto explains that the general public are prohibited from going beyond the perimeter fence into the crater unattended as there have been some fatalities over the years: "People have gone down into the crater and have become asphyxiated by the noxious fumes." While experienced personnel abseil down onto the crater floor to take samples, conduct studies and roll hot rocks, regular punters get the chance of a mini-Vesuvian cocktail of adrenaline and eggy-steamy vapours. After a short and slightly tricky 20-m scramble down the slope of the crater, Roberto encourages me to stick my face into the steamy fumaroles to feel and sniff the sulphurous heat of Vesuvius. Glasses steamed up and knees knocking, I look up and hear a young,

My favourite excursion in the National Park is definitely the one which goes right around the crater and then descends into the Valle dell'Inferno where you can see the *bocche* (volcanic fissures) and lava flows of the 1906 eruption.

Roberto Addeo

breathless English voice above: "Oh my god! What are they doing down there? They are crazy!" Roberto regularly confronts the real dangers lurking beneath our feet: "The only things that remind you that the volcano is active, apart from the fumaroles, are the small earthquakes, which start with a muffled sound and then there are the occasional landslides that fill the crater with dust. In those moments you get a little edgy," says Roberto.

Trekking in Vesuvius National Park

For National Park headquarters, visitor centre and transport options to the summit see page 201. For further information and maps contact the park wardens or official guides, T081-777 5720, T337-942249 (mobile), guidevesuvio.it.

Within the Vesuvius National Park there are nine colour-coded trails, varying in difficulty. Trail 4 (orange) is a seven-hour round trip and covers over 8 km of rough terrain including the Tirone Alto Forestry Nature Reserve, established in 1972. On the trail you can hear and see lizards, martens, cuckoos, foxes and hares. Trail 9 (grey) *Il Fiume di Lava* (the Lava Flow) is a much easier 90-minute circular track that starts and ends at via Osservatorio. Amid the 1944 lava flows is a unique yellow lichen species, *stereocaulon vesuvianum*, that thrives on mineral-rich magma and whose very mention can set a botanist's heart pounding.

Picnics & places to eat

Just over the road from the entrance to the ruins at Herculaneum is a great local shop for picnic goodies and refreshments, **F/lli de Luca Bossa** (via IV Novembre 4/6, Ercolano). To sample the area's famed tomatoes as well as the curious local speciality of imported Norwegian stockfish (*stucco* or *stoccafisso*) head to **La Lanterna**, at Somma Vesuviana, a favourite of the vulcanologists.

Pompeii & around

Around 20,000 people lived in Pompeii when Vesuvius spewed and spat ash, pumice and wave upon wave of scorching pyroclastic debris on the town in AD 79, sealing a bubble of Roman life for 2000 years. Built on a lava plateau the city was ruled by Oscans, Etruscans and Samnites – Italic tribes – as well as by Greek colonists, before the Roman Empire ceded it. Walking around Pompeian streets, houses, baths and shops among its graffiti, artworks and artefacts of horror is a spellbinding experience that warrants a couple of days' exploration.

Mind-boggling time-travel explorations of AD 79's victims continue at the dreamlike, epicurean gardens of Villa Oplontis, where Nero's colourful second wife Poppaea Sabina sojourned. At Boscoreale, further up the slopes of Vesuvius, visitors can discover life on a Roman farm and vineyard. Four villas were found at Roman Stabiae and more artefacts will be unearthed in the coming years as part of a US$200 million archaeological project.

Shoddy management and millions of visitors (2.6 million visited the ruins at Pompeii in 2007) have taken their toll on the area's ancient treasures; the government has declared a state of emergency with new emphasis placed on protecting the excavations. With Italian state heritage funding slashed and a former fast-food chain chief appointed new cultural heritage 'tsar' in 2008, the archaeological sites have been told that they must pay their own way by generating more income. It remains to be seen whether Mario Resca will 'McDonaldize' Pompeii's Thermopolia inns during his three-year reign.

Pompeii

Pompei Scavi, via Villa dei Misteri 2, Pompei, information T081-857 5347, ticket office T081-536 5154, pompeiisites.org.

Apr-Oct 0830-1930 (last entry 1800), Nov-Mar 0830-1700 (last entry 1530), closed 1 Jan, 1 May, 25 Dec, €11, €5.50 EU citizens 18-24/school teachers, free EU citizens under 18/over 65. See also page 173 for details of combined ticket for all 5 Vesuvian sites. Porta Marina entrance is just over the road from the Scavi-Villa dei Misteri station.

Fascination in the beauty and sophistication of Pompeii's everyday objects, buildings and society is tempered with the horror of its devastation. Thousands stayed behind after the first deluge of volcanic debris: some perhaps to save their possessions from looting, some no doubt just unable to flee. Roofs collapsed under the weight of ash and pumice, crushing many before the massive pyroclastic surges engulfed everyone and everything. Haunting casts of human and animal victims created by archaeologist Giuseppe Fiorelli, who poured plaster into cavities left by bodies in the ash, freeze the mortal positions of the incinerated victims.

Pompeii covers 67 ha, 44 ha of which have been excavated. Its walls are punctuated by seven gates: Marina, Ercolano, Vesuvio, Nola, Sarno, Nocera and Stabia. Many of its older Greek-influenced buildings and irregular sixth-century BC street

Fiorelli plaster cast.

Essentials

❶ Getting around The **Circumvesuviana** railway is the cheapest and most convenient way of getting to and around the archaeological sites.

By road Take the A3 Autostrada and exit at Pompei Ovest then follow signs to Pompei Scavi; Torre Annunziata and follow signs for Boscoreale; Torre Annunziata Sud then signs for Scavi di Oplonti; Castellammare di Stabia and the SS145.

By bus SITA (T081-5522176, sitabus.it) runs various buses from piazza Garibaldi in Naples to Pompei and along the Amalfi coast.

By tour guide Itinera (T081-664545, itineranapoli. com) run tours around the sites.

By train From Naples or Sorrento: take the **Ferrovia Circumvesuviana Railway** (T800-053939, vesuviana.it), which departs regularly from the Stazione Vesuviana (Corso Garibaldi; Metro: Garibaldi) and along the coast from the Sorrento station – it stops at Pompei, Boscoreale, Torre Annunziata-Oplonti Villa di Poppea and Castellammare di Stabia.

❺ ATM Banca Monte dei Paschi di Siena at piazza Longo B40, T081-863 6511.

❹ Hospital Hospital Pronto Soccorso, Via Colle San Bartolomeo 50, T081-535 9111.

✚ Pharmacy Farmacia Pompeiana, via Roma 12, Pompei, T081-850 7264.

⌕ Post office Piazza Esedra 3, T081-5365200, Mon-Fri 0800-1330, Sat 0800-1230.

❶ Tourist information Ufficio AASCT, piazza Esedra 12, T081-536 3293.

Tip...

The vast scale of the Pompeii ruins makes it worthwhile having a planned route around the site. However, the heat of the sun and stamina will also play a part in your day out – bring lots of sun protection, water and energy-giving snacks. Set out early in the morning if you can and plan a rest for the hottest part of the day in a cool spot – the trees around the amphitheatre provide welcome shade. Expect lots of walking on uneven ancient surfaces, so pace yourself and mind your step!

Around the region

plan are around the Foro Triangolare (Triangular Forum) area. The later grid layout, with rectangular *insulae* (urban blocks), *decumani* (east-west streets) and *cardi* (north-south streets) date from the fourth century BC onwards.

Orientation The amount of ground you cover will depend on your stamina and the weather, so it's good to have an outlined route that includes the most compelling sights. Bear in mind though that some villas may be closed. The description below divides the sprawling 44 ha area into mini-itineraries that roughly follow the classic route from porta Marina, opposite the Circumvesuviana station, ending up at the amphitheatre. To take in

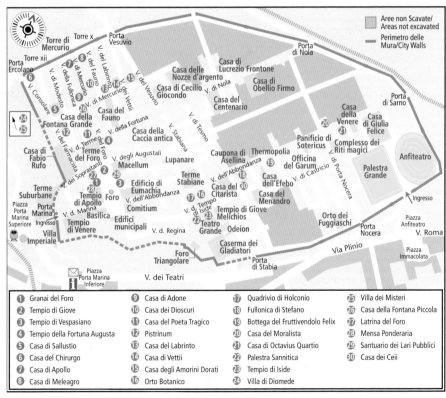

❶ Granai del Foro	❾ Casa di Adone	⓱ Quadrivio di Holconio	㉕ Villa dei Misteri
❷ Tempio di Giove	❿ Casa dei Dioscuri	⓲ Fullonica di Stefano	㉖ Casa della Fontana Piccola
❸ Tempio di Vespasiano	⓫ Casa del Poeta Tragico	⓳ Bottega del Fruttivendolo Felix	㉗ Latrina del Foro
❹ Tempio della Fortuna Augusta	⓬ Pistrinum	⓴ Casa del Moralista	㉘ Mensa Ponderaria
❺ Casa di Sallustio	⓭ Casa del Labrinto	㉑ Casa di Octavius Quartio	㉙ Santuario dei Lari Pubblici
❻ Casa del Chirurgo	⓮ Casa di Vettii	㉒ Palestra Sannitica	㉚ Casa dei Ceii
❼ Casa di Apollo	⓯ Casa degli Amorini Dorati	㉓ Tempio di Iside	
❽ Casa di Meleagro	⓰ Orto Botanico	㉔ Villa di Diomede	

Above: Around the Forum. Opposite page: 2000 year-old beard growth.

Tip...

The **Quadrivio di Holconio** (Holconius Crossroads) is a good spot to meet if your group splits up. It allowed cart traffic north and south along via Stabiana, and east along via dell'Abbondanza. Access westwards to the Forum was blocked by a tufa stone barrier, an ancient traffic-calming and security measure. Truncated pillars of a monumental tetrapylon stand here, which were a focal point of inscriptions and statues.

all these sights and the suburban villas and baths requires a couple of full days, so pick out the most interesting ones to visit.

Here is a five-hour route that starts at the porta Marina and ends at the amphitheatre: around the Forum, Casa del Fauno, Casa di Vettii, Casa degli Amorini Dorati, Lupanare, Terme Stabiane, the Theatre district, the western section of Via dell' Abbondanza, Palestra Grande and the Anfiteatro.

Forum On entering through Porta Marina you come to the **Tempio di Venere** (Temple of Venus), dedicated to the city of Pompeii's guardian goddess, then the **Basilica**, seat of the law courts, before the Roman **Foro** (Forum) opens out to your left. The Forum was the centre of the city's public life, covering 17,400 sq m and containing governmental buildings and temples.

Starting clockwise, the **Tempio di Apollo** (Temple of Apollo) was erected on the site of an

earlier building constructed by the southern Italian Samnites in the fifth century BC. Seek out the bronze statue of Artemis shooting arrows here. The **Granai del Foro** (the *holitorium* or grainstore) houses archaeological finds and some poignant plastercasts of some of the victims of the AD 79 eruption (other examples can be seen at the Garden of the Fugitives and the Stabian Baths). At the north end, flanked by two triumphal arches, is the **Tempio di Giove** (Temple of Jupiter), which became the Roman Capitolium – the raised podium once had statues of Jupiter, Juno and Minerva.

Pompeian graffiti

Pompeian graffiti ranges from political posturing to witty put-downs and some fruity flirting. Here are some examples:

"Primigenia – would that I might become the gem in your fine ring for no more than an hour, so that as you use it to seal a letter I might kiss your lips."

"Whoever loves, go to hell. I want to break Venus's ribs with a club and deform her hips. If she can break my tender heart why can't I hit her over the head?"

"Postpone your tiresome quarrels if you can, or leave and take them home with you."

"Walls, you have held up so much tedious graffiti that I am amazed that you have not already collapsed in ruin."

"Chie, I hope your haemorrhoids rub together so much that they hurt worse than they have ever before!"

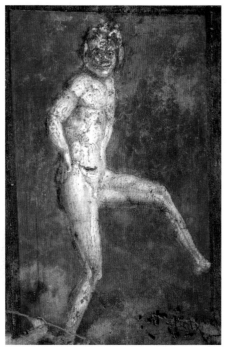

Above: Impish jig. Opposite page: Archaeologist at work.

The Forum is still the meeting place of a motley flock, nowadays consisting of tour parties, snoozing stray dogs and Italian school kids who hop on the empty plinths and strike poses. There is little shade but it's worth lingering here by the patch of grass to view the architectural fragments backdropped by Vesuvius. On the east side you'll find the **Macellum** (market), the **Sacrarium** (more venerated deities) and the **Edificio di Eumachia** (Building of Eumachia), the headquarters of the wool fullers, who cleaned (with a brew of urine and potash) and thickened woollen cloth. Exquisite marble decoration depicts birds and insects amid acanthus leaves here, while the marble altar of the **Tempio di Vespasiano** (Temple of Vespasian) has bas-reliefs of a sacrificed bull. Municipal elections were held at the Comitium.

North of the Forum   The **Terme del Foro** (Forum Thermal Baths), built around 80 BC, have rich architectural details including a stuccoed *tepidarium* (warm water baths) and terracotta *telamones* (male figures supporting the ceiling). At the junction of via del Foro and via della Fortuna is the **Tempio della Fortuna Augusta** (Temple of Fortuna Augusta) whose once-magnificent Corinthian columns, double staircase and towering marble-faced entrance were built in honour of an imperial cult by Marcus Tullius, a military man, imperial knight and ally of Augustus.

Towards Porta Ercolano   On the way to Porta Ercolano and the suburban villas (which is a fabulous detour for those with extra time and stamina, see page 193) is the area first excavated by archaeologists – it may have consequently faded and been damaged but has a striking atmosphere and views. On via Consolare is the mighty old **Casa di Sallustio** (House of the Sallust) dating from the third century BC. It was split into various commercial uses, becoming an inn with a *thermopolium* (restaurant) after the AD 62 earthquake, and suffered the indignity of a 1943 US air attack. Beyond the grand frontage of *opus quadratum* pillars of tufa stone are cavernous interiors, a clever *viridarium* (garden) with an Ionic portico and a luxuriant *trompe l'œil* garden scene painted on the back wall. The nearby **Casa del Chirurgo** (House of the Surgeon) is a colossal building where grisly looking surgical instruments were found.

Via del Mercurio Starting at the **Torre del Mercurio** (Tower of Mercury) and heading south on via del Mercurio, there are some grandiose dwellings. The **Casa di Apollo** (House of Apollo) has a mosaic of Achilles at Skyros, the **Casa di Meleagro** (House of Meleager) contains a fountain, fish pond and a simple fridge, while the **Casa di Adone** (House of Adonis) is named after a painting of a wounded Adonis tended by Venus and some cupids. The grandest though is the **Casa dei Dioscuri** (House of Castor and Pollux) with its imposing colonnade and mythological paintings of Apollo and Daphne, Adonis and Scylla. Paintings of the Dioscuri, the Divine twins Castor and Pollux, that adorned the entrance, and of Perseus and Andromeda, are in the Archaeological Museum in Naples (see page 108).

Further along is the **Casa della Fontana Piccola** (House of the Little Fountain), with its *trompe l'œil* effects and a cute cherub grasping a goose, while neighbouring **Casa della Fontana Grande** (House of the Large Fountain) has a mosaic fountain and tragicomic masks. More mosaics and theatricality fill the **Casa del Poeta Tragico** (House of the Tragic Poet), where a much-reproduced mosaic in the floor of the vestibule warns visitors to '*Cave Canem*' ('Beware of the dog').

House of the Faun Crowds gather around the copy of the statuette of a dancing faun at the **Casa del Fauno** (House of the Faun), a large house covering over 3000 sq m. Its best finds include the *tesserae* mosaic of Alexander the Great tussling with Darius at the Battle of Issus, now at the Archaeological Museum in Naples (see page 108). Around the corner on vicolo Storto is the best-preserved Pistrinum (bakery), whose millstones and bulbous ovens were owned by one Popidius Priscus.

Casa di Vettii and around vicolo di Mercurio
On vicolo del Labrinto at the **Casa del Labrinto** (House of the Labyrinth) there's a mosaic maze depicting Theseus slaying the Minotaur, while the must-see **Casa di Vettii** (House of the Vetti) has lavish paintings in the Fourth Style (the most intricate decorative style that was all the rage around the time of the AD 62 earthquake), peppered with mythology and mischievousness. Owned by the Vettii family of freedmen, who prospered around the time of the AD 62 earthquake (look out for the electoral slogans on the south wall) and commissioned quality restoration after the quake, it is much visited and consequently damaged by footfall. It has been undergoing restoration in recent years.

The Vettii's conversation pieces include a modestly endowed and demi-proud Priapus, and a witty frieze lined with endearing cherubs (or psyches) busy peddling gold and perfume, lobbing stones at a target and topsy-turvy chariot racing. Look out for the cherub cracking the whip astride a crab. The sumptuous *triclinium* (dining room) and *oecus* (living area) have a compendium of mythology and include lots of romantic couples (Perseus and Andromeda, Dionysius and Ariadne, Poseidon and Amymone) and Hellenistic scenes, including Ixion bound to a spinning wheel, punishment for leering at Zeus's wife. Statues of Bacchus and cupids clutching grapes and a goose were rigged up to a sophisticated system of fountain jets in the *peristyle* (porticoed garden). Other highlights include erotic paintings in the

Around the region

Above: Terme Stabiane. Opposite page: Via dell'Abbondanza.

servants' quarters (some scholars guess that it was a private brothel) and the frescoed *lararium* (shrine) with household gods (*lares*) and a snake.

Historians reckon the well-to-do Poppaei family owned the **Casa degli Amorini Dorati** (House of Gilded Cherubs), at the junction with via del Vesuvio, renowned for its marble relief bacchanalian scenes, Egyptian gods and gold cupids.

Around porta di Nola

On via di Nola is the extensive **Casa del Centenario** (House of the Centenary), excavated in 1879, 18 centuries after Vesuvius's eruption. A certain A Rustius Verus owned and enjoyed its baths with Egyptian flourishes, a *nymphaeum* and garden fountain portraying a young satyr pouring wine. In the servants' atrium – now in the Archaeological

Museum in Naples (see page 108) – was a celebrated scene showing Bacchus with a cape of grapes among birds, snakes, a panther and a vine-strewn Vesuvius.

Eastern section of via dell'Abbondanza

Starting at the Forum, Pompeii's wide high street slopes down to porta di Sarno and is lined with shops, workshops and hostelries. The inscriptions and scribblings along the way offer insights into the commercial, political and sexual lives of the people of Pompeii. Stepping stones would have been handy to hop over water and detritus. Deep ruts attest to the busy cart traffic that would have rumbled along here. Imagine the onslaught of movement, sound and pongs, with Vesuvius brooding in the corner of your left eye.

Terme Stabiane

Entering the Stabian Baths, along the via dell'Abbondanza, the men's *tepidarium* is a whirl of intricate stucco work and camera shutters. In the footsteps of ancient bathers, you enter the antechamber (dressing room) with its *clipei* (shields) decorated with nymphs and cupids, then the *tepidarium* and circular *frigidarium* with its plunge pool and twinkling, lapis lazuli dome. The niches held towels and massage ointments. Bathers would then brave the *calidarium*'s 40°C steam and hot baths, followed by a massage in the *tepidarium*. Patrons would relax with a drink under the porticoes of the *palaestra*. According to some scholars, women paid almost double to enter their baths, which are adjacent to the mens' and were accessed on the vicolo del Lupanare.

Tip...

Don't miss the **Orto Botanico** (Botanic Garden), along via dell'Abbonadnza (opposite the Terme Stabiane), which offers a welcome break from the ruins. Run by botanical researchers of the Antica Erboristeria Pompeiana, it's filled with fruit trees and herbs grown in the Pompeii era, and you can sometimes buy plant seeds of ancient varieties here.

Side-trip to the Lupanare

Expect a lot of eye-bulging images advertising personal services in the compact brothel quarters of the **Lupanare** (named after the howl of a lupa: she-wolf) on the vicolo del Lupanare. Among the tiny cubicles are pieces of Latin graffiti, including: "Long live lovers, death to those who do not know how to love! Double death to those who hinder love!"

Western section of via dell'Abbondanza

Upon reaching the **Nuovi Scavi** (new excavations begun in 1911 yet largely untouched to the north), there are a number of small businesses such as the **Fullonica di Stefano** (Stefano's Laundry), **Thermopolia** (inns serving hot food and drink), and the **Bottega del Fruttivendolo Felix** (Shop of Felix the Fruit Merchant), with its amusing Bacchic scenes. There are lots of middle-class dwellings along here. The **Casa del Moralista** (House of the Moralist) has a fine loggia and gardens, and the **Casa di Octavio Quartio** (House of Octavius Quartius) has scenes from *The Iliad* and a long marble pool shaded by a pergola. Don't miss the huge **Casa di Giulia Felice** (Villa of Julia Felix) with its extensive gardens and baths.

Five of the best

Controversial Graeco-Roman deities

❶ **Dionysus/Bacchus** The god of wine, fruits and ecstasy is associated with a popular cult, initially worshipped by women. The Bay of Naples was the natural home of wild Bacchanalian rites, where tales spread of untamed shenanigans and mysterious rituals that led to Bacchanalia being outlawed by the Roman Senate in 186 BC.

❷ **Isis** Egyptian goddess and the idealized mother and wife, Isis was a focus of magic and mysterious cults especially amongst slaves and Graeco-Roman bigwigs. Emperor Augustus (27 BC-AD 14) was so threatened by the cult that he outlawed it and promoted state-sponsored gods.

❸ **Persephone/Proserpina** Springtime goddess and Greek Queen of the Underworld who chomped on pomegranate seeds with Hades.

❹ **Priapus** Son of Aphrodite and Dionysus and god of fertility – his phallus is all over Pompeii, on walls, doorknobs and candle holders.

❺ **Vulcan** Fire god worshipped on 23 August (the Vulcanalia) outside city walls when fish were flung into the flames. Little did they know that Vulcan would appear from the seemingly serene mountain bearing juicy grapes above them.

Around the region

Towards porta di Stabia

On via Stabia is the main entrance to the sprawling **Casa del Citarista** (House of the Lyre Player) which has a copy of a statue of a wild boar and snarling dogs. Victims were crushed by a shaky peristyle at the **Casa del Menandro** (House of the Menander) along nearby vico Meridionale. It was excavated by celebrated archaeologist Amadeo Maiuri in 1930-31 and is important for its lavish furnishings, decoration and jewellery, including cluster earrings of gold globes and green semi-precious gems strung on golden thread. Don't miss the painting of the poet Menander and exquisite mosaic flooring in the private *thermae* depicting a bunch of acanthus with a bird and sea creatures including dolphins. A rib-tickling multi-coloured mosaic in the *oecus* shows porky pygmies punting along the Nile. It's reckoned that the villa was owned by the magistrate and friend of the Empress Poppaea (who liked a milky bath), Nero's second wife.

Theatre district

Hellenistic influences between the sixth and second centuries BC feature in the layout and history of the theatre district. The monumental **Foro Triangulare** (Triangular Forum), with its Ionic portico leading to a Doric colonnade and temple, was a venue for religious and athletics events, while the **Palestra Sannitica** (Samnite Palaestra) had a statue of Doryphorous (now in Naples, see page 108). The **Tempio di Giove Melichios** (Temple of Jupiter Meilichios) was dedicated to a Greek cult as well as Jupiter, Juno and Minerva. Greek-aping turns into the capers of the Egyptian cult of Isis at the **Tempio di Iside** (Temple of Isis) where small bones were found on the main altar. Picture the scene: shaven-headed priests in black robes and men with dog-faced masks performing weird rituals.

The **Teatro Grande** (Large Theatre) had a two-storey Greek-style *scaenae frons* at the back of the stage, with doorways for the thesps and

niches with honorary statues, all framed with entablatures and columns. Next door is the **Odeion** (Odeon), a small covered theatre built around 80 BC. The **Caserma dei Gladiatori** (Gladiatorial Barracks) has the Quadriporticus, a large square surrounded by a portico.

Around the amphitheatre & porta Nocera
Welcome shade is provided by the tunnel entrances, porticoes and surrounding trees around the amphitheatre and Great Palaestra. The **Anfiteatro** (Amphitheatre) is an elliptical structure begun around 70 BC and completed around the turn of the new millennium. It's the oldest surviving Roman amphitheatre and an incredible arena to explore, making a fitting climax to a day in Pompeii. Gladiatorial battles were watched by around 20,000 spectators, seated in three tiers, or the *cavea* (sections for different social classes). Roman chronicles and inscriptions found outside the arena, where spectators gathered to eat and chant at the popular inns, attest to the popularity of star gladiators: Felix was the "bear fighter", Thracian Celadus was dubbed "a heart-throb" and Oceanus was the "barmaid's choice". Boisterous rivalry spilled over into hooliganism in AD 59 when Pompeians clashed with rivals from Nuceria. In 1823 tons of volcanic debris was cleared from the site but it was not until the 20th century, under the archaeological eye of Amedeo Maiuri, that it was properly excavated.

The **Palestra Grande** (Great Palaestra) was built under the reign of the state-strengthening Emperor Augustus as a place where the *collegia iuventum* (youngsters) could train body and mind, primarily in preparation for Roman army service. It has a sloping pool that was continually fed water by a lead pipe, and the 141 x 107 m area is enclosed on three sides by a handsome portico. Stucco reliefs found here depict Dionysus as a wrestler and an athlete resting on an exercise hoop. Rows of plane trees have been planted recently to recreate the layout of AD 79.

In 1961 13 victims of the eruption were revealed near the porta Nocera, at the **Orto dei Fuggiaschi** (Garden of the Fugitives).

Above: L'Anfiteatro. Opposite page: Teatro Piccolo.

Suburban villas & baths
Outside the city walls, at Porta Marina, erotic artworks were recently exposed in the **Terme Suburbane** (Suburban Baths). Built in the first century BC, the multi-storey complex was the only unisex baths in Pompeii and probably had a brothel on the top floor. It has lots of mosaics and stuccoed cherubs. Nearby, the Villa Imperiale has frescoed rooms splashed in Pompeian red.

The via dei Sepolcri, outside Porta Ercolano, is lined with tombs and leads to two opulent residences. The **Villa di Diomede** (Villa of Diomedes) had the largest garden in Pompeii. During the excavations in the late 1700s, 18 skeletons of unlucky souls who tried to escape were found in the vaulted cellar. The **Villa dei Misteri** (Villa of Mysteries) has a colourful history: this sumptuous pile was turned into a large winery but it's the Dionysian Cycle in the so-called Hall of Mysteries – nine scenes from a ritual dedicated to the Greek god of wine and revelry, Dionysus – that really captures the imagination. Although outlawed by Rome, the cult thrived further south in this Hellenistic region and perhaps explains some of those exuberant Neapolitan traits.

Around the region

Modern Pompeii

Modern Pompeii has nondescript shopping streets fanning out from piazza B Longo, which has four patches of grass interspersed with a fountain, palm trees and benches. The focal point is the impressively flamboyant pilgrimage shrine dedicated to the Madonna of the Rosary, **Santuario della Madonna del Rosario** (Piazza B Longo 1, T081-857 7111, santuario.it, May-Oct daily 0900-1300, 1530-1830, Nov-Apr Mon-Fri 1500-1700, Sat-Sun 0900-1300, free), built in the late 19th century. Weekend and festival services are particularly worth attending, when you can inhale much Neapolitan piety and incense amid atmospheric surroundings.

Oplontis – Villa di Poppaea

Via Sepolcri, Torre Annunziata, T081-862 1755, pompeiisites.org.
Circumvesuviana railway to Torre Annunziata. Turn left at the front of the station and walk for 5 mins.

Villa di Poppaea is a large and lavish suburban Roman villa at Oplontis, near the port of Torre Annunziata, around 7 km from Pompei and 20 km southeast of Naples. It's reckoned that Nero's second wife Poppaea Sabina lived here. *Trompe l'œil* architectural details and lively landscape scenes filled with birds, butterflies, theatre players and fruits of the land fill the atrium, *triclinium, caldarium* and gardens. Bodies, gold jewellery, coins and statues were found crammed in the storeroom, making it likely that the villa was being restored at the time of the AD 79 eruption.

Boscoreale

Antiquarium Nazionale Uomo e Ambiente nel Territorio Vesuviano, via Settetermini 15, Località Villaregina, T081-857 5347, pompeiisites.org.
Circumvesuviana railway to Boscotrecase, then shuttle bus to Villa Regina.

Once a rural hamlet and Pompeian suburb, Boscoreale is located to the north of Pompei on the slopes of Vesuvius. It's worth seeking out for its archaeological museum which houses finds from the area's working Roman villas. Exhibits bring the workings of a Roman farm to life and a visit to Villa Regina with its vineyards, *torcularium* (grape press) and wine cellar is a must for vino quaffers. Fabulous frescoes and a hoard of silver were discovered in the 1800s at two nearby villas, the Villa di Pisanella and Villa di Publius Fannius Synistor. Their treasures can be seen in the Archaeological Museum in Naples, the Louvre in Paris and the Metropolitan Museum of Art in New York.

Stabiae (Scavi di Stabia)

Via Passeggiata Archeologica, Castellammare di Stabia, T081-871 4541, pompeiisites.org.
Circumvesuviana railway to Castellamare or Via Nocera then red No 1 bus.

Castellammare di Stabia, a spa town with shipbuilding traditions, is 33 km southeast of Naples and marks the start of the Sorrentine Peninsula. Its excavated Roman villas and *antiquarium* (museum) are currently being transformed by one of the largest archaeological projects in Europe since the Second World War. The plan is to create a 60-ha Stabiae archaeological park that will encompass the four villas already discovered at Roman Stabiae, which were excavated in the 18th century and from the 1950s onwards. Named after a wall painting of the mythological Ariadne found asleep by Dionysus, the **Villa di Ariana** (via Piana di Varano, T081-274200) is just outside the modern town at Varano. Nearby is the **Villa di San Marco** (via Passeggiata Archeologica, T081-871 4541), a wealthy residence with frescoes, stucco work and the remains of a swimming pool. The walk is well worth it for the views alone and you may even be lucky to glimpse ancient treasures coming to light.

Tip...

Near the Castellammare di Stabia Circumvesuviana station is a *funivia* (cable car) service to Monte Faito, with stunning views and trails, including a walk to the church of San Michele (1280 m). For further details, see page 212.

Tip...

Oplontis, Boscoreale and Stabiae's opening hours are the same as those for Pompeii (see page 185). If you haven't already bought a combined ticket for all five Vesuvian sites (see page 173), a one-day combined ticket to the three minor sites costs €5.50/€2.75.

Santuario della Madonna del Rosario.

Sleeping

Bel Vesuvio Inn €€
Via Panoramica 40, San Sebastiano al Vesuvio, T081-771 1243, agriturismobelvesuvioinn.it.
Take the San Giorgio a Cremano exit off the A6 Napoli–Salerno road.

This attractive 18th-century farmhouse with modern comforts is set amid vineyards on the slopes of Vesuvius. It's especially good for nature lovers and families as there are farmyard animals, a playground, horse riding, local walking trails and a *bocce* area where you can enjoy Italian boules. Meals are served on a large terrace with spectacular views and feature local produce including *piennolo* tomatoes, apricot jam, cheeses, chicken and *salume*.

Miglio d'Oro Park Hotel €€
Corso Resina 296, 80056 Ercolano, T081-739 9999, migliodoroparkhotel.it.
The 18th-century Villa Aprile is within easy reach of Herculaneum, has awe-inspiring views of Vesuvius (ask for a room with *una vista del Vesuvio* at the back), and is surrounded by fabulous grounds. Its fountains and garden follies reveal the whimsical tastes of its first owner, the Count of Imola and Forlì, Gerolamo Riario Sforza. It's all very modern with some crazy artworks spanning various cubed spaces around a lounge bar. A smart glass and

chrome lift whisks you to the guest rooms, which range from a reasonably priced Classic to the spacious Suite – all have fabulous bathrooms (some with jacuzzi baths, others with jet showers), air conditioning, internet and satellite TV. The high-ceilinged restaurant serves a buffet breakfast although service is a tad lax.

La Murena B&B €€
Via Osservatorio 10, Ercolano, T081-777 9819.
This small B&B is a good base for exploring Vesuvius National Park and visiting the Vesuvian Observatory and Herculaneum. The accommodation includes suites and an apartment with a kitchen and a terrace for alfresco dining, while the wonderful grounds are a great place to eat breakfast and relax. There's also the option of renting the entire house for €260 per night.

Il Cavaliere €
Via Gramsci 109, 80040 Massa di Somma, T081-574 3637, agrodelcavaliere.altervista.org.
From Naples take the SS162, exit at Cercola and follow signs to Massa di Somma.
Good value accommodation, an *agriturismo* farmyard,

stunning views, a pool and superb food make 'The Knight' a hit with Neapolitan families and couples seeking a rural getaway. Their *casalinga* (homemade cooking) fixed menu (€25) meal starts with an antipasto selection of meats, cheeses, *frittelle* and local vegetables, followed by a pasta dish and barbecued meat. A children's menu is available, and their local white wine is made with an old variety of Catalan grape, *l'uva catalanesca*.

Crowne Plaza Stabiae €€€
SS145 Sorrentina, Località Pozzano, 80053 Castellammare di Stabia, T081-394 6700, ichotelsgroup.com.
As you curve around the Vesuvian coast towards the Sorrentine peninsula, there is a striking vision of a former factory

Top: Miglio d'Oro Park Hotel.
Above: Crowne Plaza Stabiae.

Eating & drinking

building and its strangely alluring modernist shapes. Luxury and stylish accommodation, a choice of indoor and outdoor pools, and a private beach make this Crowne Plaza far more glamorous than its industrial origins would suggest. The 157 rooms have clean contemporary lines and some have terraces with stunning views of the bay of Naples. There is one obvious downside: unless you have a car you'll have to rely on the free shuttle bus to Vico Equense and the train station.

Hotel Forum €€
Via Roma 99, 80045 Pompei, T081-850 1170, hotelforum.it.
Beyond the recently added contemporary façade, set back from busy via Roma, the Forum offers good value near the piazza Anfiteatro, the modern town and Santuario. The staff in the lobby are friendly and helpful. The best of the 36 guest rooms are in the new wing, which have smart modern bathrooms and better soundproofing than the other rooms. Buffet breakfast is served in a rather scruffy space but fortunately there is a leafy garden in which to enjoy your morning *cornetto* and coffee.

Hotel Santa Caterina €€
Via Vittorio Emanuele 4, Pompei, T081-856 7494, hotelsantacaterinapompei.com.
Conveniently located on via Roma opposite the entrance to the ruins, this pleasant hotel has 20 cosy guest rooms in which Pompeian red hues and classical paintings abound. There are impressive views of either Vesuvius or the amphitheatre from some rooms while another two have been customized for disabled access. The English-speaking staff are helpful and there's free parking.

Hotel Diana €
Vico Sant'Abbondio 10, 80045 Pompei, T081-863 1264, pompeihotel.com.
This modern and well-run hotel is near the Pompei Scavi, Santuario and town amenities. It won an Italian hospitality award in 2007. Expect good service and immaculate, brightly decorated rooms in various sizes to suit most needs, even if the bathrooms are a little on the small size. Facilities include a laundry and dry-cleaning service, while the garden filled with citrus and palm trees is a considerable bonus.

Ercolano & Vesuvius

Casa Rossa al Vesuvio €€€
Via Vesuvio 30, Ercolano, T081-777 9763.
Wed-Mon 1230-1500, 1900-2300.
The sister restaurant of the renowned Casa Rossa 1888 in Torre del Greco, the Pink House is all about elegant Neapolitan dining. The house specialities include Parthenopean pasta dishes like *vermicelli ai frutti di mare* and *paccheri al ragù di mare*. They also do pizza and have a selection of the very best Lacryma Christi del Vesuvio wine.

Viva lo Re €€€
Corso Resina 261, Ercolano, T081-739 0207, vivalore.it.
Tue-Sat 0930-0100, Sun 0930-1600.
This cozy osteria-enoteca run by serenely suave Maurizio Focone has handsome wooden interiors lined with hundreds of bottles of wine. Some may find the presentation of the food a tad pretentious (it comes on fancy flat, angular plates) but the food itself is expertly prepared. *Piatti del giorno* are written on a board and often include a plate of *pesce crudo* (raw seafood), grilled cuttlefish with bitterly delicious *friarelli* (a type of broccoli and an acquired taste) and chunky steaks. They also have three stylish rooms overlooking Villa Campolieto.

La Lanterna €€
*Via Colonnello Aliperta 8,
Somma Vesuviana, T081-899 1843.*
Tue-Sun 1200-1500, 1930-2300.
After a day on the slopes of
Vesuvius, vulcanologist guide
Roberto Addeo enjoys coming
here to try their various *baccalà*
dishes: the imported Norwegian
stockfish (*stucco* or *stoccafisso*)
is a traditional ingredient in
Somma Vesuviana cuisine.
Their classic pasta dish is the
much imitated *paccheri con lo
stucco* and they also make pizzas
including *pizza al baccalà*, which
is best eaten outside under the
garden pergola.

Il Cavaliere €
*Via Gramsci 109, 80040 Massa di
Somma, T081-574 3637.*
Sat-Thu 1200-1500, 1930-2300.
Booking is essential at this
popular *agriturismo* known for its
excellent cooking – see page 196.

Cafés & bars
L'Angolo degli Scavi
Via IV Novembre 1, Ercolano.
Daily 0730- 2100.
Just over the road from the Scavi
entrance, on the 'Corner of the
Excavations', this small and often
busy bar is convenient but the
prices are geared to tourists –
a cappuccino at the bar costs €2
and a filled panino €2.50. You are
better off walking further up via
IV Novembre to one of the many
bars used by the locals.

President €€€
*Piazza Schettino 12, Pompei,
T081-850 7245,
ristorantepresident.com.*
Tue-Sun 1200-1500, 1930-2330.
Il President's elegant rooms
often host themed evenings
with historic culinary creations
served from ancient times to
the Bourbon era. Their *la cucina
povera napoletana extravaganza*
sees tiny 17th-century-style
Neapolitan pizzas on the menu.
They also organize candlelit

Pick of the picnic spots

Herculaneum Pick up provisions
from F/lli de Luca Bossa and head
for the amphitheatre where there
is plenty of shade.

Pompeii If you like people
watching there is plenty of
space but not much shade at
the Forum.

**Parco Nazionale del
Vesuvio** Take a picnic on a walk
in Vesuvius National Park. There's
welcome shade in the Tirone
Alto wood.

Below Vesuvius Find a spot in
the grounds of the *agriturismi*,
Bel Vesuvio Inn and Il Cavaliere,
both of which sell produce and
prepare meals.

Castellammare di Stabia
There are great views on the
lungomare prom and the nearby
Casa Armonica park with its
bandstand and fountains.

Tip...

Cross over via IV Novembre to the small *alimentari* (food shop) F/lli
de Luca Bossa, where you can pick up more reasonably priced picnic
supplies and refreshments.

Entertainment

walks around the ancient city – their website has details of all their latest gastronomic events. Reservations recommended.

Il Principe €€€

Piazza Bartolo Longo 8, Pompei, T081-850 5566, ilprincipe.com.
Tue-Sat 1200-1500, 1945-2230, Sun 1200-1500.

Ancient Roman recipes with multi-ethnic origins (especially Arabic, African and Greek) dominate the menu at this large restaurant brimming with Pompeian design. Some courses have culinary antecedents from Roman times, including the *garum pompeianum*, a piquant anchovy-based sauce served with pasta. Other inventive creations include *arselle con scampi su timballo di riso selvatico*: clams and scampi with wild rice.

Addu' u Mimi €

Via Roma 61, Pompei, T081-863 5451.
Sat-Thu 1200-1500, 1930-2300.
This is a relaxing place to eat near the centre of modern Pompei, serving good-value food, although service is often charmless and portions are not generous, so you will probably need a few courses. They serve salads and pizzas for veggies and tasty seafood pasta dishes.

Cafés & bars

Caffè Spagnolo

Via Giuseppe Mazzini 45, Castellammare di Stabia, T081-871 1272.
Thu-Tue 0800-2200.
A *stile-Liberty* (Italian art nouveau) gem near Roman Stabiae at Castellammare di Stabia. The surroundings are handsome and everything is top quality, from the coffee and pastries to the focaccia and ice cream.

De Vivo

Via Roma 36/38, Pompei, T081-863 1163.
Daily 0730-2200.
This gelateria cum pasticceria on via Roma does savoury snacks including panini, a range of gelati, *sorbetti* and *semifreddi*, as well as sweet creations including *sfogliatelle, pastiera* and *Babà al limoncello*.

Ercolano & Vesuvius

Clubs

Bunker Bar

Via G Semmola 141, Ercolano, T081-739 7900.
Thu-Tue 2000-late.
There's something not right about a military-styled bar with camouflage and bullets. Don't expect a Russian roulette scene reminiscent of *The Deer Hunter* though – the most disturbing spectacle to be found here is seeing 20-somethings doing the conga to *molto* cheesy Euro-house. It's popular for special occasions when locals eat pizza around the tables.

Sciuscià Club

Via Viulio 2, Ercolano, T081-771 9898, sciusciaclub.it.
Commercial house music and latino pumps out under the vaulted ceilings, and there's a garden where you can sample Neapolitan classics. Check in advance for latest programme.

Right: *Espresso cremoso.*
Opposite page: *Limoni.*

Shopping

Activities & tours

Food & drink
F/lli de Luca Bossa
Via IV Novembre 4/6, Ercolano.
Daily 0800-1300, 1600-2100.
This tiny *alimentari* near the
entrance to the Scavi is where the
locals come for their supplies. As
well as decent bread and snacks
like *taralli di finochietto*, you can
pick up a bottle of Valdobbiadene
prosecco for just €5 and a large
bottle of water for €1 here.

Markets
Mercato di Resina
Piazza Pugliano, Ercolano.
Daily 0730-1300.
Famous since the Second World
War, when impoverished locals
peddled objects and clothes
stolen from the Allied forces,
colourful Resina second-hand
market often throws up a quirky
clothing item. Just take care of
con artists offering dodgy
electronics goods and cigarettes.

Food & drink
Melius
Via Lepanto 156, Pompei.
Daily 0800-1300, 1600-2100.
A fabulous deli with homemade
meals as well as cheeses and
salame to fill your panini bought
from the *paneficio* (bakery) next
door. Great too for food and
wine to take home.

Mirto
Via Lepanto 142, Pompei.
Daily 0830-2000.
A decent supermarket in the
modern town which is useful
for picnic products and food
to take home.

Photographic supplies
Foto Shop
Via Sacra, Pompei,
T081-850 7816.
A handy shop for camera
equipment and spare memory
cards in the centre of town.

Cultural
Arethusa
T0823-448084, arethusa.net.
This company provides
group tours all over Italy
including guided visits to the
archaeological sites around
Vesuvius, starting from €14 for
a tour around the Terme
Suburbane, Pompeii.

Itinera
Corso Vittorio Emanuele 663,
Naples, T081-664545,
itineranapoli.com. Metro to
Corso V. Emanuele.
Friendly, English-speaking
Francesca del Vecchio organizes
a host of tours along the Bay of
Naples including trips around
the Vesuvian sights. A two-hour
guided tour around Pompeii or
Herculanuem costs €130 (for up
to four people) while a four-hour
tour of Pompeii or Herculanuem,
plus Vesuvius, costs €160.

Lacryma Christi wine.

Postcards on the precipice.

L'Ultima Notte di Ercolano
*T081-8631581, tappetovolante.
org. €25 – check for latest
programme.*
This is a tour under the stars
with a theatrical performance
thrown in – 40 costumed actors
perform Domenico Maria
Corrado's musical version of
Virgil's *Aeneid* amid Ercolano's
ancient baths and villas.

Sogno Pompei
*T081-1930 3885,
sognopompei.com.
€20, €14 with Artecard or Easy
Napoli.*
An atmospheric 70-minute tour
of the Scavi at night, with the
sights and sounds of ancient
Pompeii and some creepy
lighting thrown in.

Ufficio Scavi
*Villa dei Misteri 2, T081-857 5347,
pompeiisites.org.*
For details about guided tours,
themed adventures and latest
access to restricted areas around
the Scavi, contact this office.

Walking
Guide Alpine della Campania
*Piazzale di Quota 1000, Ercolano,
T081-777 5720.*
Alpine guides for walks around
Vesuvius and beyond. Tours from
€20.

Presidio Vulcano Vesuvio
*Via S Vito 151, Ercolano, T081-777
5720, guidevesuvio.it.*

Roberto Addeo is one of the
vulcanological guides who take
people around the Vesuvius
National Park. The 90-minute
guided walk around the crater
costs €6. Roberto can be
contacted on his mobile
T347-351 6815 or via email
at vesuviotrek@libero.it.

Wellbeing
Terme di Stabia
*Viale delle Terme 3/5,
Castellammare di Stabia,
081-391 3111, termedistabia.com.
Daily 0900-1900.*
Alas concrete and crazy paving
covers most of the ancient baths
here but the complex does still
provide mineral waters with
curative properties, a Centro
Benessere offering spa beauty
treatments and medical
programmes for sports injuries.
Prices start at €20 for a sauna or
Turkish bath plus use of thermal
baths and gym.

Ercolano Scavi
Frequent Circumvesuviana train
services to Napoli (20 mins),
Pompei Scavi (20 mins),
Torre Annunziata-Oplonti
(15 mins), Castellammare di
Stabia (30 mins) and Sorrento
(50 mins).

Pompei Scavi-
Villa dei Misteri
Frequent Circumvesuviana train
services to Napoli (35 mins),
Torre Annunziata-Oplonti
(5 mins), Castellammare di Stabia
(10 mins), Ercolano (20 mins) and
Sorrento (30 mins).

Torre Annunziata-Oplonti
Frequent Circumvesuviana train
services to Napoli (30 mins),
Castellammare di Stabia
(15 mins), Pompei (10 mins),
Ercolano (20 mins) and
Sorrento (35 mins).

Castellammare di Stabia
Frequent Circumvesuviana train
services to Napoli (45 mins),
Pompei (10 mins), Torre
Annunziata-Oplonti (15 mins),
Ercolano (30 mins) and Sorrento
(20 mins).

Parco Nazionale del Vesuvio
Vesuviana Mobilità bus from
Naples – Piazza Garibaldi
(65 mins), Pompei – Piazza
Anfiteatro (90 mins), Ercolano
Circumvesuviana station
(35 mins).

Contents

Sorrentine Peninsula & Amalfi Coast

Amalfi, early November.

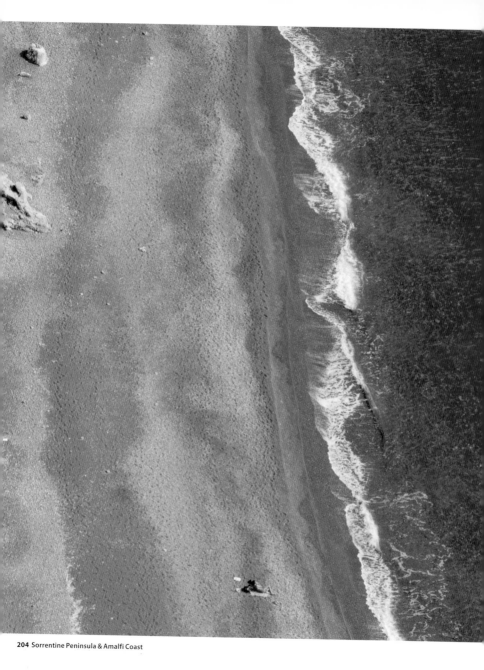

Introduction

Tectonic forces lifted limestone rock from the ocean floor to create the spectacular coastline of the *Penisola Sorrentina* (Sorrentine Peninsula) and *Costiera Amalfitana* (Amalfi Coast). Bewitching natural beauty abounds from its milk-and-cheese producing Monti Lattari that plunge down to an azure sea. Hidden coves and grottoes, those natural pirate hideouts, now attract yachts and swimmers. Despite the comparatively recent arrival of roads, including the famously meandering SS163 Amalfi Drive, and mass tourism, rustic traditions and the tastiest produce thrive amid the terraced olive and citrus groves, campanile-chiming villages and intimate fishing harbours.

The Sorrentine Peninsula extends from the ancient Roman spa town of Castellammare di Stabia to wild Punta Campanella. Touristy Sorrento and Vico Equense retain some elegance. The Amalfi Coast starts after Sant'Agata sui Due Golfi which sits astride the gulfs of Naples and Salerno. Positano defines the pastel-painted picturesque harbour turned chic resort. Escaping the SS163 traffic, the coast is studded with pebbly beaches, wild headlands and dramatic fjords, while up high there are stunning walks – such as the *Sentiero degli Dei* (Trail of the Gods) – covering mule tracks, mills and craggy escarpments.

Amalfi basks in its glorious past as a maritime republic. Sublimely high Ravello has ethereal gardens and vistas that have inspired novels and operas. Salerno has Moorish cathedral cloisters, while towards the untamed Cilento Coast, Graeco-Roman Paestum is a captivating vision of a lost civilization.

Spiaggia deserta.

What to see in...

...one day
Head straight for **Amalfi** by hydrofoil, then up to rarefied **Ravello**. Scoop out the best bits of **Conca dei Marini** and **Positano** and perhaps dine at **La Tagliata**.

...a weekend or more

Take in Sorrento's **Chiesa di San Francesco d'Assisi** before exploring unspoilt **Massa Lubrense**, **Sant'Agata sui Due Golfi** and **Punta Campanella**. Charter a boat from **Marina di Lobra** or **Marina del Cantone** to discover stunning bays and the **Li Galli** islets. Visit gorgeous spots like **Ravello** and **Positano** between excursions: a boat trip to **Capri**; walks in the **Monti Lattari**; wine, pastry and mozzarella tasting trips; **Salerno**'s Moorish architecture and the magical Greek temples at **Paestum**.

Sorrentine Peninsula

As you follow the curves of the SS145 road along the Sorrentine Peninsula, volcanic debris deposited by Vesuvius eventually gives way to the limestone layers of the Appenines that jut into the Mar Tirreno (Tyrrhenian Sea). The first resort you come to is Vico Equense, which survived the worst of the AD 79 eruption and centuries of Saracen attacks, and has an air of faded grandeur in and around its Gothic cathedral and Catalan courtyards. Swooning around Punta Gradelle, you come to the lemon-scented terraces and sheltered *Piano di Sorrento* (Sorrento Plain), whose gentle climate was celebrated by Romans and Romantic artists – it is now popular with package holidaymakers who throng its kitschy streets and luxuriant gardens.

Away from the crammed bathing platforms and on the minor roads towards Massa Lubrense are picturesque villages and harbours, interspersed with lots of lemon and olive groves. Genuine local dialects can still be heard and traditional Sorrentine culture thrives here.

Below: Towards Punta Campanella, Li Galli and Capri. Opposite page: La Penisola.

Vico Equense

Vico Equense is probably best known these days as the home of *pizza al metro* (pizza by the metre) at **Da Gigino Università della Pizza** (see page 231). In the 12th century, Carlo I di Angio renamed this former Roman stronghold Aequa and it later became known as Vico Equense (vico from the Latin vicus for village). The Spanish Aragonese continued the rebuilding and today its centre retains elegance in its Gothic cathedral, Catalan courtyards, and some interesting small museums.

Chiesa di Santissima Annunziata

Via Cattedrale, Vico Equense.
Daily 0800-1230, 1530-1900, free.

You wouldn't believe that this peachy clean church sitting above plunging cliffs has 14th-century Gothic origins. As you approach, narrow atmospheric lanes are crammed with Catalan-style buildings from the Aragonese era. An imposing arch cuts through its lofty campanile and draws you into a belvedere area with superb seaward views.

Museo Antiquarium Equano

Casa Municipale, via Filangieri 98, Vico Equense.
Mon, Wed and Fri 0900-1300, Tue and Thu 1530-1830, Sat-Sun 0930-1230, free.

Housed in the town hall is Vico's archaeological museum, whose dusty highlights include fragments left by Etruscans and other Italic tribes as well as Greek remains from the ancient town's necropolis.

Museo Mineralogico Campano

Via San Ciro 2, Vico Equense, T081-801 5668, museomineralogicocampano.it.
Mar-Sep Tue-Sat 0900-1300, 1700-2000, Oct-Feb Tue-Sun 0900-1300, 1600-1900, year round Sun and Bank Holidays 0900-1300, €3.

Mineral-mad Pasquale Discepolo, an engineer and collector, helped open this excellent little

Essentials

❶ Getting around Line 1 of the **Circumvesuviana railway** (T800-053939, vesuviana.it) stops along the Bay of Naples and Sorrentine Peninsula, terminating at Sorrento. From there seasonal hydrofoil services connecting all the resorts along both coasts are run by **Metro del Mare** (T199-446644, metrodelmare.com). SITA (T081-552 2176) runs buses to and from Naples, and there are many local lines reaching Ravello, Vietri and smaller hamlets.

❷ Bus and train station Via Marziale, Sorrento, T800-053939/ T081-552 2176.

❸ ATM Banco di Napoli, Piazza Tasso 35, Sorrento, T081-807 3066.

⊕ Hospital Ospedale, S Maria della Misericordia, Corso Italia, Sorrento, T081-533 1111.

✛ Pharmacy Farmacia Alfani, Corso Italia 129, Sorrento, T081-878 1226.

⤴ Post office Corso Italia 210, Sorrento, T081-878 1495.

❶ Tourist information Sorrento office: piazza Tasso (via Luigi de Maio 35), Sorrento, T081-807 4033, sorrentotourism.com.

Tip...

Driving to and along both coastlines (A3 Napoli–Salerno, then SS145 and SS163) can be exhilarating but the traffic (especially the lines of coaches) and Neapolitan drivers on the narrow roads will test your patience and nerve. If your budget allows, hire a driver.

Around the region

Mineralogy Museum of Campania in 1992. It's fascinating if you have just walked around the crater of Vesuvius as some of the crystals created by the volcano can be seen here, including intensely blue lapis lazuli collected on Monte Somma. The museum's palaeontological and anthropological collections include dinosaur fossils and ancient artefacts such as Libyan arrowheads.

Marina di Equa & beaches east of Sorrento

Site of the original ancient settlement Aequana, Marina di Equa has a robust defensive tower, Il Torre di Caporivo, rebuilt in 1608, as well as a long and popular beach lined with parasols and a smattering of restaurants. The beaches at Meta, Seiano and Alimuri are often packed, so it's best to seek out isolated stretches of pebble like Tordigliano, which is accessible by boat.

Suspended 45 m above the sea, Sorrento's cobbled streets and squares combine elegance with lashings of limoncello-kitsch. Roman big shots Augustus and Agrippa sojourned in Surrentum, followed by 19th-century Romantic artists, writers and composers. Ibsen and Gorky had Sorrentine boltholes, and in 1876 the fresh, lemon-scented Piano di Sorrento air rang with the nihilist rantings of Nietzsche, who famously fell out with Wagner over the composer's religious interpretation of *Parsifal*. Nowadays sunburned Brits form the bulk of the international package-holidaymakers who spill out of the cafés and Disneyland-esque Dotto 'train' on piazza Tasso.

Piazza Tasso, Sorrento

Piazza Tasso, named after the troubled 16th-century poet Torquato Tasso whose statue stands in the centre of the square, is built upon the Graeco-Roman layout of Surrentum. Away from the traffic melee, on via Cesareo, is the **Sedile Dominova**, a 15th-century loggia with *trompe l'œil* frescoes, now a men's social club where old *signori* play cards on wooden tables. Nearby, on corso Italia, is the **Chiesa di Santa Maria del Carmine** with its Baroque stucco work and bright yellow façade.

To the south of piazza Tasso is the unexpected and rather magical sight of the inaccessible **Vallone dei Mulini** (Valley of the Mills), where the ruins of an abandoned watermill have been left to crumble in a deep, dank ravine whose microclimate supports rare ferns. For a hands-on feel of this coastline's early industrial past, you can visit various mills near Amalfi (see page 213).

Heading east from piazza Tasso towards the cathedral, there are some fine medieval palazzos to admire on via Santa Maria della Pietà: **Palazzo Veniero** (No 14) is 13th century, showing Byzantine and Arabic influences, while **Palazzo Correale** (No 24) has a handsome portal, windows and tiled courtyard.

Left: Chiesa di Santa Maria del Carmine.

Duomo di San Filippo e San Giacomo

Corso Italia 1, Sorrento, T081-878 2248.
Daily 0800-1200, 1600-2000, free.

The façade of Sorrento's Romanesque cathedral is a tad underwhelming at first glance but look carefully and you'll notice two Roman columns and a majolica-tiled clock face. Inside there's lots of multicoloured marble and naturalistic motifs at the altar, some fine 18th-century Neapolitan School paintings and striking inlaid-wood stalls.

Chiesa di San Francesco d'Assisi

Piazza Francesco Saverio Gargiulo, Sorrento.
Daily 0800-1300, 1400-1900, free.

Heading westwards towards the sea is a must-see religious sight and another panoramic garden terrace. Birdsong and bougainvillea twitter and tumble around the interlaced Arabic arches of the evocative 14th-century monastery cloisters next to the Church of San Francesco. Look out for some fascinating architectural fragments taken from ancient temples. Art exhibitions and classical concerts are held in these incredibly atmospheric surroundings, and there are two 18th-century frescoes in the Baroque church, depicting Sant'Antonio of Padova and San Giacomo. More fabulous sea views can be enjoyed from the Villa Comunale Gardens nearby.

Museo Bottega della Tarsia Lignea

Palazzo Pomarici Santomasi, via San Nicola 28, Sorrento, T081-877 1942, alessandrofiorentinocollection.it.
Apr-Oct 0930-1300, 1600-2000, Nov-Mar 0930-1300, 1500-1900, closed Mon and certain public holidays, €8 (includes conducted tour). From corso Italia take via Tasso to via San Nicola.

Sorrento is famous for its *intarsia* (marquetry) and the town's shops are crammed with traditional inlaid-wood products. Find out more about the history and art of marquetry at this gem of a museum, the Intarsia Museum and Craft Shop, where fine examples of inlaid furniture and objects crafted by the great Sorrento inlayers of the past and their modern counterparts are housed in an elegant 18th-century villa. Exquisite marquetry objects for the home are sold in the shop here.

Museo Correale

Via Correale 50, Sorrento, T081-878 1846, museocorreale.com.
Wed-Mon 0900-1400, €8.

Via Correale has some fine aristocratic residences including the former home of the Correale di Terranova family, which provides a look at the tastes and sumptuous furnishings of the Neapolitan nobility. Its 23 rooms are filled with collections of Greek and Roman marble statuary, early photographic equipment, landscape paintings of the Posillipo School, nativity scene figurines, period costumes and dainty porcelain pieces.

Long and thin.   Il Duomo.

Tip...

Take a breather and enjoy sea views at the piazza della Vittoria gardens (go west down via Tasso towards the sea). It's a great place to escape the sun, have a picnic and imagine cavorting Romans worshipping at the temple of Venus that apparently stood here.

Tip...

For drinks, ice cream, basil and chilli flavoured chocolates and a selection of pastries (including both types of *sfogliatella*: *ricce* and *frolle*) seek out 'O **Funzionista** at via San Nicola 13.

Marina Grande.

Sunbathing & swimming in Sorrento

Marina Piccola is busy with ferry traffic and backed by sheer cliff walls topped by hotels. Marina Grande (despite its name) has more of an intimate, fishing village feel and a pebbly beach strewn with boats. All along here are spindly wooden jetties crammed with sun worshippers and bathers in the summer. There are plenty of other small stony beaches nearby (to the east are Sant'Agnello and the Marinella beaches; to the west is Marina di Puolo) but the most beautiful spots are towards the wilds of Punta della Campanella.

All along here are spindly wooden jetties crammed with sun worshippers and bathers in the summer.

Massa Lubrense

The pace of life slows west of Sorrento. Minor roads wind down from the busy SS145 to small picturesque harbours. Towards the rocky end of the peninsula, Punta della Campanella, there are wild walks on old mule tracks with views of Capri, just 5 km away. The **Area Marina Protetta di Punta Campanella** has pristine waters and marine caves like Grotta della Cala di Mitigliano and the Grotta dell'Isca which are ideal for snorkelling.

Located just 5 km west of Sorrento along the peninsula, the town that gives its name to this rocky region is a good base for the adventurous and outdoorsy. Massa Lubrense's original cathedral, **Santissima Annunziata**, has Baroque stucco work and an adjoining Franciscan monastery built in the 1580s. After the havoc wrought by Saracen and Turkish pirates Massa built a new cathedral (redone in the 18th century), **Santa Maria delle Grazie**, which is worth a visit for its majolica flooring and *terrazza* sea views. A steep, meandering lane trails between the houses of old Massa Lubrense to reach the cylindrical tower and battlements of a 14th-century **Aragonese castle**, from where there are dramatic glimpses of Capri.

Marina della Lobra

This intimate little harbour filled with colourful fishing vessels and pleasure boats is just down the road from Massa Lubrense. Amid the higgledy-piggledy buildings is the cheerful *giallo-verde* (yellow-and-green) cupola of the monastery-church of Santa Maria della Lobra (1528), which contains a vaulted ceiling and majolica flooring.

Sant'Agata sui Due Golfi & Torca

Just off the SS145 is the village of Sant'Agata ('on the two Gulfs'), which sits in a commanding position overlooking the two coastlines and bays of Naples and Salerno. Its sights include the Chiesa di Santa Maria delle Grazie, which has an exquisite

Sorrento's most magical shore

Escape the crowds on a 3-km walk to the secluded Punta del Capo beach. Head west along the main street corso Italia then follow via del Capo up the hill. The walk passes lemon groves and **Il Serito** (no public entry), the villa where Maxim Gorky lived between 1924 and 1933 and where Lenin stayed during his exile), before a path (Calata Punto del Capo) descends to the sea. On the rocky shoreline, popular with swimmers and sunbathers, there are ruins of a once-sumptuous Roman villa (believed to have belonged to Pollius Felix though the jury is still out on this) and the limpid waters of the **Bagno della Regina Giovanna** (Queen Jean's Bath), a natural, steep-sided pool.

17th-century marble, lapis lazuli and mother-of-pearl Florentine altar and a majolica clock face. A minor road accesses the once thriving fishing village of **Torca** at 350 m, where there are incredible views towards Li Galli (see page 217) and the shimmering sea beyond. Pop into one of Torca's three shops (including two *salumerie*) for picnic supplies and a chinwag with friendly shopkeepers and passing maritime characters.

Fiordo di Crappola

This mini fjord hewn out of the rock and its tranquil pebbly beach was a favourite hideout of pirates. It's about a 45-minute walk away from Sant'Agata or else accessible by boat. Where there was once a Greek temple to Apollo there now stands the tiny chapel of San Pietro.

Nerano, Baia di Ieranto & Marina del Cantone

Perched on a ridge at 166 m, the small village of Nerano is the gateway to the idyllic emerald and azure waters of the Bay of Ieranto and nearby Marina del Cantone, where yachts drop anchor and film stars are spotted going for a dip and mixing with locals at seafood restaurants on stilts.

Marina della Lobra.

Deserto

Also near Sant'Agata, towards Massa Lubrense, is the religious complex of Deserto, which at 457 m affords 360-degree views across Campania, making it one of the most spectacular spots in Southern Italy. The monastery here was built by Carmelite nuns on the site of a hermitage. Remains of a Greek necropolis found here has led some people to claim that this was the site of an ancient Temple of the Sirens. An inscription on one of the towers reads 'Tempus breve est' ('Time is brief'). After taking in the jowl-dropping views and contemplating these wise words you'll probably want to crack on.

Trail of the Gods & other walks

The stunning coastline terrain is interspersed with old trails and mule tracks that provide many walking opportunities for most abilities. Early spring and early autumn may provide the mildest climatic conditions for trekking, but refreshments and suitable outdoor equipment are vital throughout the year. Many of the most popular routes are signposted but tricky trails on crumbly limestone paths make enlisting the expertise of a local walking guide like **Giovanni Visetti** (Giovis, T339-694 2911, giovis.com) a sensible choice. Giovanni leads trips along wild stretches of coastline near his home in Massa Lubrense as well as high up in the Monti Lattari, around Agerola and on the **Sentiero degli Dei** (Trail of the Gods). His website has lots of maps, descriptions and photos and is a portal for the region's outdoor specialists. Here he picks five of his favourite walks on the Sorrentine Peninsula and Amalfi Coast.

See page 126 for more about walking in Campania.

Giovanni's top walks

Termini to Punta Campanella to Termini
This 7-km circular route can be enjoyed in both directions but Giovanni recommends the anticlockwise version which involves some scrambling on tricky limestone cliffs. From the main piazza in Termini follow the signs to Monte San Costanzo: walking on a tarmac road followed by a rough trail. On the way there are spectacular views of 16th-century watchtowers – Fossa di Papa and Torre Minerva at Punta Campanella – and beyond to the Bay of Ieranto and Capri. Between January and March there are vibrant blue swathes of *lithodora rosmarinifolia*, a native flower seen all along this coast.

Monte Faito and Molare
This walk takes in an awe-inspiring limestone canyon with stratified rock layers and otherworldly rock formations. Take the cable car at Castellammare di Stabia to Monte Faito (1102 m) and then walk along a dusty trail through beech woods towards the Conocchia ridge, following the contours of the Vallone Acqua del Milo.

An undulating path eventually climbs to the Molare, which at 1444 m is the highest peak in the Monti Lattari range.

Colli Fontanelle to Malacoccola to Torca

There are numerous alternative routes along this awesome stretch of the Sorrentine Peninsula. One itinerary begins at the Colli Fontanelle and proceeds through chestnut woods and hillsides strewn with wild flowers to the promontory of Malacoccola, following the red and white signposts of the Alta Via dei Monti Lattari (Lattari Mountains High Route) to Torca. Fit walkers may like to complete a circular walk back to Colli Fontanelle through the Pineta delle Torre pine woods followed by a seat-of-the-pants descent down to the picturesque fjord of Crapolla.

Bomerano or Praiano to Colle Serra to Nocella (Trail of the Gods)

According to Giovanni this is the classic *Sentiero degli Dei* (Trail of the Gods) and is best tackled westwards for the most awe-inspiring views of the Amalfi Coast. You can reach the pass of Colle Serra (580 m) from either Bomerano or Praiano, before

taking in grassy terraces grazed by sheep and goats, fields studded with chestnut, oak and Mediterranean scrub, and then the limestone rock pinnacles and caves of the vast gorge Il Vallone di Grarelle. From the tiny village of Nocella (440 m) there is the option of rejoining the SS163 at Arienzo or more trekking adventures towards the towering cliffs of Montepertuso.

Valle dei Mulini aka Valle delle Ferriere (Valley of Mills)

The full 6-km walk in the Valley of Mills passes through olive and lemon groves and fresh streams of the Canneto River. Picturesque stone mill buildings that once drove lime, water and paper production litter the often shady route. On the way you are likely to see local characters leading sack-laden donkeys. Fitter and adventurous walkers may relish the ridge walks of the higher trail from Pogerola to Scala.

Amalfi Coast

The Amalfi Coast boasts the impossibly scenic coastal road, the SS163, otherwise known as the Amalfi Drive or *Via Smeraldo* (Emerald Road), which starts at Sant'Agata sui Due Golfi. This is connected to the SS145, *la Strada di Nastro Azzurro* (the Blue Ribbon Road), from Sorrento. Both roads glide around pulse-quickening bends offering visions of an azure and emerald sea down plunging limestone cliffs. Be warned: slow coaches and daredevil drivers of sports cars demand that you keep your eyes glued to the hairpins.

The SS163 soars above chic Positano's steep stairways and beaches before heading eastwards to Amalfi's maritime marvels and Byzantine Duomo. As an antidote to Amalfi's billowing tales of graft and glory on the high seas, you can climb 300 m to genteel and dreamy Ravello, whose refreshing air and garden vistas have inspired artists like Boccaccio and Wagner. The lush Dragone Valley is peppered with picturesque old mills. At Scala, Atrani, Minori, Cetara and Vietri majolica-tiled domes embellish the coast's natural wonders of fjord-like valleys, coves and limestone ridges as far as the city of Salerno.

Leaving the SS163, Viale Pasitea winds down into Positano, where traffic ceases and narrow lanes and *scalinatelle* (stairways) pass fragrant gardens and small boutiques. At via dei Mulini 23, Joachim Murat (1767-1815), Napoleon's brother-in-law and King of the Two Sicilies (1808-1815), built the imposing **Palazzo Murat** with its captivating *cortile* (courtyard). It's now one of the many swanky hotels here. Cool cotton threads and artisan-made sandals that hung on hipsters of the 1950s and 1960s still spill out of the shops on the way to Positano's jet-set playground, La Spiaggia Grande.

Chiesa di Santa Maria Assunta

Piazza Flavio Gioia, Positano, T089-875480.
Daily 0800-1200, 1600-1900.

The yellow, green, blue and white majolica Vietri tiles of the dome of Santa Maria Assunta dazzle near the beach and can be seen from all over Positano. The present triple-naved layout took shape in the 18th century when the church was built over the remains of a 13th-century Benedictine abbey. Inside, amid the underwhelming feast of white and gold stucco work, is *La Madonna Nera* (the Black Madonna), a Byzantine icon that holds centre stage during the town's exuberant *Festa della Assunta* (Feast of the Assumption), held each year on 15 August.

Tip...

Driving to and along both coastlines (A3 Napoli–Salerno, then SS145 and SS163) can be exhilarating but the traffic and Neapolitan driving will test your patience and nerve. If your budget allows, hire a driver from a reputable firm like **Benvenuto Limos** (via Roma 54, Praiano, T346-684 0226/089-874024, benvenutolimos.com), run by charming Giovanni and Umberto who have a fleet of air-conditioned Mercedes vehicles, and lots of local knowledge.

Essentials

❶ **Getting around** Prepare yourself for traffic on the roads along the Amalfi Coast, especially on the SS163, which is very narrow in places and often gets jammed with coaches from May to Oct. In the summer, the most comfortable way to reach Positano, Amalfi and Minori is to take a hydrofoil from Napoli Molo Beverello. There are also seasonal services connecting resorts along the both the Sorrentine and Amalfi coasts run by **Metro del Mare** (T199-446644, metrodelmare.com). **SITA** (T081-552 2176) runs buses to and from Naples, and there are many local lines reaching Ravello, Vietri and smaller hamlets.

❷ **Bus station** Piazza Flavio Gioia, Amalfi, T089-871016.

❸ **ATM** Banco di Napoli, piazza Duomo 1, Amalfi, T089-871005.

⊕ **Hospital** Croce Rossa Italiana, via Nuova Chiunzi 1, Maiori, T089-852002.

❹ **Pharmacy** Farmicia del Cervo, piazza Duomo 42, Amalfi, T089-871045.

❔ **Post office** Corso delle Repubbliche Marinare 33, Amalfi, T089-830 4811.

❶ **Tourist information** AAST, via delle Repubbliche Marinare, Amalfi, T089-871107, amalfitouristoffice.it.

Above: Looking down to Positano. Opposite page: Saint Andrew, patron saint of Amalfi, Scotland and all things fishy.

Spiaggia Grande & Positano's other beaches

Positano's main beach and ferry port, Spiaggia Grande, can be a seething mass of bodies and boat operators during the high season. Backed by restaurants and artists with easels, the western part of the shingle beach is public and free while bathing establishments cram the eastern half with parasols, loungers and deckchairs. Two defensive towers, Torre Trasita and Torre Sponda, frame this much-painted beach scene. A shady prom, via Positanesi d'America, runs along its cliffs and links with the the more secluded Spiaggia Fornillo which is less busy but has several beach bars.

Serious sun-worshippers tend to walk to or hop on a boat to one of the small coves along the coast. These include La Porta (where Palaeolithic and Mesolithic remains were found in a cave), Fiumicello, Arienzo (film director Franco Zeffirelli had a villa here), San Pietro and Laurito (with restaurants and a hotel).

Tip...

Lots of small operators, such as **Lucibello** and **Gennaro e Salvatore**, offer boat trips to nearby bathing spots, hidden coves, Li Galli and beyond – see Boat trips, page 237.

East of Positano

Praiano

Leaving Positano, to the west of Capo Sottile is the small village of Vettica Maggiore, whose main attraction is the peachy-looking **Chiesa di San Gennaro**, crowned with a majolica-tiled dome. Neighbouring Praiano, 6 km west of Positano, sits below Monte Sant'Angelo (120 m) and was the summer residence of the Amalfi Doge. Its watchtowers give it a mildly medieval atmosphere. As you approach, look out for the village houses set into the roadside rock – at Christmas these are lit up and turned into nativity scenes. Praiano's picturesque harbour and pebbly beach, Marina di Praia, lies within a small fissure between rocky cliffs. Nearby Gavitella beach has a tiny platform and an excellent seafood restaurant, La Gavitella Blu Bay (see page 213), accessed by tricky steps from Praiano or free shuttle boat from both Positano and Marina di Praia.

Furore

Continuing towards Amalfi on the SS163, it's worth stopping to admire the **Vallone di Furore**, a fjord-like gorge that cuts into the limestone rock below the Agerola plateau. The Furore gorge was known as Terra Furoris in ancient times after the almighty racket caused by the waves and wind whipping through the cleft in the towering rock walls. Gazing down at the dramatic ravine that

What the locals say

I suggest that you get a boat to explore the coast. La Praia beach is quite busy during the weekend but is still pleasant. La Gavitella has a very tiny beach but there is a platform with sunbeds and umbrellas that makes it a cute, fun place. The restaurant here does great, great fish.

Giovanni Benvenuto, Praiano resident

Li Galli – the Land of the Sirens

The turquoise waters that surround the myth-laden Li Galli islands – 'The Cockerels' – are a sublime spot for swimming, attracting fancy yachts and chartered boats. The rocky islets Gallo Lungo, La Rotonda and Castelluccia are privately owned. Russian choreographer Leonide Massine built a magnificent villa on Gallo Lungo's Roman remains in the 1930s and ballet dancer Rudolf Nureyev owned the magical place from 1989 to his death in 1993. According to Greek mythology, Sirens (feathered creatures with Avian bodies and human female heads) seduced sailors with their music onto these rocks, also known as Le Sirenuse. In Homer's *Odyssey*, as the hero Ulysses approaches the Sirens he fills his ears and those of his crew with wax and ties himself to the mast to avoid the creatures' spellbinding song.

Above: Furore footsteps. Opposite page: Spiaggia Grande.

gouges through the cliffs, you can see far below a couple of *monazzeni* (old fishermen's cottages) and a small pebbly beach filled with boats: the scene conjures up Peter Pan adventures and what JM Barrie called 'the nowhere village'.

The adventurous may enjoy approaching the fjord via the *Sentiero della Volpe Pescatrice* (Path of the Fishing Fox) from the old fishing village of **Furore**, which is now famed for its vibrant mural paintings. Other trails in the area have similarly evocative names (Mad-Bat Path, Crow's Nest Path, Path of Love). These paths offer various degrees of difficulty for walking, abundant local flora and fauna, and some intriguing buildings including three churches and old paper mills hugging the waters of a stream, the Schiato. The area makes an excellent base for walking in the Monti Lattari around Agerola and for sampling its local cheeses and Furore DOC wine. The Gran Furor Divina Costiera winery in Furore offers tours and tastings by appointment only (see page 239).

Agerola

On the Agerola plateau above Furore, amid the cows chomping on the lush meadows of the Monti Lattari, a more rural atmosphere reigns. Here you'll find spectacular walking trails (the Trail of the Gods passes through here) and new perspectives of Vesuvius. Some of Campania's finest cheeses, including *fior di latte* (cow's milk mozzarella) and *Provolone del Monaco* (well-aged cheese of stretched curd fashioned into ovoid balls) are produced on Agerola's fertile slopes.

It's a fact...

One of the *monazzeni* at Furore was the scene of a tempestuous love affair between Italian film director Roberto Rossellini and actress Anna Magnani played out after shooting the film *L'Amore* (1948). The *monazzeni* are now the focus of cultural events.

Around the region

Grotta dello Smeraldo

On SS163, 5 km west of Conca dei Marini.
Mar-Oct 0900-1900, Nov-Feb 0900-1600,
weather permitting, €6. Positano–Amalfi SITA
buses stop nearby.

Mesmerizing blue-green waters and strange
stalactite and stalagmite formations make a visit
to the Emerald Grotto an eerie – and worthwhile –
experience. Arriving by road, the grotto is accessed
by lift or a steep staircase, which may be dangerous
for some; you can also get here by boat trip. The
grotto measures 30 m x 60 m and is 24 m deep in
places; a ceramic *presepe* (nativity scene) lies in its
luminous depths.

Conca dei Marini

The dramatic defensive citadels, intimate marina
and rocky cove of Conca dei Marini lie 5 km west
of Amalfi. Conca's arresting combination of crystal
clear waters backed by handsome palazzi perched
on wild, towering cliffs make it a fabulous place to
explore for a couple of hours. At the 14th-century
Monastero di Santa Rosa, the nuns fashioned
pastry into the shape of a priest's cowl and
a special version of *sfogliatella* was born.
Neighbouring Chiesa di Santa Maria di Grado
contains lots of Baroque flourishes, Renaissance
marble reliefs and a spooky sight: a reliquary
containing the skull of San Barnaba.

Scala & Pontone

Perched on a lofty step near Ravello is the oldest
settlement on the Amalfi Coast, the fortified village
of Scala, whose origins go back to Roman times.
At the end of the 13th century Amalfi's nobles built
palaces including imposing Palazzo d'Afflitto and
Palazzo Mansi, amid stone stairways that wind

Tip...

If you want to witness the most intense light effects
at Grotta dello Smeraldo, try to get there between
1200 and 1500, and if possible arrive by boat.

between citrus and chestnut groves. Scala's
12th-century **Duomo di San Lorenzo** (piazza
Municipio 5, T089-857397, daily 0800-1300,
1800-1900) has a Romanesque portal, majolica
flooring and a crypt with wood carvings.

At the nearby village of Pontone is the
Centro Visite Valle delle Ferriere (T089-873043,
valledelleferriere.com) where you can obtain
maps and information about walking in the Valley
of the Mills, which follows the force that drove the
paper mills, the Canneto river (see Great days out,
page 213).

Below: Conca dei Marini. Opposite page: Up the Duomo steps.

Back in the sixth century, Amalfi became a prosperous port, trading salt and slaves for eastern gold. This small Duchy of Naples rose rapidly, adding an archbishop and then maritime republic status in 987. Doges, laws, taxes and enormous wealth followed. Holy Roman Emperors, the Vatican and the rival republics were just a few of the behemoths to covet its commercial influence and affluence. In the 1340s a huge tsunami smashed the port and town, followed by a terrible plague, taking the wind out of Amalfi's sails.

Walking around this Unesco World Heritage site today, it's hard to believe that between the 9th and 12th centuries Amalfi's maritime empire rivalled Venice, Genoa and Pisa. It's well worth exploring the town's medieval lanes and exotic past, including the imposing Byzantine Duomo, although the buzz and bustle of its artisan paper shops and souvenir outlets may prove too taxing on a sweltering sunny day. Early mornings and late afternoons are the best times to appreciate Amalfi's commercial and artistic colours. Other favourite pastimes include swimming and sunbathing at one its pebbly beaches (choose from half-a-dozen private beaches belonging to hotels or the free public beach by piazza Flavio Gioia) and trips to savour lofty delights at Scala, Ravello and the Valle dei Mulini (Valley of the Mills).

Duomo

Piazza del Duomo, Amalfi, T089-871324.
Summer 0900-2100, winter 1000-1700, €3 museum and cloisters, cathedral free.

Dedicated to the apostle Sant'Andrea in the 9th century, Amalfi's cathedral reflects the maritime republic's oriental trading links in dazzling, Byzantine style. Its grand central staircase leads to a columned porch and bronze Byzantine doors above which towers a richly decorated façade (1203) and Romanesque campanile. The 13th-

century Chiostro del Paradiso (Cloister of Paradise) has gardens surrounded by interlaced Arabic arches and a wavy roofline, while the museum contains 12th-century mosaics and an Angevin mitre studded with 19,000 pearls. Beside the nave is the frescoed Chapel of the Crucifix, the oldest part of the church, which leads to the crypt where part of Sant'Andrea's skull, looted from Constantinople during the Crusades, now resides.

Tip...

Don't miss a visit to historic bar-pastry shop **Pasticceria Andrea Panza 1830** (piazza Duomo 40) which is famed for its *frutti canditi*: vibrant and tangy orange, lemon and citron candied citrus fruits that adorn eye-catching ice creams and cakes.

Around the region

Above: Amalfi evening. Opposite page: Villa Rufolo.

Museo Civico

Town Hall, piazza Municipio, Amalfi, T089-873620.
Mon-Fri 0830-1330, 1630-1830, free.

Amalfi's civic museum contains the original manuscript that details the maritime code that governed the Mediterranean until 1570, *Il Tavoliere Amalfitane*. Exhibits relating to Flavio Gioia, the celebrated mariner and inventor of the dry compass, can also be seen. Down by the waterfront, in the piazza named after him, stands a statue of Flavio Gioia.

Museo della Carta

Palazzo Pagliara, via delle Cartiere 23, Amalfi, T089-830 4561, museodellacarta.it.
Mar-Oct daily 1000-1830, Nov-Feb Tue-Sun 1000-1530, €4.

Amalfi was one of the first places in Europe to bring back papermaking technology from the Orient and within this old paper mill the traditional methods are explained by a guide. The town remains one of the European capitals of *carta a mano* (hand-made paper) and the museum shop is full of posh stationery.

Atrani

A 20-minute walk east of Amalfi takes you away from the crowds to the more peaceful Atrani with its medieval buildings and atmospheric lanes interspersed with lush gardens. Amalfi's doges and judges lived here; the doges were crowned and buried at the 10th-century Chiesa San Salvatore de' Birecto (piazza Umberto 1): birecto being a reference to the doge's ceremonial cap. Down on the sheltered beach fishermen potter around with their *lampare* boats – these traditional vessels cast off at night covered in twinkling lights to attract fish.

Way up high at 350 m, some 6 km northeast of Amalfi, along a twisting, ear-popping road, is ever-so-refined Ravello. For nearly the entire second half of the last millennium Ravello's status as an independent principality meant that it was answerable only to the Pope. Prestigious villas and gorgeous religious buildings in Norman-Saracenic style sprang up amid elegant terraced gardens here in the 1400s. Illustrious visitors including Graham Greene, DH Lawrence, Wagner and JF Kennedy all found inspiration from its uplifting environs and views. Although the road to Ravello is often choked by traffic, all vehicles are left at the car park near piazza Duomo, where cafés, a ceramics shop and the elegant cathedral set the relaxed and detached-from-modernity tone. Allow at least three hours to enjoy Ravello's uniquely serene atmosphere.

Duomo

Piazza del Vescovado, Ravello, T089-858311.
Cathedral daily 0900-1300, 1700-1900, museum Easter-Oct daily 0900-1300, 1500-1900. Cathedral free, €2 museum.

The understated façade and elegant 13th-century campanile crowned with interlaced arches hint at the pleasing proportions of Ravello's cathedral. Inside, the intimate scale, exquisite artworks and refreshing lightness of it all make this a Romanesque duomo to remember. Built in 1086 and remodelled in 1786, the cathedral is dedicated to San Pantaleone – whose blood 'miraculously' liquefies without fail each 27 July. A double set of wooden doors protects enormous 12th-century bronze doors cast in Constantinople by Barisano

da Trani. The panels on the doors depicting biblical scenes have been undergoing restoration. Medieval pulpits by Bartolomeo da Foggia have intricate bas-reliefs, vibrant mosaics and twisting columns resting on six squat marble lions. A mosaic of Jonah and the Whale recalls the frescoed panel by Giotto in Padova's Scrovegni Chapel. The series of frescoes of Madonna and Child here also appear to be influenced by Giotto's genius – Giotto did some work for the Angevins at Castel Nuovo (see page 84) in the 14th century. Descend into the crypt to see some pious relics, including a striking 13th-century marble bust of Sigilgaita Rufolo, wife of the treasurer of King Charles of Anjou (ruler of Naples 1265-1285) and depicted here as a Fortuna: a classical goddess symbolizing the city's prosperity.

Villa Rufolo

Piazza Duomo, Ravello, T089-857657.
Daily 0900-1800, Apr-Sep until 2000, €5, €3 concessions.

Built in 1270 by the Rufolos, a rich merchant family, this villa has hosted and inspired royalty, celebs and plebs. The 19th-century Scots botanist Francis Reid transformed a sadly neglected villa into the magical place we know today. If the dreamlike atmosphere created by Moorish arcades, cool cloisters and an ivy-covered tower don't grab you, the awe-inspiring views from the terraced gardens certainly will. Wagner's enchanting garden of Klingsor (from the opera *Parsifal*) was inspired

Tip...

For reasonably priced refreshments and Neapolitan pastries consume *al banco* (at the bar) or pay extra to sit down at **Bar Klingsor** (4 via dei Rufolo, on piazza Duomo, T089-857407).

by the villa and its surroundings, and it may even feature, in some way, in Boccaccio's *Decameron*. Classical music concerts and art shows are often staged here as part of the world famous Ravello Festival (see page 54).

Villa Cimbrone

Via Santa Chiara 26, Ravello, T089-857459. Gardens open daily 0900 to sunset, €6.

A 10-minute walk along a hillside path from Piazza Duomo brings you to this fantastical castle that comes complete with turrets, cloisters, wonderful gardens and terraces with views to rival any in Italy. It was the brainchild of Ernest Beckett, 2nd Baron Grimthorpe, who in 1904 bought what was then little more than a ruined farmhouse and set about creating his masterpiece. The villa remained in the hands of the Beckett family until the 1960s, enchanting a succession of visitors that included Virginia Woolf, EM Forster, DH Lawrence, Henry Moore, Winston Churchill (who painted here), Greta Garbo and Gore Vidal. Although it's now a posh hotel, the gardens can still be visited during the daytime. Romantic verses by Roman poets and Persian astronomers are etched onto plaques among the fronds and flowers. Standing by the classical busts on the belvedere, there are exquisite views of the Gulf of Salerno and beyond.

Tip...

Ravello's Tuesday market near the Duomo is full of the most delicious produce, including many varieties of olives – favourites are the purplish *olive di Gaeta* and some large vivid-green beauties.

Top: Il Duomo, Piazza del Vescovado. Above: Villa Cimbrone. Opposite page: Minori.

Minori, Maiori & Tramonti

Lying between Amalfi and Capo d'Orso, the two towns of Minori and Maiori can come as a bit of a disappointment after the glories of Ravello and Amalfi.

In **Minori** there's little evidence of its cantieri, the shipyards that helped to build the Amalfi maritime republic's fleet. Instead there's a small, scruffy beach backed by a promenade where market stalls manned by some dodgy characters sell cheap threads, odds and duds. Near the prom, the 11th-century **Basilica di Santa Trofimena** contains the relics of St Trofimena, in whose honour a festival is held each July.

Dusty remains of a Roman villa from the town of Regina Minor can be seen at Minori's **Villa Marittima** (via Capo di Piazza 28, T089-852893, Mon-Sat 0900 to 1 hr before sunset), including some faded frescoes, a dank *nymphaeum* and some archaeological fragments. Terrapins sunbathe and perform bellyflops in the shallow courtyard pool here.

Minori's neighbour, **Maiori**, suffered a devastating flood in 1954 that washed away most of the town's charm, although it does have the majolica-tiled cupola of the 12th-century Chiesa di Santa Maria a Mare. Its large beach, strewn with flotsam and jetsam, is flanked by a long promenade.

Climb 600 m up the Valico di Chiunzi to the mountain villages around **Tramonti** for sublime views of seascapes and mountains. Mules carrying cheeses and fruits totter amid the tiny stone buildings. The people of Amalfi named the cold and dry wind that whipped them from the north, La Tramontana after its lofty neighbour.

Tip...

Award winning pastry chef Salvatore de Riso makes Neapolitan pastries and cakes, including *delizia di limone*, from his shop **Pasticceria Sal De Riso** (piazza Cantilena 28) in Minori.

Capo d'Orso

A few kilometres east of Maiori is Capo d'Orso, a protected reserve with jagged cliffs, a lighthouse and the **Abbazia di Santa Maria de Olearia** (open by appointment: contact Maiori tourist office T089-877452 for latest opening times). This atmospheric monastery has chapels and caves hewn out of the limestone.

Erchie, Cetara & Vietri

Erchie has a small pebbly beach strewn with fishing boats while Cetara's beach is backed by a defensive tower and restaurants serving its famous *colatura di alici* (salted anchovy sauce similar to the ancient Roman garum) and tuna in oil. In the summer Vietri's Marina di Vietri is peppered with parasols and day-tripping Salernatini (Salerno is only 5 km away). The town's celebrated ceramics are everywhere: adorning cupolas and shopfronts, and spilling out of shops on via Madonna degli Angeli. An amazing 20,000 pots cover the eccentric, conical towers of iconic factory **Ceramiche Artistiche Solimne** (via Madonna degli Angeli 7, T089-212539), designed by Paolo Soleri, a student of American modernist architect Frank Lloyd Wright. Nearby, in the village of Raito, is the **Museo della Ceramica** (Villa Giariglia, via Nuova Raito, T089-211835, museibiblioteche.provincia. salerno.it; Tue-Sat 0900-1315, 1400 to 1 hr before sunset in the summer €3).

Salerno & Paestum

Campania's second city, Salerno, located 55 km southeast of Naples, is a busy university town with some fine historic sights and a scenic *lungomare* (seaside promenade). Since its foundation in the sixth century BC, Salerno has had as many rulers as Naples. In recent times, it was the focus of frenzied skirmishes from 1943 to 1945 between the Allies, Germans and retreating Fascists. Amid the post-Second World War modernist architecture are remnants of a medieval quarter, 19th-century buildings and art nouveau palazzi. Some 40 km south of Salerno on the flat plains of the Sele River are the impressive Graeco-Roman ruins of Paestum. An archaeological museum here tells the fascinating story of a lost civilization, while 9 km up the road, amid grazing buffalo, are more Greek temple remains at the *Santuario di Hera Argiva*.

There are fabulous sea views along the recently revamped, palm tree-lined *lungomare*. At its western end is the Villa Comunale, with its verdant gardens flanked by historic buildings. The *centro storico* starts near the flamboyant Teatro Verdi building (see page 235). Beyond the smart shops on via di Porta Catena is the piazza Sedile del Campo, the old market square, which contains the spouting dolphins of La Fontana dei Delfini and arcaded palaces including Baroque Palazzo dei Genovesi (a university seat and cultural venue). Nearby via dei Mercanti turns into corso Vittorio Emanuele, Salerno's main shopping street.

Duomo di San Matteo

Piazza Alfano 1, Salerno, T089-231382.
Daily 1000-1800, free.

Salerno's cathedral was founded in 845, rebuilt in 1076, and has been renovated many times since. A Romanesque gateway leads to a Moorish atrium containing 28 columns pinched from Paestum. Towering 55 m above the beautiful colonnade is the cathedral's striking 12th-century campanile. A bronze door with niello engraving from Constantinople (1099) leads into the elegant Latin-cross interior with its two *ambones* (medieval raised platforms/pulpits). Down in the crypt is the body of the evangelist St Matthew and among the Roman and medieval sarcophagi is the tomb of Pope Gregory VII who died in exile in 1085. The adjoining Museo Diocesano contains an exquisite 11th-century altar-front with ivory panels.

Chiesa di San Benedetto

Via San Benedetto 38, Salerno, T089-231135.
Mon-Sat 0900-2000, free.

Grand interiors of the 11th-century wing of the San Benedetto convent are overflowing with antiquities organized into themed sections. There are fascinating finds from Roman Salerno (seek out

Above: Salerno. Opposite page: Magical Paestum.

the 1st century bronze head of Apollo found in the gulf in 1930) and some 5th-century burial treasures from Roscigno.

Castello di Arechi

Via Benedetto Croce, Salerno, T089-233900, castellodiarechi.it.
Mon-Fri 0830-1930, Sat-Sun 0900-1330, free.

Take a taxi or climb the steep path to this castle for fabulous views of the Gulf of Salerno. The impressive fortifications were built by Byzantines and added to by the Normans, Angevins and Aragonese. A museum contains collections of weapons, ceramics, armoury, glass and coins. Occasional concerts and firework displays light up the battlements.

Around the region

Paestum is about 40 km south of Salerno. By car, take the A3 autostrada and exit at Battipaglia (from the north) or Eboli (from the south) and follow the signs. The train from Salerno takes 35 minutes and the SCAT bus from piazza Concordio in Salerno takes 80 minutes. The entrance is a 10-minute walk from the station. During the summer months the Metro del Mare from Naples or Amalfi stops at nearby Agropoli, from where a bus serves Paestum.

Mainland Italy's most important Greek ruins and its three impressive Doric temples emerge out of the grassy Sele River plain, a place famed for its wild roses and violets back in antiquity. Poseidonia was founded by Greek settlers from Sybaris around 600 BC and continued to thrive under

Below: Tomb of the Diver. Opposite page: Paestum.

Tip...

There are three entrances to the temples: one is over the road from the archaeological museum and tourist office while the other two are by the Temple of Neptune and porta della Giustizia. It makes sense – especially in the sweltering summer – to begin at the most southerly porta della Giustizia in the morning and to head northwards towards the Temple of Ceres, ending up in the cool museum at the hottest part of the day. The site is very exposed so don't forget hats, energy-giving snacks and refreshments.

Lucanian tribes (from 410 BC) and then the Romans (273 BC), who renamed it Paestum. Poets Ovid and Virgil sung Paestum's praises before Saracen invasions and encroaching malarial swamps drove its inhabitants into the mountains. Its architectural splendours were spared looting as it became enveloped in overgrown mire and was largely forgotten about, only to be rediscovered in the 18th century when engineers excavated a road straight through the amphitheatre. Thereafter, Grand Tourists and arty adventurers like Shelley, Canova and Goethe made it the climax of their European odysseys. It was not until the 1950s that major archaeological digs started to unearth the minutiae of ancient treasures. Allow a full day if you want to get the most out of a visit to this wonderfully evocative site.

Gli Scavi di Paestum

Archaeological area open daily 0900 to 1 hr before sunset, €4.50 or €7 combined ticket with museum.

Entering through the porta della Giustizia, one heads north along the **Via Sacra** (Sacred Road) that linked the principal buildings of Poseidonia with the **Tempio di Hera** (Temple of Hera), Paestum's oldest structure, built in 550 BC. Its 50 tapering outer columns were given convex curves to give the illusion of straight lines from a distance, a process known as *entasis*. The survival of these bulging columns makes this the most well-preserved example of an early Doric temple anywhere. Seek out the sacrificial altar and a square well where the sacrificial remains were thrown.

Next to the Temple of Hera is Paestum's largest temple, the **Tempio di Nettuno** (Temple of Neptune), built around 450 BC. Its covering of Travertine marble makes the temple glow a rich hue at sunset. Confusingly, historians believe that it was dedicated to Hera Argiva, goddess of fertility. It is 6 m longer than the Temple of Hera, with 36 fluted columns (six at each end and 14 along the sides). Look carefully at the cornices and horizontal lines that curve slightly upwards in the middle: this architectural method creates an elegant appearance and less sagging look. To the east are the remains of a sacrificial altar.

Continuing along the via Sacra, the Roman Forum is one of the most complete anywhere in the world. A Doric portico surrounded it. To the north is the 1st century BC amphitheatre, which is cut in half by a modern road. The rectangular buildings next to the forum had various uses: *taberna* (shops), a *comitium* (court), basilica, *macellum* (covered market) and temples dedicated to Asclepius (the god of healing) and Fortuna Virilis (where women worshipped Venus).

The **Tempio di Cerere** (Temple of Ceres), further north, is really an Athenaion: a temple dedicated to the goddess Athena. Three Christians tombs were added in the medieval period. It has 34 fluted columns and is the smallest of the three temples.

To the west of via Sacra there was a large residential district containing some luxurious homes, some with pools. A tour of the city walls throws up more intriguing finds and layers of history including towers, bastions and medieval watchtowers.

Museo Archeologico Nazionale

Via Magna Grecia 917, Paestum, T0828-811023, infopaestum.it.
Daily 0900-1845 (closed on first and third Mon of each month), €4.50 or €7 combined ticket, reductions with Artecard.

Paestum Archaeological Museum, designed in 1952, is just over the road from the excavations, near the tourist office. Top billing goes to the Tomb of the Diver, comprising frescoed panels including a funereal banqueting scene and the famous image of a youth diving gracefully into blue water, an allegory of death. Among the burial treasures, architectural fragments and terracottas from Paestum's Greek, Lucanian and Roman eras is sculpture depicting various Homeric scenes found at the sanctuary of Hera Argiva.

Museo Narrante del Santuario di Hera Argiva

Masseria Procuriali, T0828-811016, infopaestum.it.
Daily Tue-Sat 0900-1600, free.

At the mouth of the Sele river, 9 km north of Paestum, is the Sanctuary of Hera and a new, engaging multimedia museum that spills the ancient beans and beads about ancient Greek cults and their penchant for weaving and spinning. Ancient scribes Strabo (63 BC – AD 26) and Pliny the Elder (23 BC – AD 79) wrote about this legendary place which according to Magna Grecia mythology was built by Jason and the Argonauts. Earthquakes, eruptions and conflicts smashed the lavish temples, then the increasingly marshy Sele plain and looting left us mere foundations to stumble upon. In 1934 it was discovered by archaeologists and although little remains of its former grandeur it's an evocative place to visit and a big, wallowing hit with grazing buffalo.

Tenuta Vannulo

Via G Galilei (Contrada Vannulo), Capaccio Scalo, T0828-724765, vannulo.it.

You can get up close to the mud-wallowing buffalo on a guided tour of the estate and dairy on this farm near Paestum. As well as producing arguably the best mozzarella in the world, the creative Palmieri family also sell ricotta, served here with a choice of condiments (cinnamon, honey, cocoa powder, nutmeg and kumquat jelly), and yoghurts (flavoured with local figs, hazelnuts and pomegranate). Naples resident Vicky recommends their delicious organic buffalo-milk ice cream and popular handbags made from buffalo hide.

Sleeping

All along the Sorrentine Peninsula and Amalfi Coast there is plenty of choice for most budgets, from lavish beachside hotels to out-of-the-way *agriturismi* up in the Lattari Mountains.

Self-catering
Among the companies offering affordable apartments and sumptuous villas are well-established brokers like **Cuendet** (T0800-085 7732, cuendet.co.uk) and smaller, local operations like **Amalfi Vacation** (T339-589 2551, amalfivacation.it) and **Amalfi Residence** (Largo Filippo Augustariccio 1d, 84011 Amalfi, Salerno, T089-873 588, amalfiresidence.it). Down at Marina del Cantone is the **Casale Villarena** (via Cantone 3, 80061 Nerano, T081-808 1779, casalevillarena.com) a largish complex containing a half-dozen apartments.

Tip...

La Ginestra's organically produced *miele di castagno* was deemed Campania's best honey in 2004. Vincenzo Mariniello, resident of Naples and Capri, swears by it: "When one of my family has the sniffles I always get some of La Ginestra's wonderful honey."

Sorrentine Peninsula

Hotel Michelangelo €€€
Corso Italia 275, Sorrento, T081-878 4844, michelangelohotel.it.
The Michelangelo offers good value and modern yet attractive surroundings in busy and pricey Sorrento. It's down the quieter end of corso Italia, and is handily placed for all the Sorrentine action and public transport connections. Both public areas and the 121 guest rooms are reassuringly clean and bright with warm touches. There's a small pool and a bar where barista Pepe fixes the drinks and throws in some entertaining quips.

Grand Hotel Hermitage & Villa Romita €€
Corso Sant'Agata 36, Sant'Agata sui Due Golfi, T081-878 0025, grandhotelhermitage.it.
It's not just the sublime views from the pool area and lush gardens that make these two adjoining and very differently styled hotels so special. The modern Grand Hotel offers great value while the swankier Villa Romita, a former residence of a Neapolitan philosopher, is all about extra comfort and privacy. The Grand Hotel has a kitschy bar area and a Neapolitan restaurant La Sala dei Sogni.

La Ginestra €
Via Tessa 2, Santa Maria del Castello, Vico Equense, T081-802 3211, laginestra.org.
A bus passes nearby connecting with Vico Equense and Sorrento.
Escape the tourist trails at this small farmstead-*agriturismo* up in the hills above Vico Equense. There are just seven rooms but all are cosy and of different sizes. Guests and daytime visitors can see the farm's goats, geese and deer. There's also a playground so it's great for families. The real bonus comes in the restaurant which serves La Ginestra's home-grown organic produce in classic Amalfitana dishes such as *scialatielli con pomodorini del Vesuvio* (pasta with tomatoes from the slopes of Vesuvius).

Seven H €
Via Iommella Grande 99, Sant'Agnello, T081-878 6758, sevenhostel.com.
A short walk from the station.
This stunningly renovated *conservatorio* is now the fanciest hostel imaginable. A bed in a dorm costs around €25 while a comfy double is €85 in high season. The roof terraces have stylish loungers and sofas, and offer stunning views. Interesting artworks, mood lighting and design touches in the courtyard and smart bar make it one of the first boutique hostels known to man or beast.

Camping

Villaggio Nettuno

Via A Vespucci 39, Nerano Massa Lubrense, T081-808 1051, villaggionettuno.it.

Isolation and beauty are the watchwords of a stay at enchanting Marina di Cantone, but there's no shortage of activities and seafood restaurants nearby. This dusty camping village has the usual places to pitch your tent or caravan, as well as basic bungalows sleeping 2-8 people for €65-200 per night. Expect lots of activities (snorkelling, diving and boat trips), facilities (pool, sports and shop) and boisterous night-time shenanigans.

Amalfi Coast

Hotel Santa Caterina €€€€

Via Nazionale 9, 84011 Amalfi, T089-871012, hotelsantacaterina.it.

Clinging to the cliffs west of Amalfi this fabulous hotel is immersed in terraced gardens filled with citrus fruits and vines. A Bond-style lift whisks you down to the pool and shore where you can often watch the staff fishing for octopus. Choose from dining in the relaxed café-restaurant or more formal dining around a piano bar and terrace, which requires a jacket. The best of the accommodation is a five-minute walk away – past the spa facilities and shop – in the annexe, where rooms have huge whirlpool baths and their own terrace.

Le Sirenuse €€€€

Via C Colombo 30, Positano, T089-875066, sirenuse.it.

The Amalfi Coast's most gorgeous hotel is run by the Marchesi Sarsale, who opened up their noble residence in the 1950s, hosting the likes of John Steinbeck and many famous people since. Antiques and artworks fill the elegant public rooms while the guest rooms have colourful tiled floors and vaulted ceilings – most have balconies with sea views. Alfonso and Ernesto Iaccarino (from Michelin-starred Don Alfonso, see page 231) have recently taken charge of the menu in the stunning La Sponda restaurant.

Palazzo Sasso €€€€

Via San Giovanni del Toro 28, Ravello, T089-818181, palazzosasso.com.

Opened in 1997, this place regularly wins awards for its level of luxury and service. The breathtaking sea views from its lofty Ravello perch give this 12th-century palazzo the edge over many smart hotels on the *costiera*. If you want to eat posh Neapolitan nosh there's the two Michelin-starred Rossellini's restaurant, or there's more laid-back dining on the magical Terrazza Belvedere. Facilities include a spa/wellness centre with hydro pool and Turkish steam bath, as well as a heated pool and fitness area.

Seaside pool, Hotel Santa Caterina.

Caffè dell'Arte, Hotel Palazzo Sasso.

Marina Riviera €€€
Via P Comite 19, 84011 Amalfi,
T089-871104, marinariviera.it.
Its vibrant tiles, great views and
excellent staff make this a great
base in Amalfi. The 20 guest
rooms come in many shapes and
sizes, most have sea views, and
many have intimate balconies
you can sit out on. Start the day
eating breakfast on the terrace
and perhaps spend a night at the
amiable Gargano family's elegant
Eolo restaurant nearby.

Hotel La Lucertola €€
Via Cristoforo Colombo 29, 84019
Vietri sul Mare, T089-210255,
hotellalucertola.it.
Recent refurbishment of this
1970s hotel on the Vietri coast
has created a kind of value-for-
money minimalist hotel:
boutique on the cheap if you
will. Lounge lizards and local
lucertole (the native reptile)
enjoy the beiger-than-beige
bar-restaurant. The hotel's 33
guest rooms combine modern
technology (Wi-Fi and Sky TV)
with lots of 1980s-style black
veneer with contemporary
sinks and baths, plus sea views.

Hotel Vittoria €€
Via Fornillo 19, 84017 Positano,
T089-875 049,
hotelvittoriapositano.com.
Above the popular Spiaggia
Fornillo is the Vittoria's flowery
terrace, a great place to enjoy
breakfast and their authentic
pizza napoletana made in a

forno a legna (wood-fired oven).
Each of the 34 rooms has cool
tiled floors, unfussy decor and
a balcony with sea views.

Il Castagno €
Via Radicosa 39, Fraz. San
Lazzaro, Agerola, T081-802 5164,
agriturismoilcastagno.com.
Immersed in the vineyards and
chestnut trees of Agerola, this
old farmhouse has simple but
comfortable accommodation
(10 rooms). B&B costs just €35
per person, per night, while half
board lunch or dinner (featuring
the farm's products and wine) is
€45. Friendly owner Rosa Coccia
organizes walking and cycling
trips around the region.

Salerno & Paestum

Il Cannito €€€
Via Cannito, Capaccio, Paestum,
T0828-196 2277, ilcannito.com.
Traditional stone dwellings near
Paestum's archaeological site
have been converted into a
relaxing rural retreat full of stylish
design flourishes. Whitewashed
guest rooms have all the
technology and comforts
including air-conditioning,
underfloor heating and LCD TVs,
and minimalist bathrooms have
hydro-massage baths. A free
shuttle bus takes guests to a
nearby beach and there are
lots of walks to be had in the
surrounding woods.

Oleandri Resort Hotel Residence Villaggio Club €€
Via Laura 240, Paestum,
T0828-851730,
residenceoleandri.com.
Pools with swaying palms,
extensive lush gardens leading
to the beach and sports facilities
makes this resort especially
suited to families. There
are 53 rooms and lots of
accommodation options
including suites and villas for
up to seven people. Food can be
eaten at the poolside restaurant
or else you can buy provisions
and cook in your kitchenette.
Sports and activities such as
beach volleyball, ping-pong
or whiff-whaff, and aerobics
workouts are organized daily.
It's isolated so you need a
vehicle.

Hotel K €
Via D Somma 47 (just off
Lungomare Colombo), Salerno,
T089-725515, hotelk.it.
Beyond the striking façade
covered in cascading greenery
is a functional hotel with 53
room options. As well as being
near Salerno's sights, it has
some decent facilities including
restaurant, spa, laundry service
and garage parking.

Eating & drinking

Don Alfonso €€€€
Corso Sant'Agata 11, Sant'Agata Sui Due Golfi, T081-878 0026, donalfonso.com.
Tue-Sun 1200-1430, 2000-2300 (closed Wed in low season).
This place comes with two Michelin stars and a big reputation, but some Neapolitans reckon it's overrated and overpriced. Alfonso and Livia Iaccarino are celebrity food heroes in the south and organic produce pioneers: lots of their veg is grown on their Punta Campanella land while all the cheeses and fish come from local producers. Expect simply prepared dishes like fish casserole and caciotta cheese ravioli and an aubergine and chocolate creation, served in sumptuous rooms. The *menu di degustazione* (tasting menu) costs €120. Reservations recommended.

Antico Francischiello da Peppino €€
Via Partenope 27, Massa Lubrense, T081-533 9780.
Daily 1200-1530, 1830-2400, closed Wed in low season.
Set on a hillside between Sorrento and Massa, this popular restaurant serves the freshest seafood and grilled meats accompanied by the tastiest *contorni* (vegetables). The rustic rooms are filled with Sorrentine knick-knacks and a mixture of locals and first-timers.

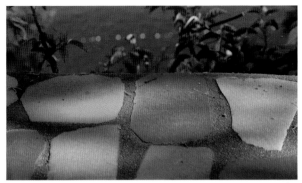

Ceramic tiles.

Il Delfino €€
Via Marina Grande 216, Sorrento, T081-878 2038.
Daily 1200-1530, 1830-2230.
Down by the Marina Grande harbour this restaurant serves fresh seafood and pasta dishes including *fettuccine con gamberetti e spinaci* (pasta ribbons with spinach and prawns). Il Delfino's long modern *salone* is lined with picture windows giving sublime shoreline views while you dine.

Da Gigino Università della Pizza €
Via Nicotera 10, Vico Equense, T081-879 8426, pizzametro.it.
Open 24 hrs.
The home of *pizza al metro* opened in the 1930s and claims to be the largest pizzeria in the world – it caters for as many as 2000 patrons at once. According to the experts a metre of pizza will feed five people but some of the Neapolitans regularly

break the norm and some buttons. For the non-purists, antipasti and dolci are brought around on a trolley.

Pizzeria da Franco €
Corso Italia 265, Sorrento, T081-877 2066.
Daily 1200-2400.
This no-nonsense pizzeria serves all the classics including *margherita* and *capricciosa* plonked on a tray in wax paper. Expect long queues.

Cafés & bars
Circolo dei Forestieri
Via Luigi de Maio 35, Sorrento, T081-877 3263.
Closed Feb-Mar.
This restaurant-bar has a large terrace with superb views, where you can hear traditional Neapolitan music live in the evening and more international tunes later on.

O Funzionista
Via San Nicola 13, Sorrento.
Great for picnic snacks, refreshments, ice cream, chocolates and pastries

Premiata Pasticceria Polli
Corso Italia 172, Sorrento, T081-877 2889.
This pastry parlour is famed for its ice cream, *spremute di arancia*

Five of the best
Culinary treasures

❶ Cetara's salted anchovy sauce, *la colatura*, resembles the ancient Roman garum.

❷ At Gragnano dried pasta-making was turned into a mass-production industry. In 1860 there were over 80 pasta factories at Gragnano.

❸ Minori is famous for *'ndunderi*, which resemble ancient Roman *gnocchi* (dumplings).

❹ At the marine nature reserve of Punta Campanella, hand-woven baskets (*nasse*) are used by local fishermen from April to September to catch *parapandolo*, small rare shrimp famed for their sweet, flavoursome meat.

❺ The Monti Lattari (Milky Mountains) are named after their dairy products which have been highly sought after since the days of the Dukes of Amalfi. The pastures of Tramonti, Scala and Agerola produce quality cheeses such as *Provolone di Monaco*, mozzarella, *caciocavallo* and *fior di latte*.

(fresh orange juice) and sweet treats including *bigne al caffè* (brioche with fruity fillings or Nutella) and *ciambelle* (doughnuts).

Amalfi Coast

Da Gemma €€€
Via Fra Gerardo Sasso 9, Amalfi, T089-871345.
Daily 1230-1445, 1930-2230.
Established in 1872, this well-respected ristorante still combines beautifully created dishes with a wonderful atmosphere. Try to book a table on the flower-filled terrace with views of the Duomo. Standout dishes include locally caught langoustines cooked in lemon oil and the classic *crostata Amalfitana* (baked tart). Reservations required.

Acquapazza €€
Corso Garibaldi 33, Cetara, T089-261606.
Daily 1230-1500, 1930-2300.
Cetara's famously fishy delights, including *colatura di alici* (anchovy sauce derived from an ancient Roman garum recipe), are served in this tiny place under and around a portico. They combine veg and seafood to yummy effect: try *totani* (type of squid) with fennel seeds and *seppie* (cuttlefish) served with *fagioli* (beans) and the ubiquitous *colatura*. Reservations recommended.

Da Lorenzo €€
Via Fra Gerardo Sasso, Scala, T089-858290.
Daily 1230-1500, 1900-2230 (closed Mon-Thu off season).
This family-run restaurant has an attractive terrace with gorgeous views and serves fabulous fish and pasta dishes, including *paccheri con cuoccio* (large pasta tubes with gurnard) and *calamari fritti* (fried squid).

Da Salvatore €€
Via delle Repubbliche 2, Ravello, T089-857227.
Apr-Oct daily 1230-1500, 1930-2300.
With jowl-dropping terrace views, friendly staff and the freshest seafood and meat creations, this is a good choice in the heart of Ravello. Book a table near the edge of the terrace and try their grilled *pescato del giorno* (catch of the day), with lots of freshly squeezed lemon juice. They also have some guest rooms.

Tip...
Costiera resident Giovanni Benvenuto says: "Da Lorenzo is a great place and does fine home cooking, but is open just on Fridays, Saturdays and Sundays off season. Also with wonderful views is Da Salvatore in nearby Ravello."

La Gavitella Blu Bay €€
Via Gavitella 1, Praiano, T089-813 1319, ristorantelagavitella.it.
Daily 1200-1530, 1900-2230.
A small boat whisks guests from Positano (Banchina di Approdo) and Marina di Praia to this elegant shoreline restaurant. The elegant glass-roofed dining room has picture windows that offer salty sights and smells of the waves lapping nearby. Complementing the freshest seafood dishes is a wine list full of the region's best labels including Furore, Falerno, Taurasi, Fiano and Greco di Tufo.

Lido Azzurro €€
Lungo Mare dei Cavalieri, Amalfi, T089-871384.
Daily 1230-1500, 1930-2230.
If you're after a no-frills trattoria, Lido Azzurro serves outstanding-value pasta and seafood dishes. Classic creations include *spaghetti alle vongole* (with clams) and *tubetti con zucchini* (tube-like pasta with courgettes). Don't leave without trying the local Furore DOC wine.

Lo Guarracino €€
Via Positanesi d'America 12, near Spiaggia Fornillo, Positano, T089-875794.
Daily 1200-1500, 1930-2330.
Perched above the waves overlooking Spiaggia Fornillo, this ristorante-pizzeria serves great-value thin-crust pizzas baked in a wood-burning oven and seafood dishes like *linguine*

guarracino (mixed seafood and little-tongued pasta speciality). The hike along the via Positanesi d'America path from Spiaggia Grande to reach the bamboo-covered restaurant is well worth the effort.

La Tagliata €
Via Tagliata 22, towards Montepertuso, Positano, T089-875872, latagliata.com.
Daily 1230-1500, 1930-late.
Way up on the hill near Montepertuso this rustic trattoria run by Enzo, Peppino and friends is the most hospitable place to eat imaginable. They eschew seafood and plump for a menu full of local meats and vegetables. A good introduction to this simply prepared, tasty cuisine is their selection of antipasti but leave some room for their *semifreddi* (creamy cakes). Most afternoons the large picture windows are opened for the welcome breeze while evenings at La Tagliata involve cups of vino, music and carousing overflowing onto the wooden tables. Reservations recommended.

Cafés & bars
Andrea Panza
Piazza Duomo 40, Amalfi, T081-871065.
Frutti canditi (candied fruits) fill the windows of this historic *pasticceria* that dates back to 1830. Conveniently close to the Duomo, it serves a refreshing *granite*, gelati, cakes and pastries.

Tip...
It's not just the food, atmosphere and hospitality that is exceptional at La Tagliata: the view from the loo, towards Li Galli, will take your breath away. Phone them in advance and if you ask nicely they'll pick you up from the Positano area.

La Tagliata dolci and semifreddi.

La Zagara
Via dei Mulini 8/10, Positano, T089-811116, lazagara.com.
All your favourite Neapolitan pastries and others including *crostatina fragolina* (strawberry tart), plus savoury snacks, cocktails and coffee, can be enjoyed to the accompaniment of piano bar tunes during the summer.

Sal De Riso
Piazza Cantilena 28, Minori, T089-853618, deriso.it.
A talented young pastry chef Salvatore De Riso opened this *pasticceria* up the road from his family's old bar along the Minori seafront. His versions of the classic pastries – such as *delizia di limone* (lemon slice), *Babà al distillato di rhum* and *profitteroles all'amaretto disaronno* – are now

renowned throughout Italy. They also do artisan ice creams, *granite* and a takeaway tray of devilish *dolci*.

Salerno & Paestum

Cenacolo €€€
Piazza Alfano I 4, Salerno, T089-238818.
Tue-Sun 1230-1500,
Tue-Sat 1930-late.
Il Cenacolo is a well-respected ristorante Salernitano, with elegant rooms over the road from the Duomo. The cuisine is based on traditional regional dishes given an innovative twist. Start with the *crespelle* (folded and filled savoury crêpes) and perhaps try one of their rustic creations, like the vegetable pie or the classic *parmigiana di melanzane* (layered aubergine, cheeses and tomatoes) which here is given a salty, tangy edge with anchovy. Reservations recommended.

Nettuno €€
Zona Archeologica, via Nettuno, Paestum, T0828-811 028.
Apr-Sep daily 1200-1500,
Oct-Mar Tue-Sun 1200-1500.
These rustic yet refined 19th-century dining rooms fill with passing tourists and locals who lap up the excellent value *crespolini* (large savoury crêpes) filled with local mozzarella, and the magical views of the ancient temples. It's run by the Pisani family who opened the doors of this famously isolated villa as a restaurant in 1929 and continue to create seafood favourites like *ricciola* (amberjack fish) served with the pepperminty herb *calamintha* and some mighty fine home-made desserts.

Antica Pizzeria del Vicolo della Neve €
Vicolo della Neve 24, Salerno, T089-225705.
Thu-Tue 1930-late.
Salerno's oldest pizzeria (going strong for over 150 years) is based next to a 10th-century church. Its old vaulted cellars were once crammed with compacted snow and preserved fish – the traditional food served here mirrors these atmospheric surroundings. Expect classic pizzas and *calzone*, as well as *polpette* (meat balls), *baccalà e patate* (salted cod and potatoes) and *carciofi e peperoni ripieni* (filled artichokes and peppers with meaty fillings).

Cafés & bars
Pantaleone
Via Mercanti 75-77, Salerno, T089-227825.
Opened in 1868, Salerno's famous *pasticceria-gelateria* is renowned for its trademark *scazzetta* (*pan di spagna* sponge, sweet *crema*, strawberries and topped with a candied strawberry) as well as a creamy *delizia al limone* and all the Parthenopaean pastry classics like *babà* and *sfogliatella*.

Pick of the region's picnic spots

All along the Sorrentine Peninsula and Amalfi coastline local *alimentari* (food stores) are filled with the area's wonderful fruits, cheeses and salame – which combined with sweet pastries from the likes of Panza, Pantaleone and Salvatore De Riso make a picnic fit for a Duke or Doge of Amalfi.

Bagno della Regina Giovanna near Sorrento Down by the ruins of a once lavish Roman villa you can enjoy Punta Campanella peaches between dive bombing in the sea.

Marina del Cantone Charter a boat from the beach here and eat your lunch between dives in sparkling pools.

Convento di San Domenico While walking the *basso* (lower) trail of the Sentiero degli Dei you come across this old convent amid olive trees, fruit-laden terraces and limestone pinnacles.

By the Canneto River in the Valle dei Mulini Seek out the cool waters of this stream lined with old stone mills.

Right: *Peperoncini.*

Entertainment

Clubs
Artis Domus
Via san Nicola 56, Sorrento, T081-877 2073, artisdomus.com.
In the bricked-up bowels of a villa that once belonged to a Sorrentine scholar you can just about squeeze onto the dance floor where the smartly dressed locals lap up cheesy Italo dance and live music acts.

Music
Teatro Tasso
Piazza Sant'Antonio, 25 Sorrento, T081-807 5525, teatrotasso.com.
Neapolitan folk music and dancing rocks the rafters of this renovated 1920s cinema building. The 75-minute Sorrento Musical Show does all the old *canzoni*, including *Funiculì funiculà*, *O' Sole Mio* and *Torna a Surriento*, and is accompanied by a meal.

Theatre
Cinema Teatro Armida
Corso Italia 219, Sorrento, T081-878 1470, cinemateatroarmida.it.
Concerts, plays and cinema screenings are staged here. Matinee theatre productions of plays by Samuel Beckett or Eduardo de Filippo might be followed by the latest film release.

Amalfi Coast

Clubs
Africana
Via Torre a Mare, Praiano, T089-874082, africananightclub.it.
Jun-Sep daily 2200-late.
You might spot a moustached-Barney Rubble gyrating to cheesy dance music on the glass-bottomed dance floor here. Opened in 1962 this beach cave club is like something out of a Connery-era Bond movie.

Music on the Rocks
Via Grotte dell'Incanto 51, Positano, T081-875874, musicontherocks.it.
Apr-Oct 2300-late,
phone for latest listings.
Soulful sounds and bangin' House are the musical staples at this stylish club in a vividly lit grotto. Expect fancy cocktails, occasional celebrity sightings and steep prices for drinks.

RoccoCò Music Bar
Via delle Cartiere 98, Amalfi, T089-873080.
Phone for latest listings.
Piano bar crooning during the week gives way to Latin American rhythms and other dancey tunes at the weekend

Music
Ravello Festival
Viale Wagner 5, Ravello, T089-858360, ravellofestival.com.
Late Jun-Oct.
A classical music and cultural festival with lots of clifftop arias and Wagnerian bombast. Highlight of the programme is the *Concerto all'Alba* (dawn concert) on 10 August.

Suoni Degli Dei Associazione Pelagos
Via Casa Rispoli 4, Praiano, T089-874557, isuonideglidei.com.
Apr-Oct.
The recently launched and more laid-back alternative to the Ravello Festival stages small classical concerts in gorgeous natural settings along the famous *Sentiero degli Dei* (Trail of the Gods).

Salerno & Paestum

Theatre
Teatro Verdi
Piazza Luciani, Salerno, T089-662141, teatroverdisalerno.it.
Salerno's lavishly decorated theatre, built in the 1860s, has exquisite medallions honouring artistic greats including Dante Alighieri, Giotto and Da Vinci. Tickets for concerts and other performances start at €12.

Shopping

Ceramics
Linea Casa
Viale Enrico Caruso 14B,
Sorrento, T081-877 2622.
For anyone interested in funky
espresso cups and kitchen kit
with that Italian design look.

Food & drink
Gelateria Latteria Gabriele
Corso Umberto I 5, Vico Equense,
T081-801 6234, gabrieleitalia.com.
As well as its famous gelati and
granite, this place has all sorts of
goodies for picnics and to take
home, including pastries,
cheeses and olives.

Pink Elephant
Piazza San Antonino 8,
Sorrento, T081-877 1011.
You can't escape the tide of
limoncello in Sorrento and this
place does lots of citrus brews
as well as other local specialities.

Market
Mercato di Via San Cesareo
Via San Cesareo, Sorrento.
Sorrento's weekly market, held
each Tuesday, is good for picking
up bargains like beach towels
and beach ware

Souvenirs
Gargiulo & Jannuzzi
Via Fuori Mura 1, Sorrento,
T081-878 1041.
G & J is world-renowned for
marquetry goods (gorgeous
boxes especially), elegant
furniture and ceramics.

Art & antiques
Amalfi nelle Stampe Antiche
Piazza Duomo 10,
T089-873 6374, artadiamalfi.it.
Luigi d'Antuono's outlet is full of
hand-made Amalfi paper as well
as lots of interesting historic
prints, books and maps.

Cartiera Amatruda
Via delle Cartiere 100, Amalfi,
T089-871315, amatruda.it.
Amatruda has been producing
fancy paper products for
generations and is a great
place to get some special
business cards made.

Ceramics
Ceramica Artistica Solimine
Via Madonna degli Angeli 7,
Vietri sul Mare, T089-212539,
solimene.com.
The shop within this iconic
factory has dinnerware to
enliven the dreariest table
scene. The rest of the street is
crammed with colourful shops.

Tip...

Record di Della Pietà Giulio

Viale Nizza 9, Sorrento, T081-807 1090.
"Although small, this is the only sportswear and outdoors shop around
with technical kit for walking and adventure sports, and is especially
good for footwear and clothing."

Giovanni Visetti, Walking guide, see pages 238 and 251.

Left: Ceramic fish.
Opposite page: Art on
Spiaggia Grande, Positano.

Activities & tours

Ceramiche Autore
Piazza Duomo 6, Ravello,
T089-858260.
It's worth having a browse in
this shop full of extravagantly
coloured ceramics, next to the
Duomo, if only to meet eccentric
owner Pino.

Beachwear & clothing
La Botteguccia
Via Trara Genoino 13,
Positano, T089-811824.
Complete your Positano-style
get-up with a pair of hand-made
sandals from this outlet.

Sartoria Maria Lampo
Viale Pasitea 12,
Positano, T089-875021.
All the VIPs come to Maria's
boutique filled with vibrant
fabrics – it was the first shop to
open after the Second World
War and started the whole
Positano fashionista scene.

Food & drink
Anastasio Nicola
Via Lorenzo d'Amalfi, Amalfi,
T089-871007.
Picnic supplies, snacks and
refreshments near the Duomo.

I Sapori di Positano
Via dei Mulini 6, Positano,
T089-812055.
All things citrus fill this shop:
limoncello, biscuits, candles,
sweets and soap.

Salerno & Paestum

Food & drink
Casa Bianca
Corso Garibaldi 231,
Salerno, T089-232125.
Lots of Campanian cheeses and
salami to fill your panini, as well
as some cooked foods for a
special picnic on the Salerno
lungomare.

Sorrentine Peninsula

Boat trips
Coop Marina della Lobra
T081-808 9380, marinalobra.com.
Boat trips from tiny Marina della
Lobra to Sorrento, Capri,
Positano, Amalfi and the marine
reserve: Riserva Marina di Punta
Campanella. For a few hundred
euros you can hire a traditional
gozzo sailing boat or one of their
yachts for an afternoon.

Cooperativa San Antonio
Via Cantone 47, Marina di
Cantone, T081-808 1638.
This cooperative organizes boat
trips around the nearby coves
and as far as Capri.

Nautica O Masticiello
Marina di Cantone,
T081-8081443, masticiello.com.
Traditional *gozzo* sailing boats,
motorized dinghies and flashy
yachts can be hired here.

Cultural
City Sightseeing Sorrento
Via degli Aranci 172, Sorrento,
T081-877 4707, sorrento.
city-sightseeing.it.
Termini: piazza Lauro (Sorrento)
and piazza Flavio Gioia (Amalfi).
The open-top sightseeing bus
company now runs services
along the coast, providing
hop-on and jump-off tours with
multilingual commentary, to and
from Sorrento, Amalfi, Ravello,
Maiori and Minori.

Listings

Diving
Diving Tour
Via Fontanelle 18,
Massa Lubrense,
T081-808 9003, divingtour.it.
This well-established outfit organizes diving trips all over the world, including forays around their own beautiful backyard. A single dive with all equipment costs €55, two dives around Capri or Li Galli €70, and a snorkelling trip €25.

Diving Sorrento
Via A Vespucci 39,
Nerano, T081-808 1051,
divingsorrento.com.
Based at the Nettuno Holiday Village at Nerano, Diving Sorrento offers PADI diving courses and snorkelling excursions. Check out the website for latest offers and details of basic accommodation available.

Tennis
Tennis courts can be booked at **Tennis Sorrento** (viale Montariello 4, Sorrento, T081-878 1246) and **Tennis Sport Sorrento** (via Califano, T081-807 4181). Best to book early for cooler evening sessions in the summer.

Walking
Giovis
Via 4 Novembre, Massa Lubrense,
T339-694 2911, giovis.com.
Experienced hiking guide Giovanni Visetti leads lots of guided walks on both coastlines and has a network of outdoor enthusiasts throughout the region. See page 251 for some of his favourite walks.

Amalfi Coast

Boat trips
Amalfi Boats
Via Lungomare dei Cavalieri,
Amalfi, T089-831890,
amalfiboats.it.
Gioacchino and Flavio skipper the boat trips, ranging from tourist cruises to fishing forays. For the experienced there are various boats for hire.

Gennaro e Salvatore
Via Trara Genoino 13,
Positano, T089-811613,
gennaroesalvatore.it.
Excursions to the Madonnina del Mare, Nerano and Li Galli.

Left: Fishing for octopus.
Above: So hoist up the John B's sails.
Opposite page: Catch the *piccione* – Cetara.

Lucibello
Via del Brigatino 9, Positano,
T089-875032, lucibello.it.
Excursions around Capri, and along the coast to the Grotta dello Smeraldo, Amalfi and Praiano.

Cycling
Genius Loci
Salerno, T089-791896,
genius-loci.it.
This company organizes cycling and walking tours throughout the region. Their eight-day Panorami della Costiera tour starts at €495.

Food & wine
Ciao Laura Cookery Courses
T1-615 478 1599, ciaolaura.com.
American Laura Faust organizes various cookery courses on the Amalfi Coast, including a four-hour Neapolitan pastry class (€130) and Pizza Pie in the Sky at Ravello with Mamma Agata (€175).

Transport

Gran Furor Divina Costiera Winery
Via GB Lama 14, Furore, T089-830348.
Tours and tastings by appointment.
Andrea Ferraioli and Marisa Cuomo produce Costa d'Amalfi DOC wines using indigenous grape varieties including whites like Ripoli, Falanghina and Bianca Tenera, as well as hardy reds Piedirosso and Aglianco. Their gnarly vines grow on steep slopes studded with old stone walls, where even mules fear to teeter.

Horse riding
Centro Ippico La Selva
Via Belvedere, Colli Fontanelle, Sant'Agnello, T081-808 3196.
Riding school in the hills of Sant'Agnello with modern facilities – they organize lessons for young and old, and stage the occasional equestrian event.

Walking
Maurizio De Rosa
84010 Praiano, T339-171 8194, sulsentierodeglidei.it.
Walking tours around Valle delle Ferriere, Monte Faito, Punta Campanella and Sentiero degli Dei. Maurizio tailors his excursions to suit most abilities and needs, and even has an interesting alternative to the classic Trail of the Gods which starts at Vettica Maggiore and visits the San Domenico monastery at 400m.

Sorrento
Frequent Circumvesuviana trains to Napoli (1 hr), Pompei (30 mins), Ercolano (50 mins). Hydrofoil to Napoli (1 hr) and Capri (25 mins).

Amalfi
Ferry and hydrofoil services from Naples, Capri, Ischia, Salerno and all along the coast. SITA bus services from Naples and other places along the coast.

Salerno
Ferry and hydrofoil services from Naples, Capri, Ischia and all along the coast. Train from Naples (1 hr) and from Paestum (35 mins).

Contents

Barche di Capri.

Capri, Ischia & Procida

Introduction

The islands of the Bay of Naples all have their own unique fascination. Capri, *L'Isola Azzurra* (the Blue Island), parades the most glamour and dizzying beauty in its 10 sq km. Emperor Augustus was so smitten with its limestone coves and plunging cliffs that he swapped it for Ischia, which is nearly five times larger. His successor Tiberius ruled the empire from his Caprese villas, and according to some Roman accounts had a knee-tremblingly good and dastardly time. Lavish lifestyles, illustrious visitors, and the jet-set entourage followed.

Capri has a magical lustre but Ischia and Procida are no bogus rocks. The Campi Flegrei volcano system plopped these islands into the sea farther west – they share the geology and earthy characteristics of Naples while limestone love child Capri was chipped off the shoulder of the Sorrentine Peninsula. Ischia, *L'Isola Verde* (the Green Island), still vents its vulcanism at its thermal springs and spa resorts. There are some fine sandy beaches and varied landscapes (including a dead volcano or two) and microclimates that allow subtropical species to thrive.

You can get around cute Procida and its 4 sq km in no time; its charm is its intimacy, down-to-earth feel and picturesque sights, including pastel-coloured fishing villages, rolling lanes lined with market gardens and a half-dozen beaches.

Il Faro, Capri.

What to see in...

...one day

Glide over the bay to **Capri** for a day excursion, dipping into Capri Town's chic shopping, **Anacapri**'s charming lanes and the azure waters around its stunning rocky shoreline. The chairlift to **Monte Solaro** should not be missed.

...a weekend or more

Depending on time constraints and your position in the bay, try to sample all the islands' charms. From the Amalfi Coast and Naples, head straight to **Capri** by hydrofoil; those starting in the **Campi Flegrei** with a week to spare could hop over to nearby **Procida**, then **Ischia** before heading to **Capri** and the **Sorrentine Peninsula**.

Capri

Capri is just 5 km from Punta della Campanella on the Sorrentine Peninsula. Despite the invasion of day-trippers who throng its boutique-lined lanes and cram its cute orange buses, Capri still has that special allure, particularly in its gorgeous hidden bays beloved of emperors and film stars and along its tranquil, flower-strewn paths. Out of season and after the last boat to Naples has departed you almost feel part of the privileged Capri set. Its chic epicentre is Capri Town, 142 m above sea level and 3 km by road from the island's main harbour, Marina Grande, which is always abuzz with the weaving and heaving of foaming boats, floppy-hatted tourists and *facchini* (porters). Anacapri, 3 km to the west by road, is less self-consciously exclusive and has a friendlier feel. The single-seat chairlift ride to Monte Solaro is a magical, must-do experience – from its summit there are wonderful walks across wild country.

Capri Town sits in a lush bowl between the limestone cliffs of Monte Solaro and Punta del Capo. Known as **La Piazzetta** (the little square), piazza Umberto I is the intimate and chic social hub of Capri Town and the island. Everyone, anyone and no one over the past two centuries has sat at one of the cafés here, plonking their feet on the flagstones and glancing intermittently over a newspaper to do some people-watching – you never know who will walk by. It must have been a less pricey pleasure, though, for the likes of Dickens, Greene, Gorky and Lenin.

Gaze beyond the entertaining ebb and flow and you'll see the **Torre dell'Orologio** (clock tower), with its majolica-tiled clock face; the **Municipio** (town hall); the Baroque **Chiesa di Santo Stefano** (with fragments of Roman flooring from Emperor Tiberius's Villa Jovis); and **Palazzo Cerio** (T081-837 6218, Tue-Wed, Fri-Sat 1000-1300, Thu 1500-1900), which has natural history collections amassed by naturalist and physician Ignazio Cerio.

A maze of medieval *vicoli* (alleyways) fans out from the Piazzetta. Via Madre Serafina, an atmospheric arcaded street, follows the town's old ramparts. Between the whitewashed buildings light-wells offer glimpses of flowery terraces. The locals would pour hot oil through the holes onto invading Saracen pirates. Via Lungano and Capri's main via Vittorio Emanuele III are lined with boutiques, bars, *pasticcerie* and glitzy hotels, including Il Quisisana (meaning 'here one heals'), originally a 19th-century sanatorium founded by a Scottish doctor.

Certosa di San Giacomo

Via Certosa, T081-837 6218.
Tue-Sun 0900-1400, free.

The Charterhouse, a 14th-century Carthusian monastery dedicated to the apostle Giacomo (James), is located southeast of the Piazzetta. The monks have long since packed their habits,

Essentials

❶ **Getting around** Capri is just 6 km by 3 km and traffic is restricted so forget about using a car. Ferries from Naples and elswhere (see pages 167, 239 and 271) arrive at Marina Grande. To reach Capri Town take the 3-min funicular ride (€1.30) or hop on a bus. Getting around on the tiny orange buses run by **SIPPC** (T081-937 0420) and **Staiano Autotrasporti** (T081-837 1544) is fun and exhilarating as you hurtle around hairpin bends and contemplate dizzying chasms. There are frequent services between Marina Grande, Capri Town, Marina Piccola, Anacapri, Damecuta, Faro, and the Grott'Azzurra; prices from €1.30 for a single bus ride to €6.70 for a day pass allowing unlimited bus travel and 2 funicular rides. **Taxis** (Capri T081-837 0543, Anacapri T081-837 1175) are very pricey, especially the open-topped vintage vehicles.

❸ **ATM** Banca di Roma, piazza Umberto I 19, Capri Town, T081-837 5942.

⊕ **Hospital** ASL Na 5 Guardia Medica, piazza Umberto I 1, Capri Town, T081-837 5716.

✛ **Pharmacy** Farmacia Internazionale, via Roma 24, Capri Town, T081-837 0485.

➋ **Post office** Via Roma 50, Capri Town, T081-837 5829, Mon-Fri 0800-1630, Sat 0800-1230.

❶ **Tourist information** AASCT Capri, piazzetta Cerio, Capri Town, T081-837 5308, capritourism.com.

What the locals say

Top Caprese moments

A drink at the Pullali wine bar, in the clock tower overlooking the Piazzetta. Marina Piccola out of season. A walk from the centre of Capri to Marina Piccola by via Via Krupp. Chairlift to Monte Solaro for the view. Anima e Cuore nightclub, typical Caprese. Capri should be seen from the sea, so take a picnic and hire a *gozzo* (wooden boat) and visit all of the little grottoes. The Grotta Verde is less famous than the Grott'Azzurra but equally pretty and you don't pay to go in.

Michelle Lowe, resident of Naples and Capri and owner of Micalò hotel in Naples.

Capri listings

① Sleeping
1 Caesar Augustus *via G.Orlandi 4*
2 Caprihouse *strada Provinciale 8*
3 Casa Ersilia *Trav. Prov. Marina Grande, 1c*
4 Casa Malua *via Sopromonte 6*
5 Casa Mariantonia *via G. Orlandi 180*
6 J.K.Place *via Prov. Marina Grande 225*
7 La Tosca *via D.Birago 5*
8 Le Terrazze
9 Stella Maris *via Roma 27*
10 Weber Ambassador *via Marina Piccola 118*

① Eating & Drinking
1 Bar Buchetto *via G. Orlandi 38*
2 Capri's *via Roma 38*
3 Da Gioia *Marina Piccola*
4 Da Paolino *via Palazzo a Mare 11*
5 Il Solitario *via G. Orlandi 96*
6 La Rondinella *via G. Orlandi 295*
7 Pasticceria Buonocore *via Vittorio Emanuele 35*
8 Torre Saracena *via Marina Piccola*

but the serene atmosphere, sombre architecture and verdant gardens makes it worth the walk here. It's rather run down but there are things to see: two cloisters, a church, panoramic terraces and the intriguing refectory museum that contains Roman statues recovered from the Grotta Azzurra and haunting paintings by the German painter, Wilhelm Diefenbach.

Continuing on via Giacomo Matteotti you come to the **Giardini di Augusto** (Gardens of Augustus), a vibrant profusion of flowers and vegetation with jowl-dropping terrace views to die for – so mind the chasm.

Belvedere Cannone

From the Piazzetta, follow the via Madre Serafina, linger at the Santa Teresa church, then climb to the impressive Castiglione (a sprawling €40 million villa still up for sale at time of writing). Steps lead to the

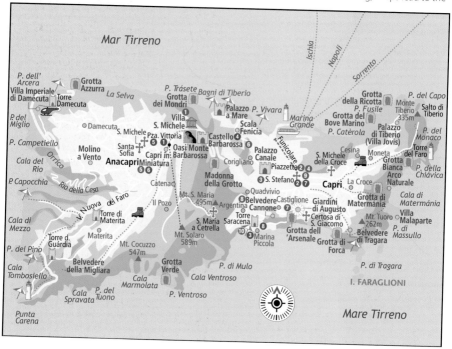

View near La Piazzetta.

belvedere that looks over the Faraglioni rocks, the Charterhouse, the Grotta delle Felci (where Bronze Age artefacts were found) and down towards the Marina Piccola (see box page 245).

Circular coastal walk from the Piazzetta

Starting at the Piazzetta, take via le Botteghe, then follow via Croce and via Matermania –before following the signs to steps that descend near the breathtaking natural archway, **Arco Naturale**. A path continues to the **Grotta di Matermania** – a cave with a Roman *nymphaeum* and lots of *opus reticulum* bricks. At the craggy outcrop **Punta Masullo** you'll glimpse red-hued **Villa Malaparte** with its trapezoidal staircase and angular shapes: this piece of Italian rationalist architecture was named after its eccentric owner, the writer Curzio Malaparte. It starred alongside Brigitte Bardot in Jean-Luc Godard's 1963 film *Le Mépris*. Climbing up to **Punta Tragara**, there are fabulous views of the Faraglioni and Monacone rocks rising from turquoise waters. Head northwest along leafy via Tragara to return to the Piazzetta. Allow at least three hours to do the entire route.

Villa Jovis & Il Salto di Tiberio

Viale Amedeo Matiuri.
Daily 0900 till dusk.

Villa Jovis, Emperor Tiberius's infamous 7000-sq-m palace from which he ruled the Roman Empire from AD 27 to 37, takes about an hour on foot to

Five of the best

Capri bathing spots

❶ Marina Piccola Capri's most famous bathing spot, on the south side of the island, is split into two small bays, the **Marina di Pennauro** and **Marina di Mulo**, which overlook the Scoglio delle Sirene (Sirens' Rock) and Faraglioni Rocks. Shoreline seafood restaurants with wooden decks, including Da Gioia (see page 265), look over tiny pebbly beaches and bathing establishments that fill from 0800 in the summer.

❷ Bagni di Tiberio West of Marina Grande is this intimate cove with the remains of one of Tiberius's villas and a Roman theatre. Take the shuttle boat (€7 return) from Marina Grande or a winding path that starts five minutes' walk above the JK Place Hotel. There are beach huts, a small pebbly beach and a seafood restaurant/bar Bagni di Tiberio, run by Carlo di Mattino, who can be seen here mending his nets off season. From August, the cliffs of Anacapri block out much of the sun so sun-worshippers prefer it in early summer.

❸ Bagni Nettuno Backed by dramatic cliffs, this picturesque rocky shoreline near Anacapri has a popular bathing establishment (via Grotta Azzurra, T081-837 1362) with two pools (for adults and kids) and a bar-ristorante, and rents out deckchairs, parasols and cabins from late March to mid-November. A bus service shuttles bathers to and from Anacapri.

❹ Lido di Faro A winding road from Anacapri reaches the southwest extremities of the island and Lido di Faro or Punta Carena (T081-837 1798, lidofaro. com). Amid the sun-worshippers and sun terrace there's a snack bar (Da Antonio's) and sun terrace built onto the jagged rocks near the lighthouse. Migliara cliffs soar 292 m above the snorkellers, divers and dive-bombers who enjoy the deep pools and marine life here – be careful of the sharp limestone rocks.

❺ Spiaggia di Marina Grande Capri's largest beach is handily placed, just a short stroll west of the port-side bustle. Around 100 m of popular pebbly beach stretches to cliffs and breakwater rocks below the swanky J.K. Place hotel. There are a couple of beach establishments with facilities, snack bars and public access so it's ideal for day-trippers seeking a dip and doze *alla caprese* before catching the return boat.

reach from Capri Town. Verdant lanes pass by colonnaded gardens (linger at Villa La Moneta at via Tiberio 32), prickly pears, abundant birdlife and lounging lizards. There's not much left of the lavish apartments (although Prime Minister Silvio Berlusconi had plans to allow luxury pads to be built here for him and his mates). Between orgies, gorging and torturing, Tiberius apparently enjoyed spending time in the loggia, with its sublime views, and in the *specularium*, where astrologers gave him the low-down perhaps. Within the site, at Monte Tiberio, there's a rustic church, **Santa Maria del Soccorso**, scene of the Festa di Santa Maria del Soccorso (7-8 September), a festival involving morning mass, music and dance.

Tiberius's Leap, near Villa Jovis, is a 300-m cliff from where the emperor apparently flung his tortured victims. According to the Roman historian Gaius Suetonius Tranquillus, sailors would wait in the sea below to finish off the unfortunates. Suetonius flung a lot of juicy muck in his opus *The Lives of the Twelve Caesars*, and a reputation for perversion, madness and cruelty has certainly stuck to Tiberius.

Anacapri & around

Sitting below Capri's highest point, Monte Solaro, Anacapri – a short bus ride from Capri – has a friendlier, more villagey feel than self-consciously chic Capri Town.

Piazza della Vittoria is always abuzz with buses, taxis, coaches and crowds. Up its steps is the chairlift to Monte Solaro, Villa San Michele and viale Axel Munthe lined with perfumed boutiques and aristocratic *alberghi*. Anacapri's main lane via Orlandi heads past some interesting shops and friendly *chiaccheroni Anacapresi* (local chit-chatters) to an intimate piazza in front of the cheery, yellow-hued **Chiesa di Santa Sofia**, a favourite meeting place and wedding venue. On the way is the **church of San Michele** (with majolica marvels) and **Casa Rossa**, a building painted in Pompeian red with Moorish detailing, a gallery of Caprese

landscape paintings and a courtyard displaying archaeological fragments. Along the craggy northwestern and western coastline are some magical natural and ancient attractions including the ethereal Grotta Azzurra cave and the fort, flora and fauna-studded trail, *Il Sentiero dei Fortini*.

Chiesa San Michele

Piazza San Nicola, Anacapri.
Daily 0930-1800, €1.

Built in 1761, the Baroque church has majolica flooring depicting Adam and Eve in a dreamlike scene, viewed from a special gallery. The beguiling small square here is a meeting place for the Anacapresi.

Villa San Michele

Viale Axel Munthe 34, Anacapri, T081-837 1401, sanmichele.org.
Mar 0900-1630, Apr and Oct 0900-1700, May-Sep 0900-1800, Nov-Feb 0900-1530, €5.

Swedish doctor and writer Axel Munthe (1857-1949) created this idyllic villa with an emphasis on bringing out the island's "light, light everywhere". After assisting the cholera epidemic relief effort in the 1880s, he put down his stethoscope and focused on constructing the villa's buildings and lush garden, with its loggia, pergolas, statues and columns, and a circular viewpoint with the most stunning views across the Gulf of Naples. Run as a museum by the Axel Munthe Foundation, temple-like interiors display Munthe's eclectic

Tip...

The 800 or so steps of the Scala Fenicia (Phoenician Steps) used to be the only means of communication between the two halves of the island. The vertiginous stairway cut out of the rock starts above Marina Grande, climbs about 200 m and emerges near Villa San Michele. It's quite a climb and will take you the best part of 45 minutes to reach the old gates of Anacapri.

Casa Rossa courtyard.

Around the region

collection of art, antiquities, bric-a-brac and personal memorabilia. There are also the remains of a Roman imperial villa. Munthe's *The Story of San Michele*, published in 1929, charts his Caprese love affair and became a worldwide bestseller, drawing many a pilgrim to this enchanting place.

Monte Solaro chairlift

Seggiovia Monte Solaro, via Caposcuro 10, T081-837 1428.
Mar-Oct 0930 till sunset, Nov-Feb 1030-1500, €8 return, €6 single.

If you don't fancy the walk, the chairlift offers a quick and easy means of reaching the highest point of the island. Feet dangle over a hiking path weaving through terraced gardens dotted with quirky ornaments and abundant produce, and as you rise to the 600-m summit the craggy ridge, wild parched landscape and shimmering seascapes become ever more spectacular. After 12 minutes you arrive just below the one-bar terrace which is pleasingly slightly run-down. You can spend a couple of hours sitting in a deckchair slurping ice cream and exploring the rough terrain and knee-knocking drops, including the vertiginous cliffs down to Ventroso and limpid

Chairlift.

blue waters. Just watch your step though. There are lots of walks from here: to Monte Capello, the small church at Cetrella and along the very tricky Passetiello path back to Capri Town (note that the Passetiello has lots of loose rocks and steep scrambles, so should only be tackled with an experienced guide.

Grotta Azzurra

0900 till dusk. Bus or by foot (3 km) from Anacapri, or boat from Marina Grande, then entry to the cave by rowing boat.

Once filled with statues from Tiberius's Gradola villa, the Blue Grotto and its ethereal light atmospherics were 'rediscovered' in 1826 and turned into a Grand Tour day trip. The lighting effects inside the cave are caused by the refraction of the sun's rays in the waters, lighting the cave from below in an eerie a shade of blue. The island's most popular tourist attraction can be approached via a footpath, lift or by boat, with many excursions around the island including a trip to the grotto. Joining the melee of bobbing rowing boats you pay €10 to board one of them and then it's time to duck down while going through the narrow entrance into the cavern beyond. It's usually all over after about five minutes, in which time the oarsmen sing and shout, point at strange rock formations and nudge you for a tip. For the best experience and lighting effects come between 1100 and 1300.

Il Sentiero dei Fortini

Along this stretch of coast there's a fabulous trail, Il Sentiero dei Fortini, that follows the crumbling forts built by Bourbon-backed British troops and enlarged by Napoleonic French after they retook the island in 1808. It passes the scenic ruins of a Roman complex, the Villa Imperiale Romana di Damecuta. Walking guide Luigi Esposito of Capri Trails (T347-368 1699, capritrails.com) reckons, "It's best to walk southwards from the Grotta Azzurra to Faro as the sun and sea are in front of you, whereas going the other way you face the cliffs."

Five of the best

Walks on Capri

Walking guide Giovanni Visetti picks his favourite Caprese walks, the first three of which are best tackled going uphill as they contain tricky and steep sections with loose rocks. None of these trails should be attempted in bad weather.

❶ Anacapri to Monte Solaro This spectacular trail starts at the circular defensive tower Torre della Guardia, rebuilt by the English during the conflicts with Murat's republican French troops 200 years ago, passing the Belvedere di Migliera and verdant slopes of Monte Cocuzzo (545 m) before arriving at Monte Solaro.

❷ Passetiello The ancient path between Anacapri and the saddle of Capri (or Due Golfi as it's also known locally) has steep sections of crumbly limestone that require great care. Best tackled with a guide, and certainly not for those who suffer from vertigo.

❸ Anginola Like the Passetiello, this path starts near the hospital in Capri, then diverges from it before merging again at the Cetrella church. Giovanni reckons the Anginola trail is safer although there is a tricky section with chains and steel cables that help you hop from ledge to ledge.

❹ Sentiero dei Fortini A coastal path that follows the old forts from the Grotta Azzurra to Punta Carena.

❺ Tragara to Belvedere delle Noci (via Dentecale) This path east of Capri Town takes in heart-pounding coastal views of the Fariglioni rocks, Arco Naturale and limpid blue coves.

For more information, maps and contact details of Capri guides check out giovis.com and whenever.it

Top: View from Monte Solaro terrace.
Above: Capri's limestone coastline. Left: One of the old forts.

Ischia

Ischia's dead volcanoes, steamy thermal fissures and curvaceous craters are evidence of its Campi Flegrei caldera origins. Follow in the sandal-steps of Greeks, Romans and today's ubiquitous German holidaymakers at one of Ischia's popular spa resorts. There are 67 fumaroles (volcanic vents) and a hundred-plus thermal springs across the island, and the island's longest and most coveted stretch of volcanic sand, La Spiaggia dei Maronti is dotted with them. Away from the swanky spas and bulging bathrobes are hilltop villages and exotic gardens sheltered by the shapely tufa-rock topped Mont Epomeo, an extinct volcano reachable on foot or donkey.

Pescatore, Ischia.

A volcanic crater was transformed into the island's main harbour, Ischia Porto, by Bourbon King Ferdinand II in 1854. The Riva Destra, along its right bank is lined with yachts and fishing boats, and popular bars and restaurants spill out onto the pitted flagstones of its quayside. Ischia's main shopping drag (via Pontano, corso Vittoria Colonna and then via Roma), known as *il corso* by the locals, connects the port with the medieval town Ischia Ponte via a 228-m-long causeway. A few sandy beaches lie to the east: Spiaggia dei Pescatori, Lido d'Ischia and the public beach, Spiaggia San Pietro e della Marina. Ischia Ponte's fortifications were first laid down in the fifth century BC and today's structure is due to the House of Aragon, hence the name Castello Aragonese.

Castello di Ischia

Piazzale Aragonese, Ischia Ponte, T081-992 834, castellodischia.it.
Mar-Oct 0930-1700, €8.

The first fortress here was built by Syracusan Greeks in 474 BC and the present towering citadel and bridge (more like a causeway these days) was begun by Alfonso of Aragon in the 1440s. Attacked by Romans, Arabs, Normans, Swabians, French and English, it was not only the strategic stronghold of the island but also a vital place of refuge for the locals. A fairytale romance is also attached to the castle: in the 1500s it became the home of the poet-princess Vittoria Colonna, who married Ferrante d'Avalos here then later became the platonic sweetheart of Michelangelo. Amid its maze of stone steps and higgledy-piggledy structures, there are atmospheric churches, spaces with art exhibitions and some creepy corners. The **Convento delle Clarisse** has the macabre sight of a ring of stone seating, where nuns were laid to rest and decompose, the fluids collected in vases beneath before their skeletons joined their sisters in the Ossarium. Other highlights of the citadel are the museum of torture instruments and the tall 15th-century tunnel.

Essentials

❶ **Getting around** Ferries from Naples (21 km), Pozzuoli (11 km) and elsewhere arrive at Porto d'Ischia (for a list of operators see page 271). A system of 19 bus routes run by **SEPSA** (T081-991 1808, orari.sepsa. it) circles the island in clockwise and anticlockwise directions: the CD (Circolare Destra) goes clockwise and the CS (Circolare Sinistra) goes anticlockwise. Unico Ischia tickets (€1.20) allow 90 mins of travel. If you are here for over a week, car hire is an option. Companies include: **Di Meglio** (T081-995222, ischia-rentacar.it) and **Mazzella** (T081-991141, mazzellarent.it).

❸ **ATM** Banca Monte dei Paschi di Siena, via Sogliuzzo 44, T081-982310.

⊕ **Hospital** Guardia Medica, T081-983499.

✚ **Pharmacy** Farmacia Internazionale, via de Luca Alfredo 117, T081-333 1275.

➲ **Post office** Via Morgioni, Porto d'Ischia, T081-507 4611, Mon-Fri 0800-1630, Sat 0800-1230.

❶ **Tourist information** AACST Ischia, via Sogliuzzo 72, Ischia, T081-507 4211, infoischiaprocida.it.

Tip...

To see Ischia in the comfort of an air-conditioned vehicle hire reliable driver **Giuseppe Lauro** (T081-992651, T339-4052691 (mobile), ischiataxiservice.com). For a fun ride, hail a Microtaxi, Ischia's tiny three-wheel Apecar taxi, at least once during your stay.

Museo del Mare

Palazzo dell'Orologio, via Giovanni da Procida 3, Ischia Ponte, T081-981124, museodelmareischia.it.
Apr-Jun 1030-1230, 1500-1900, Jul-Aug 1030-1230, 1830-2230, Nov-Mar 1030-1230, closed Feb, €3.

Approaching the Aragonese citadel you come to the attractive Palazzo dell'Orologio which houses the Museum of the Sea. The engaging collection is awash with maritime curios, nautical instruments, fishermen's tackle, marine creatures, Marconi's radio equipment and intriguing archaeological finds.

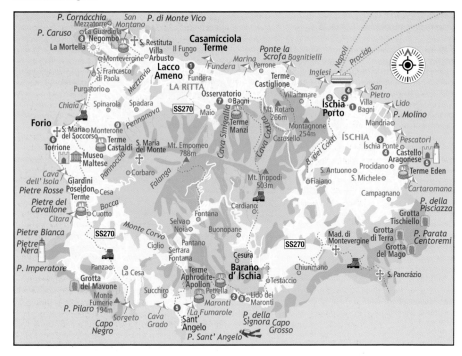

Ischia listings

Torre di Michelangelo & Baia di Cartaromana

Torre di Guevara, via Nuova Cartaromana,
T081-333 1146.
Tue-Sun, times vary, free.

The fine sands of the Cartaromana Bay have thermal spring waters and are backed by a rectangular tower, the Torre di Guevara, also known as Michelangelo's Tower. The story goes that Michelangelo stayed here and had a relationship with the poetess Vittoria Collana, who resided in the Aragonese castle over the water, spawning the romantic myth that a secret tunnel connecting the two castles enabled hush-hush rendezvous. The tower is now a cultural centre with occasional art shows.

Casamicciola Terme

This popular spa resort 6 km northwest of Ischia Porto is renowned for its 85°C iodine-rich springs. Inventive Iron Age inhabitants tapped into the area's vulcanism for cooking and pottery. In 1883 an earthquake decimated the village. The European aristocracy flocked to its spas on piazza Bagni in the 18th and 19th centuries and many offer state-of-the-art facilities today (see page 271). Casamicciola Terme's beaches – dell'Eliporto, del Convento and by the Marina – may have some fine grains of sand but they can get mighty busy in the summer and are not the island's most picturesque.

Lacco Ameno

More laid-back than Casamicciola Terme, Lacco Ameno has the most naturally radioactive waters in Italy, with alleged curative powers. The first colony of Neapolitan Magna Graecia was established here at Monte Vico before one too many earth tremors persuaded them to set sail to nearby Cumae and Megaride. The sleepy fishing village was transformed in the 1950s into an exclusive spa resort. Among its famous spa establishments today are the Hotel Regina Elisabetta on piazza Santa Restituta and the exclusive Negombo resort just out of town. Lacco Ameno's logo is the mushroom-shaped volcanic rock offshore, known as *il fungo*.

The local archaeological museum, **Museo Civico Archeologico di Pithecusae** (corso Angelo Rizzoli, T081-900356, Tue-Sun 0930-1300, 1600-2000, €5-2.50, free with Artecard), is housed in the 18th-century Villa Arbusto. It contains Roman tombs, geological exhibits and archaeological finds including the Coppa di Nestore (Nestor's Cup), a terracotta *kotyle* made in 700 BC on Rhodes and found in the tomb of a child in 1995. Further reminders of Lacco Ameno's past can be found in the **Sanctuary & Church of Santa Restituta** (piazza Santa Restituta 1, T081-980706). Next to the pink-hued church is a museum with archaeological finds (don't miss the Egyptian amulets in the form of beetles) and subterranean Graeco-Roman ruins.

Natural beauty spots off the beaten track

La Scarrupata A picturesque beach with chunky *ciottoli* (pebbles) that stretches from Punta San Pancrazio to Capo Grosso in the southeastern corner of the island. Spectacular layers of volcanic debris can be seen along this stretch of the Barano coastline, which is accessed via a path from Barano d'Ischia or by chartering a boat.

I Frassitelli a La Falanga These wild chestnut and acacia woods on the slopes of Monte Epomeo are criss-crossed with trails, where you may encounter the island's wild rabbits and abundant birdlife, including falcons. Like the locals who fled invasions and epidemics, you can live on nuts, mushrooms and berries and explore their ingenious stone dwellings hewn out of the volcanic tufa stone as well as colossal basins to store water and ice.

Spiagge di San Pancrazio e Sorgeto The stunning rocky southeastern coastline around the intimate and isolated San Pancrazio beach is reachable only by boat. Honey-coloured tufa rock cliffs are pocked with marine caves popular with snorkellers. A seafood restaurant and bar is open here in the summer.

Spiaggia dei Maronti In the southwestern corner of the island, just 2 km up the coastal road from Sant'Angelo, is one of Ischia's most beautiful beach hot spots – although it's volcanic thermal waters and steamy vents seldom scorch a non-Italian *culo*. Its balmy pebbles and pools are accessed via a long set of steps near Panza or else by taking a boat from Sant'Angelo for a few euros. After a dip in the clear waters, take care not to burn your backside on the hot rocks. When tides are low, its tepid waters make it popular with winter skinny-dippers.

Tip...

Just west of Lacco Ameno is the beautiful Bay of San Montano which is backed by verdant Mediterranean scrub and the famous **Spa & Resort Negombo** (Baia San Montano, T081-986152, negombo.it). Negombo's 12 thermal pools may be a favourite with Berlusconi and pals, but it's still a welcoming place to relax for the casual spa-seeking punter.

Visconti's Dovecote Hill retreat

Cinema legend Luchino Visconti, director of *Death in Venice* and *The Leopard*, stayed in the now sadly neglected Villa La Colombaia on a wooded hill outside Forio. Its whitewashed Moorish towers, roof terraces and great stained-glass *ascensore* (lift) are in a sorry state but there are plans to renovate the building, which hosts occasional cultural events related to the celebrated director. If you are lucky the friendly caretaker will show you around.

Giardini La Mortella

Località Zaro, T081-986220, lamortella.it. Apr-Oct Tue, Thu, Sat, Sun 0900-1900, €12 plus concessions. Take the SS Forio–Lacco Ameno, towards Chiaia.

The brainchild of garden architect Russell Page and Susana Walton, the Argentinian widow of English composer William Walton, La Mortella offers a dreamlike garden experience, with fountains, lily ponds, zen water features and subtropical species that thrive in this microclimate beneath the lava flows of Monte Zaro. Pavilions, temples and a tea room add contemplative English and Eastern atmospheres. Check online for details of their programme of Spring and Autumn chamber recitals and Summer Festival of Youth Orchestras.

Forio

The port and town of Forio, on Ischia's western coast, has traditionally been the island's home of winemaking and fishing. From the 1950s to 1970s it became an enclave for artistic types like poet Pablo Neruda and writer-directors Luchino Visconti and Pier Paolo Pasolini. Germans especially enjoy its scenic ramparts and towers. The rotund watchtower that dominates the Forio skyline is home to the **Museo Civico** (via del Torrione, T081-333 2934, iltorrione.org), with exhibits relating to Neapolitan song, artworks (lots by landscapist local hero Giovanni Maltese) and temporary exhibitions.

The elegantly outlined **Santuario della Madonna del Soccorso** (via del Soccorso) is a whitewashed church with majolica-tiled flourishes. Its terrace is the perfect place to watch the setting sun. To the north is the picturesque Spiaggia di San Francesco, with its coarse sand, and beyond it the rocky promontory Punta Caruso. Long and scruffy (but popular) Spiaggia Citara lies to the south of the town, backed by the beach-front gardens of the **Parco Termale Giardini di Poseidon** (T081-907122), one of the most attractive spas.

Panza, Sant'Angelo & Lido di Maronti

Panza, with its restaurants, roadside bustle and joyously yellow San Leonardo church runs into Sant'Angelo, the island's most appealing village, which looks over a harbour with a mound-like islet connected by a sandy isthmus. It's a sublime place to saunter, shop, eat alfresco and visit the beach Lido di Maronti, reached by water taxi in five minutes. This 2-km-long stretch of beach formed from volcanic sand and studded with steaming fumaroles, has some relaxing bar-restaurants. Close to this *spiaggia calda* (hot beach) is the Roman spa resort of Cava Scura. For a tad more exertion trek to Ischia's highest point, Monte Epomeo, for a scramble over smooth tufa rocks and gasp at some stunning views.

Walk to Monte Epomeo

Serrara and neighbouring village Fontana lie below the extinct volcano Epomeo (788 m), which is an enjoyable 45-minute walk away. Serrara has a charming piazza and pastel-coloured church, the Chiesa di Santa Maria del Carmine. The path up to Monte Epomeo begins in Fontana, near the medieval church of Santa Maria della Sacca (1374). You can cut the journey to the summit a little if you opt for a donkey-aided ascent. After negotiating a dusty trail through woods there is a scramble over strange tufa rock formations (tricky in wet conditions) pitted with volcanic bubbles. Clear days reward you with awe-inspiring views of the island, the Bay of Naples and as far as smoking Stromboli (towards Sicily) while cloudy ones evoke an eerie atmosphere that is just as memorable. A restaurant housed in a former convent building serves simple snacks and pasta dishes. Don't miss the 15th-century San Nicola church and hermitage hewn out of the volcanic rock.

Below: Sant'Angelo. Opposite page: Neglected Villa La Colombaia.

Procida

Located between Capo Miseno and Ischia, Procida is under 4 km long and has a worn, down-to-earth charm. Its old fishing villages of dishevelled pastel-painted buildings have become a favourite film backdrop, most famously in *Il Postino* and *The Talented Mr Ripley*. Don't expect tourist hordes and glitz here – although its 11,000 inhabitants and summer influx do create traffic mayhem in its centre. There are leafy lanes with attractive villas and market gardens to explore, and the island's fishing tradition lives on, making dining here a treat. Procida's circular bays Corricella and Chiaiolella are dead volcanic craters created by the Phlegrean caldera system, between which are some fine but scruffy beaches.

Below: Chiesa della Madonna delle Grazie. Opposite page: Marina della Corricella.

Marina Grande & Terra Murata

On arrival at Marina Grande (Porto Sancio Cattolico or, as the locals call it, Sent' Cò) you are greeted by an expanse of sticky, uneven flagstones hosting the usual Neapolitan traffic chaos backed by a ramshackle row of high, pastel-coloured former fishermen's dwellings. The eye-catching arches of these via Roma buildings, under which fishing boats used to be stored, are now occupied by bars and restaurants. Ischia's high street, via Principe Umberto, leads to piazza dei Martiri where the Baroque **Chiesa della Madonna delle Grazie** stands alongside a memorial to 12 Procidani – Republican martyrs killed during a Royalist backlash to a 1799 uprising.

Terra Murata ('walled land'), the highest point on the island at 91 m, offers wonderful views of the fishing port, Marina di Corricella, and beyond. The medieval quarter Terra Casata and the *cittadella* Castello d'Avolos have atmosphere aplenty: the latter was a castle turned Aragonese-built prison (1560s). Nearby the impressive noble residence Palazzo de lorio has a belvedere with more views.

Essentials

❶ Getting around Boat services from Naples and Pozzuoli (for a list of operators see page 259) arrive at Marina Grande. The island is so small that you can get around on foot but there are times when you'll need some wheels to take the strain. Four bus routes run by **SEPSA** (T081-542 9965, sepsa.it) cover just about all the island. Walking is not pleasant after dark, especially as there are no pavements, and often piles of rubbish on the roadside. Taxis and microtaxis are pretty cheap and cycling around the quieter lanes can be fun. At Marina Grande there's a taxi rank (T081-896 8785), and nearby you can hire scooters and bicycles from **Ricambio Giuseppe** (via Roma 107, T081-896 0060).

❸ ATM Banco di Napoli, via V Emanuele 158, T081-810 1489.

⊕ Hospital Guardia Medica, T081-983499.

✛ Pharmacy Farmacia Madonna Delle Grazie, piazza dei Martiri 1, Corricella, T081-896 8883.

➐ Post office Via Libertà 34, T081-896 0711.

❶ Tourist information Ufficio di Turismo, via Roma, Marina Grande, T081-810968, infoischiaprocida.it.

Procida's patron saint

The Abbazia contains Nicola Russo's painting *Saint Michael Protects the Island* which portrays Procida's patron saint stopping a 1535 Saracen attack. According to the legend, St Michael appeared as a vision in the sky, whipped up some waves and overwhelmed Barbarossa Hayreddin Pasha's pirates. Perhaps it was that disorientating meteorological phenomenon St Elmo's Fire that did the saintly work?

Abbazia di San Michele Arcangelo

Via Terra Murata, T081-896 7612, abbaziasanmichele.it.
Daily 0945-1245, 1500-1800, closed Sun afternoon, church free, museum €2.

This abbey deep in the Terra Murata was originally built in the 11th century and was repeatedly ransacked by Saracen pirates in the 16th and 18th centuries. Contrasting with the uplifting artistic highs of the exquisite inlaid marble altar, coffered ceiling and flourishes of gold leaf are some macabre sights in the catacombs.

Marina della Corricella, Marina di Chiaiolella & Isola di Vivara

The pastel-coloured buildings and alleyways of Marina della Corricella were the backdrop of the film *Il Postino*, starring the late Massimo Troisi, a Neapolitan comedy genius. Marina Chiaiolella is a crescent-shaped harbour, and also has a fair catch of fishing-harbour lure, with some swanky yachts and bar-restaurants to boot. Another curvaceous crater ridge forms the Isola di Vivara, an island nature reserve with a 109-m-high lump of Mediterranean scrub teeming with birdlife and other animals (accessed via a bridge; permission needed to enter T081-896 7400, isoladivivara.it).

Above: Higgledy-piggledy Procida.
Right: Ravishing in rosa.
Opposite page: Not impressed...

Five of the best

Procida beaches

Although often littered with flotsam and jetsam, Procida's beaches have their charms and lie in stunning positions.

❶ La Spiaggia del Ciraccio
Procida's longest and most popular beach is a continuation of Spiaggia della Chiaiolella and just around the corner from Marina di Chiaiolella, on the western shore. Afternoon breezes are welcomed by its sun-worshippers and windsurfers.

❷ Spiaggia della Silurenza
Just west of Marina Grande, with ample beach facilities and restaurants. Locals fire themselves off Il Cannone (named after an old cannon placed on the rocks).

❸ Spiaggia della Lingua
East of the port, off piazza della Marina Grande, is this intimate beach with limpid waters, popular with swimmers, snorkellers and fishermen.

❹ Spiaggia di Chiaia
Access to this busy beach's dark coarse sands on Procida's eastern shore involves a descent down 200 steps off piazza San Giacomo, or a boat ride.

❺ Spiaggia Pozzo Vecchio
In the northwestern corner of the island (reached from via Battisti) is the Pozzo Vecchio beach, which appeared in *Il Postino* - it is enclosed within a semicircular bay, making it popular with swimmers.

Sleeping

Capri is the priciest for accommodation, Ischia offers lots of choice, while planning laws have led to a dearth of decent hotels on Procida.

Capri

Caesar Augustus €€€€
Via G Orlandi 4, Anacapri, T081-837 3395, caesar-augustus.com.
Within walking distance of Anacapri, 'Cesare Augusto' – as the locals call it – is perched on cliffs, giving it the most spectacular views towards Marina Grande, Bagni di Tiberio and across the bay. A sprawling lounge with comfy sofas and piano bar looks onto the long terrace where a statue of Emperor Augustus watches the ferry and yacht traffic. Amid its citrus trees and flowers there's an infinity pool, spa and two restaurants. A secluded mini terrace is laid out for candlelit meals served by your own butler. A shuttle service is available to the port and the Piazzetta.

J.K. Place €€€€
Via Prov. Marina Grande 225, near Marina Grande, T081-838 4001, jkcapri.com.
Capri's first quality inn – the Hotel Continental – was housed in this whitewashed 19th-century palazzo. A penthouse and roof terrace have been added as well as all manner of luxuries including two pools (indoor and outdoor), spa

facilities, stylish interiors filled with artworks and a sundeck straight out of *Wallpaper* magazine. In 2007 and 2008 it was the understated new darling of the world's chic hotels, picking up awards nonchalantly and wads of celebrity scribbles in its guest book.

Casa Mariantonia €€€
Via G Orlandi 180, Anacapri, T081-837 2923, casamariantonia.com.
You get lots of choice at this welcoming place down the leafier end of Anacapri's main lane. Expect beautifully tiled rooms, spacious suites and apartments with terraces overlooking a lemon grove where a Russian revolutionary allegedly laced his *limone* with vodka. Breakfasts are a little basic but overall this is a gem of a place and the Canale family, who first registered and continue to produce Limoncello di Capri, are charming hosts. La Rondinella (see page 265) serves wonderful seafood over the road.

Stella Maris €€
Via Roma 27, Capri Town, T081-837 0452, albergostellamaris@libero.it.
Up the tiled steps of this *pensione*, opposite the bus station, is a cozy B&B that has been run by the same family for over 25 years now. Expect kitsch decor in the charming lobby-cum-lounge-cum-breakfast room, which hasn't changed

much since the late 1980s. The owners have a few apartments dotted around town. Avoid the rooms at the front unless you enjoy the sights and smells of Capri's cute buses.

Hotel Weber Ambassador €€
Via Marina Piccola 118, Marina Piccola, T081-837 0141, info@hotelweber.com.
Many rooms here look out over Marina Piccola's pebbly beaches, restaurants and shapely rocks. Rooms have tiled floors and functionality, and some have small terraces with sea views. A shuttle service takes guests to and from the Piazzetta from early morning to the wee early hours (0700-0300). Table tennis, mountain biking, fishing and various watersports are available.

Hotel La Tosca €
Via D Birago 5, Capri Town, T081-837 0989, h.tosca@capri.it.
La Tosca is ensconced down a quiet lane and is a short swagger from the Piazzetta. Breakfasts are taken on the flower-filled terrace with views of the Faraglioni rocks. The clean, simple decor throughout extends to the 11 whitewashed guest rooms with their smallish bathrooms.

Self-catering
Renting an apartment or villa on Capri starts at about €100 per night off-season for two to four people. A useful list of places to

stay can be found at capri.com, which includes small apartments like **Caprihouse** (T328-152 8750, caprihouse.it) and **Casa Malua** (T081-837 9577, casamalua.it); modest villas including **Casa Ersilia** (T081-837 0752, casaersilia.com); and the swanky **Le Terrazze** (T333-509 9565, caprilivia@virgilio.it), which sleeps up to eight.

Ischia

Aragona Palace Hotel €€€
Via Porto 12, Ischia Porto, T081-333 1229, hotelaragona.it.
Comfort and location – it's right on the Riva Destra with its harbourside restaurants and near all the transport – make the Aragona Palace a popular choice. Many of the spacious, blue-tiled rooms have terraces with harbour views. Facilities include a smart spa offering treatments.

Hotel Parco Smeraldo Terme €€€
Spiaggia dei Maronti, Barano d'Ischia, T081-990127, hotelparcosmeraldo.com.
The bright, cheery and airy hotel is well situated on magical Maronti beach, near its steaming fumaroles, and many of the 64 rooms have sea views and balconies. Relax in the hotel's subtropical gardens or its wellness centre (with two pools and spa treatments) or hit some balls on the tennis court. Most beach facilities are included and

there's a choice of restaurants along the volcanic sands.

Albergo Il Monastero €€
Castello Aragonese, Ischia Ponte, T081-992435, albergoilmonastero.it.
Atmosphere and stylish understated interiors make this hotel, housed in the former Convent of Santa Maria della Consolazione within the Castello Aragonese, a special place to stay. Room 21 has a balcony with stunning views of the Chiesa dell'Immacolata and beyond. Their café serves delicious pastries and looks over the Baia di Sant' Anna.

Hotel Continental Mare €€
Via B Cossa 25, Ischia, T081-982577, continentalmare.it.
Whitewashed walls and tiles throughout give this sprawling clifftop hotel a clean fresh feel. Head waiter Luigi is the embodiment of efficiency and the staff are generally very helpful. There are two pools –a thermal pool within the leafy grounds and a larger pool on an upper terrace. Down some stone steps is a pebbly beach, which alas is not ideal for swimming. Most of the 57 rooms have small outdoor terraces. Ischia Porto can be reached by bus, a €12 taxi ride or on foot along a path that winds through gardens. Spa treatments are offered at their sister hotel, Continental Terme.

Hotel Europa €
Via A Sogliuzzo 25, Ischia Ponte, T081-991427, hoteleuropaischia.it.
The Europa has been run by the same family since the 1950s and is near to Ischia Ponte's historic quarter and Ischia Porto's restaurants, with lots of shops in between. There are 34 reasonably priced rooms with tiled floors and unfussy decor. The hotel provides a thermal pool and spa treatments and organizes excursions and boat trips.

Camping

Camping Mirage
Spiaggia dei Maronti, Barano d'Ischia, T081-990551, campingmirage.it.
€26 for a small tent and 2 people. This typically dusty Italian campsite is right next to Maronti beach and has the usual campsite basics including washing facilities and a no-frills bar-restaurant.

Self-catering

Pera di Basso
Via Pera di Basso (loc. Rarone), T081-900122, peradibasso.it.
Deep in the woods above Casamicciola Terme, this stone farm building has comfortable accommodation and offers tranquillity and outdoor pursuits including trekking and mountain biking. The suite for two costs from €100 per night. The most basic studio apartment at **Villa Olivia** (via Baiola 129, Forio, T081-998426, villaolivia.it), which

has gardens and two pools, starts at €350 per week for two people, with various options for different-sized parties. At the other end of the scale is the luxurious **Villa Caruso** (Ville in Italia, T055-412058, villeinitalia. com/houses/PuntaCaruso.jsp), in Forio, which sleeps up to 18, has seriously swanky interiors, a large pool and extensive leafy grounds – and will set you back over €12,000 for a week.

Procida

La Vigna €€€
Via Principessa Margherita 46, Procida, T081-896 0469, albergolavigna.it.
The crenellated parapet of La Vigna's red-hued tower pokes above the vines in its clifftop vineyard setting. Atmosphere, tranquillity and luxury reign at this *castellino* in the country, a 10-minute walk from the harbour; you can quaff their vino, indulge in therapeutic baths and massages and revel in the effortless style of the place. For those fancying a splurge, the Malvasia suite has a luxury bath set within exotic wood.

Hotel La Casa sul Mare €€
Via Salita Castello 13, Procida, T081-896 8799, lacasasulmare.it.
Deep in the Terra Murata historic quarter, this 18th-century residence has 10 elegant rooms decked out in cool hues and tiled

floors. Many have small balconies with views. As it sits on a hill, some muscle is required to get around although a handy beach shuttle service is provided.

Hotel Celeste €
Via Rivoli 6, Procida, T081-896 7488, hotelceleste.it.
The Celeste offers reasonably priced basic accommodation near the Marina di Chiaiolella with its beach, bars and eateries. Many of the 35 functional rooms have a balcony or terrace and

Procida listings

Sleeping
1 Campeggio Punta Serra *via Serra 4*
2 Celeste *via Rivoli 6*
3 La Casa sul Mare *via Salita Castello 13*
4 La Vigna *Principessa Margherita 46*
5 ProcidaTour *via Santo Ianno 20*

Eating & drinking
1 Caffè dal Cavaliere *via Roma 42*
2 Caracalè *via Marina Corricella 62*
3 Il Galeone *via Marina Chiaiolella*
4 La Medusa *via Roma 116*
5 Sent' Cò *via Roma 167*

Eating & drinking

there are lots of relaxing and intimate corners (including a cozy bar and sundecks) awash with celestial blue hues. The owners collaborate with a local tour company to provide guests with stimulating excursions.

Camping
Campeggio Punta Serra
Via Serra 4, Procida, T081-896 9519, campeggioserra@simail.it.
Open Jun-Sep.
Pozzo Vecchio beach, granular star of *Il Postino,* is a short walk from this campsite which has pitches for tents and caravans and bungalows for rent (sleeps 2-6, €65-170 per night).

Self-catering
ProcidaTour
Via Santo Ianno 20, Procida, T081-896 9393. procidatour.it.
This family-run enterprise rents out a number of apartments and studios in the Collinetta di Cottimo area. Punto Faro and Pozzo Vecchio beaches are nearby.

Under the pergola at Il Solitario.

Capri

Da Gioia €€€
Marina Piccola, T081-837 7702.
May-Oct daily 1200-1500, 1900-2300, rest of year times vary.
The magical essence of Caprese dining can be found on this boardwalk platform overlooking the Marina Piccola shoreline. The Mennillo family's simple Neapolitan classics like *spaghetti ai frutti di mare* (spaghetti with shellfish), pizza and salads, washed down with a Peroni or wine, hit the epicurean spot best when outside, looking over the sea and towards the Fariglioni rocks. Reservations recommended.

Da Paolino €€€
Via Palazzo a Mare 11, T081-837 6102.
Thu-Tue 1230-1500, 1900-2400.
Down a leafy lane on the way to Bagni di Tiberio, amid lemon groves and stray cats, is legendary Paolino's, famed for simply prepared seafood dishes such as *totano con patate* – a special, seasonal type of squid served with potatoes.

Il Solitario €€
Via G Orlandi 96, 80071 Anacapri, T081-837 1382, trattoriailsolitario.it.
Daily 1200-1500, 1900-2400.
Under a pergola near the Santa Sofia church, charming Alessandra and Massimiliano carry on the family tradition started in 1960 when Il Solitario was a tavern for locals. Expect excellent pizzas (try their *pizza bianca*) and wonderful dishes like *calamari alla griglia* (grilled squid), cheese-dream filled *ravioli capresi* and their special *scialatelli pasta* (with some potato in the mix) *alle vongole*. Polish it off with home-made tiramisù.

La Rondinella €€
Via G Orlandi 295, 80071 Anacapri, T081-837 1223.
Daily 1200-1500, 1900-2300.
The Rondinella combines flavoursome food, relaxed dining and friendly service down the quiet end of Anacapri's main lane. There's a smallish but wonderful terrace (book it!) and a large dining room. The freshest seafood goes into dishes like *linguine al scampo* and *frittura di gambero e calamaro* (fried prawns and squid).

Capri's €
Via Roma 38, Capri Town, T081-837 3108, capris.it.
Near the Piazzetta on the way to Marina Grande is this sleek café-bar-restaurant with an open kitchen and superb views through large windows. As well as decent pizza and home-made ice cream, they do pasta and seafood dishes including meaty medallions of tuna and grilled swordfish.

What the locals say

Torre Saracena €€€€
Via Marina Piccola, T081-837 0646.
Apr-Oct daily 1200-1500, Sat 1900-2300.

Saturday night dinner at Torre Saracena is very special but very expensive. Right on the rocky shore of Marina Grande, they serve seafood dishes including *pezzogna all'acqua pazza* (bream cooked in "crazy" boiling water) and *zuppa di pesce con scorfano e pomodorini* (fish soup with scorpion fish and tomatoes), as well as ravioli alla caprese.

Capri resident **Michelle Lowe.**

Cafés & bars
Bar Buchetto
Via G Orlandi 38, Anacapri.
Daily 0800-2200.
Near the bus terminal, ever-reliable Bar Buchetto, with charming Michele Scarpato at the helm (68 years in the job), delivers *pizza al taglio*, ice cream and refreshments.

Caffè Michelangelo
Via Trieste e Trento 1, Anacapri.
Daily 0800 till late.
The amiable bar staff at this swish bar serve aperitivi with *taralli di finocchietto* (savoury biscuits with fennel seeds) on the terrace while you watch the Anacapresi and tourists go by.

Pasticceria Buonocore
Vittorio Emanuele 35, Capri Town, T081-837 7826.
Daily 0730-2100.
The sweet smell of Buonocore's ice cream cones stays long in the olfactory memory. Its sweet and savoury treats, like lemon-and-almond *caprilù* biscuits and

freshly prepared panini, are great for snacks and picnics.

Sfizi di Pane
Via le Botteghe 4, Capri Town, T081-837 0106.
Tue-Sun 0700-1330, 1600-2000.
Breaded treats including olive breads, cute and crusty rolls (*bacetti*) and *taralli* biscuits make this a good stop for snacks.

Ischia

Umberto a Mare €€€
Via Soccorso 2, Forio, T081-997171, umbertoamare.it.
Tue-Sun 1200-1530, 1930-2300.
Sophisticated dining and spellbinding views of the Soccorso shoreline make this a special restaurant. Innovative dishes like local *ricciola* fish with sweet artichokes, fresh basil and lemon can be accompanied by an impressive range of wines. Phone to book a table near the window to enjoy the sunset.

Neptunus €€
Via delle Rose 11, Sant'Angelo, T081-999702.
Daily 1200-1500, 1930-2400
Eating the freshest seafood on the terrace here, overlooking Sant'Angelo, is an archetypal Ischian experience. Start with the seafood salad of squid and octopus, squeeze your lemon wedge and let Giuseppe Jacono and team guide you through the menu – it may just climax with a sugar, alcohol and caffeine-combined rush of *torta caprese*, grappa and a shot of espresso.

Mezzanotte €
Via Porto 72, 80077 Ischia Porto, T081-981653.
Daily 1200-1500, 1900 till late.
A youthful throng spills out onto the Riva at weekends here and there's a cocktail bar upstairs. Expect classic seafood dishes like *spaghetti alle vongole* and a choice of pizzas.

Cafés & bars
Bar Ciccio
Via Porto 1, Ischia Porto.
Daily 0700-2200.
Open for over a hundred years, Bar Ciccio does interesting ice-cream flavours including healthy options such as organic, fat-free, doppio-zero and gluten-free.

Bar Pasticceria Calise
Via Sogliuzzo 69, Ischia Porto, T081-991270.
Sweet filled *cornetti* including the devilish *alla crema e amarene*

La Pizza.

(with cream and sour cherries) are just some of the pastries enjoyed at this popular spot.

Al Triangolo
Via Roma, Lacco Ameno,
T081-099 4364.
Daily 0700-2200.
Near Il Fungo, this is the place for refreshing *granite* in classic and crazy flavours like lemon, melon, coffee, strawberry and yoghurt.

Procida

La Medusa €€
Via Roma 116, Marina Grande,
T081-896 7481.
Daily 1200-1500, 1900-2300.
An idiosyncratic owner and excellent seafood dishes including *spaghetti ai ricci di mare* (sea urchin sauce) make this a memorable place to dine. If the *padrone* (main man) takes a liking to you expect copious amounts of charm and *cibo* (food).

Sent' Cò €€
Via Roma 167, Marina Grande,
T081-810 1120.
Tue-Sun 1200-1500, 1900-2300.
Sent' Cò is a no-frills ristorante-pizzeria serving the catch of the

day and a popular fish soup. Also worth trying are the *orecchiette* (small ear-shaped pasta) with a sauce made from the island's vegetables.

Caracalè €
Via Marina Corricella 62,
Corricella, T081-896 9192.
Daily 1200-1500, 1900-2300.
Caracalè serves seafood creations like swordfish with aubergine and is a fine spot for absorbing the picturesque Corricella harbour scene. The laid-back atmosphere and unfussy preparation of the freshest catch make it the most beguiling eatery on the *banchina* (quayside).

Cafés & bars
Caffè dal Cavaliere
Via Roma 42, Marina Grande,
T081-810 1074.
Daily 0700-2100.
Famed for their creamy pastries – *lingue di bue* (cow's tongues) – containing Procida's mightily pithy lemons.

Il Galeone
Via Marina Chiaiolella, Marina di Chiaiolella, T081-896 9622.
Daily 0800-2400.
A largish café-bar-restaurant by the harbour serving drinks, pizzas, snacks like *bruschette*, as well as meat dishes and grilled fish.

Pick of the Picnic Spots

Pick up picnic treats from a local *alimentari* (food shop) or splash out on something special at one these gourmet gems: Pasticceria Buonocore, Capri, see page 266; Ischia Sapori, Ischia; Il Ghiottone di Imputato M, Procida, see page 270.

Monte Solaro, Capri After ascending serenely on the chairlift or by foot to Capri's limestone peak, there are shimmering views to savour over the rolling island, ocean and even as far as smoking Stromboli, towards Sicily.

La Migliera, Capri The buzz of Anacapri fades as you walk down flowery lanes, through woods and grapevines to the clifftop Belvedere del Tuono, with heart-pounding panoramas down jagged cliffs to Punta Carena, Il Faro and along the spectacular coast with its forts and yacht-studded coves.

Monte Epomeo, Ischia A walk to Ischia's volcanic zenith is rewarded with the chance to eat and drink in the breathtaking views while lounging on the smooth sculptured rocks.

La Mortella, Ischia Exotic plant species, trickling water features and idyllic garden corners make this a mellifluous venue for a *merenda* (snack) – just don't leave a mess – and perhaps enjoy a drink in La Mortella's tea room.

Marina della Corricella, Procida Take a pew near the rusty rings and flaking boats on the fishing village quayside. Between bites and glimpses of salty Procida lives you can snap away at pastel and marine blue-hued views.

Entertainment

Capri

Clubs

Anema e Core
Via Sella Orta 39/e, Capri Town, T081-837 6461, anemaecore.com.
Thu-Sat 2100 till late.
The cheesiest Caprese night club, where Italian celebrities go cheek to cheek and dressed-up locals quaff cocktails, grin and gyrate to live Italo-latino music, including resident crooner Guido Lembo.

Lanterna Verde
Via G Orlandi 1, Anacapri, T081-837 1427.
Thu-Sat 2200 till late.
Piano-bar Italian tunes and live latino sway young and ageing hips at Hotel San Michele's chic nightspot.

Underground
Via G Orlandi 259, Anacapri, T081-837 2523.
Thu-Sat 2200 till late.
House music and cabaret entertain young Capresi at this *discoteca*.

Festivals & events

Procession of San Costanzo
Capri Town, 14 May.
According to legend, Capri's patron saint and protector was washed ashore here on his way back to Constantinope. A colourful procession to Marina Grande sees Capresi shower the garlanded statue with rose petals.

Procession of Sant' Antonio
Anacapri, 13 Jun.
Anacapri's saintly protector is honoured with a colourful ceremony involving lots of flower petals and eating of sweets, followed by a concert in piazza Diaz.

Santa Maria del Soccorso
Villa Jovis, 7-8 Sep.
The ancient church at Villa Jovis is lit up on the evening of 7 September and the following morning a mass is held in honour of the Virgin Mary. Music making, dancing and feasting follow.

Settembrata Anacaprese
Anacapri, late Aug to early Sep.
The town's four *quartieri* (districts) pit their wits against each other in gastronomic and other quirky contests.

Gay & lesbian

Number 2
Via Camerelle 2, Capri Town, T081-837 7078, numbertwocapri.com.
Thu-Sat 2300 till late.
The nudist beach Spiaggia Libera Via Krupp at Marina Piccola may be the traditional daytime meeting place, but this house music club on the chic Capri Town drag via Camerelle is the island's main gay nightspot.

Ischia

Clubs

L'Ecstasy
Piazzetta dei Pini 3, Ischia Porto, T081-992653.
Daily 2000 till late.
A bar-*discoteca* that hosts club nights and live music including jazz acts during September's Jazz Festival.

New Valentino
Corso Vittoria Colonna 97, Ischia Porto, T081-982569, valentinoischia.eu.
Daily 2100 till late.
A bizarre mix of majolica tiling and lurid lighting is the backdrop to wild nights of piano bar and dance music.

Festivals & events

Festa di Sant' Anna
Ischia, 26 Jul.
The island's patron saint is honoured with a lively procession of boats, fireworks and feasting around the Castello Aragonese.

Ischia Film Festival
ischiafilmfestival.it.
Each June Ischia hosts a two-week film festival dedicated to film locations.

Shopping

Procida

Clubs
GM Bar
*Via Roma 117, Marina Grande,
T081-896 7560, gmbar.it.
Thu-Sat 2200 till late.*
According to the locals this
bar-discoteca is *"il boom"* at
the moment – and it's certainly
popular with the young
Procidiani who cram in here
at weekends for live music, DJs
and free buffet food.

Festivals & events
Procida's festivals include **Festa
della Madonna delle Grazie**
(2 July), a colourful religious
procession with much feasting;
Sagra del Mare (Festival of the
Sea) in late July; **Sagra del Pesce
Azzurro** (mid-August), a fish
festival in Corricella involving lots
of eating and drinking; **Sagra del
Vino** (November), Procida's wine
festival.

Good Friday procession
Dating back to 1627, this Easter
procession was inspired by the
Spanish tradition of the mysteries.
Representations of Christ's
suffering made by local children
are displayed and then a dozen
white-robed locals haul an
18th-century wooden statue of
the dead Christ to Terra Murata.
A funereal procession takes place
the following morning.

Capri

Ceramics
Cose di Capri
*Via G Orlandi 50/a, Anacapri,
T081-838 2111.*
Interesting ceramics in unusual
colours and shapes made by
Vittoria Staiano.

Clothing
Canfora
*Via Camerelle 3, Capri Town,
T081-837 0487.*
Historic Canfora makes quality
leather sandals in lots of colours.

100% Capri
*Via Fuorlovado 27-44, Capri
Town, T081-837 7561.*
Quality luxuries such as fine
cotton beach robes and scented
candles fill this oh-so-white
outlet.

Food & drink
Fairly cheap, basic picnic
ingredients can be gathered at
Supermarket Al (via Pagliaro 19,
Capri Town, and Anacapri) and
Deco (via Matermania 1, Capri
Town).

La Capannina Più
*Via le Botteghe 39, Capri Town,
T081-837 8899.*
The posh restaurant's *enoteca*
and gourmet shop has lots of
wines and food for that very
special picnic.

Limoncello di Capri
*Via Roma 79, Capri Town,
T081-837 5561; via Capodimonte
27, Anacapri, T081-837 2927.*
Many places claim to have
invented the syrupy *digestivo*,
but the story that this family's
first brew oiled the constitution
of Russian revolutionary guests
is hard not to like.

Perfumery
Carthusia Profumi
*Via Camerelle 10, Capri Town,
T081-837 0368; via Capodimonte
26, Anacapri, T081-837 3668.*
Carthusia does famous scents –
first created by monks and made
from the fruit and flora of Capri
– and gorgeous packaging.

Ischia

Ceramics
Di Meglio
*Via Roma 42, Ischia Porto,
T081-991176.*
A large space brimming with
colourful ceramic plates and tiles.

Food & drink
Ischia Sapori
*Via R Gianturco 2, Ischia Porto,
T081-984482.*
Gastronomic goodies,
including liqueurs, olive oils,
wines, handmade pasta and
preserves.

Salumeria Manzi
Via Roma 16, Lacco Ameno.
With lots of reasonably priced
bread, cheese, meats and fruit

Activities & tours

and vegetables, this is a good place to buy picnic or self-catering provisions.

Souvenirs
Napoli Mania
Il Corso, Ischia Porto, napolimania.com.
Novelties in Neapolitan dialect that many Italians don't understand: from T-shirts and mugs to baby bibs and Maradona-related items.

Procida

Food & drink
Il Ghiottone di Imputato M
Via Vittorio Emanuele 15, T081-896 0349.
Gastronomic establishment – great for gifts and all you need for a lavish Procidano picnic.

Souvenirs
Izzo Rosana
Via Vittorio Emanuele 36, T081-896 9118.
Funky stationery and knick-knacks.

Capri

Boat trips
Gruppo Motoscafisti
Via Provinciale Marina Grande 282, T081-837 7714/5648, motoscafisticapri.com.
Capri must be experienced from the sea. Pack a picnic and hire a boat or join one of the many boat trips offered by the Società Cooperativa Motoscafisti – their distinctive wooden kiosk and fleet can be found at Marina Grande. Classic excursions include tours of the island, through the Fariglione di Mezzo and into the the Grotta Verde, from €30 for a two-hour trip.

Giovanni Aprea
T347-475 7277 (mobile), aprea.it.
Giovanni Aprea takes groups around Capri's bays and grottoes in his mildly souped-up Sorrentine *gozzo* sailing boat from €30.

Diving
Sercomor
C. Colombo 64, Marina Grande, T081-837 8781, T328-721 2920 (mobile), caprisub.com.
Scuba-diving courses and boat tours around Capri.

Sports
Capri Sporting Club
Via G Orlandi 10, Anacapri, T081-837 2612, caprisportingclub.net.
Tennis courts and *calcetto* (five-a-side) footie pitches in a spectacular setting.

Walking
Capri Trails
T081-837 5933, T3473-681699 (mobile), capritrails.com.
Luigi Esposito takes walking tours, kayaking adventures and climbing on the cliffs near Faro (€30 per hour, €180 per day).

Wellbeing
Capri Palace
Via Capodimonte 14, Anacapri, T081-978 0505, capripalace.com.
Mar-Nov 0900-1300, 1600-2000.
Specialist medical spa and beauty treatments in the most luxurious surroundings. Rates range from €225 for a day's pampering to €4000 and upwards for one of their seven-night programmes.

Left: Bagni di Tiberio.
Opposite page: Marina Grande, Procida.

Transport

Ischia

Adventure sports
Indiana Park Pineta
Loc. Fiaiano, Barano,
T0773-474473.
Apr-Oct.
Six colour-coded arboreal assault courses (they call it) allow anyone over 110 cm in height to experience adrenaline-fuelled "tarzanning", which involves lots of climbing, swinging and abseiling around this forest park.

Sailing
Scuola Vela Ischia
Hotel Villa Carolina, Forio,
T081-997119, scuolavelaischia.it.
Sailing school in Forio with courses starting at €100 for two outings.

Walking
Ischia Trekking
T368-335 0074 (mobile),
ischiatrekking.it.
Guided treks exploring the caves of Pizzi Bianchi, Piano Liguori and Mont' Epomeo (four hours) from €15 per person.

Wellbeing
Parco Termale Castiglione
Via Castiglione 62, Casamicciola Terme, T081-982551,
termecastiglione.it.
Historic spa now with luxurious

spaces and outdoor pools. A day ticket costs €30 and entitles use of thermal pools, sauna, sunbeds and changing facilities.

Spa Resort Negombo
Baia San Montano,
T081-986152, negombo.it.
Arguably Ischia's most beautiful spa resort, frequented by both minted megalomaniacs and everyday Giuseppes. Massage treatments involving the use of hot healing stones start at €75.

Terme Manzi
Piazza Bagni, Casamicciola Terme, T081-994722,
termemanzihotel.com.
Amid the chic interiors, mood lighting and techie spa equipment is the tub a wounded Giuseppe Garibaldi sat in when convalescing during his 1862 Risorgimento campaign. A pricey yet serene and stylish spa.

Procida

Sport
De Sanctis
Via G da Procida, Procida,
T081-896 7571.
Tennis and *calcetto* (five-a-side) facilities, best booked for the cool evenings.

Lots of companies run services to the islands from Naples, Pozzuoli and Sorrento (for a list of operators and services see pages 167 and 239 respectively). Large ferries (Navi) and TMVs or Traghetti Veloci (fast ferries) now operate out of Calata Porta di Massa. Molo Beverello handles most of the faster vessels and *gli aliscafi* (hydrofoils). Mergellina is handy for Ischia. Seasonal timetables apply: check latest *Qui Napoli* booklet and/or *Il Mattino* newspaper.

Capri

Ferries, TMVs and hydrofoils to Naples, Ischia, Positano, Sorrento and Salerno. Journey times 35-80 mins. Seasonal timetables apply.

Ischia

Ferries, TMVs and hydrofoils to Naples, Pozzuoli and Capri. Journey times 50-90 mins. Seasonal timetables apply.

Procida

Ferries, TMVs and hydrofoils to Ischia, Pozzuoli and Naples. Journey times 20-60 mins. Seasonal timetables apply.

Tip...

For a taster at the Parco Termale come an hour before closing and try the facilities for just €3.

Contents

Practicalities

Metronapoli.

Practicalities
Getting there

 Air

From UK and Ireland
Flying to Naples International Airport (Aeroporto Internazionale di Napoli, also known as Aeroporto Capodichino) is the most convenient option as it's within easy reach of the city and other attractions. Year-round direct flights leave from Dublin, London Heathrow, London Gatwick and London Stansted airports. The main airlines providing year-round direct flights are **Alitalia**, **Aerlingus**, **British Airways** and **easyJet**. Some carriers like **Thomson** run charter flights in the spring and summer months from London and other UK airports including Belfast, Birmingham, Bristol, East Midlands, Glasgow, Manchester and Newcastle. Liverpool is served by **easyJet** from June to October.

From North America
There are no year-round direct flights to Naples from North America. Rome Fiumincino is the nearest airport you can fly direct to, with **Alitalia** and **Delta** flights from New York and Toronto. **Alitalia**, **Air Canada**, **Air France**, **British Airways**, **Delta** and **KLM** also fly to large Italian airports Milan Malpensa and Venice Marco Polo. London, Munich and Paris are other possible hubs with lots of connecting flights to Naples.

From rest of Europe
There are direct flights to Naples from many European cities including Amsterdam, Athens, Basel, Berlin, Brussels, Bucharest, Frankfurt, Geneva, Hanover, Kiev, Madrid, Monaco, Munich, Paris, Prague, Stockholm, Stuttgart, Vienna and Zurich. Carriers include **Aerosvit**, **Air One**, **Air France**, **Alitalia**, **Brussels Airlines**, **easyJet**, **Clickair**, **Lufthansa**, **Meridiana**, **My Air**, **Tuifly** and **Sky Europe**.

Airport information

Naples International Airport (NAP, T081-789 6259, gesac.it), also known as Capodichino Airport, is situated about 7 km northeast of the centre of Naples. Recent additions to the airport complex have not drastically changed its feel as a small airport of a manageable size. Buses to central Naples are fairly reliable – they all stop at the main train station, Napoli Centrale, and many drop passengers near the port – so connections with other transport services are usually straightforward. In the Arrivals hall there's an EPT (local tourist board) desk where you can find out tourist information and buy the Artecard (see page 77), and car hire desks including Avis (T081-751 6052, avis.co.uk), Europcar (T081-780 5643, europcar.co.uk) and Hertz (T081-780 2971, hertz.co.uk).

Airport transport
The cheapest means of reaching the centre of Naples is to take the **3S bus** (for 'Service, Save money and Satisfaction'), a standard orange city bus, from outside the terminal. Buy UnicoNapoli tickets (see page 76) at the Sunstore in Arrivals, or from *tabacchi* (tobacconists) or *edicole* (news-stands). Buses run roughly every half hour between 0520 and 2320 and stop at via Volta (the Brin car park), corso Garibaldi (outside the Circumvesuviana station) and piazza Garibaldi (Napoli Centrale train station). Journey times are 20-25 minutes. It's cheap but not ideal if you have lots of luggage. The **Alibus** is a slighty smarter service with a luggage hold that runs every 30 minutes from 0630 to 2330 between the airport, piazza Garibaldi and the port terminal at piazza Municipio. Tickets cost €3 and can be bought on board: they are valid for 90 minutes and can be used on public transport. If you opt for a **taxi**, you are plunged into Neapolitan chaos at the taxi rank outside Arrivals. Make sure you get an authorized cab (most are white and should have a laminated

card with tariff list on the back seat) and either agree to a *prezzo fisso* (fixed price: a journey to a hotel in central Naples is around €30) or that the *tassista* (taxi driver) puts on his *tassimetro* (metre).

Rail

There are no direct rail links to Naples from the UK. However there are train services to Milan, Turin, Venice, Padua and Verona from European cities, including Paris, Munich, Vienna and Geneva; you can then use **Trenitalia** (trenitalia.com) trains to reach Naples. Travel by rail from the UK involves taking the **Eurostar** (eurostar.com) service from London St Pancras to Paris Gare du Nord (from £59 return, 2 hrs 25 mins) and then crossing Paris to the Gare de Bercy to catch a direct overnight sleeper (from £60 return) to Milan or Venice Santa Lucia in northern Italy, from where you can catch a train to Naples which takes another six hours. Daytime travel is also possible but you'll have to spend a night in either Paris, Milan or Geneva. Another alternative is an overnight train from Paris Bercy to Roma Termini, which takes 18 hours. Buy tickets through **Rail Europe** (T0870-584 8848, raileurope. co.uk, raileurope.com) or **SNCF** (voyages-sncf.com). For comprehensive information on rail travel throughout Europe, consult seat61.com.

Road

Car

If you're up for the 2000-km journey and can afford the petrol, you could drive from the UK to Naples in a leisurely 30 hours (if you're lucky) – a few overnight stops on the way would make for a more pleasant adventure. The classic route from the UK is through France, entering Italy through the Mont Blanc tunnel where you will arrive in the gorgeous Italian Alps, just north of Turin. Italian *autostrade* take you down to Naples; perhaps choose a route to take in towns and sights on the way. Having a car is a bonus if you want to explore Campania but it's more of hindrance for those based in Naples itself as Neapolitan traffic can be a frightening prospect, especially for the uninitiated. Car theft and parking is also a big problem in the city so think thrice before opting to drive in Naples.

Bus/coach

Eurolines (T041-538 2118, eurolines.com) run long-distance coaches across Europe. The tortuous journey from London to Naples (return fare around £125) takes about 36 hours, stopping at Paris and Milan on the way. Coaches arrive at and depart from piazza Garibaldi.

Sea

Naples is very much on the Mediterranean cruise liner route. Colossal ships dock around the impressive Fascist-era **Stazione Marittima** (T081-551 4448, terminalnapoli.it) terminal building on the Molo Angioino. A good place to research into the pros and cons of cruise holidays and operators is cruises.co.uk, which contains a wealth of reviews.

As well as the many hydrofoil and ferry services that operate to and from the islands and resorts around the Bay of Naples (see page 167), there are also overnight ferry services further afield, to and from Catania and Palermo in Sicily, the various Aeolian islands off the north coast of Sicily (Stromboli, Panarea, Salina, Lipari and Vulcano), Cagliari and Olbia in Sardinia and the Pontine islands of Ventotene and Ponza, off the Lazio coast. The main operators of these services are: **Di Maio Lines** (dimaiolines.it), **Siremar** (siremar.it), **SNAV** (snav.it), **TTT lines** (tttlines.it) and **Tirrenia** (tirrenia.it).

Getting around

Rail

Italy's hugely extensive, efficient and affordable rail network is the best way to get around the country on a city-based trip. It is served by air-conditioned and splendid Eurostar Italia trains (ES); direct and convenient InterCity trains (IC); and the slightly less regular Regionale (REG) and Interregionale (IR) trains, both of which stop at many more stations. All can be booked at trenitalia.com; booking is advised for Eurostar Italia and InterCity services.

Ticket prices are sure to be a pleasant surprise: a single from Rome to Naples, for example, costs €11 for an IR train (2 hrs 40 mins); €20 for a reserved second-class seat on an IC train (2 hrs 10 mins); and €33 on an ES fast train (1 hr 21 mins). As well as standard fares there are also cheaper Amica fares, available in advance, and first-class tickets, which are not that much more expensive. Booking and buying tickets at the counter in a station usually involves a long wait so look for the ticket-dispensing machines. These take cash and/or credit or debit cards, have a number of language functions and offer all the options, prices and timings. Remember, you must validate train tickets at the yellow stamping machines before boarding, although on many Italian trains it is possible to travel 'ticketless' by quoting a booking reference to the conductor instead. In general, it's cheaper and more convenient to book individual journeys online or to buy the ticket at the station than it is to buy a pass for multiple journeys; Eurostar Italia and InterCity services often have a surcharge which makes rail passes less cost-effective. To avoid queues, frustration and fumbling with cash at ticket machines register at trenitalia.com, where you can buy and book your journey well in advance: ticketless and discounted.

The city's central train station, **Napoli Centrale**, is on crazy, traffic-ridden piazza Garibaldi. Be especially careful in and around the crowded station, keeping a close eye on your valuables and your wallet, as its frenzied and humid environment can be disorientating and the area is frequented by some dodgy characters and pickpocket squads. The main train line runs north to Rome and south to Salerno and Calabria. Many regional trains (at least two per hour) serve Caserta and Capua (40-60 mins) from Napoli Centrale, with most stopping at stations in the sprawling and scruffy suburbs. Some trains from the north also stop at: **Stazione Mergellina** (T081-761 2102), northwest of the city centre on piazza Piedigrotta, which is handy for people staying in Posillipo, Mergellina and Chiaia; and the Campi Flegrei station in Fuorigrotta, which is convenient for those staying in the seaside towns around Pozzuoli.

Trenitalia (T89-20-21 from within Italy, T+39 0668-475475 from outside Italy, trenitalia.com) has details of all routes, service issues and latest discount offers.

Local railways
The **Ferrovia Circumvesuviana** (T800-053939, vesuviana.it) runs between Naples (Stazione Circumvesuviana, just off piazza Garibaldi) and the satellite towns east of the city, below Vesuvius (including Ercolano and Pompei) and along the Sorrentine Peninsula as far as Sorrento. It's a reliable service and cheap to use, although overcrowded at peak times. The **Cumana** and **Circumflegrea** railways (which will eventually form part of the updated Metronapoli system) link Naples (Montesanto being the main hub) with the Campi Flegrei – the Cumana is especially handy for those visiting the coastal resorts here.

Public transport in Naples
Naples has a comprehensive transport system of buses, trams, funiculars and metro trains, see page 76.

Road

Car

Having your own vehicle is more of a burden than a bonus in Naples as the traffic is horrendous and car crime is rife. Put it this way – running a car in this city demands some of the highest insurance premiums on the planet! However, if you plan to brave the roads and tour Campania's mountainous interior, having your own transport will allow you to visit more rural destinations that are difficult to reach by bus or train. For those heading into the city and the islands, the most convenient and central car park is **Parcheggio Buono Molo Beverello** (piazza Municipio, T335-499658, parcheggiobeverello.com, daily 0600-2100, €16 per day for a medium sized car), which is next to the Molo Beverello port.

EU nationals taking their own car into Italy need to have an International Insurance Certificate (also known as a *Carta Verde*) and a valid national or EU licence. Those holding a non-EU licence need to take an International Driving Permit with them.

Speed limits are 130 kph on *autostrade* (motorways), 110 kph on dual carriageways and 50 kph in towns. (Limits are 20 kph lower on motorways and dual carriageways when the road is wet.) The **A1** links Rome and Naples, passing Capua and Caserta and through the northern suburbs before it becomes the **A3**, which runs eastwards below Vesuvius and towards Salerno. Approaching the city, vehicles use the **Tangenziale di Napoli**, a huge ring road on stilts that sweeps westwards above the city. It has various exits and can be a tad confusing and overwhelming for those not used to the fluid Neapolitan traffic – Uscita 1 (Exit 1) on the Tangenziale is for Capodichino and Naples International airport. For those staying north or west of the city at Capodimonte, Vomero, Fuorigrotta or the Campi Flegrei, it's best to use the Tangenziale to avoid the city's traffic mayhem downtown. Drivers heading to the port or east of the city towards Ercolano, the Sorrentine Peninsula and Amalfi Coast should continue to the intersection near San Giovanni a Teduccio, where the A3 starts.

Autostrade are toll roads, so keep cash in the car as a back-up even though you can use credit cards on the blue 'viacard' gates. **Autostrade** (T055-420 3200, autostrade.it) provides information on motorways in Italy and **Automobile Club d'Italia** (T06-49981, aci.it) provides general driving information. It also offers roadside assistance with English-speaking operators on T116.

If you intend to drive in the Apennine and Lattari mountains along the Amalfi Coast, take extra care, certainly in winter due to the icy conditions but also in summer when there are a lot of cyclists on the road. The winding Amalfi Drive (SS163) is particularly taxing in the summer, when its narrow hairpins are clogged with holiday traffic and coaches. Wet conditions combined with often-oily, poorly maintained roads throughout the region make for treacherous driving conditions, requiring care.

Be aware that there are restrictions on driving in historic city centres, indicated by signs with black letters ZTL (*zona a traffico limitato*) on a yellow background. If you ignore these signs, you are liable for a fine. Parking is usually available outside the *centro storico* for €2-5 an hour depending on the location. City hotels will either provide parking for guests or be able to direct you to the nearest car park.

Since July 2007 on-the-spot fines for minor traffic offences have been in operation; typically they range from €150 to €250 (always get a receipt). Note the following legal requirements: the use of mobile telephones while driving is not permitted; front and rear seatbelts must be worn, if fitted; children under 1.5 m may only travel in the back of the car. Italy has very strict laws on drink driving: the legal limit is 0.5 g per litre of blood compared to the UK's 0.8 g). If your car breaks down on the carriageway, you must display an emergency triangle and wear a reflective jacket in poor visibility. Car hire companies should provide both of these but check the boot when you pick up your car.

Car hire

Car hire is available at Naples airport. You are advised to book your hire car before you arrive in the country,

> ## Tip…
> Unleaded petrol is *benzina*; diesel is *gasolio*.
> Expect to pay €1.25 for a litre of petrol and €1.30
> for a litre of diesel.

especially at busy times of year. Car hire comparison websites and agents are a good place to start a search for the best deals: try avis.com, europcar.co.uk and hertz.co.uk. Check what each hire company requires from you: some companies will ask for an International Driving Licence alongside your normal driving licence; others are content with an EU licence. You will also need a credit card, so, if you book ahead, make sure that the named credit card holder is the same as the person renting and driving the car. Most companies have a lower age limit of 21 years, with a young driver surcharge for those under 25, and require that you've held your licence for at least a year. Confirm the company's insurance and damage waiver policies and keep all your documents with you when you drive.

Bicycle
If your thighs are up to it and you are confident on roads populated with fast and crazy drivers, cycling around the rural areas of Campania can be memorable. Arm yourself with a good map: Edizioni Multigraphic and Touring Club Italiano do excellent road maps and Kompass cater for outdoor enthusiasts seeking wilder climbs. Bikes are allowed on many train services: check out trenitalia.com for more information. Bike hire is available at **Napoli Bike** (Riviera di Chiaia, T081-411 934, napolibike.com). The **European Cycling Federation** (ecf.com) promotes cycling in Europe and has some good advice as well as links to companies that provide biking tours in the region.

Bus/coach
With trains so fast, cheap and efficient, it is only in the more rural areas that buses provide a useful service. Check with the local tourist information office to confirm times and pick-up points, as well

as to find out where to buy tickets (it's often a nearby newsagent or tobacconist). Travelling around cities by bus is easier as these services are regular. Again you can buy tickets from newsagents, tobacconists (look for a big T sign) and even some cafés: if you intend to make a number of journeys, buy a stash of tickets or a travel card like UnicoNapoli and UnicoCampania (see page 76). Always remember to validate your ticket when you board by stamping it in the machine located at the front and sometimes also at the back of the bus. The main bus companies in the region are **ANM** (anm.it), who run buses around the city and the suburbs, and **SITA** (sitabus.it), who provide regional services.

Sea
There are many operators who provide maritime passenger services to and from the islands (Capri, Ischia and Procida), along the Sorrentine Peninsula (including Sorrento) and along the Amalfi Coast (Amalfi and Positano) towards Salerno. The new (opened in 2008) port terminal at **Calata Porta di Massa**, off via Cristoforo Colombo, now handles the bulk of the ferry (*navi/traghetti*) services whereas nearby **Porto Beverello**, near piazza Municipio, is where to go for the swifter hydrofoils (*aliscafi*) and catamarans (*catamarani*). The smaller and less hectic quayside at **Mergellina** now handles the bulk of the faster services (hydrofoils) to Ischia. Further west in the Campi Flegrei at the port of **Pozzuoli** there are services to and from Ischia (Ischia Porto, Casamicciola and Forio) and Procida (Marina Grande). The main carriers are: **Alilauro** (T081-497 2211, alilauro.it), **Caremar** (T081-017 1998, caremar.it), **Linee Marittime Artenopee** (T081-807 1812, consorziolmp.it), **Medmar** (T081-552 2838, medmargroup.it), **Metro del Mare** (T199-600700, metrodelmare.com), **NLG** (Navigazione Libera del Golfo, T081-552 0763, navlib.it), **Procidalines** (T081-896 0328), **Procidamar** (T081-497 2278, procida.net) and **SNAV** (T081-761 2348, snav.it).

Directory

Customs & immigration

UK and EU citizens do not need a visa but will need a valid passport to enter Italy. A standard tourist visa for those outside the EU is valid for up to 90 days

Disabled travellers

Italy is beginning to adapt to the needs of disabled travellers but access can still be very difficult due to the age of many historic buildings or the lack of careful planning. For more details and advice, contact a specialist agency before departure, such as **Accessible Italy** (accessibleitaly.com) or **Society for Accessible Travel and Hospitality** (sath.org). **Oltre La Disabilità** (T081-790 1596, oltreladisabilita. com), is a local organization that looks after the interests of disabled people in the Campania region.

Emergencies

Ambulance T118; **Fire service** T115; **Police** T112 (with English-speaking operators), T113 (*carabinieri*); **Roadside assistance** T116.

Etiquette

Facendo la bella figura (projecting a good image) is important to Italians but down in Naples there is a more laid-back, humorous outlook – the locals are famed for flouting rules and dodging barriers. Neapolitan chattiness is one of the infectious aspects of the region. However, as in the rest of Italy, you should check your change, prices and tariffs. Being *furbo* (sly) and dishonest dealings to gain commercial advantage do not have the same negative connotations in Italy as they do in other cultures. Learn the phrase *non è giusto* (it is not right) as a firm word will be needed from time to time. Unfortunately, *La Dolce Vità Italiana* often leaves a bitter taste.

Take note of public notices about conduct: sitting on steps or eating and drinking in certain historic areas is not allowed. Covering arms and legs is necessary for admission into some churches – in rare cases even shorts are not permitted. Punctuality, like queuing (*facendo la coda*), is an alien concept in Italy, so be prepared to wait on occasion – but not necessarily in line or order.

Families

The family is highly regarded in Italy and children are well treated (not to say indulged), particularly in restaurants (although more expensive restaurants may not admit children). Naples is particularly famed for its family-orientated lifestyle and Neapolitans generally welcome children with open arms. There's plenty to do in Naples and Campania besides endless museum visits: there are seaside attractions aplenty of course, as well as theme parks and a zoo in Fuorigrotta. Note that lone parents or adults accompanying children of a different surname may sometimes need proof of guardianship before taking children in and out of Italy; contact your Italian embassy for current details (Italian embassy in London, T020-7312 2200).

Health

Comprehensive medical insurance is strongly recommended for all travellers to Italy. EU citizens should also apply for a free European Health Insurance Card (ehic.org), which replaced the E111 form and offers reduced-cost medical treatment. Late-night pharmacies are identified by a large green cross outside. To obtain the details of the three nearest open pharmacies dial T1100; out-of-hours pharmacies are also in most local newspapers. The accident and emergency department of a hospital is the *pronto soccorso*.

Practicalities

Insurance

Comprehensive travel (and medical) insurance is strongly recommended for all travellers to Italy. You should check any exclusions, excess and that your policy covers you for all the activities you want to undertake. Keep details of your insurance documents separately. Scanning them, then emailing yourself a copy is a good way to keep the information safe and accessible. Ensure you are fully insured if hiring a car, or, if you're taking your own vehicle, contact your current insurer to check whether you require an international insurance certificate.

Money

The Italian currency is the Euro (€). To change cash or travellers' cheques, look for a *cambio* (exchange office); these tend to give better rates than banks. Banks are open Monday to Friday 0830 to 1300 with some opening again from 1500 to 1600. ATMs that accept major credit and debit cards can be found in every city and town (look around the main piazzas). Many restaurants, shops, museums and art galleries will take major credit cards but paying directly with debit cards such as Cirrus is less common than in the UK, so having a ready supply of cash may be the most convenient option. You should also keep some cash handy for toll roads if you're driving.

Police

There are five different police forces in Italy. The *carabinieri* are a branch of the army and wear military-style uniforms with red stripes on their trousers and white sashes. They handle general crime, drug-related crime and public order offences. The *polizia statale* is the national police force, dressed in blue with a thin purple stripe on their trousers. They are responsible for security on the railways and at airports. The *polizia stradale* handles crime and traffic offences on the motorways and drives blue cars with a white stripe. The *vigili urbani* are local police who wear dark blue (in summer) or black (in winter) uniforms with white hats and direct traffic and issue parking fines in the cities. The *guardia di finanza* wears grey uniforms with grey flat hats or green berets (depending on rank). They are charged with combating counterfeiting, tax evasion and fraud.

In the case of an emergency requiring police attention, dial 113 or approach any member of the police or visit a police station (below). If it's a non-emergency, dial 112 for assistance.

Naples: via Medina 5, T081-551 1190.
Pozzuoli: piazzetta Italo Balbo, T081-303 0611.
Pompeii: via Sacra 1, T081-856 3511.
Sorrento: vico Bernardini Rota 14, T081-807 5311.
Salerno: via Amendola Generale Adalgiso, T089-613111.
Capri: via Roma 68, T081-837 4211.
Ischia: via Delle Terme, T081-507 4711.
Procida: via Libertà 96, T081-896 0086.

Post

The Italian post service (poste.it) has a not entirely undeserved reputation for unreliablility, particularly when it comes to handling postcards. Overseas post will require *posta prioritaria* (priority mail, which is actually just ordinary mail). You can buy *francobolli* (stamps) at post offices and *tabacchi* (look for T signs). A postcard stamp costs from €0.60 for both EU and transatlantic destinations. For letters over 20g and parcels, there is a maze of prices and options.

Safety

Naples has a reputation for petty theft and elaborate street scams which is often exaggerated – unfortunately, the stigma has stuck, which combined with its hectic traffic and general sense of chaos tends to frighten many people away. In reality, random acts of violence are less of a problem here than in many cities around the world. As long as you are extra careful (don't flaunt your wealth and valuables), pickpockets and bag snatchers shouldn't bother you. The use of a money belt to store credit cards, passports and large denominations is advisable – especially when using crowded public transport and visiting chaotic and poor neighbourhoods like Spaccanapoli and the Quartieri Spagnoli. Don't leave bags and valuables unattended in your vehicle, and remove everything from the boot at night. Beware of scams, con artists and sellers of fake goods: if someone offers you electrical goods (camcorders and mobiles are current favourites) or a box of cigarettes on the street, just say *no grazie, non mi interessa* (no thanks, I'm not interested) firmly – and walk on.

Telephone

The dialling codes for the main cities and provinces in Campania are: **Naples** 081; **Salerno** 089; **Caserta** 0823. You need to use these local codes, even when dialling from within the city or region. The prefix for Italy is +39. You no longer need to drop the initial '0' from the area codes when calling from abroad. For directory enquiries call T12.

Time difference

Italy uses Central European Time, GMT+1.

Tipping

It is increasingly common for service to be included in your bill on top of the cover charge. Where this isn't the case (and, sometimes, even when service is included in the bill), tipping is expected wherever there is waiter/waitress service: 50 cents to €1 is fine if you've only had a drink but, for a meal, 10-15% of the total bill is the norm. If you're ordering at the bar, a few spare coins might speed up your coffee and even result in a smile. Taxis may add on extra costs for luggage but an additional tip is always appreciated. Rounding-up prices always goes down well, especially if it means avoiding having to give change – not a favourite Italian habit.

Voltage

Italy functions on a 220V mains supply. Plugs are the standard European two-pin variety.

Language

In hotels and bigger restaurants, you'll usually find English is spoken. The further you go from the tourist centre, however, the more trouble you may have, unless you have at least a smattering of Italian. Luckily, Neapolitans are generally gregarious and very encouraging of anyone speaking Italian, although many of them communicate between themselves in Neapolitan dialect, a branch of the Napoletano-Calabrese language spoken throughout Southern Italy.

Napoletano (pronounced nabuledan') has a very different rhythm and phonology to the Tuscan dialect that forms the basis of standard Italian – indeed most Northern Italians find it very tricky deciphering a Neapolitan's clipped vowels, voiced and double consonantal sounds, and exotic Greek, Arabic and Spanish linguistic influences. So a trip to Naples not only gives visitors the opportunity to dip into the city's rich tradition of music, literature and theatre: there's also the chance to hear Neapolitan language and its witty proverbs.

When communicating in shops and restaurants stick to Italian. Stress in spoken Italian usually falls on the penultimate syllable. Italian has standard sounds and is the most phonetically true language: unlike English you can work out how it sounds from how it is written and vice versa.

Vowels

a like 'a' in cat

e like 'e' in vet, or slightly more open, like the 'ai' in air (except after c or g, see consonants below)

i like 'i' in sip (except after c or g, see below)

o like 'o' in fox

u like 'ou' in soup

Consonants

Generally consonants sound the same as in English, though 'e' and 'i' after 'c' or 'g' make them soft (a 'ch' or a 'j' sound) and are silent themselves, whereas 'h' makes them hard (a 'k' or 'g' sound), the opposite to English. So *ciao* is pronounced 'chaow', but *chiesa* (church) is pronounced 'kee-ay-sa'.

The combination 'gli' is pronounced like the 'lli' in million, and 'gn' like 'ny' in Tanya.

Basics

thank you   *grazie*
hi/goodbye   *ciao*
good day (until after lunch/
mid-afternoon)   *buongiorno*
good evening (after lunch)   *buonasera*
goodnight   *buonanotte*
goodbye   *arrivederci*
please   *per favore*
I'm sorry   *mi dispiace*
excuse me   *permesso*
yes   *si*
no   *no*

Right: Francesco e figlio.

Gestures

Italians are famously theatrical and animated in dialogue and use a variety of gestures.

Side of left palm on side of right wrist as right wrist is flicked up   Go away

Hunched shoulders and arms lifted with palms of hands outwards   What am I supposed to do?

Thumb, index and middle finger of hand together, wrist upturned and shaking
What are you doing/what's going on?

Both palms together and moved up and down in front of stomach   Same as above

All fingers of hand squeezed together   To signify a place is packed full of people

Front orside of hand to chin   'Nothing', as in 'I don't understand' or 'I've had enough'

Flicking back of right ear   To signify someone is gay

Index finger in cheek   To signify good food

Numbers

one	*uno*	17	*diciassette*
two	*due*	18	*diciotto*
three	*tre*	19	*diciannove*
four	*quattro*	20	*venti*
five	*cinque*	21	*ventuno*
six	*sei*	22	*ventidue*
seven	*sette*	30	*trenta*
eight	*otto*	40	*quaranta*
nine	*nove*	50	*cinquanta*
10	*dieci*	60	*sessanta*
11	*undici*	70	*settanta*
12	*dodici*	80	*ottanta*
13	*tredici*	90	*novanta*
14	*quattordici*	100	*cento*
15	*quindici*	200	*due cento*
16	*sedici*	1000	*mille*

Questions

how?   *come?*

how much?   *quanto?*

when?   *quando?*

where?   *dove?*

why?   *perché?*

what?   *che cosa?*

Problems

I don't understand   *non capisco*

I don't know   *non lo so*

I don't speak Italian   *non parlo italiano*

How do you say ... (in Italian)?
   come si dice ... (in italiano)?

Is there anyone who speaks English?
   c'è qualcuno che parla inglese?

Shopping

this one/that one   *questo/quello*
less   *meno*
more   *di più*
how much is it/are they?
  quanto costa/costano?
can I have …?   *posso avere …?*

Travelling

one ticket for…   *un biglietto per…*
single   *solo andata*
return   *andata e ritorno*
does this go to Pompeii?
  questo va a Pompei?
airport   *aeroporto*
bus stop   *fermata*
train   *treno*
car   *macchina*
taxi   *tassi*

Hotels

a double/single room
una camera doppia/singola
a double bed   *un letto matrimoniale*
bathroom   *bagno*
Is there a view?   *c'è un bel panorama?*
can I see the room?   *posso vedere la camera?*
when is breakfast?   *a che ora è la colazione?*
can I have the key?   *posso avere la chiave?*

Time

morning   *mattina*
afternoon   *pomeriggio*
evening   *sera*
night   *notte*
soon   *presto/fra poco*
later   *più tardi*
what time is it?   *che ore sono?*
today/tomorrow/yesterday   *oggi/domani/ieri*

Days

Monday   *lunedi*
Tuesday   *martedi*
Wednesday   *mercoledi*
Thursday   *giovedi*
Friday   *venerdi*
Saturday   *sabato*
Sunday   *domenica*

Conversation

alright   *va bene*
right then   *allora*
who knows!   *bo! / chi sa*
good luck!   *in bocca al lupo!* (literally, 'in the
  mouth of the wolf')
one moment   *un attimo*
hello (when answering a phone)
  pronto (literally, 'ready')
let's go!   *andiamo!*
enough/stop!   *basta!*
give up!   *dai!*
I like …   *mi piace …*
how's it going?   (well, thanks) *come va?* (bene, grazie)
how are you?   *come sta/stai?* (polite/informal)

Index

Index

Credits

Footprint credits

Text editor: Tim Jollands
Assistant editor: Alice Jell
Picture editor: Kassia Gawronski
Layout & production: Angus Dawson
Maps: Compass Maps Ltd

Managing Director: Andy Riddle
Commercial Director: Patrick Dawson
Publisher: Alan Murphy
Editorial: Sara Chare, Ria Gane,
Jenny Haddington, Felicity Laughton,
Nicola Gibbs
Design: Mytton Williams
Cartography: Sarah Sorenson, Rob Lunn,
Kevin Feeney, Emma Bryers
Sales & marketing: Liz Harper,
Hannah Bonnell
Advertising: Renu Sibal
Business Development: Zoë Jackson
Finance & Administration: Elizabeth Taylor

Print

Manufactured in Italy by EuroGrafica
Pulp from sustainable forests

Footprint Feedback

We try as hard as we can to make each
Footprint guide as up to date as possible
but, of course, things always change.
If you want to let us know about your
experiences – good, bad or ugly – then
don't delay, go to footprintbooks.com
and send in your comments.

Every effort has been made to ensure
that the facts in this guidebook are
accurate. However, travellers should still
obtain advice from consulates, airlines etc
about travel and visa requirements before
travelling. The authors and publishers
cannot accept responsibility for any loss,
injury or inconvenience however caused.

Publishing information

FootprintItalia Naples & Amalfi Coast
1st edition
© Footprint Handbooks Ltd
April 2009

ISBN 978-1-906098-60-5
CIP DATA: A catalogue record for this
book is available from the British Library

® Footprint Handbooks and the Footprint
mark are a registered trademark of
Footprint Handbooks Ltd

Published by Footprint
6 Riverside Court
Lower Bristol Road
Bath BA2 3DZ, UK
T +44 (0)1225 469141
F +44 (0)1225 469461
www.footprintbooks.com